The Short Novels of John Steinbeck

The Short Novels of John Steinbeck

Critical Essays with a Checklist to Steinbeck Criticism

Edited by Jackson J. Benson

Duke University Press   *Durham and London 1990*

© 1990 Duke University Press
All rights reserved.
Printed in the United States of America
on acid-free paper ∞
Library of Congress Cataloging-in-Publication Data
appear on the last printed page of this book.
Permission for quotations from Steinbeck's published works has been
given by McIntosh & Otis, Inc., agents for the John Steinbeck Estate.

For Sue Ellen

Contents

Acknowledgments ix

Introduction I

My Short Novels, John Steinbeck 15

I Tortilla Flat

1 *Tortilla Flat* and the Creation of a Legend, 19
Joseph Fontenrose

2 Nonteleological Thinking in Steinbeck's *Tortilla Flat*, 31
Robert Gentry

II Of Mice and Men

3 A Historical Introduction to *Of Mice and Men*, Anne Loftis 39

4 *Of Mice and Men*: John Steinbeck's Parable of the Curse 48
of Cain, William Goldhurst

5 Of George and Lennie and Curley's Wife: Sweet Violence 59
in Steinbeck's Eden, Mark Spilka

III The Red Pony

6 *The Red Pony* as Story Cycle and Film, Warren French 71

7 John Steinbeck's *The Red Pony*: A Study in Narrative 84
Technique, Howard Levant

IV The Moon Is Down

8 Dr. Winter's Dramatic Functions in *The Moon Is Down*, 95
Tetsumaro Hayashi

9 Steinbeck's "European" Play-Novella: *The Moon Is Down*, 101
John Ditsky

V Cannery Row

10 *Cannery Row*: Escape into the Counterculture, Peter Lisca 111

11   "Some Philosophers in the Sun": Steinbeck's *Cannery Row*,   119
      Robert S. Hughes, Jr.

12   *Cannery Row* and Steinbeck as Spokesman for the "Folk   132
      Tradition," Jackson J. Benson

      VI   The Pearl

13   The Shadow and the Pearl: Jungian Patterns in *The Pearl*,   143
      John H. Timmerman

14   Precious Bane: Mining the Fool's Gold of *The Pearl*,   161
      Michael J. Meyer

15   Steinbeck's *The Pearl*: Legend, Film, Novel,   173
      Roy S. Simmonds

      VII   Sweet Thursday

16   Steinbeck's Version of the Pastoral, Charles R. Metzger   185

17   Critics and Common Denominators: Steinbeck's *Sweet*   195
      Thursday, Louis Owens

18   Steinbeck's Bittersweet Thursday, Richard Astro   204

      VIII   Burning Bright

19   *Burning Bright*: The Shining of Joe Saul, Carroll Britch   217
      and Clifford Lewis

20   Straining for Profundity: Steinbeck's *Burning Bright* and   234
      Sweet Thursday, Mimi Reisel Gladstein

      IX   The Short Reign of Pippin IV

21   Steinbeck's "Deep Dissembler": *The Short Reign of*   249
      Pippin IV, Louis Owens

22   The Narrative Structure of *The Short Reign of Pippin IV*,   257
      Howard Levant

      X   Overview

23   Steinbeck and the Stage, Robert E. Morsberger   271

      Notes   295
      Steinbeck's Short Novels: 315
      Comprehensive Checklist of Criticism
      Contributors   347

Acknowledgments

Permission to reprint "My Short Novels," by John Steinbeck, which originally appeared in the Literary Guild Review *Wings* (October 1953), has been granted by McIntosh and Otis, Inc., agents for the Steinbeck estate. They have also given permission for the use of parts of two unpublished Steinbeck letters in the essay by Roy S. Simmonds.

Permission to quote from "Lapis Lazuli" in *The Poems of W. B. Yeats: A New Edition* (edited by Richard J. Finneran; copyright 1940 by Georgie Yeats, reviewed 1968 by Bertha Georgie Yeats, Michael Butler Yeats, and Anne Yeats) as used in the Introduction to this book was granted by Macmillan Publishing Company.

Permission to reprint *"Tortilla Flat"* from Joseph Fontenrose's *John Steinbeck: An Introduction and Interpretation*, was granted by Holt, Rinehart, and Winston, Inc. Permission to reprint William Goldhurst's "*Of Mice and Men*: John Steinbeck's Parable of the Curse of Cain" and Jackson J. Benson's "*Cannery Row* and John Steinbeck as the Spokesman for the 'Folk Tradition' " (part of "John Steinbeck's *Cannery Row*: A Reconsideration"), appearing in *Western American Literature*, was granted by the Western Literature Association. Permission to reprint Mark Spilka's "Of George and Lennie and Curley's Wife: Sweet Violence in Steinbeck's Eden" and Charles R. Metzger's "Steinbeck's Version of the Pastoral," which appeared in *Modern Fiction Studies*, was granted by Purdue Research Foundation; both articles copyrighted by the Purdue Research Foundation. Permission to reprint Howard Levant's "John Steinbeck's *The Red Pony*: A Study in Narrative Technique" was granted by the *Journal of Narrative Technique*.

Permission to reprint Tetsumaro Hayashi's "Dr. Winter's Dramatic Functions in *The Moon Is Down*" has been granted by the author. John Ditsky's "Steinbeck's 'European' Play-Novella: *The Moon Is Down*" was written for joint publication in this volume and in the *Steinbeck Quarterly*—the editor is grateful to the editor of the *Quarterly*, Tetsumaro

Hayashi, and the John Steinbeck Society for this arrangement and for permission to reprint Richard Astro's "Steinbeck's Bittersweet Thursday." Permission was granted by the author, Peter Lisca, for "*Cannery Row:* Escape into the Counterculture" from his *John Steinbeck: Nature and Myth*. Permission to reprint Howard Levant's "The Narrative Structure of *The Short Reign of Pippin IV*" was granted by the University of Missouri Press.

Introduction

When he was good, he was very, very good, and when he was bad, he was terrible. John Steinbeck's writing was often so good—a prose so smooth, a touch so delicate, an insight into human nature so precise—that few readers really appreciated just how much skill and talent was involved. More often they simply felt it. If some critics have demurred from his greatness, it is probably in part because his best work seems so effortless that he gets very little credit for it, while his poorer work is so heavy-handed that it is impossible to forgive him.

The Grapes of Wrath is most commonly thought of as Steinbeck's masterpiece, although he considered another long novel, *East of Eden*, his best work. But the short novel was the form that he most frequently returned to and most consciously theorized about, and with constant experimentation he made the form his own. Nearly everyone has heard of *The Grapes of Wrath*, but because they are taught in schools here and abroad and because they remain among the well-loved works of parents who pass them on to their children, the best of Steinbeck's short works—*Tortilla Flat, Cannery Row, The Red Pony, Of Mice and Men,* and *The Pearl*—have remained in the currency of our culture. At the same time, much of his worst writing appears also in the short novels, in such works as *Burning Bright* and *Sweet Thursday*. The writing in another, *The Short Reign of Pippin IV*, is usually fine, but the conception of this satire seems weak and shallow. Or is it? Perhaps readers, rather than the writer, have fallen short here.

The purpose of this collection, gathered some twenty years after Steinbeck's death in December 1968, is to look back at what has been taken to be the "good" and the "bad"—and look more carefully beyond the cant and careless labeling that has characterized all too much of the commentary on Steinbeck's work—at what has made it so, if indeed it is so. As these essays will testify, there is much yet to discover. However, the main thrust of these essays is neither to praise nor condemn, but to inform.

Even in the short novels most frequently taken to task, there may be more depth and sophistication of technique than has generally been acknowledged. Like his near contemporary, the poet Robert Frost, Steinbeck early developed the technique of writing on several levels, starting with a clear, lyrically told surface story which has made his work accessible to nearly any reader, young or old, literary or nonliterary by taste or training. While this is no doubt the key to Steinbeck's long-lived success, it was also a matter of discouragement for him, for like Frost he was often considered simple-minded by academics and elitist critics. And while Frost was eventually discovered to be the complex and sophisticated poet he had been all along (not soon enough for Frost, who held a deep resentment toward the "critical establishment" for most of his life), the same acknowledgment has not yet been made for Steinbeck, who, sadly, ended his life thinking of himself as something of a failure.

Of course, it is not just New York book reviewers and Ivy League academics who establish our literature. If it were up to them we would have Henry James, but not Mark Twain, William Faulkner, but not Ernest Hemingway. Writers such as Steinbeck and Hemingway have been blessed and cursed by popularity. In our book culture one finds a paradox: If an author does not have at least one great popular success, he or she may well be ignored by the media, but if he or she is constantly popular, then the critics become suspicious of the writer's serious intentions. From a financial point of view, Steinbeck was lucky. Nearly every book he wrote, starting with his fourth, *Tortilla Flat* (1935), sold well, even though he never wrote fiction with an eye to potential sales. Even the short novel *The Short Reign of Pippin IV*, which he wrote as a tongue-in-cheek experiment and thought would have almost no sales at all, was, much to his amazement—and amusement— chosen as a Book-of-the-Month Club selection.

The popularity of such works led the critics to accuse him of writing junk to please a mass audience, and the author himself, feeling put-upon by a barrage of criticism, began to wish for more modest sales, particularly for works that in retrospect he realized had not achieved the artistic success he had aimed for. What argues against the idea of Steinbeck as a writer of potboilers in his seriousness of purpose, even in a light and funky—too funky, as it turned out—comedy such as *Sweet Thursday*, as well as his dedication throughout his life to the art of fiction. He was not a lightweight either as man or as writer. A well-educated and thoughtful man, he was an intellectual in the best sense of the word—a person who read constantly and widely and who loved to consider and discuss ideas. And, like all artists who achieve some measure of greatness, he was a risk taker. He tried something new with every story and every novel, so that as one reads through his work, his fictions are so different from one another that it is hard to believe that the same person wrote them all. These are certainly not the works of someone writing by a formula.

He was also a man of some complexity, full of contradictions. One such was that he could display, as in that little jewel of a book *Of Mice and Men*, an almost perfect ear for colloquial speech and for the most suitable prose rhythms. (And to my ear, at least, Steinbeck's imitation of Spanish in English in *The Pearl* sounds a good deal more natural than Hemingway's in *The Old Man and the Sea*.) At other times, however, his ear unaccountably went deaf, and the speech, as in *Burning Bright*, seems completely false—irritatingly so—or the prose, as in the windier parts of *East of Eden*, appears so overwritten that it is nearly unendurable. At the bottom of this particular contradiction was Steinbeck's unfortunate affection for the lilt of Irish English, which he thought he derived from his maternal grandfather (but didn't, really, since the grandfather died before Steinbeck could have had any memories of him).

Following this attraction early in his career, he was heavily influenced by the style of a very mediocre writer, Donn Byrne (author of *Blind Raftery and His Wife, Hilaria*), who sometimes wrote in brogue. Later, Steinbeck became very fond of the poetry and plays of the Irish playwright John Millington Synge, who constructed an artificial language composed of what sounded like Irish syntax combined with the simple formality of the King James Bible. (Indeed, the prose of *Burning Bright* sounds very much like overdone Synge, and the experimental setting changes in the play—putting the same set of characters in three different settings of circus, farm, and sea—may remind us of the combination of farm and sea used by Synge as the setting in his *Riders to the Sea*.)

One thing (or really two connected things) that kept John Steinbeck from becoming *the* great writer of his time was his wrong-headed devotion to poetic prose rather than to the colloquial, and to the fabulous rather than the realistic. They were convictions that he strayed from for a time when he was caught up in the ongoing drama of the Great Depression (and wrote his best prose—always lyrical, but at the same time natural-sounding), but which he always returned to as aspects fundamental to most of those works we consider part of the canon of great literature. He was right in his diagnosis of the history of Western literature, but there was a terrible irony in his use of it to defeat his own best talents. Although a modest man by comparison to most other famous writers, he was also, as another contradiction, somewhat arrogant in his own sense of literature and language, and it was this arrogance, I suspect, that sustained him in the face of hostile reactions.

Another reason for what might charitably be called Steinbeck's "unevenness" was, despite the conservatism of his literary idea, the penchant for experimentation that I have already noted. He resisted becoming a one-instrument player, a one-tune soloist. He was always trying new ways of expressing things, but all too often these strike our sensibilities as discordant or inappropriate. A writer, like a composer, must, if he is going to gain and keep some audience, find and attune himself somewhat to his audience's expectations. But his arrogance led him to react against anything that he considered popularization and to discount, perhaps too completely, his audience's tastes and ideas. There is a terrible irony in a stubbornness that expressed itself throughout his career as just the opposite of the popular artist he was often taken to be.

While on the one side he was severely criticized for his offbeat experimentation, on the other side he was attacked for *not* repeating himself. A number of critics in the post-World War II period who were on the militant political left were disappointed that he did not write *The Grapes of Wrath* over and over again, and many, such as Stanley Edgar Hyman, expressed their disappointment in strident personal abuse. Presumably, pure political motives can justify any kind of behavior. Steinbeck was a writer with a sense of humor and fun, and whenever he expressed these—departing from the deep seriousness that some critics insisted that he maintain as a sort of moral duty—he was lambasted as somehow betraying his calling.

Even his serious work aroused anger when it did not meet critical expectations in tone or treatment. The leftists, in particular, were unhappy with *The Moon Is Down* because it was told as a fable and the "invaders" (used by the author to characterize a generic condition, but who would, of course, bring to mind the Nazis) were not treated as monsters. James Thurber even went so far as to accuse Steinbeck of sabotaging the war effort. But the book that seemed to anger these critics most was *Cannery Row,* which the author had written near the end of the war after returning from a stint as a war correspondent.

This short novel came at a turning point in Steinbeck's career. The work that had made him famous during the years just prior to the war had dealt mostly with the dispossessed and farm labor, which pleased the Left and angered the Right. Although his wife, Carol, and many of their friends in the Monterey–Pacific Grove area were active in the support of farm labor, Steinbeck did not see the plight of the migrants, for whom he had great sympathy, in political terms. He saw himself as an artist trying to create works that had a universal meaning and would stand the test of time. As subjects came to him, whether the paisanos of *Tortilla Flat* or the striking fruit pickers of *In Dubious Battle*, he invariably investigated to learn more about them so that his fictions, no matter how far they departed from literal fact, would always have the ring of truth. Most of his fictions have some appearance of reality, but he was not an author who felt that realism in itself had any special virtue, but rather that it was often less able to convey truth than the fabulous or fantastic. And as he grew older he became less and less tolerant of the realism that seemed for many to give power to the works like *Of Mice and Men* and *The Grapes of Wrath* that had brought him to fame.

The fantasy of *Tortilla Flat*, an early work, was forgiven, but the fantasy of *Cannery Row* aroused outrage—not too strong a word— among those who felt the author had abandoned his social responsibility. The book was inconsequential; it "smells," one reviewer declared, "of fish and reeks with kindness" and was "as sentimental as a book can be." "Sentimental" is the ultimate pejorative in modern literary criticism, tending to disqualify anything so labeled from further serious consideration. The term has stuck to Steinbeck, partly because he was so little understood, partly because his themes—even when they were recognized—seemed irrelevant to Eastern, urban critics, and partly because he was, in fact, sentimental at times.

The picture is complicated. A kind and compassionate man, Steinbeck obviously cared deeply for people in trouble, and it shows in his work. It is this sense of caring that has endeared him to generations of readers around the world, but it can also degrade his fiction when on occasion it lapses into mere tearful sadness. If there is one episode in *Cannery Row* that qualifies as "sentimental," it is chapter 10, concerning the mentally retarded boy, Frankie, who wants desperately to please but cannot deal with society's rules. Designed to break the reader's heart with the injustice of Frankie's fate, the segment reflects two themes that are almost Steinbeck obsessions: society's failure to accept the handicapped on their own terms, and the intolerance and hypocrisy of respectability. Here, as occasionally elsewhere, the author's emotions have led him into artistic excess, but it is certainly an excess that most will find forgivable.

What saved Steinbeck from constant excess was a compassion that was, in much of his writing, balanced and disciplined by a very objective view of the world and of man. My favorite Steinbeck anecdote illustrates this. When he was at Stanford, he once tried to sign up for a class in the medical school on dissection of cadavers. It was an odd request from an English major, and he was asked by the dean of the medical school to justify it. "I want to learn about human beings," he explained. He was, needless to say, turned down, since cadavers are a valuable resource not to be wasted on literature students. The story illustrates an aspect of Steinbeck's thinking that many critics of his work have overlooked: a naturalism more thoroughgoing and a view of life colder and less sentimental than almost any other American writer we might classify as a naturalist, including Crane, Norris, London, and Dreiser. Unlike Steinbeck, these other writers were disillusioned romantics who found it difficult to accept man's role as just another animal in a very large and indifferent universe. They believed it, but they didn't like it.

Although not an expert, Steinbeck wrote out of a more-than-casual knowledge of biology, anthropology, and astronomy, and a biological-ecological view of man's nature and place dominated his thinking. He saw man not at the center of creation but as just another species, one, after the advent of nuclear weapons, that he had little faith would survive its own "self-hatred," as he called man's propensity toward war, terrorism, and brutality. When he wrote of the plight of Lennie and George in *Of Mice and Men*, he did so with a strange mixture of compassion and distance. There is no motivation for social reform behind the novelette at all; it is simply the presentation of a story, of "Something that Happened," as he first called his manuscript. It was the social reformers who made this very deterministic picture of man's fate a novel which calls for social action.

Despite his tribute to medical science in *The Forgotten Village*, he had little faith in progress; and despite Tom Joad's stirring call to action near the end of *The Grapes of Wrath*, he had little faith in political solutions. And as a further contradiction, although he cared about people in need, he was very skeptical about human nature, and that skepticism brings a hard edge on nearly everything he wrote. So one is inclined to believe that for the most part, those who have felt that Steinbeck "sentimentalized the folk," to use Richard Hofstadter's phrase, have brought their own sentimentality with them. As early as *In Dubious Battle*, he showed that he had no illusions about the dispossessed, whom he presented in that novel as sometimes careless, greedy, and easily manipulated. Although the tourists that flocked to Monterey after the publication of *Tortilla Flat* may have considered the paisanos quaint or cute, that did not reflect the author's attitude, which was a distanced respect for their dignity and for their best attributes in a grasping, materialistic society. The picture he drew of them, which omits the realistic details of their physical discomfort and the ravages of alcoholism, is not so much sentimentalized as it is stylized to fit the telling of a fable, or, as Joseph Fontenrose shows in chapter 1, the generation of a legend.

The paisanos, like the down-and-outers of *Cannery Row* and *Sweet Thursday*, are material not for the sociological study or political tract that the Marxists would have desired, but for fables which alter our perspective so that we might reexamine our values. What bothered the political minded was that these works dealing with the dispossessed in our society were essentially apolitical. Accusing the author of sentimentality, leftists would have substituted their own brand: the melodrama of the proletarian novel with its noble workers and wicked bosses.

Perspective is a key word here, for the short novels invariably ask us to step out of our traditional way of looking at things to take another point of view. Here again, as so often in studying Steinbeck, we are led back to science, for it is more important to him that we look than do, more important that we understand than accomplish. We might note that in *Cannery Row* Doc is often seen with his microscope, and in *Sweet*

Thursday he is given a telescope, so that the whole range of seeing is thereby covered. The range is crucial, for what leads Steinbeck to object to politics, in the immediate, shortsighted sense, is its narrow view of the world. Other groups also have blinders on: the narrowly religious, the socially respectable, the greedy for success and/or money—whatever is egocentric or ethnocentric in our makeup. From the early *Tortilla Flat* to the late *Pippin*, as Louis Owens shows in his essay on that rarely discussed short novel (chapter 21), the author is a critic of an American society that is self-absorbed, bigoted, and materialistic.

Not only should we stop to look and understand as a scientist might, but we should approach life with the scientist's objectivity and distance. For Steinbeck, one can be detached in his observations, on the one hand, while at the same time one can express compassion, on the other. This is a combination that one might see in the field or laboratory work of a zoologist, for example, working with endangered species. This combination, which has been often mistaken for sentimentality by negative critics of Steinbeck, is really quite the opposite when examined closely. Detachment and compassion together are major components of an overall attitude toward the universe—nature, including that speck of dust called "man"—which Steinbeck calls "acceptance."

Acceptance is an attitude that is very difficult for Americans, and particularly middle-class Americans, to understand or adopt. We believe in change, progress, and "can do." We want to believe that nothing is impossible, that if you work hard enough, you are bound to succeed, and that people get what they deserve. The ideas that one should learn to accept a condition or situation that is uncomfortable or distressing and that change is not necessarily good are largely foreign to our thinking. But acceptance is, in my mind, the one concept that can put Steinbeck's work in proper critical perspective. To accept, in the sense that Steinbeck employed it, is to stand aside from all those factors that limit our vision and confine our sympathies and to see people and events within the indefinite continuums of time and space. It is to be broad-minded in the largest possible sense.

Distrust of outsiders and hatred for those of a different race or class or style of living are subjects touched on in nearly all of Steinbeck's fiction. In our daily experience we observe in ourselves and others reactions for which that fiction might serve as an antidote. As we walk down the streets of our cities, if we are middle-class and proper, we are likely to view anyone who doesn't fit our model with suspicion or disdain. Of course, today's homeless differ from Steinbeck's Cannery Row bums in that a large percentage of our homeless are not cut off from society voluntarily. How many of us who are more fortunate view the homeless as "untouchables," people we would rather not even see, let alone try to understand? We look the other way or cross the street with a shudder. How many of us in our hearts believe that if these people *really* wanted to, they could easily get a job and get off the streets? For Steinbeck, the challenge was to escape the early conditioning which has led us into the habits of suspicion or disgust, to accept individuals on their own terms for what they in fact are, rather than as representatives of categories.

Contrary to the behavior of the weepy-eyed, sentimental liberal, the person who practices acceptance is open-eyed and realistic—he or she not only casts aside preconceptions and prejudice but also looks to see people and events clearly for what they actually are. Sentimentality, within Steinbeck's scheme, is simply another kind of blinder and self-deception, another mode of categorizing so that we can feel superior. We would do well not to approach Mac and the boys from the motives of the do-gooder or naïve bleeding heart, for we are likely to be, first, taken to the cleaners, and second, shocked by their independence and ingratitude.

In an age dominated by the horrors of terrorist bombs and sub-machine guns in the hands of young men and women of absolute certainty used against unarmed and helpless men, women, and babes whose only crime was to be in the wrong place at the wrong time, in an age of intractable conflicts of politics and religion in the Near East, in Northern Ireland, in South Africa—to mention but a few—we can easily view the fruits of nearsightedness, the inability to accept. Acceptance does not mean to agree or endorse, but rather to see within a larger perspective and to refrain from imposing views or standards on others. Steinbeck loved his country, but he did not treat his country like a football team. Cheering for "the best" inevitably implies that other countries are worse and that other peoples are somehow inferior. Instead, it was just as important to him to have a respect for all mankind as it was to love his native land. It is not accidental that he was a strong supporter of the United Nations and a close friend of Dag Hammarskjöld, the secretary general, and of Adlai Stevenson when he was the American ambassador to the UN, and of Norman Cousins, who was constant in his support of the UN as editor of *Saturday Review*.

Acceptance is a quality displayed by many of the world's great prophets and wise men. Christ certainly displayed it, although Steinbeck was more likely to think of it as a quality more frequently expressed in Eastern literature and philosophy than in Western forms. The marine biologist Edward F. Ricketts, who for many years was the novelist's best friend and discussion partner, was very interested in Eastern philosophy and probably turned Steinbeck's attention in that direction. Ricketts was the model for a number of "self-characters," as Steinbeck called them, characters that stand in for the author in his work, as does Doc in *Cannery Row*, Doctor Winter in *The Moon Is Down*, and Friend Ed in *Burning Bright*. His friend was used this way so frequently because the author admired him so much, and the quality he admired most was Ricketts's acceptance. That quality was so prominent in Ricketts's thinking and character and reached out to such an extent that it was sometimes difficult for John Steinbeck to go as far. Although neither was conventionally religious, and Ricketts was no saint, one may still be reminded of the Disciples, who found that their human limitations made it hard for them to follow their Master.

One occasion which illustrates this occurred when Steinbeck was working on the semidocumentary *The Forgotten Village* in Mexico. This project came out of his growing interest in film as a medium for communicating his ideas and out of a concern for needed improvements in public sanitation realized during his research in the field for *The Grapes of Wrath*. He became aware of the problems faced by public health nurses attempting to deal with the prejudices of Okie and Mexican migrant workers, which were resulting in needless illness and death. Film seemed to be the best way of getting across the message to those most concerned.

Ricketts came down to the filming site to join Steinbeck and his first wife, Carol. Almost immediately there was trouble. Ricketts heartily disagreed with the direction the script was taking. Any "progress," as far as he was concerned, would be corrupting of "the deep smile," the rich "relational life" enjoyed by the Mexican people, and for that reason the situation should be accepted as it was. While outwardly, in the realm of material things, we might be ahead of them, the Mexican people were ahead of us in the more important "region of inward adjustment." Steinbeck was put in a position where his own sense of compassion, his interest in science, and his wife's very vocal social activism were set against a position that he had generally endorsed and which was espoused by the man he admired most. He finished the film successfully but remained troubled by his decision.

Steinbeck consciously worked hard throughout his life to become a better person by becoming more accepting. It wasn't easy, particularly at that point in his life when he became famous and had money. But in the long run he was successful in fighting off the lures of pride and ego (and rather less successful in resisting materialism—he was very fond of cars and boats and mechanical gadgets of all kinds). A record of one stage of this battle to achieve more acceptance in his life is his short novel *Burning Bright*.

This book is probably the least successful of his works, and yet, when read in the context of the author's life, it can become one of his most moving. In it he brings together two stories. One is the story of a couple he had known, made up of a husband who was impotent and a wife who, with her husband's approval, searched diligently for a substitute biological father. (The story is that Ed Ricketts became that father and that the husband proudly claimed the children as his own.) The second story is Steinbeck's. When his second wife, mother to his two sons, told him that she wanted a divorce, she claimed that she had never loved him, that she had been unfaithful to him for years, and that his second son, John IV, was not his. The latter claim, apparently used as a weapon of spite, was false, and it would seem that Steinbeck did not really believe her. Yet it created doubt and, as it was designed to do, made him suffer.

At about the same time that his wife asked for a divorce, he suffered a second loss, the accidental death of Ed Ricketts, whose car was hit by a train. Steinbeck slid into a period of deep despair, suffering a mental and emotional breakdown that threatened to destroy him until he was able, after more than a year, to get his own thinking in order. One of the ways he was able to do this was to squash his ego and stretch his acceptance so that it didn't matter whether his son was born of someone else's seed or not—this was his son, in any event, and he could love him no less. A couple of years later, after remarrying, he brought the two stories together as the basis for a novelette-play. In that play Joe Saul, with the counsel of Friend Ed, is finally able to accept his child, born of his wife Mordeen by Victor, with the declaration, "I had to walk into the black to know—to know that every man is father to all children and every child must have all men as father." It is one of the noblest sentiments ever penned.

In his own writings, unpublished until after his death, Ed Ricketts refers to a concept of W. B. Yeats, the "tower beyond tragedy." This phrase may remind us of Yeats's late poem "Lapis Lazuli," which begins with hysterical women responding to fears of the "times"—bombs and airships—complaining about artists and poets who are "always gay" and never involved, never *doing* anything. (One almost thinks here of the tone of voice of the critics who were so angry with Steinbeck for writing *Cannery Row*—he had, they thought, given up politics and therefore wasn't doing anything.) By way of reply, Yeats writes of the figures in Shakespearian tragedy—Hamlet, Lear, Ophelia, Cordelia—who, like all of us, "perform their tragic play," but when the end comes, the supporting players do not "break up their lines to weep." They know that "Hamlet and Lear are gay; / Gaiety transfiguring all that dread."

Further emphasizing the role of art and artist as detached and separated from ongoing events, and contemplating them from the perspective of man's long history wherein "all men have aimed at, found and lost," Yeats describes a scene carved in lapis lazuli. Two Chinamen climb toward a little halfway house, while overhead a crane, symbol of longevity, flies. With them is a serving man carrying a musical instrument. The speaker of the poem says that he likes to imagine these figures seated at the house,

> There, on the mountain and the sky,
> On all the tragic scene they stare.
> One asks for mournful melodies;
> Accomplished fingers begin to play.
> Their eyes mid many wrinkles, their eyes,
> Their ancient, glittering eyes, are gay.

Some may think of John Steinbeck as the great political writer of his time or—our most accomplished social novelist—observer and recorder of the farm family, the farm worker, and the Great Depression. But I am inclined to see him somewhat differently. He had witnessed and often shared great pain and suffering. The sight of Okie children needlessly starving or of workers beaten by company thugs so paralyzed him with helpless anger that it was many months before he could approach the writing of his masterpiece with the detachment he needed. For almost two years after World War II he could not shake from his mind or his dreams the scenes of bloody pieces of women and children after bombardments in Italy. He had suffered much in his personal life, and he had endured more public abuse for his art than any man can rightly be asked to undergo: The day after he won the Nobel Prize for literature, the "newspaper of record," the *New York Times*, announced to the world in an editorial that he didn't deserve it.

Yet somehow he was always able to rise above his anger and pain. Near the end of his life I see him, "the great stage curtain about to drop," at his desk in his own little halfway house, Joyous Garde. He is writing. He does not pause to weep but plays out his scene.

Explanatory Note   In 1953 the Viking Press published a volume called *The Short Novels of John Steinbeck*, which collected six novellas into one book: *Tortilla Flat*, *The Red Pony*, *Of Mice and Men*, *The Moon Is Down*, *Cannery Row*, and *The Pearl*. In order to make this critical survey as complete and valuable as possible, I have added Steinbeck's other three short novels—*Burning Bright*, *Sweet Thursday*, and *The Short Reign of Pippin IV*—even though these have generally been considered less successful than the original six.

Of the twenty-three essays included in this collection, twelve are printed here for the first time, and one was written for joint publication with the *Steinbeck Quarterly*. The ten essays I have chosen to reprint (marked by a note on the first page of each essay), such as the article by Joseph Fontenrose on *Tortilla Flat* and the one on *Cannery Row* by Peter Lisca, are in my estimation classic pieces that deserve to remain in print.

Since most of Steinbeck's short novels have some connection to drama (indeed, with *Of Mice and Men* the author can be said to have invented a form of his own, the play-novella), many of the essays in this volume deal with play or film versions of the short novels as well as with the fiction; and the overview by Robert E. Morsberger at the end of the selections deals with Steinbeck as dramatist.

My Short Novels

John Steinbeck

I have never written a preface to one of my books before, believing that the work should stand on its own feet, even if the ankles were slightly wobbly. When I was asked to comment on the six short novels of this volume, my first impulse was to refuse. And then, thinking over the things that have happened to these stories since they were written, I was taken with the idea that what happens to a book is very like what happens to a man.

These stories cover a long period of my life. As each was finished, that part of me was finished. It is true that while a work is in progress, the writer and his book are one. When a book is finished, it is a kind of death, a matter of pain and sorrow to the writer. Then he starts a new book, and a new life, and if he is growing and changing, a whole new life starts. The writer, like a fickle lover, forgets his old love. It is no longer his own: the intimacy and the surprise are gone. So much I knew, but I had not thought of the little stories thrust out into an unfriendly world to make their way. They have experiences, too—they grow and change or wane and die, just as everyone does. They make friends or enemies, and sometimes they waste away from neglect.

The Red Pony was written a long time ago, when there was desolation in my family. The first death had occurred. And the family, which every child believes to be immortal, was shattered. Perhaps this is the first adulthood of any man or woman. The first tortured question "Why?" and then acceptance, and then the child becomes a man. *The Red Pony* was an attempt, an experiment if you wish, to set down this loss and acceptance and growth. At that time I had had three books

Previously published.

published and none of them had come anywhere near selling their first editions. *The Red Pony* could not find a publisher. It came back over and over again, until at last a brave editor bought it for the *North American Review* and paid ninety dollars for it, more money than I thought the world contained. What a great party we had in celebration!

It takes only the tiniest pinch of encouragement to keep a writer going, and if he gets none, he sometimes learns to feed even on the acid of failure.

Tortilla Flat grew out of my study of the Arthurian cycle. I wanted to take the stories of my town of Monterey and cast them into a kind of folklore. The result was *Tortilla Flat*. It followed the usual pattern. Publisher after publisher rejected it, until finally Pascal Covici published it. But it did have one distinction the others had not: it was not ignored. Indeed, the Chamber of Commerce of Monterey, fearing for its tourist business, issued a statement that the book was a lie and that certainly no such disreputable people lived in that neighborhood. But perhaps the Chamber of Commerce did me a good service, for the book sold two editions, and this was almost more encouragement than I could stand. I was afraid that I might get used to such profligacy on the part of the public, and I knew it couldn't last. A moving-picture company bought *Tortilla Flat* and paid four thousand dollars for it. Thirty-six hundred came to me. It was a fortune. And when, a few years later, the same company fired its editor, one of the reasons was that he had bought *Tortilla Flat*. So he bought it from the company for the original four thousand dollars and several years later sold it to M-G-M for ninety thousand dollars. A kind of justification for me, and a triumph for the editor.

Of Mice and Men was an attempt to write a novel in three acts to be played from the lines. I had nearly finished it when my setter pup ate it one night, literally made confetti of it! I don't know how close the first and second versions would prove to be. This book had some success, but as usual it found its enemies. With rewriting, however, it did become a play and had some success.

There were long books between these little novels. I think the little ones were exercises for the long ones. The war came on, and I wrote *The Moon Is Down* as a kind of celebration of the durability of democracy. I couldn't conceive that the book would be denounced. I had written of Germans as men, not supermen, and this was considered a very weak attitude to take. I couldn't make much sense out of this, and it seems absurd now that we know the Germans were men, and thus fallible, even defeatable. It was said that I didn't know anything about war, and this was perfectly true, though how Park Avenue commandos found me out I can't conceive.

Subsequently I saw a piece of war as a correspondent, and following that wrote *Cannery Row*. This was a kind of nostalgic thing, written for a group of soldiers who had said to me, "Write something funny that isn't about the war. Write something for us to read—we're sick of war." When *Cannery Row* came out, it got the usual critical treatment. I was wasting my time in flippancy when I should be writing about the war. But half a million copies were distributed to troops, and they didn't complain. We had some very warlike critics then, much more bellicose than the soldiers.

In Mexico I heard a story and made a long jump back to the *Tortilla Flat* time. I tried to write it as folklore, to give it that set-aside, raised-up feeling that all folk stories have. I called it *The Pearl*. It didn't do so well at first either, but it seems to be gathering some friends, or at least acquaintances. And that's the list in this volume. It is strange to me that I have lived so many lives. Thinking back, it seems an endless time and yet only a moment.

1 Tortilla Flat

Joseph Fontenrose

1 *Tortilla Flat* and the Creation of a Legend

Steinbeck has loved no town so much as Monterey. It has been his town in a way that Salinas, Pacific Grove, and New York have not. It has an Old World flavor that has lingered from the days when it was the seat of Spanish and Mexican governments. The Steinbeck Monterey, which is not necessarily the same thing as the real Monterey, fights a losing battle against twentieth-century civilization, but has not yet gone under. "Monterey sits on the slope of a hill, with a blue bay below it and with a forest of tall dark pine trees at its back. The lower parts of the town are inhabited by Americans, Italians, catchers and canners of fish. But on the hill where the forest and the town intermingle, where the streets are innocent of asphalt and the corners free of street lights, the old inhabitants of Monterey are embattled as the Ancient Britons are embattled in Wales. These are the paisanos." This purlieu is Tortilla Flat, a purely fictitious subcommunity of Steinbeck's Monterey which represents the town's paisano population. "What is a paisano? He is a mixture of Spanish, Indian, Mexican and assorted Caucasian bloods. His ancestors have lived in California for a hundred or two years."

The paisanos are a people to whom Steinbeck is sympathetic. Paisano characters had appeared in *To a God Unknown* and in short stories later to be collected in *The Long Valley.* Steinbeck himself knew paisanos, talked and drank with them, listened to their tales, and some paisano lore, Moore* says, he learned from Susan Gregory, a resident of Monterey, to whom *Tortilla Flat* is dedicated. He put these people into a

Previously published.   *Harry Thornton Moore [ed.].

novel which has delighted many readers, but the book's unexpected popularity had its disconcerting features: readers liked the paisanos for wrong reasons, for being quaint curiosities, contrary to Steinbeck's intention.

Tortilla Flat at first sight appears to have a loose construction like *The Pastures of Heaven*, several stories set within a frame and written about the same people. It is, in fact, much more tightly constructed. Every story has the same central characters, Danny and his friends; we do not move from one family to another as in *The Pastures*. And it has a perceptible plot with a gradual rise and a swifter fall.

Danny, returning from the war, found that he had inherited two houses in Tortilla Flat. He rented one to Pilon, who never had money to pay rent. Pablo Sanchez and Jesus Maria Corcoran moved in with Pilon, but they never had money either. Relations between Danny and Pilon were becoming strained when Pilon's house burned down. Then the three friends moved in with Danny. The four admitted the Pirate, a half-witted man, and his five dogs to the house, hoping to get the Pirate's hoard of money; and he did bring a big bag of quarters to them for safekeeping, explaining that he had vowed a golden candlestick, worth a thousand quarters, to Saint Francis for the recovery of a dog. The friends were loyal to their trust, and the bag of quarters became "the symbolic center of the friendship." Soon afterward Joe Portagee joined the group and stole the Pirate's bag. His housemates gave him a beating and, recovering most of the money, found that the Pirate had enough to buy his candle. Several adventures occurred before and after the fulfillment of the vow; but finally the good days of the fellowship came to an end. Danny deserted his friends and ran wild; when he came back, he was listless and melancholy. To rekindle his spirits his friends gave a big party, which all Tortilla Flat attended. Danny had a last uproarious fling, surpassing all his past exploits of drinking, wenching, and fighting, until he ran outside to fight "The Enemy who is worthy of Danny," fell into a gulch, and was killed. The evening after the funeral his house burned down and the friends scattered.

It is a picaresque novel: Danny and his friends are pleasant rogues who never work unless extremity drives them to it. They pick up food, drink, and fun as chance offers, thinking nothing of petty theft, prevarication, and trickery, and they get along quite well without running water, electric lights, and a change of clothes. They live for the pleasures of the passing day: all they want is enough to eat, plenty of red wine, a cozy place to sit and talk, an occasional amour or brawl. "Love and fighting, and a little wine," said Pilon, "then you are always young, always happy." They use money and barterable goods mainly for buying wine or presents for women. Although they literally break the law often enough, they are not criminals. Nor do they lack conscience and moral feelings (except perhaps Joe Portagee). Still, they are hardly paragons of virtue and reliability, and he who puts his trust in them is likely to regret it. We may give them credit for keeping faith with the Pirate and keeping his bag of quarters inviolate; yet we should remember that the Pirate's quarters were devoted to Saint Francis, and also that Danny's second house burned down because Pablo, having bought a candle for Saint Francis, had used it profanely instead. "Have you forgotten that this candle was blessed? . . . Here is the principle which takes the waxen rod outside the jurisdiction of physics." Danny and his friends could not risk offending the saint again: they had but one house left.

The paisanos are great moralizers, but their moralizing too often consists in finding noble reasons for satisfying desires at a friend's expense, as when Pilon took Joe's serge trousers. Wanting wine as he sat beside the sleeping Joe on the beach, Pilon pretended to himself that he wanted it for Joe. Searching his own and Joe's pockets for money or some exchangeable object and finding none, he noticed Joe's serge pants. Now Joe's friends wore jeans; the trousers were much too small for Joe anyway, and besides Joe had stolen a blanket from Danny's house and needed punishment. So off came the trousers, which Pilon exchanged for a quart of wine (having asked for a gallon). Drinking the quart at once, he then "thought sadly of his friend out there on the beach," liable to arrest for indecent exposure, because a harpy (Mrs. Torrelli) "had tried to buy Pilon's friend's pants for a miserable quart of miserable wine." As he left Torrelli's he recovered the trousers and, posing as Joe's benefactor, returned them to the awakened and embarrassed Joe.

This is the sort of picaresque episode which has caused many readers to enjoy *Tortilla Flat* as an entertaining account of amiable rascals. The book, however, is a good deal more than a picaresque novel, and we have not said all that there is to say about its characters when we have called them rogues. As "good people of laughter and kindness" Steinbeck sets them in contrast to the commercial civilization that surrounds them; they "are clean of commercialism, free of the complicated systems of American business." This is a recurring theme of Steinbeck's fiction: the values of a simple people are opposed, as more healthy and viable, to the values of a competitive society.

That income property may damage human relations is an important thesis of *Tortilla Flat*. When Danny told Pilon that he had inherited two houses, Pilon said, "Now the great times are done. . . . Thou art lifted above thy friends. Thou art a man of property." The final phrase, one feels, is deliberately reminiscent of Galsworthy's Soames Forsyte, the man of property who got income from rented houses. The ownership of a rented house did aversely affect Danny's friendship with Pilon, and so when that house burned, Danny gladly gave up the status of rentier, saying, "Now we can be free and happy again." But Danny still owned one house; it was still true that as a house owner he could no longer smash windows at will or joyously destroy property with a clear conscience. "Always the weight of the house was upon him; always the responsibility to his friends." So he fled, and that was the beginning of the end.

The house was the body of an organism. In *Tortilla Flat* Steinbeck's biological point of view becomes explicit, and for the first time he makes deliberate, if humorous, use of the conception of the group as organism. The first words are, "This is the story of Danny and of Danny's friends and of Danny's house. It is a story of how these three became one thing, so that in Tortilla Flat if you speak of Danny's house you do not mean a structure of wood flaked with old whitewash. . . . No, when you speak of Danny's house you are understood to mean a unit of which the parts are men, from which came sweetness and joy, philanthropy and, in the end, a mystic sorrow." The group organism is more than just the sum of its parts, and the emotions of its unit parts coalesce into a single group emotion. When the friends discovered Joe Portagee's theft of the Pirate's money, they waited in the house for his return: "No words were spoken, but a wave of cold fury washed and crouched in the room. The feeling in the house was the feeling of a rock when the fuse is burning in toward the dynamite." So *Tortilla Flat* is on one level the life history of an organism, which was conceived when Danny, just out of jail, met Pilon and told him about the two houses. When Pilon, Pablo, and Jesus Maria moved in with Danny, the organism was born. It grew (when the

Pirate and Joe Portagee came in), thrived for a time, had good and bad experiences, became sick, and died; and the burning of the house was the cremation of the organism's body.

Just as individual organisms are units of a group organism, so smaller group organisms may be units of larger group organisms. Danny's household was part of Tortilla Flat, and Tortilla Flat was part of Monterey. Tortilla Flat as a whole had qualities like those of Danny's fellowship, but other qualities too, since each paisano household had its peculiarities. In Monterey as a whole paisano characteristics mingle with other kinds; yet Monterey is in certain respects like Danny's house: "There is a changeless quality about Monterey. . . . On Tortilla Flat, above Monterey, the routine is changeless, too. . . . In Danny's house there was even less change." Monterey too can behave like a single organism: "All Monterey began to make gradual instinctive preparations against the night"; then Steinbeck reports the unvarying acts of several persons and creatures at this time of day, not as acts of autonomous individuals but as coordinated movements of a single organism's parts. The group organism has a nervous system—the pathways of rumor—which carries information and emotions through the whole collective body. In several books Steinbeck expresses his wonder at the uncanny speed and operation of rumor, as in *Tortilla Flat:* "One evening, by that quick and accurate telegraph no one understands, news came in that a coast guard cutter had gone on the rocks near Carmel." Again, when Danny's friends began to plan the final party, the rumor of it flew about Tortilla Flat and beyond into Monterey: "The morning was electric with the news."

This organismic complex—Danny, Danny's fellowship, Tortilla Flat, Monterey—is doomed to defeat before the forces of twentieth-century civilization. Monterey becomes just another American city, and Tortilla Flat fades away into it. The old organism was changeless— that was its *hamartia*—and lacked the resilience and vigor needed for resistance. It was too easily infected by the insidious pride of property ownership.

The organismic complex may also be seen as an ecological community, for Steinbeck's interest in ecology first makes itself plainly felt in *Tortilla Flat*. The paisanos illustrate the ecological principle that every niche in the environment is likely to be filled and that some kind of creature will adapt itself to every possible source of subsistence. In his later foreword, Steinbeck says that the paisanos are "people who merge successfully with their habitat. In men this is called philosophy, and it is a fine thing." The Pirate brought his friends scraps and leftovers collected at the back doors of restaurants, very good fare sometimes, "fresh fish, half pies, untouched loaves of stale bread, meat that required only a little soda to take the green out"; once he had "a steak out of which only a little was missing." After the Pirate had bought his votive candlestick, he spent his daily quarter, earned by selling kindling wood, for food, which he brought to the house. Sometimes the friends threw rocks at fishing boats from the wharf and picked up the fish thrown back at them. They also pilfered food from restaurants and stores and got wine in devious ways. Some paisanos gleaned the bean fields. We perceive, therefore, that the paisanos, particularly of Danny's kind, are symbiotics or commensals (some would say parasites) of the Monterey community, depending upon others for their food, living on the pickings. So in one aspect *Tortilla Flat* is the story of this symbiosis. The paisanos, trying to preserve their own values, pushed into a corner of the habitat, are forced to become scavengers and jackal-like snatchers of others' food.

But more important than the organismic and ecological themes, though merging with them, is the Arthurian theme; for the Arthur story, as Steinbeck has said plainly, provided *Tortilla Flat* its central structure. On the first page Steinbeck says, "For Danny's house was not unlike the Round Table, and Danny's friends were not unlike the knights of it. And this is the story of how that group came into being, of how it flourished and grew to be an organization beautiful and wise. This story deals with the adventuring of Danny's friends, with the good they did, with their thoughts and their endeavors. In the end, this story tells how the talisman was lost and how the group disintegrated." This broad hint was ignored by readers of the manuscript and by reviewers of the published book. The failure of publishers' readers to recognize the Arthurian theme puzzled Steinbeck. In a letter to his agents, early in 1934, he said,

> I had expected that the plan of the Arthurian cycle would be recognized, that my Gawaine and Launcelot that my Arthur and Galahad would be recognized. Even the incident of the Sangreal in the search of the forest is not clear enough I guess. The form is that

of the Malory version, the coming of Arthur and the mystic quality of owning a house, the forming of the round table, the adventures of the knights and finally, the mystic adventures of Danny. However, I seem not to have made any of this clear.

When the book appeared in 1935 Steinbeck had provided it with chapter headings in the style of Caxton's Malory: e.g., chapter 1, "How Danny, home from the wars, found himself an heir, and how he swore to protect the helpless."

As recently as 1957 Steinbeck said that *Tortilla Flat* was deliberately based on Malory's book. An author's own statement of his structural plan should be of prime importance for the study and interpretation of a book. Yet in dealing with *Tortilla Flat* critics usually brush aside the Arthurian theme with the remark that there is nothing more to say about it than what Steinbeck himself has said, that the structural similarities which Steinbeck mentioned are so general as to lack significance, and that it is vain to look for detailed parallels. Of course, one must not look for one-to-one correspondences throughout; and if we say, truly enough, that Danny corresponds to Arthur and Pilon to Launcelot (Pablo seems to be Gawaine and Jesus Maria to be Galahad), we need not suppose that Danny is always Arthur, Pilon always Launcelot. This is to misconceive a creative writer's use of a mythical theme. Faulkner's *A Fable* illustrates nicely what a writer does with a myth: the old French Marshal is now God the Father, now Satan, and again Pontius Pilate; the Messiah is married to Mary Magdalene. In taking the Arthurian ingredient of *Tortilla Flat* seriously one is not reading the work as a modern version of the Arthur legend, since obviously the novel is not an Arthurian legend, any more than Faulkner's novel is the gospel story. The structural plan of Malory's *Arthur* had to be condensed for use as model for *Tortilla Flat*, and one rescue of a maid in distress will do for twenty. But Malory's Arthur story did in fact determine the narrative sequence and pervade the whole content.

First notice the narrative sequence. Arthur [Danny] after an obscure boyhood unexpectedly inherited a kingdom [house] and was transformed from ordinary manhood to heaven's viceroy as lord of the land [a landlord who experienced "the mystic quality of owning a house"]. The new king had trouble with subject kings and barons [Pilon, Pablo], who refused to pay homage [rent], but were finally defeated [the rented house burned down] and reconciled. Arthur [Danny], chastened by experience of rule, gathered knights [friends] to his Round Table [house] and gave them lands [shelter and a place to sleep]. The knights swore an oath of devotion and fealty [Danny's friends promised to see that Danny should never go hungry]. Arthur and his knights gave their attention to Pelles, the Maimed King, and the Grail which he kept [Pirate and his treasure]. Percival, undervalued by the knights (a simpleton in the pre-Malory legend), was placed among humble knights [the Pirate was given a corner of Danny's house, where he slept among his dogs]. The knights (but not Arthur) set out in search of the Grail for the welfare of Arthur's kingdom [the friends, without Danny, searched on Saint Andrew's Eve for mystic treasure for Danny's welfare]. Launcelot [Pilon, who said, "It is because my heart is clean of selfishness that I can find this treasure"] achieved a vision of the Grail [a phosphorescent light above the spot], but failed in the quest [found a Geodetic Survey marker]. Demon women [Sweets Ramirez] tempted Percival and Bors [Danny], who were finally saved from their machinations (the partly successful efforts of Launcelot's friends to draw him away from Guinevere, a later episode in Malory, are merged with the demon women's temptations in the successful effort of Danny's friends to separate him from Sweets). An old man came to Arthur's court with the boy Galahad [a Mexican corporal came to Danny's house with his infant son], who would be greater than his father [as the corporal intended his son to be]. Then the Grail appeared to the knights at supper and supplied them with meat and drink [Danny and his friends "were sitting in the living room, waiting for the daily miracle of food"; soon the Pirate (keeper of the true Grail) came in with a bag of mackerels]. Arthur and his knights, finishing their supper, went to look at the Siege Perilous, where Galahad sat [after their meal Danny and his friends went to look at the corporal's son lying in an apple box]. Galahad did not live long [the child died]. Percival [Joe Portagee] came upon a damsel [Tia Ignacia] who gave him wine to drink; he fell asleep in her pavilion [chair] and afterward made love to her (here Joe with his ill-fitting trousers is also La Cote Male Taile, whom a lady first scorned and then loved). Percival, Galahad, and Bors achieved the quest of the Grail [the friends' true treasure was the Pirate's bag of quarters, "the symbolic center of the friendship, the point of trust about which the fraternity revolved" (and the Pirate kept the house supplied with food, as the Grail provided often for the Round Table)].

After the quest the Round Table knights reassembled [the friends became reconciled with Joe Portagee], Launcelot saved Guinevere from death and again from capture [the friends rescued Teresina Cortez in the bean shortage] and had amorous trysts with her [Teresina found herself pregnant again]. The knights, as formerly, enjoyed tournaments and the fellowship of the Round Table ["Of the good life at Danny's House (chapter 14)], until Arthur became Launcelot's enemy. Arthur left England to fight elsewhere [Danny left the house and took to fighting elsewhere]. In Arthur's absence Mordred claimed the throne, relying upon the regency which Arthur had granted him and upon forged letters [Torrelli, carrying a deed signed by Danny, claimed ownership of the house]. Arthur's loyal subjects opposed Mordred's claim [Danny's friends foiled Torrelli's attempt to occupy the house]. Arthur returned to England [Danny came back to the house] and in a great last battle defeated his enemies [at the final big party "roaring battles . . . raged through whole clots of men," and "Danny defied and attacked the whole party," prevailing over everybody], but mortally wounded, went off over a lake to Avalon with supernatural companions [Danny, going outside to fight The Enemy, met him and fell into a gulch to his death]. None of Arthur's knights [Danny's friends] was present at his funeral and burial.

The parallels, of course, should not be more obvious than they are. Steinbeck started with tales, true and legendary, about paisanos. He perceived something in paisano behavior that reminded him of Arthur's knights, farfetched as any similarity may seem offhand, and he believed the likeness worth developing. The manner in which he could assimilate paisano deeds and habits to knightly ways is perhaps even better revealed in narrative details than in the more general structural parallels.

Like the knights of old, Danny, Pilon, and Joe Portagee were warriors, having enlisted in the American army in the First World War. And Danny, like every knight, was a horseman: "At twenty-five his legs were bent to the exact curves of a horse's sides," and few men could handle mules as well. Danny's company liked fights with one another or with anybody: Arthur's knights loved jousts and hostile encounters on the road. Both paisanos and knights fought over women, who were likely to favor the victor. Danny and Pilon had "a really fine fight" in the presence of two girls, who "kicked whichever man happened to be down." The knights' ladies were sometimes like that too. It hardly mattered to a certain damsel whether Palomides or Corsabrin won their fight, for she was ready to go with either (Malory 10:47). Another cheerfully spent the night with Epinogris after he had killed her father and a companion knight; the next morning she went off with Helior when he wounded Epinogris; later, Palomides restored her to Epinogris (Malory 10:83). Sometimes several knights attacked one man and took his lady from him; likewise several soldiers twice took the hardly reluctant Arabella Gross from Jesus Maria, and the second time Arabella helped them beat him up. Nor for all their chivalrous talk were Arthur's knights less lecherous than the paisanos. Arthur himself had amorous relations with Lyonors and Lot's wife Margawse, Launcelot with Guinevere and Elaine, Tristram with Isoud, Gawaine with Ettard. Moreover, the knights enjoyed good food and wine quite as much as did Danny and his friends.

Tortilla Flat has the same Catholic background as Malory's *Arthur*. In both books references to masses, rituals, and sacred objects are frequent; the characters in both speak as men to whom the Faith is second nature. Miracles occur, visions are seen, in Tortilla Flat as in the kingdom of Logres. The Pirate's dogs saw a vision of Saint Francis—so the Pirate believed—and he almost saw it too. As Jesus Maria lay on the beach near Seaside, the waves washed an empty rowboat ashore. He rowed it to Monterey, sold it for seven dollars, and bought both wine and a gift for Arabella. "God floated the little rowboat to you," said Pilon; and God sent a self-moving boat to Jesus Maria's Arthurian counterpart, Galahad, who on boarding it found a silk crown and a marvelous sword. Another time an empty boat came to Arthur as he stood on a riverbank, and carried him to a castle where he was served with wines and meats.

Danny's bed was the Siege Perilous. When Big Joe tried to lie in it, a stick came down hard on the soles of his feet "so that even he learned the inviolable quality of Danny's bed." Pilon taking the sleeping Joe's trousers and going off in search of wine is Launcelot taking the sleeping Kay's armor and going off in search of adventure (Malory 6:11). Even the paisanos' habit of sleeping in the open likens them to the knights, who often lay down in a forest or by a well; and as harts and deer crossed the knights' paths, so chickens crossed the paths of Danny and his friends. Danny in Monterey jail is Arthur imprisoned in Sir Damas's castle. Petey Ravanno at last won Gracie Montez's love when he tried suicide: Ettard finally loved Pelleas when she thought him dead. Old Man Ravanno, lovesick over a girl, is like Merlin besotted over Nineve; and as Merlin, entering a rock at Nineve's request, was shut therein and died, so when old Ravanno entered a tool house to win Tonia's love by feigning suicide, the door slammed shut, nobody saw him, and he really hanged himself. In many details like these, the paisanos show their kinship with Arthur's knights. They even use the same kind of speech: in courteous expression, statements of moral sentiment, accepted codes of conduct, even in their hypocrisy and insincerity, the paisanos resemble the knights. The use of the familiar second person and the literal translation of Spanish expressions into English have the effect of giving the paisanos a speech like that of Malory's knights.

Having observed the pervasive Arthurian tone of *Tortilla Flat*, we can no longer deny significance to Steinbeck's own statements about his debt to Malory. But how does the Arthurian reading of *Tortilla Flat* harmonize with the organismic and ecological reading? The Round Table, of course, was a group, a community, and therefore a social organism. There may appear to be a great gap between the nobility of the Arthurian cycle and the squalor of the meaner sort of commensal organism. However, it is just this contrast that gives *Tortilla Flat* much of its picaresque quality. And it has a deeper meaning too, a meaning like that of Mark Twain's *A Connecticut Yankee in King Arthur's Court*. After all, the knights were no more industrious and productive than Danny's band: the fact is that they too lived on the products of others' labor. In reading Malory we are now and then reminded that lands which other men tilled gave the knights their living. If these amiable and idle paisanos are parasites, so were the knights. If the knights were courteous men, so are the paisanos.

But the term "mock-heroic" seems misleading if applied to *Tortilla Flat*. Steinbeck is too fond of both paisanos and Arthurian legend to be guilty of belittling either. *Tortilla Flat* both illuminates the Dark Ages and dignifies the paisanos. We are again confronted with an antithesis: the actual lives of men who enjoy fighting, live on others' labor, and shun work are opposed to the legendary lives of men whose mode of life was much the same. If anything, the paisanos are more amusing and less dangerous than the knights. The sort of thing that they do is the stuff that legends are made of, as Steinbeck tells us in his preface: "It is well that this cycle be put down on paper so that in a future time scholars, hearing the legends, may not say as they say of Arthur and of Roland and of Robin Hood—'There was no Danny nor any group of Danny's friends, nor any house. Danny is a nature god and his friends primitive symbols of the wind, the sky, the sun.'"

This quotation may be called the primary oracle of *Tortilla Flat;* for again Steinbeck hints at the pagan myth behind Arthurian legend: Danny is the sun that rises, rules the sky and the wind, has his high noon and brilliant afternoon, and then sets into darkness. The burning of the house is the glory of the sunset—we should notice that in Steinbeck's first five novels (including *In Dubious Battle*) a fire or parching drought (which was a fire in an early draft of *To a God Unknown*) occurs either at the climax or at the conclusion. Notice the portents which posterity will attribute to the great climactic party: "It must be remembered . . . that Danny is now a god. . . . In twenty years it may be plainly remembered that the clouds flamed and spelled DANNY in tremendous letters; that the moon dripped blood; that the wolf of the world bayed prophetically from the mountains of the Milky Way." Thus Steinbeck resumes his opening jest. We are not expected to take Danny's divinity seriously, and yet Steinbeck tells us how gods and heroes are made.

Tortilla Flat thus mingles seriousness with jest, enjoyment with deeper meanings. Its tone blends humor, bittersweet pathos, and the objectivity of a sympathetic and amused narrator of legendary events in a language just different enough from ordinary speech to be distinctive and to place the narrative at one remove from the commonplace. Again and again the reader encounters expressions both surprising and delightful, as Pilon's "One feels a golden warmth glowing like a hot enchilada in one's stomach," Danny's "I have here two great steaks from God's own pig," and the narrator's "Big Joe abhorred the whole principle of shoveling. The line of the moving shovel was unattractive. The end to be gained, that of taking dirt from one place and putting it in another, was, to one who held the larger vision, silly and gainless." Surely not only Mordred, but also Launcelot, had no more love for a shovel.

Robert Gentry

2   Nonteleological Thinking in Steinbeck's *Tortilla Flat*

In 1940 John Steinbeck and marine biologist Edward F. Ricketts made a scientific expedition to the Gulf of California. A year later, the two friends jointly published *Sea of Cortez*, made up of a catalog of specimens and a narrative, published separately in 1951 as *The Log from the "Sea of Cortez"*. Chapter 14 of the narrative defines and explains nonteleological thinking, also called "is" thinking. This chapter from *The Log* has caused many critics to link Steinbeck with nonteleological thinking, which consists of looking at what *is* rather than what *was* or what *may be*. More important, one examining life using "is" thinking does not look for *why;* he looks at life as it is without looking for the reasons or causes for its present state. The teleologist looks for the causes and the reasons for events; the nonteleologist accepts life as it is.

Steinbeck was a nonteleologist during the peak of his career. He used this theory before he met Ricketts in the late 1930s and continued until after Ricketts's death in 1948. This is not to say that Steinbeck was strictly a nonteleologist, for all evidence points to the author's devotion to experimentation rather than to any one approach, and he cannot be tied to any one method. Still, a key theory appearing in his best writing is "is" thinking.

Steinbeck consistently followed nonteleological thinking during the 1930s, 1940s, and 1950s, especially in drawing his Mexican-American characters, who form a major link connecting the author's novels of this period. Spanning the time from 1932 through 1954, Steinbeck's Mexican-Americans appear in seven works: *The Pastures of Heaven, To a God Unknown, Tortilla Flat, The Long Valley, Cannery Row, The Wayward Bus*, and *Sweet Thursday*.

In 1935 Steinbeck published *Tortilla Flat*. Whereas *Pastures* and *God Unknown* simply contain Mexican-American characters, *Tortilla Flat* is built totally around this ethnic group. In addition, this novel is primarily humorous, whereas the previous two novels involving Mexican-Americans are primarily serious.

Tortilla Flat preceded the original *Log from the Sea of Cortez* (1941) by several years, yet it contains key nonteleological ideas. Many of the characteristics of *Tortilla Flat* follow the definition of "is" thinking found in chapter 14 of *The Log*. The novel examines what "is" rather than what should be. Little valuable time is spent seeking causes: the novel is a presentation of facts. This acceptance of what "is," without imposing previous experience, provides a balanced approach between optimism and negativism; it substitutes understanding and acceptance for moral judgment. *Tortilla Flat*, while concentrating on the simple pastoral life, touches on the struggle between man as an entity and man as a member of a group.

Tortilla Flat tells the story of a group of paisanos who are very poor inhabitants of a hilly district of Monterey, ironically called Tortilla Flat. The paisano's life-style is characterized by freedom, acceptance, living for the moment, nonmaterialism, oneness with nature, and natural friendship—ideas that are reflected in the definition of "is" thinking in *The Log;* that is, seeking freedom and life for the moment. Living for the moment usually results in a nonmaterialistic approach to life; materialists are often destroyed in Steinbeck's novels. Steinbeck also explores the oneness with nature that his nonteleologists possess. In *Tortilla Flat* this oneness is extended to include one's true friends, for the "is" thinker accepts not only life and nature but also the others with whom he comes into contact.

The situation in *Tortilla Flat* almost demands that the novel be written from a nonteleological viewpoint, for an acceptance of things as they occur is a part of the paisano's life-style. Each episode is a moral parable in which a paisano is tempted by symbols of American business, but he resists and survives with his soul intact.[1] In this setting the characters learn that personal freedom is their only possession, but that their freedom is in conflict with economics.[2] This conflict seems to be no real problem because the group puts friendship first. The paisanos can survive because they have learned to accept the world as being good enough for their purposes. They simply avoid situations beyond their control.[3]

One of the key ideas of "is" thinking is a love of freedom, and this love is certainly the cornerstone of the paisano's life-style. He resists responsibility of any type, for accepting responsibility usually means some loss of freedom. Since he has such sparse possessions, he has nothing that could be "stolen, exploited, or mortgaged,"[4] making him immune to the monetary problems of the 1930s and 1940s.

In a weak moment Big Joe, Pilon, and Danny join the army: as the wine goes down in the bottles, patriotism goes up in the three paisanos (p. 12). It is ironic that from the moment the three actually volunteer for responsibility, they are each assigned menial jobs that have little or nothing to do with the war. Pilon, the most philosophical of the group, seems to sum up the paisano's love for freedom as he and Pablo drink wine and remember their childhood: " 'No care then, Pablo. I knew not sin. I was very happy.' 'We have never been happy since,' " Pablo sadly agrees (p. 45).

None of the paisanos give up their freedom for very long except for Danny. His inheritance of his grandfather's two old houses causes the major conflict in the story, and eventually causes Danny's death. The "weight of responsibility" motivates Danny to get drunk when he is told of his inheritance (p. 17). Pilon philosophizes on the event: "Now it is over. . . . Now the great times are done. Thy friends will mourn" (p. 25). When Danny enters one of the houses to survey his new possession, "Pilon [notices] that the worry of property [is] settling on Danny's face. . . . one cry of pain [escapes] him before he [leaves] for all time his old and simple existence" (p. 28).

Pilon observes Danny's loss of freedom, but he also sees some of his own disappear when he moves in with Danny. "I am getting in debt to him. . . . My freedom will be cut off. Soon I will be a slave because of the Jew's house" (p. 30).

The freedom of the paisano's life is reflected well in the changelessness of his surroundings. "On Tortilla Flat, above Monterey, the routine is changeless, too. . . . In Danny's house there was even less change. The friends had sunk into a routine which might have been monotonous for anyone but a *paisano*—up in the morning, to sit in the sun and wonder what the Pirate would bring" (pp. 259–60). Amid this casualness Danny's loss of freedom begins to prey upon his mind. He has become too integrated into the group. He spends more and more of his time remembering his life before he owned a house; finally he leaves his house and his friends. He steals, he breaks windows, he gets into fights. In the ultimate attempt to break free from his burden of responsibility, he sells his house to Torrelli, a local wine merchant, for twenty-five dollars. This bid for freedom fails—the friends grab the bill of sale and burn it before Torrelli can stop them (pp. 262–81).

Danny's loss of freedom eventually causes his death. A gigantic party is held for Danny to bring him out of his doldrums. He seems to be returning to his old self until suddenly he leaves his house to find a fight, only to stumble into the gulch behind the shack and be killed (pp. 283–304).

A second nonteleological aspect stressed in *The Log* and then in *Tortilla Flat* is an acceptance of things as they are. These Mexican-Americans avoid inner conflicts by adopting an accepting nature. As Edwin Berry Burgum said, "They recognize that happiness is more consistent, spreads over a broader area of time, when one does not over stimulate by conscious attention those deep urges from within, but takes them, after [D. H.] Lawrence's bidding, as they come. . . . Experience has taught them that the world as it is, is quite good enough for their purposes. . . . They have long since learned to avoid situations beyond their control."[5] Frederick Bracher added, "The inhabitants of Tortilla Flat . . . have no wish to become involved in the contradictions of a civilization which drives itself to the verge of a nervous breakdown finding new ways to cure the sick and kill the healthy, to pamper the body and stultify the spirit."[6]

The simple-minded Pirate is the ideal accepting person. Pilon tells the Pirate that the Pirate's friends worry about him. The Pirate is surprised that he has friends, much less that they care for him. "It did not occur to him to doubt them [Pilon's words] since Pilon was saying them" (p. 103).

Acceptance is as much a part of the paisano's life-style as it is a part of "is" thinking. Pilon seldom has any money, but one night he acquires a dollar "in a manner so astounding that he tried to forget it immediately for fear the memory might make him mad." A man gives him a dollar, asking him to go get him four bottles of ginger ale. Pilon says that such things are miracles and should not be questioned but taken on faith (p. 36).

An accepting attitude is often directed toward God, the church, or other religious matters. For instance, Pilon explains to Pablo that God is a very accepting deity. God is not concerned about the source of the money used in a mass: "A mass is a mass. . . . And where a mass comes from is of no interest to God. He just likes them the same as you like wine" (p. 50).

Nonteleological thinking stresses living for the present rather than dwelling on the past or worrying about the future. Living for the moment seems to epitomize the paisano's life-style. The friends feel that being concerned about any time other than the present can bring only heartache and pain. On Saint Andrew's Eve, as Pilon and the other members of the group wander through the forest looking for buried treasure, the wind makes the trees talk to each other, foretelling fortunes and deaths. Pilon knows it is not good to listen to the trees talking: "No good ever came of knowing the future" (p. 128).

For those who meditate on the past or plan for the future, clocks are important. For a paisano who lives for the moment, a timepiece is an unnecessary luxury.

> Clocks and watches were not used by the *paisanos* of Tortilla Flat. Now and then one of the friends acquired a watch in some extraordinary manner, but he kept it only long enough to trade it for something he really wanted. Watches were in good repute at Danny's house, but only as media of exchange. For practical purposes, there was the great golden watch of the sun. It was better than a watch, and safer, for there was no way of diverting it to Torrelli. (p. 237)

Many of the episodes that emphasize living for the moment deal in some way with money or wine or both. For the paisanos, having wine at the moment is important; it is not something to be kept for the future. Pilon and Pablo talk Jesus Maria out of two dollars because they need to pay Danny some portion of the overdue rent. Then they decide to buy two gallons of wine for Danny to give to Mrs. Morales instead of letting Danny buy his own gift for her (pp. 61–64). Because Danny "is a man who knows little restraint in drinking," Pilon and Pablo drink one of the two gallons rather than giving both to Danny (p. 66). Eventually Pilon and Pablo drink all of the wine except a small portion, which is in the house when it burns (pp. 68–78).

One reason that Steinbeck's paisanos are so successful at accepting their situation and living for the moment is that they are nonmaterialistic. They are often tempted by the things of the world, but they seem to survive each temptation. The author depicts a group of men whose materialistic drives are subordinate to their love of freedom and living for the present. When Danny learns of his inheritance, the "worry of property" settles on his face. His shoulders straighten "to withstand the complexities of life" (p. 28). Danny tells Pilon, "I wish you owned it and I could come to live with you" (p. 29). When Jesus Maria runs to Danny's house to tell him that his other house is on fire, Danny asks only if the fire department is there. Finding that the trucks have arrived, Danny returns to Mrs. Morales without further concern (p. 79). The morning after the fire, Danny indulges in a little "conventional anger against careless friends" and thinks over "the ruin of his status as a man with a house to rent" (p. 81). His true emotion, though, is "one of relief that at least one of his burdens" is removed (p. 82).

No one in the novel really seems concerned about material things, especially money. After deciding not to give Danny money, Pilon summarizes the paisano financial philosophy: "Happiness is better than riches. . . . If we try to make Danny happy, it will be a better thing than to give him money" (p. 144). Happiness cannot be bought; therefore the happy person is no slave to money. In a typical instance, "On Alvarado Street, Hugo Machado, the tailor, put a sign in his shop door, 'Back in Five Minutes,' and went home for the day" (p. 66).

The pastoral life and a closeness to nature are identified as characteristics of nonteleological thinking in both the definition of the philosophy and in Steinbeck's earlier works. Steinbeck presents the paisanos as a natural part of their surroundings. They need not beautify nature; they *are* nature. Steinbeck says this in one of his descriptions of the group: "Danny is a nature God and his friends primitive symbols of the wind, the sky, and the sun" (p. 10). As Pablo and Pilon sit on their front porch wiggling their toes only when flies light on them, Pablo says, "If all the dew were diamonds, . . . we would be rich. We would be drunk all our lives" (p. 48). In other words, they neither have nor need money, but they abound in the riches of nature.

In one bit of purple prose Steinbeck elevates Pilon to great heights as he describes his closeness to nature. Feeling guilty about never paying Danny any rent, Pilon cleans enough squid to make two dollars. On the way to Danny's house to pay him the money, Pilon buys wine but thinks he will share it with Danny. The dusk is purple; the trees are dark against the sky; the gulls are flying lazily home. In this setting

Pilon is described as "a lover of beauty and a mystic" (p. 38). At this moment Pilon figuratively joins the gulls—he is beautiful and his thoughts are "unstained with selfishness and lust" (p. 39). There is no soul purer than his. A mean bulldog sniffs at Pilon but knowingly goes away without biting him. Pilon returns from his heavenly "journey" only to be lured off by Pablo to Pilon's house, where they drink the two gallons of wine (pp. 41–43).

The paisanos are careful to protect the integrity of the friendship within the group. Steinbeck balances the freedom of the individual and the strength of friendship within the group in a way not repeated in his later nonteleological novels. When Big Joe steals Danny's blanket and trades it for wine, the friends do not get very upset (p. 138). On the other hand, the group cannot tolerate Big Joe's theft of the Pirate's money from beneath Danny's pillow. The paisanos beat him severely but then doctor his bruises in a loving manner (pp. 202–4).

The paisano's philosophy is to share with his friends, but he does not always divide with the group as he should. Sometimes he talks about sharing without really doing it. Pilon is angry when Danny asks for the rent. He says to Pablo as they stalk off to get the money, "We have been his friends for years. When he was in need, we fed him. When he was cold, we clothed him." Pablo asks when they have done these things, and Pilon replies, "Well, we would have, if he needed anything and we had it. That is the kind of friends we were to him" (pp. 54–55).

The friends value friendship above money. Danny is secretly glad when one of his houses burns because he no longer has to pressure the paisanos to pay the rent, which they never pay anyway. "My friends have been cool toward me because they owe me money. Now we can be free and happy again" (p. 82). To be a friend to others is of prime importance for the paisano. Pilon is representative; he has "neither the stupidity, the self-righteousness nor the greediness for reward ever to become a saint. Enough for Pilon to do good and to be rewarded by the glow of human brotherhood accomplished" (p. 99).

It is one of the ironies of the novel that Danny seems to keep the group's unique friendship intact. When he dies, the ring of friends who lived with him are unable to attend his funeral. None of them have decent clothes, and clothes cannot be borrowed because everyone in Monterey plans to attend the funeral (p. 307). At the end of the novel Danny's remaining house accidentally catches fire, but the friends let it burn; afterward they walk away, and no two walk together, marking the end of this circle of paisanos (p. 317).

Steinbeck said that he wrote *Tortilla Flat* for relaxation and not as a serious exploration. Therefore the novel presents the author at ease and writing naturally from a nonteleological viewpoint. At the time he published the novel this viewpoint seemed to reflect the true Steinbeck, an author who enjoyed experimenting with characteristics which would later be solidified into a philosophy called "is" thinking. Using these Mexican-American characters as his vehicles, Steinbeck depicted a view of life as it is, without examining the causes. "Is" thinking was not the only way Steinbeck viewed life. Nevertheless, it seems to be one of his major focuses, and his Mexican-American creations are his most consistent examples of this view.

II Of Mice and Men

Anne Loftis

3 A Historical Introduction to *Of Mice and Men*

Steinbeck wrote *Of Mice and Men* midway through the 1930s, the most creative decade of his career. During this time he was becoming increasingly concerned about current social and economic problems in California, and he published three successive novels about farm workers, each distinctive in tone and conception.

Of Mice and Men was a deliberate change from his previous book, *In Dubious Battle* (1936), an imaginative interpretation of a contemporary farm strike and a study of the movement and action of crowds. In the new project he set out to work within a narrow framework, concentrating on a small number of characters in carefully detailed settings, telling his story as economically and dramatically as possible. He explained that he was teaching himself to write for the theater, and in fact he soon did translate the novel into a play.

The subject was less controversial than that of his previous book. He was writing about people who were isolated in the society of their time, who belonged to a group that was fast disappearing from the American scene. Only a short time before, thousands of itinerant single men had roamed the Western states following the harvests. Their labor was essential to the success of the bonanza grain-growing enterprises that had been started in the second half of the nineteenth century and had proliferated so rapidly that by the year 1900 some 125,000 threshers were migrating along a "belt" that extended from the Brazos Bottoms in Texas north to Saskatchewan and Manitoba, and from Minnesota west to the state of Washington. Many of them traveled by rail, arriving in the fields in empty boxcars that were later used to transport the grain.

In the early years they were paid an average wage of $2.50 to $3 a day plus board and room. The "room" was frequently a tent: living conditions were spartan. But wages rose at the time of the First World War when the price of wheat was high, partly through the action of the Industrial Workers of the World, which established an eight-hundred-mile picket line across the Great Plains states.

In California, where grain was the chief farm commodity in the 1870s and 1880s before the advent of irrigated agriculture, some of the early harvesters were disappointed miners returning from the goldfields. In the social and occupational hierarchy they were on a level considerably below the mule drivers, who, like Steinbeck's character Slim, were valued for their skill in handling as many as twenty animals "with a single line" and who were generally employed permanently on the ranches.

Steinbeck's recognition of the status of the mule driver epitomizes his re-creation of a working culture that was undergoing a historic change even as he wrote about it. In 1938, the year after *Of Mice and Men* was published, about half the nation's grain was harvested by mechanical combines that enabled 5 men to do the work that had been done formerly by 350. The single farm workers who traveled from job to job by train, or like George and Lennie by bus, were disappearing. They were being replaced by whole families migrating in cars, like the people in Steinbeck's next novel, *The Grapes of Wrath*.

The physical background for *Of Mice and Men* came from Steinbeck's own early years in a California agricultural valley. His native city of Salinas, eighty miles south of San Francisco, is the seat of Monterey County. (His father was the county treasurer for a number of years.) In his childhood he spent a good deal of time on a ranch near King City, south of Salinas, that was owned by relatives of his mother, and during his high school years he worked summers in the fields and orchards near home.

More important in planting the germ of the novel was an experience he had during a period when he dropped out of college. He entered Stanford in 1919, already ambitious to become a writer and determined to follow his own particular interests in the curriculum. Experiencing some difficulty with courses and grades the following year, he decided to break away, shed his identity as a university student, and make his way for a while as a workingman. "I was a bindle-stiff myself for quite a spell," he told reporters some years later. "I worked in the same country that the story is laid in."[1]

Tall and husky, he was hired as a laborer on a ranch near Chualar, a short distance—in miles—from the prosperous neighborhood in Salinas where he was born, and for a time he became a part of this very different world. The fact that he was promoted to straw boss[2] suggests that he got on well with his fellow workers. He had a talent for being inconspicuous: they probably learned very little about him while he was gathering impressions of them.

After he returned to the campus, he published a story in the *Stanford Spectator* about a runaway girl who takes shelter during a storm in the bunkhouse of some Filipino farm workers. She marries the crew leader, who alternately showers her with presents and beats her. Eventually she leaves him.[3] Although the prose is vigorous, this sketch, full of bizarre details that strain the reader's credulity, is an amateur's experiment.

It is instructive to compare this apprentice effort with Steinbeck's achievement as a mature artist a dozen years later. *Of Mice and Men* is a work of symmetry and balance in which the action moves with a compelling momentum toward an inevitable conclusion. The social history which he had learned firsthand is woven seamlessly into the fabric of the story.

In the first scene by the river he introduces the mute evidence of the past: the ash pile left by previous campers and the tree limb overhanging the water, worn smooth by tramps who have come there over the years to jungle up. Linking the past with the present, George and Lennie make their entrance in the tradition of bindle stiffs, carrying blankets on their backs. The story then moves into the opening dialogue, justly famous in American literature, through which we come to know and believe in the touching partnership of the moronic giant and his gruff protector.

The next scene at the ranch opens with a description of the empty bunkhouse with its tiers of beds, each with an apple box nailed to the wall to hold the meager possessions of men who travel light. The place is not particularly clean. Flies dart through the motes of dust stirred up by the push broom of Candy, the old swamper; a can of bug powder suggests lice or bedbugs in the mattress ticking.

The characters who come in one by one create the social dimension of the place. This rough lodging in which nothing has been provided beyond the bare necessities is governed by the harsh code of the men who live there for a week, a month, or a year. It is a society intolerant of weakness or difference. Old Candy, helpless to stop the shooting of his dog, knows that he too will be banished when he is no longer useful. Crooks, the black stable hand, is excluded except on Christmas when the boss brings in a gallon of whiskey for the entire crew. The rest of the year Crooks plays horseshoes outside with the others, but when they come indoors to sleep, he goes off alone to his bed in the harness room of the barn.

Women are not welcome in this male enclave. Curley's wife, wandering around the ranch in a wistful quest for some kind of human contact, is stereotyped by the men, whose experience of women comes from "old Suzy" and her girls in town. Curley's wife (in the novel she has no other name) goes along with the typecasting by playing the vamp, inflaming her jealous huband, who, as the son of the boss, is as powerful as he is vicious. It is on this explosive situation that the plot turns. Lennie, sensing trouble too complicated for a simple mind to unravel, begs to leave after George tells him that Curley's wife is "poison" and "jail bait."

Steinbeck had a different view of her, as he explained in a letter to the actress who played the role in the Broadway production of the play. Curley's wife acts seductively because she "knows instinctively that if she is to be noticed at all, it will be because someone finds her sexually attractive." But her pose is deceptive. "Her moral training was most rigid." She was a virgin until her marriage and had had no sexual experience outside her unfulfilling union with Curley. She had grown up "in an atmosphere of fighting and suspicion" and had "learned to be hard to cover her fright." But she is fundamentally "a nice, kind girl" who has "a natural trustfulness. . . . If anyone—a man or a woman— ever gave her a break—treated her like a person—she would be a slave to that person."[4]

Steinbeck captured this aspect of her character in her final scene with Lennie. In the presence of this childlike man she drops her defenses and expresses her real feelings. Her rambling monologue of blighted hopes and tawdry fantasies is, in effect, a last confession.

Steinbeck has prepared his readers for the shocking climax of the novel through his portrait of Lennie. He might have created a caricature in the mental defective who crushes soft creatures in his powerful hands. He had worked with a real-life Lennie, he told reporters when he was writing the stage version of *Of Mice and Men*. "He didn't kill a girl. He killed a ranch foreman. Got sore because the boss had fired his pal and stuck a pitchfork right through his stomach."[5] The fictional Lennie is passive and nonviolent. Would he be capable of a murderous rage if George was threatened? Perhaps. It is through his connection with his intelligent partner that he becomes believable. In the opening scene Steinbeck establishes the dynamics of their relationship, in which George's exasperated bossing of Lennie appears as a form of protectiveness that masks their mutual dependence.

Loneliness is a recurrent theme in the novel, articulated in George's speech that begins: "Guys like us, that work on the ranches, are the loneliest guys in the world. They got no family. They don't belong noplace."

"*But not us,*" Lennie replies. "*And why. Because . . . because I got you to look after me, and you got me to look after you, and that's why.*"

Their plan to find a place of their own, which Candy and Crooks, outcasts on the ranch, are hungry to share, is straight out of the American Dream. They have set down the details in a kind of litany which George recites while Lennie chimes in with the chorus. They repeat the comforting words from time to time like an incantation to ward off trouble and rekindle hope. In the last scene—a final irony in a work compounded of ironies—George, in order to calm Lennie, utters the familiar refrain, which becomes an epitaph for his friend.

Before he found the apt title from Robert Burns's poem, Steinbeck called his work in progress "Something That Happened." While he was at work on the book he sent revealing bulletins to his literary agent and his friends. Describing a state of mind familiar to writers, he commented in February 1936, "I have to start and am scared to death as usual—miserable, sick feeling of inadequacy. I'll love it once I get down to work."[6]

It was as he predicted. In a postcard to the same friend he reported that "after two months of fooling around my new work is really going and that makes me very happy—kind of an excitement like that you get near a dynamo from breathing pure oxygen." He explained, "I'm not interested in the method as such but I am interested in having a vehicle exactly adequate to the theme."[7]

On April 4: ". . . my new work is moving swiftly now."[8]

Eleven days later: "Pages are flying."[9]

Toward the end of May he reported a setback. His setter pup had "made confetti" of half of the manuscript. "Two months work to do over again. . . . There was no other draft." He tried to be philosophical. The pup may have been "acting critically. I didn't want to ruin a good dog for a ms. I'm not sure is good at all."[10] He finished the work during the summer.

Almost immediately after sending the manuscript to his publishers he set out on a research trip around California in preparation for writing a series of newspaper articles on newly arriving Dust Bowl migrants and the employers who were making life difficult for them. While starting in a direction that led eventually to *The Grapes of Wrath*, he could not ignore the book he had just completed. He reported that there was a mixed reaction to the manuscript. (He didn't say *whose* reaction.) His publisher, Pascal Covici, liked it.[11]

Steinbeck said that he was not expecting a large sale, and he was surprised that *Of Mice and Men* was chosen as a Book-of-the-Month Club selection and that 117,000 copies were sold in advance of the official publication date, February 25, 1937. The reviews were enthusiastic. "The boys have whooped it up for John Steinbeck's new book," Ralph Thompson wrote in the *New York Times*.[12] The novel was praised by, among others, Christopher Morley, Carl Van Vechten, Lewis Gannett, Harry Hansen, Heywood Broun, and Eleanor Roosevelt. Henry Seidel Canby wrote in the *Saturday Review of Literature* that "there has been nothing quite so good of the kind in American writing since Sherwood Anderson's early stories."[13]

In early April it was on the best-seller list in six cities across the country, and it continued to be among the top ten best-sellers in fiction into the fall. Steinbeck, who said that he would never learn to conceive of money in larger quantities than two dollars, was surprised by the large checks he received from his agents. He was not by any means an unknown writer. *Tortilla Flat* (1935) had been a popular success, and *In Dubious Battle* and some of his short stories had been praised by critics. But he was now treated as a celebrity, something he had always feared.

As he and his wife Carol passed through New York en route to Europe, his appearance in his publisher's office was considered newsworthy in literary circles.

On his return he worked with playwright George F. Kaufman, who was going to direct the stage version of *Of Mice and Men*. Kaufman wrote Steinbeck that the novel "drops almost naturally into play form," but he had a couple of suggestions for changes. He thought that Curley's wife "should be drawn more fully: she is the motivating force of the whole thing and should loom larger." He told Steinbeck: "Preserve the marvelous tenderness of the book. *And*—if you could feel it in your heart to include a *little* more humor, it would be extremely valuable, both for its lightening effect and the heightening of the subsequent tragedy by comparison."[14]

Steinbeck seems to have ignored the latter idea, but he considerably enlarged the role of Curley's wife, who is presented in the play as a person with strongly articulated feelings about her past history and family relationships. Another change was his decision to end the play with George's speech to Lennie just before he pulls the trigger, an improvement over the anticlimactic group scene in the novel.

Of Mice and Men opened at the Music Box Theater in New York on November 23, 1937, with Wallace Ford as George and Broderick Crawford as Lennie. Claire Luce appeared as Curley's wife. Will Geer, who was prominent in many plays in the 1930s, took the part of Slim. The reviews were ecstatic, and the play drew enthusiastic audiences during a season in which *Tobacco Road*, *Golden Boy*, *Stage Door*, and *You Can't Take It with You* were among the offerings on Broadway. It ran for 207 performances and won the New York Drama Critics' Circle Award in competition with Thornton Wilder's *Our Town*.

The film version of *Of Mice and Men*, written by Eugene Solow from the novel and the play, is considered by Joseph R. Millichap to be the most faithful screen adaptation of any of Steinbeck's works.[15] It was a labor of love on the part of the director, Lewis Milestone, who consulted with Steinbeck and visited ranches in the Salinas Valley in his company. Although he shot most of the outdoor sequences in southern California, the landscape has an authentic look. He commissioned Aaron Copeland to compose the background music, and he took pains with the casting. He hired Burgess Meredith to play George, Lon Chaney, Jr., was Lennie, and Betty Field played Curley's wife, called

Mae. Charles Bickford appeared as Slim. Milestone brought Leigh Whipper from the Broadway cast to repeat his performance as Crooks.

The movie, released in 1939, was not a box-office success. Never as famous as John Ford's *The Grapes of Wrath*, it deserves more recognition than it has received. An excellent television version of *Of Mice and Men* based on Milestone's film was brought out in 1981, featuring Robert Blake, Randy Quaid, Pat Hingle, and Lew Ayres. In 1970 an opera by Carlisle Floyd, who wrote both the music and libretto, had its premiere in Seattle. The composer changed the story slightly (he eliminated Crooks, the black stable buck, and created a chorus of ranch hands), but he was faithful to Steinbeck's theme. One critic, obviously no lover of the original work, thought that the new form was an improvement: "The operatic conventions impose a frame that makes Steinbeck's basic sentimentality infinitely more acceptable."[16]

Warren French has suggested that readers who spoke of *Of Mice and Men* as sentimental should "think of it as an expression of Steinbeck's outraged compassion for the victims of chaotic forces."[17] Criticism of the novel became noticeable at the end of the 1930s when there was an evaluation of Steinbeck's total literary achievement up to that point. On the one hand, he was praised for his versatility, and on the other, denounced for trying to do too much, for mixing romance and realism,[18] for "weakness in characterization" and "puerile symbolism."[19] The most damaging assessment, one that would be echoed by later critics, was Edmund Wilson's statement that Steinbeck's preoccupation with biology led him "to present life in animal terms," to deal "almost always in his fiction . . . either with lower animals or with human beings so rudimentary that they are almost on the animal level." Wilson found a prime example of his point in the character Lennie.[20] (More recently Jackson Benson has given a different interpretation of Steinbeck's concern with biology. According to this view, science and nature provided a philosophical framework for Steinbeck's writing, his conviction that meaning and stability came from a sense of connection with the natural universe.[21] This thesis supports Peter Lisca's emphasis on the importance in *Of Mice and Men* of the camp by the river, "a retreat from the world to a private innocence," and of George and Lennie's dream of the farm, "a safe place," as a symbol of happiness.)[22]

Wilson summarized the novel as "a compact little drama, contrived with almost too much cleverness, and a parable which criticized humanity from a nonpolitical point of view."[23] During the 1940s and 1950s Steinbeck's fiction, in particular the three farm-worker novels on which his reputation was largely based, were criticized on ideological grounds. His work had been popular when it appeared because it expressed the values of the Depression decade: a passion for social justice and concern for the common man. Yet, fittingly for a man of independent judgment, he was attacked by both radicals and conservatives. Left-wing critics complained of his nonconformity to the doctrines with which he was identified by the growers' groups whose actions he had exposed in *In Dubious Battle* and *The Grapes of Wrath*.

It is interesting that *Of Mice and Men*, which represents a break in the sequence of Steinbeck's "problem" novels, took on some political coloration from his other writings and from his ongoing connection with the controversies of the 1930s. In the summer of 1937 the Theatre Union of San Francisco, which supported maritime workers in their fight for unionization, gave what was probably the first stage performance of the work, creating their own script from the novel. Two years later Steinbeck gave permission to some Stanford students to give a benefit reading from the book to raise money to help the migrants. In the 1970s scenes from the play were presented to the supporters of Cesar Chavez's United Farm Workers Union.

Yet the continuing popularity of *Of Mice and Men*, both as a drama and in its original novel form, indicates the degree to which it has transcended its historical context. As a work of literature, it has attained the status of a modern classic. A staple of the middle-school curriculum in England and the United States, it has been translated into a dozen foreign languages. The arguments of the critics will go on, no doubt, but we have come to acknowledge that Steinbeck's "little book"[24] has a quality that defies analysis. It touches our deepest feelings and enlarges our understanding of the human condition. As a tragedy, with the power to arouse pity and terror implicit in that art form, it has drawn readers for half a century and, it seems safe to predict, will reach new generations in the century to come.

William Goldhurst

4   *Of Mice and Men:* John Steinbeck's Parable of the Curse of Cain

Critical opinion on John Steinbeck's *Of Mice and Men* is surprisingly varied, miscellaneous, and contradictory. One critic calls the novella a dark comedy and says that it descends from myths of King Arthur. Other critics think of it as a tragedy, and at least one advances the idea that it has no mythic background at all. A few commentators feel very definitely that *Of Mice and Men* is political in its drift, that it illustrates "tensions created by the capitalistic system" or dramatizes "the role of the radical organizer attempting to lead the masses towards a workmen's utopia." Others contend that it has little or no political content but rather stresses sociological points such as our unenlightened treatment of old people and the mentally retarded. Several other critics have observed that Steinbeck's story emphasizes a simple thesis, variously identified as (1) each man kills the thing he loves, (2) our pleasures often oppose and thwart our schemes, and (3) the nonmorality of Nature. Basic differences of opinion may be illustrated by the comments of two well-known literary historians who sum up their reactions to the story in almost antithetical terms: Joseph Warren Beach stressed "the tone of humanity and beauty with which Steinbeck invests his tragic episode . . . without the use of sentimental phrase or direct statement," while Alfred Kazin spoke of "the calculated sentimentality of *Of Mice and Men*" which makes Steinbeck's fable "meretricious in its pathos, a moment's gulp."[1]

Perhaps this diversity reflects the sort of critical individualism which Steinbeck had in mind when he said that many critics fall under the heading of "special pleaders [who] use my work as a distorted echo chamber for their own ideas."[2] Two significant points do emerge, in any case, from a consideration of this body of critical comment. First, it affirms and reaffirms the inherent fertility of Steinbeck's novella; already *Of Mice and Men* has furnished two generations of readers with

Previously published.

material for intellectual sustenance. Second, and perhaps this is a bit unforeseen, no one of the critics, as I see it, has penetrated to the essential meaning which luxuriates under the surface of Steinbeck's story. The present study offers for consideration what seems to me a more basic and accurate interpretation than is currently available. I ought to say at the outset that my emphasis is on the religious sources of *Of Mice and Men* and its mythic-allegorical implications.

Of Mice and Men is a short novel in six scenes presented in description-dialogue-action form that approximates stage drama in its effect (about this fact there is no critical disagreement). The time scheme runs from Thursday evening through Sunday evening—exactly three days in sequence, a matter of some importance, as we shall see presently. The setting is the Salinas Valley in California, and most of the characters are unskilled migratory workers who drift about the villages and ranches of that area picking up odd jobs or doing short-term fieldwork and then moving on to the next place of employment. Steinbeck focuses on two such laborers who dream of one day saving up enough money to buy a small farm of their own. One of these is George Milton, small of stature, clever, sensitive, and compassionate; the other is Lennie Small, who is oversized, mentally retarded, enormously strong, and prone to getting into serious trouble. Early in the story the prospect of their ever realizing their dream seems remote, but as the action develops (they meet a crippled bunkhouse worker who wants to go in with them on the scheme, and who offers to chip in his life savings), the probability of fulfillment increases. If the three homeless migrants pool their salaries at the end of the current month, they can quit and move on to their farm, which, as Steinbeck emphasizes repeatedly, is a place of abundance and a refuge from the hardships of life.

Lennie manages to avoid disaster for exactly three days. He gets involved, innocently at first, with the flirtatious wife of Curley, the boss's violent son; and through a series of unfortunate circumstances he becomes frightened and unintentionally kills the girl. Curley organizes a posse to apprehend Lennie—with the idea either of locking him up in an asylum or, more likely, of killing him on the spot. George gets to Lennie first and out of sympathy for his companion shoots him in the head to spare him the pain of Curley's shotgun or the misery of incarceration.

The title of the story has a twofold application and significance. First,

First, it refers to naturalistic details within the texture of the novella: Lennie likes to catch mice and stroke their fur with his fingers. This is a particularly important point for two reasons: it establishes Lennie's fatal weakness for stroking soft things and, since he invariably kills the mice he is petting, it foreshadows his deadly encounter with Curley's wife. Second, the title is, of course, a fragment from the poem by Robert Burns, which gives emphasis to the idea of the futility of human endeavor or the vanity of human wishes.

> The best laid schemes o' mice and men
> Gang aft a-gley
> An' leave us nought but grief an' pain
> For promised joy.

This notion is obviously of major importance in the novella, and it may be said to be Steinbeck's main theme on the surface level of action and development of character.

Other noteworthy characters and incidents in *Of Mice and Men* include Crooks, the Negro stablehand who lives in the harness room. Here on one occasion he briefly entertains Lennie and Candy, the bunkhouse worker who wants to be a part of the dream farm. Crooks tells them they will never attain it; he says he has known many workers who wanted land of their own, but he has never heard of anyone who has actually realized this ambition. Then there is Carlson, the blunt and unfeeling ranch hand who insists on shooting Candy's aged sheep dog, which having outlived its usefulness has become an annoyance to the men who occupy the bunkhouse. This is a significant episode which anticipates George's mercy killing of Lennie at the conclusion. ("I ought to of shot that dog myself," says Candy later. "I shouldn't ought to of let no stranger shoot my dog.") Steinbeck is also at some pains to establish an important aspect of the ranch workers' existence: their off-hours recreation, which consists of gambling, drinking, and visiting the local brothel. Upon such indulgences, which they find impossible to resist, these men squander their wages and thereby remain perpetually penniless, tied to a monotonous pattern of work, transitory pleasure, homelessness, and dependence upon job bosses for the basic needs of existence.

Of Mice and Men was published early in 1937 and was a Book-of-the-Month Club selection and one of the year's top best-sellers. In the closing months of 1937 Steinbeck adapted the novella for the Broadway stage, where it enjoyed immediate popular success, winning in addition the award of the Drama Critics' Circle. The Hollywood version, released in 1941, became one of the most widely discussed motion pictures of the decade. If my own high school experience was at all typical, spontaneous parodies of Lennie's speech and behavior were a common feature of adolescent get-togethers in the 1940s. But from that time to the present *Of Mice and Men* has been a favorite topic for serious discussion in college literature classes; and a sensitive television production in the late 1960s revealed new subtleties and power in the little tale which, critical controversy or no, has now assumed the status of an American classic.

Viewed in the light of its mythic and allegorical implications, *Of Mice and Men* is a story about the nature of man's fate in a fallen world, with particular emphasis upon the question: Is man destined to live alone, a solitary wanderer on the face of the earth, or is it the fate of man to care for man, to go his way in companionship with another? This is the same theme that occurs in the Old Testament, as early as chapter 4 of Genesis, immediately following the Creation and Expulsion. In effect, the question Steinbeck poses is the same question Cain poses to the Lord: "Am I my brother's keeper?" From its position in the scriptural version of human history we may assume with the compilers of the early books of the Bible that it is the primary *question concerning man as he is*, after he has lost the innocence and nonbeing of Eden. It is the same question that Steinbeck chose as the theme of his later book *East of Eden* (1952), in which the Cain and Abel story is reenacted in a contemporary setting and where, for emphasis, Steinbeck has his main characters read the biblical story aloud and comment on it, climaxing the discussion with the statement made by Lee: "I think this is the best-known story in the world because it is everybody's story. I think it is the symbol story of the human soul." *Of Mice and Men* is an early Steinbeck variation on this symbolic story of the human soul. The implications of the Cain and Abel drama are everywhere apparent in the fable of George and Lennie and provide its mythic vehicle.

Contrary to Lee's confident assertion, however, most people know the Cain and Abel story only in general outline. The details of the drama need to be filled in, particularly for the purpose of seeing how they apply to Steinbeck's novella. Cain was a farmer and Adam and

Eve's firstborn son. His offerings of agricultural produce to the Lord failed to find favor, whereas the livestock offered by Cain's brother, Abel, was well received. Angry, jealous, and rejected, Cain killed Abel when they were working in the field, and when the Lord inquired of Cain, Where is your brother? Cain replied: "I know not: Am I my brother's keeper?" For his crime of homicide the Lord banished Cain from his company and from the company of his parents and set upon him a particular curse, the essence of which was that Cain was to become homeless—a wanderer and an agricultural worker who would never possess or enjoy the fruits of his labor. Cain was afraid that other men would hear of his crime and try to kill him, but the Lord marked him in a certain way so as to preserve him from the wrath of others. Thus Cain left home and went to the land of Nod, which, the story tells us, lies east of Eden.

The drama of Cain finds its most relevant application in *Of Mice and Men* in the relationship between Lennie and George, and in the other characters' reactions to their association. In the first of his six scenes Steinbeck establishes the two ideas that will be developed throughout. The first of these is the affectionate symbiosis of the two protagonists, their brotherly mutual concern and faithful companionship. Steinbeck stresses the beauty, joy, security, and comfort these two derive from the relationship:

> "If them other guys gets in jail they can rot for all anybody gives a damn. But not us."
>
> Lennie broke in, "But not us! An' why? Because . . . because I got you to look after me and you got me to look after you, and that's why." He laughed delightedly.

The second idea, which is given equal emphasis, is the fact that this sort of camaraderie is rare, different, almost unique in the world George and Lennie inhabit; other men, in contrast to these two, are solitary souls without friends or companions. Says George in scene 1: "Guys like us, that work on ranches, are the loneliest guys in the world. They got no family. They don't belong no place. They come to a ranch an' work up a stake and then they go into town and blow their stakes, and the first thing you know they're poundin' their tail on some other ranch." The alternative to the George-Lennie companionship is Aloneness, made more dreadful by the addition of an economic futility that

Steinbeck augments and reinforces in later sections. The migratory ranch worker, in other words, is the fulfillment of the Lord's curse on Cain: "When thou tillest the ground, it shall not henceforth yield unto thee her strength; a fugitive and vagabond shalt thou be in the earth." Steinbeck's treatment of the theme is entirely free from a sense of contrivance; all the details in *Of Mice and Men* seem natural in the context and organically related to the whole; but note that in addition to presenting Lennie and George as men who till the ground and derive no benefits from their labor, he also manages to have them "on the run" when they are introduced in the first scene—this no doubt to have his main characters correspond as closely as possible to the biblical passage: "a fugitive and a vagabond shalt thou be. . . ."

To the calamity of homelessness and economic futility Steinbeck later adds the psychological soul corruption that is the consequence of solitary existence. In scene 3 George tells Slim, the mule driver on the ranch:

> "I seen the guys that go around on the ranches alone. That ain't no good. They don't have no fun. After a long time they get mean."
>
> "Yeah, they get mean," Slim agreed. "They get so they don't want to talk to nobody."

Again, in scene 4, the Negro stable buck Crooks tells Lennie: "A guy needs somebody—to be near him. . . . A guy goes nuts if he ain't got nobody. Don't make no difference who the guy is, long's he's with you. I tell ya, I tell ya a guy gets too lonely and he gets sick."

This is Steinbeck's portrait of Cain in the modern world, or Man Alone, whose fate is so severe that he may feel compelled to echo the words of Cain to the Lord: "My punishment is more than I can bear." In *Of Mice and Men* Steinbeck gives us the case history of two simple mortals who try to escape the homelessness, economic futility, and psychological soul corruption which Scripture embodies in the curse of Cain.

If in scene 1 Lennie and George affirm their fraternity openly and without embarrassment, in scene 2 George is more hesitant. "He's my . . . cousin," he tells the ranch boss. "I told his old lady I'd take care of him." This is no betrayal on George's part, but a cover-up required by the circumstances. For the boss is highly suspicious of the Lennie-George fellowship. "You takin' his pay away from him?" he asks

George. "I never seen one guy take so much trouble for another guy." A short time later Curley also sounds the note of suspicion, extending it by a particularly nasty innuendo: when George says, "We travel together," Curley replies, "Oh, so it's that way." Steinbeck is implying here the general response of most men toward seeing two individuals who buddy around together in a friendless world where isolation is the order of the day: there must be exploitation involved, either financial or sexual. At the same time Steinbeck is developing the allegorical level of his story by suggesting that the attitude of Cain ("I know not: Am I my brother's keeper?") has become universal.[3] Even the sympathetic and understanding Slim expresses some wonder at the Lennie-George fraternity. "Ain't many guys travel around together," Slim says in scene 2. "I don't know why. Maybe ever'body in the whole damned world is scared of each other." This too, as Steinbeck interprets the biblical story, is a part of Cain's curse: distrust. Later on, in order to give the theme of Aloneness another dimension, Steinbeck stresses the solitude of Crooks and Curley's wife, both of whom express a craving for company and "someone to talk to."

Notwithstanding the fact that they are obviously swimming against the current, Lennie and George continue to reaffirm their solidarity all along, right up to and including the last moments of Lennie's life in scene 6. Here a big rabbit, which Lennie in his disturbed state of mind has hallucinated, tells the half-wit fugitive that George is sick of him and is going to go away and leave him. "He won't!" Lennie cries. "He won't do nothing like that. I know George. Me an' him travels together." Actually Steinbeck's novella advances and develops, ebbs and flows, around the basic image of the Lennie-George relationship. Almost all the characters react to it in one way or another as the successive scenes unfold. In scenes 1, 2, and 3, despite the discouraging opinions of outsiders, the companionship remains intact and unthreatened. Midway into scene 3 the partnership undergoes augmentation when Candy is admitted into the scheme to buy the little farm. Late in scene 4 Crooks offers himself as another candidate for the fellowship of soul brothers and dreamers. This is the high point of optimism as regards the main theme of the story; this is the moment when a possible reversal of the curse of Cain seems most likely, as Steinbeck suggests that the answer to the Lord's question might be, "Yes, I am my brother's keeper." If we arrive at this point with any comprehension of the author's purposes, we find ourselves brought up short by the idea: what if this George-Lennie-Candy-Crooks fraternity were to become universal?

But later in the same scene, the entrance of Curley's wife signals the turning point as the prospects for the idea of brotherhood-as-a-reality begin to fade and darken. As throughout the story she represents a force that destroys men and at the same time invites men to destroy her, as she will finally in scene 5 offer herself as a temptation which Lennie cannot resist, so in scene 4 Curley's wife sows the seeds that eventually disrupt the fellowship. Entering into the discussion in Crooks's room in the stable, she insults Crooks, Candy, and Lennie, laughs at their dream farm, and threatens to invent the kind of accusation that will get Crooks lynched.[4] Crooks, reminded of his position of impotence in a white man's society, immediately withdraws his offer to participate in the George-Lennie-Candy farming enterprise. But Crooks's withdrawal, while extremely effective as social criticism, is much more. It represents an answer to the question Steinbeck is considering all along: Is man meant to make his way alone or accompanied? Obviously this is one occasion, among many others in the story, when Steinbeck suggests the answer. Crooks's hope for fraternal living is short-lived. At the conclusion of the scene he sinks back into his Aloneness.

From this point on, even though the dream of fellowship on the farm remains active, the real prospects for its fulfillment decline drastically. In scene 5, after George and Candy discover the lifeless body of Curley's wife, they both face the realization that the little farm is now unattainable and the partnership dissolved. Actually the plan was doomed to failure from the beginning; for fraternal living cannot long survive in a world dominated by the Aloneness, homelessness, and economic futility which Steinbeck presents as the modern counterpart of Cain's curse. Immediately following his discovery of Curley's wife's body, George delivers a speech that dwells on the worst possible aftermath of Lennie's misdeed; and this is not the wrath of Curley or the immolation of Lennie or the loss of the farm, but the prospect of George's becoming a Man Alone, homeless, like all the others and a victim as well of economic futility: "I'll work my month an' I'll take my fifty bucks and I'll stay all night in some lousy cat house. Or I'll set in some poolroom til ever'body goes home. An' then I'll come back an' work another month an' I'll have fifty bucks more." This speech represents the true climax of the novella, for it answers the question which is Steinbeck's main interest throughout. Now we know the outcome of the Lennie-George experiment in fellowship, as we know the Aloneness of man's essential nature. In subtle ways, of course, Steinbeck has been hinting at this conclusion all along, as, for example, in the seven references spaced throughout scenes 2 and 3 to George's playing solitaire in the bunkhouse. For that matter the answer is implied in the very first line of the story when the author establishes his setting "a few miles south of Soledad. . . ," Soledad being at one and the same time a town in central California and the Spanish word for solitude, or aloneness.

But there are still other suggested meanings inherent in the dream farm and the failure of the dream. The plan is doomed not only because human fellowship cannot survive in the post-Cain world, but also because the image of the farm, as conceived by George and Lennie and Candy, is overly idealized, the probability being that life, even if they obtained the farm, would not consist of the comfort, plenty, and interpersonal harmony they envision. The fruits and vegetables in abundance, the livestock and domestic animals, and the community of people involved ("Ain't gonna be no more trouble. Nobody gonna hurt nobody nor steal from 'em")—these are impractical expectations. George and Lennie, who were to some extent inspired by questions growing out of the story of Cain in chapter 4 of Genesis, want to retreat to chapter 2 and live in Eden! Of all ambitions in a fallen world, this is possibly the most unattainable; for paradise is lost, as the name of Steinbeck's hero, George Milton, suggests. And though there will always be men like Candy, who represents sweet hope, the view of Crooks, who represents black despair, is probably a more accurate appraisal of the human condition: "Nobody never gets to heaven, and nobody gets no land. It's just in their head. They're all the time talkin' about it, but it's jus' in their head." Obviously in this context Crooks's comment about nobody ever getting land refers not to literal ownership but to the dream of contentment entertained by the simple workmen who come and go on the ranch.

To pursue the Milton parallel a step further, we perceive immediately that Steinbeck has no intention of justifying the ways of God to man. On the contrary, if anything, *Of Mice and Men* implies a critique of Hebrew-Christian morality, particularly in the area of the concept of punishment for sin. This opens up still another dimension of meaning in our interpretation of Steinbeck's novella. If George and Lennie fail to attain their dream farm (for reasons already explored), and the dream farm is a metaphor or image for heaven (as suggested by Crooks's speech in scene 4) then the failure to achieve the dream farm is most likely associated with the question of man's failure to attain heaven. Steinbeck's consideration of this last-named theme is not hard to find. Along this particular line of thought, Lennie represents one essential aspect of man—the animal appetites, the craving to touch and feel, the impulse toward immediate gratification of sensual desires.[5] George is the element of Reason which tries to control the appetites or, better still, to elevate them to a higher and more sublime level. As Lennie's hallucinatory rabbit advises him near the conclusion: "Christ knows George done ever'thing he could to jack you outa the sewer, but it don't do no good." Steinbeck suggests throughout that the appetites and Reason coexist to compose the nature of man. ("Me an' him travels together.") He goes on to suggest that the effort to refine man into something rare, saintly, and inhuman is another unattainable ambition. Even when Reason (George) manages to communicate to the appetites (Lennie) its urgent message ("You crazy son-of-a-bitch. You keep me in hot water all the time . . . I never get no peace") the appetites are incapable of satisfying Reason's demands. This submerged thesis is suggested when Aunt Clara—like the big rabbit a product of Lennie's disturbed imagination—scolds Lennie in scene 6:

> "I tol' you an' tol' you. I tol' you. 'Min' George because he's such a nice fella an' good to you.' But you don't never take no care. You do bad things."
>
> And Lennie answered her, "I tried, Aunt Clara, ma'am. I tried and tried. I couldn' help it."[6]

The animal appetites, even though well attended and well intentioned, cannot be completely suppressed or controlled. Thus, the best man can hope for is a kind of insecure balance of power between these two elements—which is, in fact, what most of the ranch hands accomplish, indulging their craving for sensual pleasure in a legal and commonplace manner each payday. Failing this, man must suppress absolutely the appetites which refuse to be controlled, as George does in the symbolic killing of Lennie at the conclusion of the novella. Possibly this is a veiled reference to the drastic mutilation of man's nature required by the

Hebrew-Christian ethic. At the same time the theological implications of *Of Mice and Men* project the very highest regard for the noble experiment in fraternal living practiced by George and Lennie; and possibly the time scheme of their stay on the ranch—from Friday to Sunday—is a veiled reference to the sacrifice of Christ. He too tried to reverse the irreversible tide of Cain's curse by serving as the ultimate example of human brotherhood.

At this point, without, I hope, undue emphasis, we might attempt to answer some specific objections which have been raised by critics of *Of Mice and Men*. The faults most often cited are the pessimism of Steinbeck's conclusion, which seems to some readers excessive; and the author's attempt to impose a tragic tone upon a story which lacks characters of tragic stature.[7] Both of these censures might be accepted as valid, or at least understood as reasonable, if we read the novella *on the surface level of action and character development*. But a reading which takes into account the mythical-allegorical significance of these actions and characters not only nullifies the objections but opens up new areas of awareness. For example, although Lennie and George are humble people without the status of traditional tragic characters, their dream is very much like the dream of Plato for an ideal Republic. And their experiment in fellowship is not at all different from the experiment attempted by King Arthur. And at the same time it is reminiscent of at least one aspect of Christ's ministry. These are remote parallels to *Of Mice and Men*, yet they are legitimate and lend some measure of substance, nobility, and human significance to Steinbeck's novella. Its pessimism is not superimposed upon a slight story, as charged, but has been there from the opening line, if we know how to read it. Furthermore, the pessimism is not inspired by commercialism or false theatrics but by the Hebrew Testament. ("And Cain said unto the Lord, 'My punishment is greater than I can bear.'")

But let us tie up our loose ends, not with reference to critics but with a brief summary of our discoveries during this investigation. *Of Mice and Men* is a realistic story with lifelike characters and a regional setting, presented in a style highly reminiscent of stage drama. Steinbeck's technique also includes verbal ambiguity in place names and character names, double entendre in certain key passages of dialogue, and a mythical-allegorical drift that invites the reader into areas of philosophical and theological inquiry. Sources for the novella are obviously Steinbeck's own experience as a laborer in California; but on the allegorical level, *Of Mice and Men* reflects the early chapters of the Book of Genesis and the questions that grow out of the incidents therein depicted. These consist primarily of the consideration of man as a creature alone or as a brother and companion to others. In addition, Steinbeck's story suggests the futility of the all-too-human attempt to recapture Eden, as well as a symbolic schema which defines human psychology. Steinbeck also implies a critique of the Hebrew-Christian ethic, to the effect that the absolute suppression of the animal appetites misrepresents the reality of human experience.

Finally, we should say that Steinbeck's emphasis, on both the allegorical and realistic levels, is on the nobility of his characters' attempt to live fraternally. Even though the experiment is doomed to failure, Steinbeck's characters, like the best men of every age, dedicate themselves to pursuing the elusive grail of fellowship.

Mark Spilka

5 Of George and Lennie and Curley's Wife: Sweet Violence in Steinbeck's Eden

Nearly everyone in the world has appetites and impulses, trigger emotions, islands of selfishness, lusts just beneath the surface. And most people either hold such things in check or indulge them secretly. Cathy knew not only these impulses in others but how to use them for her own gain. It is quite possible that she did not believe in any other tendencies in humans, for while she was preternaturally alert in some directions she was completely blind in others. Cathy learned when she was very young that sexuality with all its attendant yearnings and pains, jealousies and taboos, is the most disturbing impulse humans have.

My epigraph is from Steinbeck's postwar novel *East of Eden*, published in 1952. It concerns a woman called Cathy Ames who deserts her husband and newborn twins to become the successful proprietor of a California whorehouse. In his diaries for the composition of the novel

Previously published.

Steinbeck calls this woman a "monster" and says he will prove to his readers that such monsters actually exist. His choice of her as the archetypal mother of a California family, his peculiarly Miltonic view of her as an exploiter of men's lusts, and his awareness of the exploitability of such feelings—this complex of psychological tendencies in the later Steinbeck has much to do, I think, with the force behind his early social fiction. I want to examine one of his early social tales, *Of Mice and Men*, with that possibility in mind.

A minor classic of proletarian conflict, *Of Mice and Men* was written in 1937, first as a novel, then as a play. Both versions proved enormously popular and established Steinbeck as a leading writer of the decade. The play won the Drama Critics' Circle Award, and the film produced from it in 1941 was widely applauded. A recent television version testifies to the dramatic power of the basic story.

Certainly the novel's dramatic force has much to do with its continuing appeal. Steinbeck conceived it as a potential play, with each chapter arranged as a scene and the action confined to a secluded grove, a bunkhouse, and a barn. In the play itself each chapter does in fact become a scene; the dialogue is transferred almost verbatim, and the action—except for a few strategic alterations—remains unchanged. Plainly Steinbeck was able to convert the novel with comparative ease.

It may have helped that a paper-chewing dog destroyed his original manuscript. Thanks to that fateful interference he rewrote the tale completely, proceeding now at a high pitch of masterful control. The opening scene epitomizes the new compactness, the new surcharge of meaning, which sets the book off from all his previous work, and which testifies—as we shall see—not only to its dramatic but to its psychological power.

The sycamore grove by the Salinas River, so lovingly described in the opening lines, is more than scene setting: it is an attempt to evoke the sense of freedom in nature which, for a moment only, the protagonists will enjoy. By a path worn hard by boys and hobos two migrant laborers appear. The first man is mouselike: "small and quick, dark of face, with restless eyes and sharp, strong features. Every part of him was defined: small, strong hands, slender arms, a thin and bony nose." He is the planner from the poem by Robert Burns: as with other mice and men, his best arrangements will often go astray. A bus driver has just tricked him and his friend into getting out four miles from the ranch where jobs await them. Now he decides to stay in the small grove near the river because he "like[s] it here." There will be work tomorrow, but tonight he can "lay right here and look up" at the sky through sycamore leaves; he can dream and plan with his friend of the farm they will never own.

The nearest town is Soledad, which means "lonely place" in Spanish; the town where they last worked, digging a cesspool, was Weed. Their friendship is thus quickly placed as a creative defense against rank loneliness; it will be reinforced, thematically, by the hostility and guardedness of bunkhouse life, and by the apparent advance of their dream toward realization. But the secluded grove, the site of natural freedom, provides the only substantiation their dream will ever receive; and when our mouselike planner tells his friend to return there in case of trouble, we sense that the dream will end where it essentially begins, in this substantiating site.

The second man to appear is "opposite" to the first: "a huge man, shapeless of face, with large, pale eyes, with wide, sloping shoulders" and loose-hanging arms; he walks heavily, "dragging his feet a little, the way a bear drags his paws." This bearlike man becomes equine when they reach the grove: flinging himself down, he drinks from the pool there, "snorting into the water like a horse." Then again like a bear, he dips his whole head under, "hat and all," sits up so the hat drips down his back, and "dabble[s] his big paw in the water."

These animal actions and his childish speech place him for us quickly as an idiot. What the first man plans for, the second already has. Like other Steinbeck idiots—Tularecito in *The Pastures of Heaven* (1932), Johnny Bear in *The Long Valley* (1938)—he participates in natural life freely, has access to its powers, and his attraction for Steinbeck is his freedom to use those powers without blame or censure. More nearly animal than human, more nearly child than man, he eludes responsibility for his actions. Again like the natural artist Tularecito and the uncanny mimic Johnny Bear, he is extraordinarily gifted; he has superhuman strength which inevitably threatens a society whose rules he cannot comprehend. He is thus the perfect denizen of the secluded grove where, for a moment, natural freedom reigns; the perfect victim, too, for an intruding social world which will eventually deny that freedom.

In his pocket the idiot carries an actual mouse, dead from too much handling. Later he kills a puppy with playful buffeting. A child fondling "lesser" creatures, he is Steinbeck's example of senseless killing in nature. He is also part of an ascending hierarchy of power. His name is Lennie *Small*, by which Steinbeck means subhuman, animal, childlike, without power to judge or master social fate. His friend's name, George Milton, puts him by literary allusion near the godhead, above subhuman creatures, able to judge whether they should live or die. The title and epilogue of *In Dubious Battle* (1936) were also drawn from Milton, whose grand judgmental abstractions take humble proletarian forms in Steinbeck's world. Thus, in a later set-up scene (which may have been inspired also by Steinbeck's paper-chewing dog), old Candy, the lowly bunkhouse sweeper, says that he should have shot his own decrepit dog—should not have let a stranger do it for him. George too will decide that he must shoot Lennie, like a mad rather than a decrepit dog, for the unplanned murder of another man's wife; that he cannot allow strangers to destroy him.

Both shootings have been sanctioned by the jerkline skinner, Slim, "prince of the ranch," who moves "with a majesty achieved only by royalty" and looks with "calm, God-like eyes" upon his bunkhouse world. Since his word is "law" for the migrant farmhands, and since Milton, a rational farmhand, can recognize and accept such godlike laws, he must choose to shoot his friend. By *East of Eden* Steinbeck would conclude that it is choice which separates men from animals, a belief which supports one critic's view of George's decision as "mature." But it is not his "ordinariness" which George will accept in destroying Lennie and the comforting dream they share, as this critic holds: it is his *humanness*, his responsibility for actions which the animal Lennie, for all his vital strength, cannot comprehend.

And yet George will be diminished—made "ordinary"—by his choice. As many critics insist, he uses Lennie selfishly, draws from him a sense of power, of superiority, which he sorely needs. If he is sensitive to Lennie's feelings—cares for and about him in demonstrable ways—he also "lords" it over him almost vengefully. The opening scene indicates nicely how much petty satisfaction he takes in giving Lennie orders and complaining about the burden of thinking for him. But more than this: the scene creates a causal expectation—that one way or another Lennie will always feed this satisfaction, will always do, in effect, what George desires—which means that George himself invites the troubles ahead, makes things go astray, uses Lennie to provoke and settle his own quarrel with a hostile world.

This is evident enough when he tells Lennie not to talk, to leave job negotiations to him so as not to expose his idiocy before his strength has been displayed. Inevitably bosses are annoyed when Lennie fails to speak for himself; suspicions are aroused, and future troubles more or less ensured. This is exactly what George desires, first with the boss of the Soledad ranch, then with two extensions of the boss's power—his son Curley and Curley's straying wife. George resents these people so much, and pins such frightening taboos on them, that Lennie is bound to panic when he meets them, to clutch with his tremendous strength— like a child caught with some forbidden object—and so punish people whom George openly dislikes. In a very real sense, then, George lordfully creates the troubles for which Lennie will himself be blamed and punished—though he only obeys his master's vengeful voice.

This is to move from social into psychological conflict: but Steinbeck, in taking a boss's son and his wife as sources of privileged pressure on migrant farmhands, has moved there before us. He has chosen aggressive sexuality as the force, in migrant life, which undermines the friendship dream. This variation on the Garden of Eden theme is, to say the least, peculiar. There is something painfully adolescent about the notion of a cooperative farm run by bachelor George and idiot Lennie, with the probable help of a maimed old man and a defiant black cripple. The grouping is not unlike the Arthurian circle around Danny in *Tortilla Flat* (1935): four good-hearted lads sticking together against the world, who can drop work and go into town whenever they want to see "a carnival or a circus . . . or a ball game." Their self-employment seems more like freedom from adult supervision than from harsh conditions; and their friendship seems more like an escape from the coarseness of adult sexuality than from bunkhouse loneliness. Even their knightly pledge to help each other seems oddly youthful. That Steinbeck read the Arthurian legends at an early age, and that he also worked on ranches during boyhood summers, may be relevant here: for the world of friendship he imagines is a boy's world, a retreat from the masculine grossness and insecurity of the bunkhouse, from whorehouse visits and combative marriages like Curley's, which in his youth he must have found disturbing. George Milton shows enough insecurity and disgust about sex, and enough hostility toward women, to make these speculations about Steinbeck's choices worth pursuing.

In *Tortilla Flat* the approach to predatory sex is comic. The periodic forays into ladies' chambers, and the retreats therefrom to the safety of the male preserve, are treated as paisano versions of Arthurian gallantry. Late in the novel, however, the gentlest of the paisanos tells a disturbing story which tends to conflate these different treatments of sexuality. It concerns Petey Ravanno, who tries to commit suicide for love of Gracie Montez, and who wins her in marriage by that desperate strategy. What makes him desperate is her elusiveness: Gracie is always running away, and though men sometimes catch her, they cannot "get close to her"; she always seems to withhold "something nice" from them. This elusiveness has another strange effect on desperate admirers: "It made you want to choke her and pet her at the same time. It made you want to cut her open and get that thing that was inside of her. . . ." In *Of Mice and Men* Lennie first pets Curley's wife, then breaks her neck, without any awareness that she provokes both reactions. His conscious desires are simple: to stroke something furry, and to stop the furry thing from yelling so George won't be mad at him. But George had predicted this episode, has called Curley's wife a rattrap, a bitch, a piece of jailbait; and he has roundly expressed disgust at Curley's glove full of Vaseline, which softens the hand that strokes his wife's genitals. Lennie has obligingly crushed that hand for George, and now he obligingly breaks the rattrap for him, that snare for mice and men which catches both in its furry toils.

In the play Steinbeck goes out of his way to make it clear that George's hostility to Curley's wife prefigures Lennie's. In a scene not in the novel, he arranges an exchange in the Negro Crooks's room in which George's arm is raised in anger against this woman: he is about to strike her for threatening the friendship dream, for trying to "mess up what we're gonna do." Then Curley's father arrives, the girl retreats from the room, and George lowers his hand as the scene closes.

As such manipulations imply, Steinbeck projects his own hostilities through George and Lennie. He has himself given this woman no other name but "Curley's wife," as if she had no personal identity for him. He has presented her, in the novel, as vain, provocative, vicious (she threatens Crooks with lynching, for instance, when he tries to defy her), and only incidentally lonely. Now in the play—perhaps in response to the criticisms of friends—he reverses her portrait. She is no longer vicious (her lynching threat has been written out of the script), and she is not even provocative: she is just a lonely woman whose attempts at friendliness are misunderstood. Thus she makes her first entrance with a line transferred from a later scene in the novel: "I'm just lookin' for somebody to talk to," she says, in case we might think otherwise. In her final scene, moreover, in a sympathy speech written expressly for the play, she joins Lennie in the lost world of childhood:

> CURLEY'S WIFE: My ol' man was a sign-painter when he worked. He used to get drunk an' paint crazy pitchers an' waste paint. One night when I was a little kid, him an' my ol' lady had an awful fight. They was always fightin'. In the middle of the night he come into my room, and he says, "I can't stand this no more. Let's you an' me go away." I guess he was drunk. *(Her voice takes on a curious wondering tenderness.)* I remember in the night—walkin' down the road, and the trees was black. I was pretty sleepy. He picked me up, an' he carried me on his back. He says, "We gonna live together. We gonna live together because you're my own little girl, an' not no stranger. No arguin' and fightin'," he says, "because you're my little daughter." *(Her voice becomes soft.)* He says, "Why you'll bake little cakes for me, and I'll paint pretty pitchers all over the wall." *(Sadly.)* In the morning they caught us . . . an' they put him away. *(Pause.)* I wish we'd a' went.

Here Steinbeck overcompensates, creates a new imbalance to correct an old one. His sentimentality is the obverse side of his hostility. We see this in the novel when it breaks through in another form, as a mystic moment of redemption for Curley's wife. Thus, as she lies dead in the barn, "the meanness and the plannings and the discontent and the ache for attention" disappear from her face; she becomes sweet and young, and her rouged cheeks and reddened lips make her seem alive and sleeping lightly "under a half-covering of hay." At which point sound and movement stop, and, "as sometimes happens," a moment settles and hovers and remains "for much, much more than a moment." Then time wakens and moves sluggishly on. Horses stamp in the barn, their halter chains clink, and outside, men's voices become "louder and clearer."

Restored to natural innocence through death, Curley's wife is connected—for a timeless moment—with the farm dream. Then men's voices and stamping horses indicate the sexual restlessness she provokes in adult life. Only when sexually quiescent—as in death or child-hood—can she win this author's heart.

Interestingly, Steinbeck shares this predilection with William Faulk-ner, whose idiot Benjy in *The Sound and the Fury* (1929) wants his sister Caddie to smell like trees and is troubled when perfume or sexual odors suffuse that smell. Benjy is gelded, not shot, when he later innocently tries to "say" to little girls; but his brooding brother Quentin has meanwhile killed himself over the sexual turn which childhood love has taken, and his bachelor brother Jason has settled for lifelong hostility toward women. This troubled passage from innocence to carnal knowl-edge is as much Steinbeck's subject as Faulkner's; and like Faulkner, he sees it as a life-and-death ordeal.

Herein lies his strength and weakness in *Of Mice and Men:* for the pas-sage from stroking rabbits to stroking genitals is both profoundly and ridiculously conceived. As literary zanies like Max Schulman and Steve Allen have been quick to see, Lennie's oft-repeated line, "Tell about the rabbits, George," comes perilously close to self-parody. Lifted only slightly out of context, it reduces the friendship farm to a bad sexual joke. As a sentimental alternative to the emptiness, divisiveness, and gross sexuality of bunkhouse life, it seems fair game for satire. But Steinbeck is never that simple. He is fascinated not by Lennie's inno-cent pleasures but by the low threshold which his innocent rages cross whenever he is thwarted. Consider Lennie's reaction when George imagines that striped cats may threaten his beloved rabbits: "You jus' let 'em try to get the rabbits," he says, breathing hard. "I'll break their God damn necks. I'll . . . I'll smash 'em with a stick."

In *The Red Pony* (1933) young Jody similarly plans to smash mice with a stick, saying lordfully: "I'll bet they don't know what's going to happen to them today." To which his friend Billy rejoins, unsettlingly, "No, nor you either, . . . nor me, nor anyone." Jody takes a great deal of pleasure nonetheless in lordful violence: he kicks in melons, stones birds' nests, sets traps for his dog's nose, hits him with a clod when his pony is sick, kills a buzzard pecking at the pony's dying body, stones a thrush and cuts it up so as to hide the evidence from grownups. His awareness of the low threshold between rage and pleasure increases, moreover, in the sexual stage, when he watches horses mating and is appalled by the stallion's violence: "He'll hurt her, he'll kill her. Get him away," he cries out; and, in fact, the mare is later killed so that her colt can be delivered by Caesarean section.

This frightening capacity for violence is what Lennie brings into the unsuspecting bunkhouse world: he carries within him, intact from childhood, that low threshold between rage and pleasure which we all carry within us into adulthood. But by adulthood we have all learned to take precautions which an idiot never learns to take. The force and readiness of our feelings continue: but through diversions and disguises, through civilized controls, we raise the threshold of reaction. This is the only real difference, emotionally, between Lennie and ourselves.

A great deal of Steinbeck's power as a writer comes, then, from his ability to bring into ordinary scenes of social conflict the psychological forcefulness of infantile reactions: his creation of Lennie in *Of Mice and Men* is a brilliant instance of that ability—so brilliant, in fact, that the social conflict in this compact tale tends to dissolve into the dramatic urgencies of Lennie's "fate." In his next novel, *The Grapes of Wrath* (1939), Steinbeck would find a situation commensurate with his own low threshold for idiot rage. The epic scope of the Okies' tribulations, of their forced migration from their farms and later exploitation in California, contains and absorbs his immense capacity for anger. It is no accident that this novel begins with the return of a blameless murderer, Tom Joad, imprisoned for an almost pointless crime involving sexual rivalry (when a jealous friend knifes him at a dance, Tom smashes him with a nearby shovel); nor that the problem for Tom, for the rest of the novel, is how to control his easy rages (once he leaves the state he violates parole; any brush with police will return him to prison); nor that the novel ends with his commission of another blameless but now socially significant murder (when a strikebreaker kills ex-preacher Casy, now a Christ-like labor leader, Tom smashes him with his own club). Nor is it an accident that the erotic potential of sensual innocence is diffused, in the novel's closing scene, by an act of social compassion. With Lennie's pathetic fate in mind, the meaning of Rose of Sharon's mysterious smile as she breastfeeds a starving middle-aged man is not hard to fathom: she has found in the adult world what Lennie has never been able to find—an adequate way to satisfy inchoate longings, a way to nurture helpless creatures, perform useful tasks, indulge innocent pleasures, without arousing self-destructive anger. Steinbeck has called

Of Mice and Men "a study of the dreams and pleasures of everyone in the world" and has said that Lennie especially represents "the inarticulate and powerful yearning of all men," their "earth longings" for land of their own, for innocent-pleasure farms. In a profoundly psychological way he was right about the pleasures, though strangely neglectful of the rages which, in his world at least, accompany them. Tom Joad's confident smile, his flaunting of homicide to a truckdriver as *The Grapes of Wrath* begins, and Rose of Sharon's mysterious satisfaction as it closes, suggest that fuller accommodation of universal urges which gives his greatest novel much of its extraordinary power.

Of Mice and Men helped him to release that power by making murder seem as natural and innocent as love. He had been trying his hand at blameless murders in stories like "Flight," where a young Indian reaches manhood through a killing, then flees to his own death in the wilderness; or like "The Murder," where a husband kills his foreign wife's lover and then beats her into admiring submission. There are natural killings too in *The Red Pony*, where the little boy, Jody, cuts up the bird he has stoned and hides the pieces out of deference to adults: "He didn't care about the bird, or its life, but he knew what older people would say if they had seen him kill it; he was ashamed because of their potential opinion." Jody is too small to push these primitive sentiments very far; but Lennie, a more sizable child, is better able to amplify their meaning. After killing Curley's wife, he flees to the grove near the Salinas River, as George has told him to. Back in his own element, he moves "as silently as a creeping bear," drinks like a wary animal, and thinks of living in caves if George doesn't want him any more. Then out of his head come two figures: his aunt Clara and (seven years before Mary Chase's *Harvey*) a giant rabbit. These figments of adult opinion bring all of George's petty righteousness to bear against him, shame him unmercifully, and threaten him with the only thing that matters: the loss of his beloved bunnies. Then out of the brush, like a third figment of Miltonic pettiness, comes George himself, as if to punish him once more for "being bad." But for Lennie as for Jody, badness is a matter of opinions and taboos, not of consequences and responsibilities. He doesn't care about Curley's wife, who exists for him now only as another lifeless animal. Nor does Steinbeck care about her except as she arrives at natural innocence; but he does care about that, and through Lennie, who possesses it in abundance, he is able to affirm his belief in the causeless, blameless animality of murder. Of course, he also believes in the responsibility of those who grasp the consequences of animal passion, and it is one of several paradoxes on which this novel ends that George comes humbly now to accept responsibility for such passions, comes not to punish Lennie, then, but to put him mercifully away, to let him die in full enjoyment of their common dream. So he asks him to face the Gabilan Mountains, which in *East of Eden* are said to resemble the inviting lap of a beloved mother; and, like a bedtime story or a prayer before execution—or better still, like both—together they recite the familiar tale of the friendship farm.

What makes this ending scary and painful and perplexing is the weight given to all that Lennie represents: if contradictory values are affirmed—blameless animality, responsible humanity, innocent longing, grim awareness—it is Lennie's peculiar mixture of human dreams and animals passions which matters most. George's newfound maturity is paradoxically an empty triumph: without Lennie he seems more like a horseless rider than a responsible adult. "The two together were one glorious individual," says Steinbeck of the boy Jody and his imagined pony, Black Demon, the best roping team at the rodeo. Without such demonic vitality, by which any kind of meaningful life proceeds, George is indeed friendless and alone. With it, needless to say, he is prone to destructive rages. On the horns of that adolescent dilemma— that inability to take us beyond the perplexities of sexual rage—Steinbeck hangs his readers. Impales them, rather, since the rich tensions of this poignant perplex, however unresolved, are honestly and powerfully presented.

In *Tortilla Flat* the story of Petey Ravanno and Gracie Montez has an unfortunate sequel which helps to explain that honest power. Petey's father, in trying to emulate his son's suicidal strategy as a way of winning Gracie's sister, accidentally kills himself. The irony and pathos of this conclusion disturb one paisano but please another:

> Pilon complained, "It is not a good story. There are too many meanings and too many lessons in it. Some of those lessons are opposite. There is not a story to take into your head. It proves nothing."
> "I like it," said Pablo. "I like it because it hasn't any meaning you can see, and still it does seem to mean something, I can't tell what."

Steinbeck himself liked simple stories well enough to write straight allegories like *The Pearl* (1947). But chiefly he liked the puzzling kind. In *Tortilla Flat*, an otherwise comic novel, he shows, for instance, how Danny tires of the chivalric life and reverts to the "sweet violence" of outlawry. "Sweet violence" means something more here than the joys of boyish rebellion: it means delight in pulling the house down on one's own and other people's heads, which is what Danny does when the friendship dream proves insubstantial, and he pays with his life—and later, with his friends' help, with his house—for the pleasure of destroying it. Lennie too pays with his life for the pleasure of destructive rages; but he serves in this respect as an extension of his friend's desires: he is George Milton's idiot Samson, his blind avenger for the distastefulness of aggressive sexuality. Which may be why their friendship seems impossible from the first, why the pathos of their dream, and of its inevitable defeat, seems less important than the turbulence it rouses. Once more, "sweet violence" is the force which moves these characters, and which moves us to contemplate their puzzling fate.

By *East of Eden* Steinbeck would learn that rages generally follow from rejected love, that parental coldness or aloofness breeds violence in youthful hearts; and he would come also to accept sexuality as a vulnerable condition, a blind helplessness by which men and women may be "tricked and trapped and enslaved and tortured," but without which they would not be human. Oddly, he would create in Cathy Ames a monstrous projection of his old hostility toward women as exploiters of the sex impulse; and he would impose on her his own preternatural alertness to its selfish uses and his own fear of being absorbed and blinded by it in his youth. But by accepting sex now as a human need, he would redeem his Lennies and Dannys from outlawry and animality, and he would finally repair the ravages of sweet violence. *Of Mice and Men* remains his most compelling tribute to the force behind those ravages, "the most disturbing impulse humans have," as it moves a selfish master and his dancing bear to idiot rages. And once more it must be said to move us, too. For however contradictory it seems, our sympathy for these characters, indeed their love for each other, is founded more deeply in the humanness of that impulse than in its humanitarian disguises.

III The Red Pony

Warren French

6 *The Red Pony* as Story Cycle and Film

The two works entitled *The Red Pony* are of unique interest among John Steinbeck's fictions as the only example of the writer's being solely responsible for the film script version of one of his earlier fictional works. The pair is, in fact, of uncommon interest in American literature and twentieth-century writing generally because few major artists have produced such a pair of related works.[1] I do not speak here of Steinbeck's adapting his earlier work for another medium, because that term does not adequately describe this particular transformation.

The original *Red Pony* is a compilation of four short stories that were first published independently and that are among Steinbeck's earliest preserved writings. "The Gift," which is the only one of the four stories about the red circus pony that provides the title for the cycle, appeared in the *North American Review* (November 1933) and was followed the next month by "The Great Mountains," narrating another experience of Jody Tiflin, the boy who had owned the pony, in the same literary journal.

Although the third story in the cycle, "The Promise," appears to have been written at the same time as the other two stories, in the early 1930s, it did not appear in *Harper's* monthly magazine until October 1937; and the final story, "The Leader of the People," was not published in the United States until Steinbeck collected his early short stories in *The Long Valley* in 1938, although the manuscript was in a book with other stories that had been published as early as 1934, and the story had appeared in the English magazine *Argosy* in August 1936. In *The Long Valley* only the first three stories mentioned above appeared under the collective title "The Red Pony." All four stories were not collected under this title until the first separate publication of *The Red Pony* in a large-format edition lyrically illustrated by Wesley Dennis in 1945.

Even though the four stories were not brought together in this final form until more than a decade after their composition, they are closely linked accounts of Jody Tiflin's significant formative experiences during the crucial period of his painful passage from childhood into adolescence. "The Promise" continues the story of "The Gift." The other two stories are not so specifically linked to that pair or each other, but they all deal with similar kinds of experiences of continuing characters, which makes the quartet what Forrest L. Ingram calls a short story cycle, "a set of stories so linked to one another that the reader's experience of each one is modified by his experience of the others."[2] Longer collections exemplifying this genre are James Joyce's *Dubliners* and Dylan Thomas's *Portrait of the Artist as a Young Dog*, and, among American writings, William Faulkner's *The Unvanquished*, Sherwood Anderson's *Winesburg, Ohio*, and Steinbeck's *The Pastures of Heaven* and *Tortilla Flat*.

In "The Gift" Jody Tiflin is given his first horse (an act symbolizing the ranch boy's initiation into manhood), a red pony that his father has bought from a bankrupt traveling circus, where it had been trained to perform tricks. Jody begins to develop a sense of responsibility for more than routine chores when he is charged with caring for the pony and training it. When the delicate show animal is left exposed to the elements by Billy Buck, the ranch hand whom Jody childishly trusts, it becomes ill and dies. The boy expresses his frustration by killing a carrion buzzard that tries to feed on the carcass.

The only connection between "The Gift" and "The Great Mountains," the story that always appears second in collections, is the character of Jody. The time of the action in this story in relation to any others in the cycle is not specified, but it is usually taken for granted that it occurs some time after the autumn death of the red pony and before the birth of the colt that replaces it in "The Gift." This somber story tells of Jody's encounter with Gitano, an aged Mexican-American whose family once owned the land that is now the Tiflin family ranch. Gitano has come home to die, but Jody's father will not allow the old man to stay on the property. Jody watches helplessly as Gitano disappears with a dying horse named Easter into the great dark mountains that brood over the valley.

The third story, "The Promise," picks up where "The Gift" leaves off, with the ranch hand Billy Buck, who feels responsible for the death of the red pony, promising Jody the next colt of one of the ranch's mares, Nellie, if Jody will take her to the stud and care for her during the long pregnancy. Jody carries out these duties faithfully; but, unfortunately, Billy Buck's promise can be fulfilled only by sacrificing the life of the mare when the unborn colt moves into a position that makes its live delivery otherwise impossible.

The relationship of the time of the action of the last story, "The Leader of the People," to the others is not clear, although since it takes place in March, when Jody apparently does not have a horse, it seems most likely that it occurs just before the spring climax of "The Promise," which narrates the events of an entire year. In contrast, the final story relates the events of only a single twenty-four-hour period during which Jody's visiting maternal grandfather, who has guided parties of pioneers on their dangerous migrations to the West Coast, makes the disheartening discovery that his time, like old Gitano's in "The Great Mountains," is over and that the next generation is annoyed by his constant retelling of the story of his vital role in the conquest of the West. Jody, however, is entranced by his grandfather's stories, to the annoyance of his sedentary father. When Jody expresses the hope that he may some day lead the people himself, his grandfather gloomily observes that there is no place left to go and that the spirit of "westering" has died out.

Like most of Steinbeck's early fictions, these four stories have strong dramatic structures that would make it possible for them to be adapted with little change as successive episodes in a motion picture depicting the crucial events in a perceptive and impressionable child's maturing into a responsible young man. Although specific links are not provided between all four stories, they are not simply autonomous tales of Jody's separate confrontations with a series of crises that provide his rites of passage into manhood. As I pointed out in summarizing the interrelationships of the stories in an analysis of their individual and collective meanings in my book *John Steinbeck*, the cycle depicts the way in which this boy has learned compassion in the course of undergoing four crucial tests very much like those imposed upon appellants for knight-hood in the Middle Ages, a subject that fascinated Steinbeck.

These experiences teach Jody "the fallibility of man," through a trusted mentor's inadvertent neglect of the delicate red pony; "the wearing out of man," through old Gitano's death; "the unreliability of nature," through the death of the mare Nellie as the result of a defect in a natural process that man is powerless to remedy; and "the exhaustion of nature" that left Jody's grandfather and other leaders of the westward migration of his generation sitting along the Pacific shore hating the ocean because it has left them with no more lands for their restless "westering" spirits to conquer.[3]

This same progressive maturation of the boy's sensibilities could have been presented through a four-part film following faithfully the original stories. A precedent existed for such films in the work of French director Julien Duvivier, who, while working in exile in the United States during World War II, had experimented in *Tales of Manhattan* and *Flesh and Fantasy* with fashioning feature-length films from separate but related episodes (the former consisted of three short fables about different wearers of the same full-dress suit). While these frivolous efforts to divert and lift the spirits of war-weary moviegoers lacked the high seriousness of Steinbeck's stories, they demonstrated how visual motifs as well as verbal devices could be used to link episodes that could also be viewed as autonomous presentations.[4]

However, nothing of the structure of the original story cycle is retained in Steinbeck's film script. The closely connected stories of "The Gift" and "The Promise" are used, with some important changes, to provide a single, continuous plot line for the eighty-six-minute film, so that it is much more like a conventional film derived from a traditional novel than it is an attempt to duplicate the form of the story cycle. Although Steinbeck derives most of the material for the film from the stories, he drops a good deal, including the entire second story, "The Great Mountains." He also adds some entirely new material and makes a drastic and controversial change in the climax of the film to provide an entirely new upbeat ending.

If a producer who had acquired the rights to an original work made such extensive changes in it, admirers of the original could justifiably raise cries of protest against the treatment of the source. With *The Red Pony*, however, these drastic alterations were made not just with the author's consent but by the author himself as part of a project in which he collaborated and over which he exercised artistic control. Steinbeck was obviously not interested in simply transferring his story cycle to the screen; he wished to tell the story of Jody Tiflin's initiation into manhood in a way that he deemed suited to the new medium.[5]

Before we examine the film version of *The Red Pony*, however, something more needs to be said about the complex nature of the original story cycle. In an article assessing the significance of Steinbeck's contribution to American literature, I moved beyond my original thesis about the story cycle's portraying a particular young man's coming of age in a particular culture to argue that the four stories viewed collectively also provide a dramatization of Northrop Frye's famous schematic analysis in "The Archetypes of Literature" (1951) of the archetypal forms of literary genres as they constituted a seasonal cycle of the year from birth to death and rebirth.[6]

In that article I observed that Steinbeck does not begin his cycle, as might be anticipated, with a story of spring and rebirth, but with a tale of what Frye describes as "the sunset, autumn and death phase" that provides the archetypes of "tragedy and elegy," myths of "the dying god, of violent death and sacrifice, and of the isolation of the hero," terms that are all precisely applicable to the ironically titled tale of "The Gift."[7]

The article then proceeds to describe the second story, "The Great Mountains," as a winter's tale, even though it begins on a summer afternoon. The heat of the day, however, is in contrast to the coldness of the situation, and the ironically sunny backdrop renders particularly pathetic the tale as an example of what Frye describes as "myths of darkness and dissolution," "of floods and the return of chaos, of the defeat of the hero, and Götterdämmerung myths," as an old man returns to his birthplace to die only to be denied this attempt to recover his history.

"The Promise," however, is a spring tale of dawn and birth, especially if one sees the real focus of the tale as the colt that is ripped from its dying mother's womb, like heroes of ancient legend. This extraction of life from death provides a pattern of seasonal rebirth, of the revival and resurrection that Frye calls the archetype of romance.

The most ironic of the four tales, in the way in which it follows a mythical pattern and yet subverts it, is "The Leader of the People."

Jody's grandfather's reminiscences of "westering" do contain an archetypal summer myth of "apotheosis, of the sacred marriage, and of entering into paradise"; but the entry into paradise it describes—the marriage of wild nature and civilization—is now in the past, and the paradise has been lost. "Westering" has died out among the people, and the mouse hunt that Jody suggests to his grandfather as an alternative in the boy's aspiration to become a new leader himself shows Steinbeck, like Robert Frost in "The Oven Bird," depicting his contemporaries trying to determine "what to make of a diminished thing."

The point of comparing Steinbeck's stories with Northrop Frye's theories promulgated a quarter century later is to suggest that Steinbeck created not just a story of one youth's coming of age but a movingly realistic tale that recapitulates a basic pattern in human experience, as he acknowledged when he wrote in the proposed introduction to Aaron Copland's *The Red Pony* suite, derived from the composer's score for the film, "the path has been travelled before [and] the little boy is not a fresh created uniqueness in the universe."[8]

The modest motion picture, however, fails to live up to a mythic model as successfully as the original story cycle, for some of the tough truths that Steinbeck faced unflinchingly in raising his childhood memories to mythical proportions are omitted (like the death of old Gitano) or mitigated (like the death of the mare Rosie) in the film. It needs, therefore, to be approached on its own terms as an autonomous work of art rather than denigrated for failing to do justice to the potential of the story cycle.

The question of what the film retains of the story cycle can be dealt with briefly. The carefully structured film may be divided into twenty-four episodes, or "sequences," as groups of related scenes are usually called in film analysis. (A "scene" is a single continuous action, though it may be composed of a variety of "shots"—each the product of a single, uninterrupted running of a camera—taken from different perspectives.) It is on the basis of these sequences that the relationship of the material in the film to the stories can be most precisely calculated.[9]

Actually, most of the original material reused for the film comes from the opening story, "The Gift." More than half of the film's twenty-four sequences (thirteen) and more than half of the film's length (about forty-five of its eighty-six minutes) employ material from this original story of the red pony. The pony's death, which occurs at the end of the first story in the cycle, occurs near the end of the film. Only the last twelve minutes are used to relate the events of the year that passes during the narration of "The Promise," the third story in the cycle. Nothing is used in the film from the second story, "The Great Mountains"; and the grandfather's confrontation with Jody's father that provides the climax for the story is interpolated into the action from "The Gift" early in the film.

On the other hand, about four minutes of new material that could have provided the basis for a previously untold story about Jody's father taking a trip to town, during which he is tempted to give up the ranch and move the family back to where he could work in the family store, is introduced early in the film. While this could also be shaped into a winter's tale about the death of a dream and a loss of the land, this middle-class dilemma provides no match for the chilling dramatic power of the tale of the disinherited old man.

A major change is also made in the ending of "The Promise," which now provides the climax for the film. In the original story Billy Buck is obliged to kill the mare in order to deliver her colt and fulfill his promise to Jody. In the film, however, tragedy is averted so that a happy ending may be manufactured. Billy Buck only dreams that the colt has been mispositioned and that Rose (as the mare is called in the film) must be killed. Although the next morning he makes preparations in expectation of the worst, Jody creates a distraction that allows Rosie to make a perfectly normal delivery unaided (and unseen, since the film was produced in the days when a strict production code forbade the showing of the birth of even animals on the screen). The film ends not with Jody being forced to recognize the frightful cost of his victory but with the whole family, including the grandfather (who in an unexplained change has apparently been reconciled to joining the son-in-law's household permanently), gathered in a circle beaming blissfully at the manger scene composed by the uninjured mare and her beautiful offspring.

The title *The Red Pony* thus actually suits the film better than it does the cycle of four stories; but in its transformation it has become a simple variation on the typical Hollywood formula of the 1930s and 1940s— boy meets girl, boy loses girl, boy gets girl—though as is more fitting to a tale about a prepubescent ranch boy, the formula is altered to boy meets horse, boy loses horse, boy gets horse (not the same horse, it is true, but one better suited to the situation—a native of the region and not a pampered show pony—in a commonsensical amendment that Dickens used to the basic formula in *David Copperfield*).

The four deaths (including the death of his grandfather's dream) that Jody must confront in the story cycle are thus reduced to one that is more than compensated for by the end of the film. Jody is able to maintain his place as a true son of the pioneers, having learned only that while those not suited to an environment, like his red pony, may be doomed, generally things work out for the best for good little boys who want to maintain Western traditions and not move to the city (as Rosasharn's despicable husband does in *The Grapes of Wrath*).

Despite Steinbeck's own statement in his proposed histrionic introduction to Aaron Copland's musical suite, that the character will never be a little boy again but has become a man, the cinematic Jody has not gone through the grueling initiation portrayed in the story cycle that might indeed prepare him for leadership of the people. Rather he has been given an assurance that if he is patient enough to learn from experience and control his temper, all will work out well in maintaining his established way of life.

Readers who come to the film from the story cycle may, of course, like Joseph Millichap, be upset to find that Jody at the end of the film has not become the man-boy who offers his dispirited grandfather the bitter refreshment of lemonade and a mouse hunt in a compassionate gesture, but rather one of what Hemingway satirizes in "The Short Happy Life of Francis Macomber" as "the great American boy-men," who sometimes stay little boys all their lives.

Thus, although the film *The Red Pony* uses much of the same material as the story cycle, the differences from the earlier work far outnumber and outweigh the similarities. The most important difference is that the Jody in the film has not really begun to understand the meaning of his experiences, as is shown when he throws a tantrum like the earlier one during which he killed a buzzard just before the end of the film. Although the story cycle is frequently assigned to young readers to provide one of their earliest experiences with thoughtful literature, it is not likely that readers of Jody's own age can grasp the implications of the stories, which were written by an adult recalling boyhood experiences for readers of adult literary magazines.

The film of *The Red Pony* is, however, one of Hollywood's infrequent productions designed for a preteen audience, for which it provides a central figure with whom the audience can identify. This was evidently the audience that Steinbeck had in mind when he rearranged and altered his story line to reach the comfortable conclusion that things can work out all right as long as the family remains unified. No such reassurance is provided by the story cycle, which repeatedly portrays growing up as the terrifying process it always has been.

The story cycle is finally, in terms of Frye's archetypes, a comedy, but not a funny or even cheering one. It is an example of the classic mode of comedy—a myth about the ultimate triumph of common sense and goodwill over the delusions of what Jane Austen castigated as pride and prejudice, of sense over sensibility. *The Red Pony* story cycle foreshadowed what Steinbeck would achieve in his greatest works to follow—*Of Mice and Men*, *The Grapes of Wrath*, *Cannery Row*, even his harder-hitting film *The Forgotten Village*. *The Red Pony* as a film, however, is melodrama—a comforting work in which a situation that seems doomed to end in disaster is miraculously reversed at the last moment, if not by some *deus ex machina*, then by, as in this film, threatened calamity proving only a bad dream.

I am not, however, even in view of this comparative evaluation of these related but very different works, willing to go along with Joseph Millichap's disgruntled attribution of the changes for the worse that he perceives between the story cycle and the film to the notorious movie moguls who have often been justifiably impugned for even more dreadful transformations, like that of J. D. Salinger's short story "Uncle Wiggily in Connecticut" into the tear-jerking film *My Foolish Heart* that resulted in the author's refusal to sell film rights to any other works.

Millichap argues that Steinbeck's "complicity in the film's artistic compromises indicates how much his ideals had been altered by Hollywood" and goes on to complain that the author sent "no telegrams to protest the alteration of his work or asking to remove his name."[10] He speculates that Steinbeck may have needed the money.

Beset by domestic problems as Steinbeck was in the late 1940s, he may indeed have needed money (though, for reasons to be explained subsequently, this film never made much money, and was, in fact, originally conceived by the novelist as a charitable contribution); but it would have been odd if he had complained about a script that he had written. With this film, unlike the dreadfully mutilated and financially disastrous *Tortilla Flat* and the subtly altered and triumphant *The Grapes of Wrath*, the author, and not the production company, was responsible for the changes; and he remained actively involved in the production. We need to look beyond Hollywood's usual whipping boys to find possible reasons for Steinbeck's drastic alterations of his basic story line two decades after he had shaped it and after his own life-style and point of view had been drastically changed by the harrowing experiences of becoming a celebrity, going through World War II and the breakup of two marriages, and becoming a father.

To begin with, by the time Steinbeck wrote the final script for the film, he knew a great deal about filmmaking, and his expectations about films were different from those that he had about his novels. He had become intensely interested in filmmaking back in the 1930s after viewing Pare Lorentz's much-admired documentaries *The Plow that Broke the Plains* and *The River*, sponsored by the federal government to help promote pioneering agricultural conservation projects for saving overexploited farmland. Steinbeck studied with Lorentz during the making of a medical documentary, *The Fight for Life*; and he went to Mexico to join another independent filmmaker, Herbert Kline, in producing the pseudo-documentary *The Forgotten Village* to escape the furor following the publication of *The Grapes of Wrath*. The hour-long film was released in 1940, about the time that Steinbeck first became involved in projects for filming *The Red Pony*.

The too-little-studied *Forgotten Village* is Steinbeck's closest work in plot and theme to *The Red Pony* story cycle. It tells the story of a remote village in the Mexican mountains that is stricken by a cholera plague from a polluted well and of the effort of public health authorities to break the grip of a *curandera* (woman witch doctor) on the superstitious indigenous community, whose language is not even Spanish but an ancient local tongue. The film appears to be a documentary because it was shot in a remote mountain village using a nonprofessional cast recruited locally; but like *The Red Pony* it is a fiction, telling through pictures and a voiced-over narration in English the idealistic story of a teenaged native boy's struggle to become a doctor who will be the savior of his community.[11]

This Juan Diego very much resembles a slightly older Jody Tiflin in his irrepressible determination to become a leader of the people; the wrathful *curandera*, seeking to maintain her status and keep out the despised city doctors, resembles Jody's frustrated grandfather; the boy's family reflects the troubled irresolution of Jody's parents; and Billy Buck is transformed into a determined and dedicated team of technicians from the public health service. The boy undergoes his rite of passage by defying his parents and disapproving community and making a frightening night journey to Mexico City to bring the light of modern medicine to the benighted community. Like the film version of *The Red Pony* (in contrast to the story cycle), *The Forgotten Village* is an upbeat work in which the boy succeeds in his quest. Actually it is even more upbeat than the later *Red Pony* because the incredibly resourceful Mexican lad does not even display Jody's residual childishness.

Subsequently Steinbeck took responsibility for two more film scripts. The script for *The Pearl* (1948) was written at the same time as the popular novelette and resembles it as closely as is possible in the different medium. *Viva Zapata!* (1952) grew out of Steinbeck's friendship with film director Elia Kazan and was conceived as the script for a film about the Mexican revolutionary leader Emiliano Zapata that Kazan filmed with Marlon Brando in the title role. Both films have distinctly upbeat endings. Despite the popularity of Steinbeck's novelette as wholesome moral fiction for high school students, the Mexican-made film version of *The Pearl* (there are slightly different versions with Spanish and English soundtracks) is rarely shown in the United States, because the realistic visualization of the fantastic tale makes the farfetched nature of the story too conspicuous.

Although the incontrovertible facts of history forced Steinbeck and Kazan to kill off Zapata, they portray him as still present in spirit riding his white horse high on the mountains to lead his people to eventual liberty and light.

The implication of these comments is not that Steinbeck viewed the movies as a mass medium to be used only for dispensing upbeat inspirational messages, although the authorities governing the old Production Code certainly preferred that films be used that way. But that was the kind of message Steinbeck was disseminating through his works during the comparatively short period that he was involved in filmmaking. Though the much-debated final tableau in *The Grapes of Wrath* is only equivocally optimistic, his principal works of the 1940s and 1950s—*The Moon Is Down, The Wayward Bus, Cannery Row, Burning Bright, East of Eden*—end with hopeful, if not always convincing, visions in contrast to the bleakly ironic endings of the earlier *Cup of Gold, The Pastures of*

Heaven, *Tortilla Flat*, *In Dubious Battle*, and *Of Mice and Men*. Thus the ending of the film version of *The Red Pony* may not be in keeping with the ending of the story cycle, but it is certainly in keeping with the endings of the works that he was writing during the period when the film was produced.

The idea of basing a film upon the Jody Tiflin stories was a long time coming to fruition. As early as 1939 in a letter to his agent-confidante Elizabeth Otis, Steinbeck disclosed that Victor Fleming (at the peak of his fame for *Gone with the Wind*) and superstar Spencer Tracy, who had starred in the film adaptation of Steinbeck's *Tortilla Flat*, wanted to make a film from *The Red Pony* stories, presumably with Tracy in the most suitable role of Billy Buck. Steinbeck added that he would donate the rights to the stories and work on the script free if the others would also contribute their efforts so that all proceeds could be given to children in local hospitals. Fleming thought they might raise $2 million.[12]

There is no evidence that Steinbeck did any work on a script at this time, and such wild-eyed philanthropy must have given fits to famed Metro-Goldwyn-Mayer studio boss Louis B. Mayer, to whom Fleming and Tracy were under contract, because the next year the studio would not even allow Tracy to read the over-voiced narration for *The Forgotten Village*. Steinbeck retaliated by threatening to take M-G-M to court if it used the name Jody in the film version of Marjorie Kinnan Rawlings's best-selling novel *The Yearling*, in which an unenthusiastic Tracy was scheduled to star.[13] By the time *The Red Pony* was filmed, Steinbeck had changed his boy-hero's name to Tom. Joseph Millichap thinks that this change may have been made to avoid the name that had been used in *The Yearling*, but it seems more likely that by the time the film was made, Steinbeck wanted to use the name of his own first son Tom, born August 2, 1944.

By April 1940 Steinbeck could advise Elizabeth Otis that arrangements were being made with Lewis Milestone (director of *Of Mice and Men*, one of the most impressive film versions of a Steinbeck novel) to film the story cycle, but financial problems had caused delays.[14] By April 1940 they did have a contract with RKO (at the height of its prestige for Orson Welles's *Citizen Kane*) to make the film, and Steinbeck was preparing to write a synopsis,[15] but production was delayed again, and the film did not materialize until after World War II when Milestone directed it at Republic Studios. Steinbeck did mention in 1941 that he was working with only three of the stories, and his concept of the story line may have been approaching its final form.

Since the film was not actually produced until 1949, there is another consideration in evaluating the final story line. During the long interval that the war delayed the project, Steinbeck had two sons of his own from his short-lived marriage to Gwyn Conger. Steinbeck made no secret when he was beginning work on what he considered his most ambitious novel, *East of Eden*, at about the same time *The Red Pony* was filmed, of his intention to dedicate the novel to providing some account of his own childhood background in the valleys and mountains around Salinas, California, for his sons when they were old enough to read and understand it. Certainly *The Red Pony* film could serve much the same purpose as an easier introductory work for the boys, so that the ultimate reason for his shaping the film script as he finally did could have been to provide a realistic but suitably entertaining and inspiring introduction to these childhood years for his own sons to enjoy when they were the age of the Tom in the film.[16]

Steinbeck could exercise this kind of control over his project because by the time the film was shot on the Republic lot, the slowly dying company was serving principally as a distributor for independently produced films made by refugees from the old studio system who wanted to escape the domination of the exclusively profit-dominated New York bankers in order to produce what they considered works of artistic and humanistic value. John Ford, for example, freed from his long subjection to the bosses at Twentieth-Century-Fox, set up with others an independent producing company to make films like *The Quiet Man*, his favorite tribute to his Irish heritage, on the Republic lot.

Republic had been founded in the 1930s as one of the so-called poverty row studios that supplied the insatiable demand for "B" Westerns (films made quickly on very low budgets) for double features and Saturday matinees in small towns and poor urban neighborhoods. Hour-long pictures, long on chases and short on dialogue, were shot on location in the San Fernando Valley using the same few ramshackle sets in film after film. After the war, as television began to cut deeply into movie audiences, the logos identifying Monogram and Mascot films, among others, began to disappear from the screen, and their old pictures were sold off to the new medium.

Republic had managed to outclass the competition in the 1930s when it acquired the services of Gene Autry, who developed an enormous following as a singing cowboy. His films continued to do well even after the war, while Republic kept afloat for a while by leasing its facilities to the independent producers in return for distribution rights for the films. Thus the backers of *The Red Pony* finally had a freedom in making the film that would have been impossible in the days when it was first conceived.

Unfortunately, Republic did not have very good distribution facilities, so that despite Steinbeck's reputation in 1949, the presence of such stars as Robert Mitchum and Myrna Loy in the cast, and the attraction of a soundtrack by the distinguished American composer Aaron Copland, it was difficult to book first-run engagements in major cities. Reviewers were little help, for as Robert Morsberger observes, some of them found the modest, upbeat film "unexciting" at a time when the *films noirs* that made stars like Robert Mitchum famous were all the rage.[17] As a result, the film was not widely circulated, and for many years—after Republic Studios closed down—it was difficult to locate copies of it.

Perhaps videotape will now keep it permanently available as a minor but significant part of Steinbeck's work. It is one of those rare American films that proves it is possible to create well-crafted, dignified, emotionally moving films for preteenagers. Even if the film version does not do justice to the dramatic possibilities of the story cycle, the two offer an extraordinary opportunity to compare a major author's handling of the same basic story in two different media at two different points in his career.[18]

Howard Levant

---

7   John Steinbeck's *The Red Pony:* A Study in Narrative Technique

---

The Red Pony is a very early and a completely successful instance of the organic relationship between structure and materials which distin-

Previously published.

guishes Steinbeck's most important fiction.[1] It is set off from much of
Steinbeck's work by a relative absence of extraneous devices intended
to force order into the work of art.

This long short story consists of three episodes: "The Gift," "The
Great Mountains," and "The Promise." The structure is panoramic
with a strong thematic unity which binds the three episodes together.
Their shared reference is to one important experience, the process of
growing up, and their shared focus is on one character, the boy Jody.
The episodes provide concrete evidence that the meaning of growing up
is chiefly a development of a sense that life and death are involved in
each other; this awareness is equated with a growth of a sense of
tragedy. Detail is presented consistently in terms of Jody's progressive
awareness of the reality of death. The objective events and their implied
meanings are self-contained.

Because Jody's is the point of view, we tend to accept his innocence as
our own. The events are developed so that each episode is an objective
record of Jody's experience and deepening awareness. One episode
flows into the next, and the last episode fuses with the first because it
ends as the first begins, with the present of a pony for Jody; but any
sense of a purely mechanical progression is subordinated to Jody's
innocent point of view.

There are some minor mechanical connections between characters
and events which serve only to tighten the story. Thus, each episode
begins with a focus on Jody's childish faith in adults or a child's game
or daydream, but an adult problem intrudes and absorbs the child's
world. The specific content in the process is that death and imperfection are everywhere, and that people try to conquer death and overcome imperfection in spite of their failures, while nature is a merely
neutral element.

Death is a natural and fairly innocent presence in the opening division of "The Gift." Jody's world is ordered by kindly and severe adults,
but contains cows and pigs that are to be butchered, a dog that has killed
a coyote and been lamed, unseen dead animals, and highly visible
buzzards. At night Jody hears owls hunting mice. Of all the evidence of
death, Jody hates only the buzzards "as all decent things hate them" (p.
206). They are natural enough, and so necessary "they could not be
hurt" (p. 207). Yet, in feeding on carrion, buzzards mark the point at
which death becomes an ugly imperfection that cannot be accepted

serenely. Buzzards prove that nature feeds on nature. They dramatize the ugly fact. And, within Jody's experience, their realistic function connotes their symbolic role at the conclusion—as the ultimate images of Death.

Into this flawed ranch world, and into Jody's formless innocence, Jody's father brings the red pony. In keeping with the theme, the pony is not quite perfect. He is untrained, acquired at an auction after the bankruptcy of a "show." The red saddle he comes with is too frail for ordinary use, and he has been paid for by money from the butchered cows. Also this random gift emphasizes Mr. Tiflin's own imperfection. Jody's father is a stern disciplinarian, implicitly afraid to express his affection for Jody (p. 205). Mr. Tiflin's materialistic gift and his claim that the pony will be useful mask his effort to express a love for Jody that he cannot express in words. The ironies increase. Once he sees the red pony, Jody is filled with wonder and affection for it, not for Mr. Tiflin, but the pony bites Jody's hand.

These narrative details suggest a weight of imperfection, but, for the moment, that weight is lifted by Jody's happiness. He loves the stylish red saddle and feels that biting proves the pony's high spirits. Even the doubts of his playmates, when they learn the pony is untrained, fail to diminish Jody's happiness. He even rises somewhat out of childhood. When his friends leave, he speaks to the pony "in a deep voice," and directs all of his attention to this new love; and his mother points to this development when she feels "a curious pride rise up in her" as she sees Jody falling in love with the pony (pp. 214–15).

The pony's training can be read in abstract terms as the bending of nature to man's will, or paralleled with Jody's growing up, but the specific details of the training carry their own conviction. The fact is that Billy Buck, the kindly stable hand, teaches the pony with Jody's help; implicitly, Billy teaches Jody how to be a man by way of using a horse without showing fear. Still, the first time that Jody thinks of riding the pony as a fact, he is afraid of being hurt if the pony should fall. This reality merges with Jody's distanced fantasies of imperfection, for he imagines at times that the pony has been hurt, but only to indulge the childish luxury of self-torture. The final sentence in this passage sets aside fears and fantasies; Jody's happiness is predominant: "When the two came back from an expedition they smelled of the sweet sage they had forced through" (p. 222). Nonetheless, happiness and imperfection are so mingled in the details of this episode that very often they cannot be separated. Jody's mother speaks "irritably" and his father "crossly" to Jody on the morning he gets the pony, since they do not know how to express the love or joy that they do feel (pp. 209–11). Jody's mother says to Carl Tiflin, "Don't you let it keep him from school," and his father "walked up a side-hill to be by himself, for he was embarrassed" (pp. 210–11). Yet the objective narrator, not Jody, records these details. Again, the pony connotes power, quite as strongly as love, as when the visiting boys are awed: "They knew instinctively that a man on a horse is spiritually as well as physically bigger than a man on foot" (p. 213). And love is balanced by the mixed stages of the training; the carrots and the petting occur in a context of details such as this: "The first time the pony wore the bridle he whipped his head about and worked his tongue against the bit until the blood oozed from the corners of his mouth . . . and his eyes turned red with fear and with general rambunctiousness. Jody rejoiced, for he knew that only a mean-souled horse does not resent training" (p. 220).

The illness and death of the pony occur in this context of imperfection that even happiness does not negate. The central human fact is that Jody tends to transfer an implicit belief in his father's perfection to the less awesome Billy Buck, who is aware that he cannot bear to seem fallible to Jody. Partly because of this self-knowledge, Billy claims too much good sense, and he is badly mistaken on three occasions. The pony gets wet because Billy misjudges the weather (by quiet irony it is near Thanksgiving, when Jody can ride the pony); the pony gets sick in spite of Billy's assurance that he will not; and the pony fails to get better in spite of Billy's careful doctoring. To complete the round, Jody's need to place the whole blame for human imperfection on Billy dissolves when Jody goes to sleep in the stable, while the pony might yet recover, and wakes up to find that the pony has wandered outdoors into the chilly night. Jody does not mention this lapse, but he falls asleep again and lets the pony wander off to its death.

Carl Tiflin, Billy Buck, and Jody Tiflin are imperfect, then, in their various human ways. But the ultimate fusion of death with imperfection (and a human striving after perfection) is presented in one brilliant narrative image in the final division of the episode, in Jody's fight with the buzzard. When Jody finds the pony's body, he catches one buzzard and beats it to death. Jody wishes to protect the dead pony because he was unable to protect the sick, living pony, but his "punishment" of the carrion eater is worse than futile. The imagery indicates that nature is an indifferent process to which men assign meaning. The buzzard cannot be hurt even by its death, for it is not human; as Jody struck, "the red fearless eyes still looked at him, impersonal and unafraid and detached" (p. 238). Carl Tiflin cannot understand Jody's act (or, probably, the foregoing image), so, in the last paragraph of the episode, Billy Buck expresses Jody's feelings: "His father moved the buzzard with his toe. 'Jody,' he explained, 'the buzzard didn't kill the pony. Don't you know that?' 'I know it,' Jody said wearily. It was Billy Buck who was angry. He had lifted Jody in his arms, and had turned to carry him home. But he turned back on Carl Tiflin. 'Course he knows it,' Billy said furiously, 'Jesus Christ! man, can't you see how he'd feel about it?'" (p. 238). There is no loading of meaning; the passage's intensity and the shifts in tone are implicit in the objective narrative, as a sequence of human responses on the basis of everything that has gone before. Jody has learned that nothing can be blamed, given human imperfection and uncaring nature. The fallible but fatherly Billy Buck—Jody in his arms—being closer to nature, and more involved in Jody, can understand better than the well-meaning but detached Carl Tiflin, who presumes that Jody is inwardly as young as his physical age. The one positive touch is that Jody and Billy Buck share an awareness of human imperfection and of an impersonal nature.

So, by a completely unspoken implication, Jody leaps into the sense of tragedy that defines manhood. As silently, that leap is an ironic byproduct of the circumstances of the pony's illness and death. More than in much of his later work, Steinbeck is willing here to let an extensive texture of imagery, events, and characters produce their own implicit meanings. Steinbeck's later concept of "is" thinking (nonteleological observation) is intended to produce a precise language; that precision is organically justified here because many of the details of the pony's training, illness, and death are new to Jody. And those details serve implicitly to indicate Jody's development from childish innocence to a mature, tragic awareness; they are not merely an aspect of Steinbeck's technique. Particularly Steinbeck avoids any suggestion of the allegory that is so common in the later novels. For example, the buzzards are really, and therefore organically, the chief images of Death that a country boy would know about. The imagistic richness of the Death figure is precisely its natural quality, which corresponds perfectly with its larger meaning. A buzzard is a natural and necessary beast, and a terrible one, and in these qualities it approximates our feelings about death itself. Hence the image grows out of its surroundings and fulfills its own nature; its objectivity precludes allegorical pumping.

The second episode, "The Great Mountains," is an interlude that continues a development of the themes of Death, imperfection, and a sense of tragedy, but with some decline of narrative intensity.

The episode begins with a seemingly aimless introduction. Jody plays around the ranch—he tortures the lamed dog that he had kissed and relieved of a tick during the pony's illness; he kills a "little thrush" with a slingshot, cuts it up because he is ashamed, and finally throws the parts away; and he asks his father, mother, and Billy about the large seaward mountains that suggest death to him in contrast with the "jolly" landward mountains, the Gabilans (pp. 240, 242). The key to Jody's play is his fascination with death. Having become aware of it, he must understand its human meaning. He poses "the possibility of ancient cities lost in the mountains" to justify his deeper fascination (p. 242). "Ancient cities" is an impossible fantasy, but the mountains become even more suggestive to Jody as a strictly private image; they are "dear to him, and terrible" in their mystery (p. 242). Jody's secret fascination is drawn to one imagistic point by the appearance of Gitano, an old paisano, who comes back to his birthplace to die. After learning that the family adobe hut has washed away, and after staying a day and night with the Tiflins, Gitano travels into the great mountains that rim the Pacific, and he takes the old, useless horse, Easter; for the journey is to death.

All of this is a little too contrived. Nonetheless, it is made clear that Jody's mind works as a child's mind often does, through symbols in its preoccupation. That explains why Jody is so excited when Gitano appears. Jody can sense the painful reality of Gitano's wish to die, having learned about death in his own right, and he feels a kinship because he senses that Gitano's thoughts are like his own. Jody feels "irresistibly drawn" to the bunkhouse where Gitano is put up, since, in Jody's mind, Gitano's wish to die is associated with the seaward mountains (p. 252). Indirectly but clearly, the narrative moves forward in a subsequent action, a fusion of the question that death raises with the theme of fatherhood. Jody finds Gitano with a rapier, and Gitano's initial anger at being spied on is changed to sympathy as he realizes the boy's need: "Jody put out his hand, 'Can't I see it?' Gitano's eyes smouldered angrily and he shook his head. 'Where'd you get it? Where'd it come from?' Now Gitano regarded him profoundly, as though he pondered. 'I got it from my father'" (p. 253). Jody understands in turn that Gitano's reply is a sudden insight—the end of his search for a place to die. The privacy of the insight is shared in the objective fact of the rapier: "Jody knew . . . he must never tell anyone about the rapier. It would be a dreadful thing to tell anyone about it, for it would destroy some fragile structure of truth. It was a truth that might be shattered by division" (p. 254). The truth seems to be that death is only a natural fact, and it is natural because it is really a search for origins, for one's father. It is quite to the point that Jody's earlier eager questioning about treasure cities in the mountains forces Gitano to understand that his own search is really for a place to die that is his father's; for, as Jody questions, Gitano remembers that his father had taken him into the mountains once when he was a boy, and he comes to feel that only the mountains belong now to his father. This range of insight is not limited to the supporting phallic symbolism (mountains, rapier), or to the socially apt suggestion that Mr. Tiflin is not a warm father (a real father?) to Jody, or to the religious implications of "father," although all of these elements are relevant to the fragile structure of truth, which cannot be expressed simply.

Steinbeck is perhaps too simple at the climax of the episode, in the report the next morning that a neighbor has seen Gitano going into the seaward mountains, leading Easter and carrying a sword. Until that moment, the episode is developed surely.

Gitano's father contrasts sharply with Carl Tiflin. Gitano's father was a great man and was loved by his son, but Carl Tiflin is a fool. Interestingly, Steinbeck uses a version of his later allegorical method at its worst to suggest Mr. Tiflin's inability to sense that Gitano wishes to die. Mr. Tiflin is afraid of having to support the old man, and parallels him with Easter in a bad associative joke, suggestive of narrow stupidity, although Mr. Tiflin likes the joke so much (it *is* typical of him) that he repeats it: "Jody's father had a humorous thought. He turned to Gitano. 'If ham and eggs grew on a side-hill I'd turn you out to pasture too,' he said. 'But I can't afford to pasture you in my kitchen'" (pp. 249–50). Having innocently set off this exchange, Jody listens. Later, in the scene in the bunkhouse, Gitano is given the insight that Jody lacks a father he can respect fully. Still later, Gitano senses Jody's feeling that the rapier is a secret. And, for Jody, keeping the secret means keeping it especially from his father. Jody's lack of a respected father is emphasized—by ironic reversal—when Gitano goes into the mountains to find a place he can associate with his father. These narrative details draw together at the close. Mr. Tiflin thinks that Gitano has robbed him by taking Easter, but, with a deeper understanding, Jody walks out alone to look at the great mountains and to think about Gitano: "He lay down in the green grass . . . covered his eyes with his crossed arms . . . and he was full of a nameless sorrow" (p. 256). Jody's sorrow is for Gitano, for his probable death, and for the mystery of it. Even more, it is the sorrow of self-discovery, that imperfection is worse than death. Thus, Jody passes from a fascination with death, even from an older sorrow for the death of the red pony, to the profounder sorrow of recognizing that his father's limitations create or reveal imperfection at such close hand.

Clearly this episode is superior narrative work. Its relative inferiority to the surrounding episodes is due to some narrative strain. Mr. Tiflin's lack of sensibility is a much smaller point than the reality of death, and Mr. Tiflin's jovial stupidity cannot be elevated into a perfect correlation with Gitano's passion for his father. And the parallel between Gitano and Easter is much too self-conscious and slick in its surface emphasis. These imperfections keep "The Great Mountains" from attaining a thorough organic unity. The strength of the episode is in its success as an interlude, and its somewhat mechanical quality may have been intended precisely to relax the narrative tension to some extent. Certainly it occupies the mid-position between two very intense episodes. Finally, there is a thorough success in Steinbeck's transfer of Jody's awareness of death from the animal to the human sphere.

The third episode, "The Promise," is abolutely an organic unity. It is one of Steinbeck's most impressive works. "The Promise" opens with a series of games that Jody plays by himself on the way from school. The games modulate from pure fantasy into the real world, from leadership of "a phantom army with great flags and swords, silent but deadly," through a batch of small animals that Jody stores, "moist and uncomfortable" in his lunch pail, to his eager collection of the mail from the box in front of the ranch, and finally to his mother's news that his father wants to see him (pp. 256–58). Here the real world intrudes clearly, and the game becomes adult—a game of creation that is "silent but deadly," that involves pain, yet more new experience than a weekly paper or a mail catalog can provide.

Mr. Tiflin has been convinced by Billy Buck that one of the ranch mares, Nellie, should be bred; her colt will replace the red pony. Mr. Tiflin masks the idea with a typical coldness; his offer is based on Jody's previous good behavior, and his condition is that Jody must earn the five-dollar stud fee by work around the ranch. Jody's response is a joyful fearfulness and respect for the stern father, and "a sudden warm friendliness" for Billy Buck as he realizes that the idea is Billy's (p. 260). A forward movement containing the emotional content of the earlier episodes is clear now: Billy becomes Jody's substitute father, and Mr. Tiflin is allowed only a minimal role. Billy's stake is that he loves Jody as a father might; his benevolent idea is to let Jody help to create the new pony in the sense of helping at the birth of Nellie's colt. Mr. Tiflin's love is more objective and abstract. It is rooted in the virtue of duty and the value of money. So the idea is enmeshed from the beginning in Mr. Tiflin's private imperfections as a father and as a man.

Events deepen this suggestion. Jody brings Nellie to a neighbor who has a stallion; imagery controls the result:

> The stallion came on so fast that he couldn't stop when he reached the mare. Nellie's ears went back; she whirled and kicked at him as he went by. The stallion spun around and reared. He struck the mare with his front hoof, and while she staggered under the blow, his teeth raked her neck and drew an ooze of blood. Instantly, Nellie's mood changed. She became coquettishly feminine . . . Jess Taylor sat the boy behind him on the horse. "You might have got killed," he said. "Sundown's a mean devil sometimes. He busted his rope and went right through a gate." (p. 263)

Nellie's mild injury, Jody's very probable danger, and the natural violence of the breeding, all presented from Jody's point of view, engender a train of imagery suggesting that violence, joy, and the chance of death are involved in creation—in an event more complex than a stud fee would imply through its reduction of the event to a calculated price. Mr. Tiflin, and Jody through him, tends to deny this complexity in the rationality of work. Jody's grinding schedule, set by Mr. Tiflin, repays the stud fee and pays for Nellie's special diet. As metaphor, father and son presume the colt's life has been paid for beforehand, hence assured, and Jody is his father's son to the extent that he expects the rational bargain to be kept.

But at birth the colt is twisted around in the womb; Billy has to kill Nellie to save the colt. Thus human and natural imperfection continue, and death remains the price of life.

The episode reaches a tragic plane, a heightening of the irony that we cannot buy a life, through Jody's shared awareness of Billy's suffering. Billy does what is "right" because he is determined to keep his promise to give Jody a colt, and he knows the mare has to die if the colt is to live. "Right" as it is, Billy's act is as bad, in effect, as the fact of a buzzard's endless hunger. Billy knows this; therefore he is stricken with guilt. A buzzard feels no guilt, nor does a man as unsubtle as Mr. Tiflin. The forward narrative movement from the first episode is in Billy's tragic awareness that the best he can do is imperfect, and Jody is able to comprehend this scale of moral awareness because it echoes his own earlier experience. Thus the narrative movement is completely organic and self-contained.

Steinbeck is very careful about this. Jody's point of view remains constant; it is through his essentially innocent perception that we realize the depth of Billy's sense of guilt. Always Jody's understanding is the center of the action, not the violence of birth in its bloody detail. And Jody's point of view is justified. He tends to substitute Billy Buck for his father, as human warmth for inhumanly chilly abstraction, but that does not lull his conviction that Billy is a fallible man. Hence, Jody wants to be certain that everything goes well. He makes Billy promise "you won't let anything happen" to the colt, and he insists on attending the birth (p. 275). The price that Jody pays is a vision of Billy's self-torment. Billy's strain as the birth develops badly is established through his increasingly violent way of speaking to Jody. In the final sentence, Jody's concentration on having the colt he has paid for and arranged to have is shifted completely under these influences to Jody's awareness of Billy's torment: "He tried to be glad because of the colt, but the bloody face, and the haunted, tired eyes of Billy Buck hung in the air ahead of him" (p. 279). So, fusing natural imperfection, death, and fatherhood, the episode ends in a human environment that is more significant than the colt, given Jody's established point of view. Human relevance is at one with the clarity of the narrative.

Like "The Gift," "The Promise" is an organic whole. Its events and characters imply a larger meaning that is implicit without strain in the narrative. There are no purely mechanical links, as there are in "The Great Mountains." Certain mechanical connections are evident, as in "The Gift," but they remain minor details that only tighten the events. Thus, Jess Taylor, who saw Gitano going away, owns the stallion in "The Promise." Jody's colt is intended to replace the red pony. A year passes and Jody thinks he will be too old before he can ride the new colt. In fact, he is growing mature enough to comprehend tragedy, not merely death. The major themes are always kept in view and focus the organic development of the narrative. In brief, details are not ends in themselves; they support the whole.

Clearly, then, *The Red Pony* can stand with *In Dubious Battle*, much of *The Grapes of Wrath*, and *The Pearl* as among Steinbeck's most impressive successes in the art of narrative.

IV   The Moon Is Down

Tetsumaro Hayashi

8 Dr. Winter's Dramatic Functions in *The Moon Is Down*

Dr. Winter, a supporting character who appears as Mayor Orden's friend, adviser, and confidant in John Steinbeck's play-novella *The Moon Is Down* (1942), performs extraordinarily complex functions. "Bearded and simple and benign, historian and physician to the town,"[1] Dr. Winter strengthens the mayor's political leadership in crises by supporting his fading self-respect, healing his wounded pride, and helping him to restore his courage, integrity, and vision. Mayor Orden is too weak to cope with the challenge that comes from Colonel Lanser and the terror the colonel's army has created in the occupied town. With Dr. Winter's loyal friendship, his unfailing support and defense, and his calm but wise advice, however, Mayor Orden, in spite of being nervous, frightened, tempted, and intimidated, can still function as the leader of the people.

The dual purpose of this essay is to investigate and define the nature and extent of Dr. Winter's dramatic functions and then to discover how his roles affect Mayor Orden and the novel as a whole—to discuss why John Steinbeck juxtaposes the physician/historian with the politician/humanist in the confrontation with tyranny. To expose Mayor Orden's ambivalence, Steinbeck places Dr. Winter in marked contrast to Colonel Lanser and the soldiers sent by the Leader to impose the New Order upon the townspeople. While Dr. Winter is a healer, Colonel Lanser is a destroyer. If Dr. Winter, the local historian, represents the collective past, Colonel Lanser, though a man of memories himself, behaves like a man without respect for tradition or the past. Colonel Lanser tells Mayor Orden: "I, an individual man with certain memories, might

Previously published.

agree with you, might even add that one of the tendencies of the military mind and pattern is an inability to learn, an inability to see beyond the killing which is its job. But I am not a man subject to memories" (p. 80).

Dr. Winter also plays the part of the chorus, or a choragus, enunciating the dramatic significance of each encounter Mayor Orden has with Colonel Lanser. Dr. Winter, for example, notes the temporal nature of the invaders as he tells Joseph, the mayor's servant: "Eleven o'clock, and they'll be here then, too. A time-minded people, Joseph." He also comments that "they push the rolling world along with their shoulders" (p. 15). Thus he identifies the mentality of the invaders with the relentless movement of time. Dr. Winter's view explains the way Steinbeck begins the novel: "By ten-forty-five it was all over. The town was occupied, the defenders defeated and the war finished. The invader had prepared for this campaign as carefully as he had for larger ones" (p. 11).

Colonel Lanser's trial of Alexander Morden in the mayor's office is interpreted by Dr. Winter, acting as chorus, as a calculated act: "I would guess it is for the show. . . . The invaders will have a trial and hope to convince the people that there is justice involved. Alex did kill the captain, you know" (p. 79). Colonel Lanser testifies to the truth of Dr. Winter's interpretation when he tells the mayor: "You know as well as I that punishment is largely for the purpose of deterring the potential criminal. Thus, since punishment is for others than the punished, it must be publicized. It must even be dramatized" (pp. 85–86).

Dr. Winter also reassures Tom Adams of the worthiness of the mayor's plan as the only way to fight the armed invaders effectively: "If they will even give us dynamite to hide, to bury in the ground to be ready against need, then the invader can never rest again, never! We will blow up his supplies" (p. 143). His reassurance inspires not only Tom but also Molly Morden: "Yes, we could fight his rest, then. We could fight his sleep. We could fight his nerves and his certainties" (p. 143). Thus Dr. Winter's influence as chorus becomes contagious.

As a local historian Dr. Winter perceives the confusion of the citizens caused by the sudden invasion and military occupation of their beloved country. Dr. Winter candidly comments on the situation. "I don't know. It's been so long since we conquered anybody or anybody conquered us. I don't know what is proper" (p. 25). As he tells Colonel Lanser, his function is to remain a nonteleologist, a man who objectively observes and reports what happens. Like his fellow townspeople, he cannot understand why the Leader and his soldiers suddenly "rape" a beautiful, democratic country that has long enjoyed peace, freedom, and independence.

When Colonel Lanser intimidates Mayor Orden by blackmailing him—"If you say yes, we can tell them you said no. We can tell them you begged for your life" (p. 185)—Dr. Winter angrily cuts in as Mayor Orden's articulate defender: "They would know. You do not keep secrets. One of your men got out of hand one night and he said the flies had conquered the flypaper, and now the whole nation knows his words. They made a song of it. The flies have conquered the flypaper. You do not keep secrets, Colonel" (p. 185).

With humor, determination, and objectivity Dr. Winter is able to understand the situation in the occupied town and show the way the townspeople may regain their self-respect to fight against the enemy. He identifies the invaders as time-minded men who behave as if they were driven to defy the laws of civilization. Thus he causes both Mayor Orden and the townspeople to confront the enemy with more courage. Just as he is a doctor willing to cure his patients, he is willing to help the mayor out of political, psychological, and moral crises and give him the courage and confidence desperately needed to rescue the town from the enemy terror. While becoming Mayor Orden's "secret sharer" by going through hell with him until the dying moment, Dr. Winter can also precipitate the mayor's courage, dignity, and enlightenment. Both of them choose to die for their country rather than collaborate with the enemy.

As well as his various functions as a fictional character, Dr. Winter also seems to represent the seasons. The title of the novel, *The Moon Is Down*, hints that darkness prevails because the moon is down, as in Shakespeare's *Macbeth*, but the sun shall rise again. Winter's name hints at the seasonal metaphor of Percy Bysshe Shelley's "Ode to the West Wind," which ends with these two famous lines: "The trumpet of a prophecy! O, wind, / If Winter comes, can Spring be far behind?" In the darkness there is the hope of light; in despair, salvation. In this context Dr. Winter may well represent the dormant powers of winter as well as a brighter future full of hope, the awakening vitality of spring. Thus Steinbeck seems to suggest Dr. Winter as the sustaining metaphor of the life-giving and life-sustaining forces in the universe.

The name Dr. Winter, reminding one of *The Winter of Our Discontent*, paradoxically reinforces the image of the Waste Land. As Annie, the mayor's old cook, disapprovingly declares, "The soldiers brought winter early. My father always said a war brought bad weather, or bad weather brought a war" (p. 124). The physical world and the psychological world become one. The two worlds merge into the one world— the Waste Land—cold, frozen, dry, and dead, thereby inviting sterility as well as depravity. This world of anxiety, despair, and sterility reminds one of approaching death in the occupied town. Steinbeck's description of the novel's surroundings reinforces this idea: "In the dark, clear night a white, half-withered moon brought little light. The wind was dry and singing over the snow, a quiet wind that blew steadily, evenly from the cold point of the Pole. Over the land the snow lay very deep and dry as sand" (p. 147). At another point in *The Moon Is Down*, as Steinbeck narrates: "The cold hatred grew with the winter, the silent, sullen hatred, the waiting hatred. . . . And the hatred was deep in the eyes of the people, beneath the surface" (p. 101).

Dr. Winter himself is so conscious of the destructive nature of time that he sees it as the force driving the conquerors. Throughout the novel Dr. Winter rises to the level of prophet—a visionary who can foresee the future in spite of the darkness that prevails in the occupied town.

It is Dr. Winter who precipitates Mayor Orden's prophecy to Colonel Lanser: "You see, sir, nothing can change it. You will be destroyed and driven out. . . . The people don't like to be conquered sir, and so they will not be. Free men cannot start a war, but once it is started, they can fight on in defeat" (pp. 185–86). Dr. Winter inspires Mayor Orden to predict that the townspeople shall first endure and then prevail:

COLONEL LANSER: We have taken on a job, haven't we?
MAYOR ORDEN: Yes. The one impossible job in the world, the one thing that can't be done!
COLONEL LANSER: And that is?
MAYOR ORDEN: To break man's spirit permanently. (p. 89)

As the major critic of the Leader's New Order, Dr. Winter, at first a nonteleologist, becomes emotionally committed in his defense of Mayor Orden's secret but gallant guerrilla war against the enemy. Dr. Winter comments, "It's funny for a doctor to think of destruction, but I think all invaded people want to resist. We are disarmed; our spirits and bodies aren't enough. The spirit of a disarmed man sinks" (p. 141). When the mayor gives precise instructions on how to fight the enemy with "little bombs to use, to hide, to slip under the rails, under tanks" (p. 142), the doctor endorses the mayor's plan, "They'll never know where it will strike. The soldiers, the patrol, will never know which of us is armed" (p. 142). Dr. Winter, like the mayor, knows why the people resort to the drastic political action—the enemy's own method of "a war of treachery and murder"—because he perceives that this is "no honorable war" (p. 142), as Mayor Orden declares.

As Dr. Winter becomes an involved patriot, he inspires Mayor Orden to declare with pride and dignity: "You know, Doctor, I am a little man and this is a little town, but there must be a spark in little men that can burst into flame. I am afraid, I am terribly afraid, and I thought of all the things I might do to save my own life and then that went away, and sometimes now I feel a kind of exultation, as though I were bigger and better than I am" (pp. 177–78). Dr. Winter helps Mayor Orden become a hero and a champion of freedom by restoring the mayor's faith in humanity and democracy. Steinbeck writes, "Dr. Winter was a man so simple that only a profound man would know him as profound" (p. 14); and Mayor Orden is the one who appreciates this profound man and depends on him. Wherever Mayor Orden is, Dr. Winter is invariably found near him—as if he were the mayor's alter ego. Even Colonel Lanser recognizes the interdependent and inseparable relationship between the mayor and the doctor. That is why the colonel eventually has to arrest and execute both men.

At one point when Mayor Orden asks Dr. Winter, "Will you come back this evening?" because "I just won't like to be alone," Dr. Winter assures him: "I will be here" (p. 84). This dialogue innocently but clearly testifies to the supreme importance of their relationship as "secret sharers"—the relationship that sustains the occupied town in its struggle against dictatorship.

When the mayor confesses thinking of the coward's way out, Dr. Winter comforts him by saying, "But you haven't done it." The mayor says, "No, I haven't," and Dr. Winter assures him, "And you won't do it." When Mayor Orden then tells the doctor, "No, I won't but I have thought of it," Dr. Winter tells him: "How do you know everyone

doesn't think of it? How do you know I haven't thought of it?" (p. 177).
Thus Dr. Winter unfailingly comforts Mayor Orden, helps him regain
his self-esteem, and heals the mayor's self-doubts and guilt.

When Mayor Orden and Dr. Winter are arrested together, the doctor, the town historian, predicts: "A time-minded people . . . and the
time is nearly up. They think that just because they have only one
leader and one head, we are all like that. They know that ten heads
lopped off will destroy them, but we are a free people; we have as many
heads as we have people, and in a time of need leaders pop up among us
like mushrooms" (p. 175).

The mayor then reacts: "Thank you. I know it, but it's good to hear
you say it. The little people won't go under, will they?" (p. 176) as he
searches Dr. Winter's face anxiously. The doctor, however, reassures
him: "Why no, they won't. As a matter of fact, they will grow stronger
with outside help" (p. 176). Thus Dr. Winter continues to infuse in the
mayor the conviction that democracy will win out.

Dr. Winter's support enables Mayor Orden to gain spiritual strength
in the face of impending execution. It is Dr. Winter who gives Mayor
Orden the tranquility and faith needed to behave as the "leader of the
people" ready to die for freedom and democracy. With Dr. Winter
beside him, the mayor can understand his approaching death in relation
to Socrates' death. Remembering the ending of *Apology*, Mayor Orden
states: "There you are mistaken: a man who is good for anything ought
only to consider whether he is doing right or wrong" (p. 178).

Dr. Winter, a prophet himself, encourages the mayor to predict the
future as Socrates did: "I prophesy to you who are my murderers that
immediately after my departure punishment far heavier than you have
inflicted on me will surely await you" (p. 181). The mayor further tells
Colonel Lanser: "If you think that by killing men you can prevent
someone from censuring your evil lives, you are mistaken" (p. 182). Dr.
Winter again reassures the mayor by saying, "The debt shall be paid."
He repeats, "Yes, you remembered. The debt shall be paid" (p. 188).
The dramatic ending of *The Moon Is Down* thus enforces Steinbeck's
implied message that the sun shall rise again and makes this book "a
kind of celebration of the durability of democracy,"[2] as Steinbeck
declared in *East of Eden* in 1952: "And this I believe: that the free,
exploring mind of the individual human is the most valuable thing in
the world. And this I would fight for: the freedom of the mind to take

any direction it wishes, undirected. And this I must fight against: any idea, religion, or government which limits or destroys the individual."[3] In *The Moon Is Down* Steinbeck does "declare and celebrate man's proven capacity for greatness of heart and spirit—for gallantry in defeat—for courage, compassion, and love"[4] through such men as Dr. Winter and Mayor Orden.

John Ditsky

---

9   Steinbeck's "European" Play-Novella: *The Moon Is Down*

The famous turtle in *The Grapes of Wrath*, which cannot be deterred from its inexorable progress southwestward, and Candy's old dog in *Of Mice and Men*, which has to be shot because it is no longer fit for human society, are instances of what an earlier era of criticism would have routinely considered to be Steinbeck's naturalistic association—or even identification—of humans with animals. Such an application of the critical cookie cutter would have blurred the fact that while the turtle is a device that Steinbeck uses to swell the scope of his narrative until it takes on the dimensions of a romantic epic, the dog is simply a means by which a play-novella is given a heightened sense of ritual dramatic inevitability.

In other words, those earlier critics who insisted upon seeing Steinbeck primarily in terms of traditional naturalistic practice would have in the process obscured the fact of the writer's capacity for formal innovation. And they would have compounded the muddle by blurring the distinction between naturalism in fiction, on the one hand, with its underlying adherence to the principle of determinism, and dramatic naturalism, on the other, with its emphasis upon replication of the observable external reality of the world around us. Such a limited vision can produce no coherent overall statement about the process by which the writer of *Of Mice and Men* was eventually to produce *Burning Bright*—a process which had reached its transitional stage by the time Steinbeck wrote *The Moon Is Down* (1942).[1] The uniqueness of the latter

Previously published.

work, in great part a matter of the strangeness of Steinbeck's Europe and his Europeans, deserves the critical attention on its own terms that this essay is intended to initiate.

I have already used the word *ritual* in connection with another of Steinbeck's play-novellas, and indeed all three of them are possessed of moments of ritual—in the form of killings that serve as dramatic climaxes which are for the most part markedly different from the crucial events of the "straight"-novel versions.[2] Yet ritual is just one of the ways in which the play-novellas do differ in style and structure from those other writings, and relatively little has been said about these differences even though without considering them, there is little chance that the Europe and its inhabitants in *The Moon Is Down* will be seen as anything but artistic failures. If this essay is meant to be an apologia for Steinbeck's practices, it is not also meant to be an apology; it is simply a fact that a great deal remains to be said about Steinbeck's notions of drama.[3]

The Moon Is Down begins, oddly enough, not *in medias res* but with a recapitulation of already completed action. "By ten-forty-five it was all over" (p. 275), the book starts out; and the narrator proceeds to move briskly—with a speed that matches the celerity with which the unnamed town has been occupied by unnamed foreign invaders—through less than a page of summarized events seen as if from a distance, rather like when the credits are rolling in a film. It remains 10:45 for all of that single page, because all of that summarized action is being deliberately *excluded* from what is to come by reason of its different style—which is not like the closely observed and specific bits of action which are mentioned, like stage directions, once the dialogue begins. In effect, these lines are the playwright's prefacing notes, and they are therefore not a part of the "play" itself at all. Steinbeck is making little attempt to blur the line between genres. A single paragraph of description of setting follows (p. 276), without any real effort to conceal its patent function. We are shown two persons who occupy the stage alone, for the moment. A scene begins whose first words predict that in precisely fifteen minutes—"Eleven o'clock?" (p. 276)—a representative of the occupiers, "a time-minded people" (p. 277), will be there for a meeting with the mayor, who is said to be dressing to receive him. In other words, the scene begins by showing persons getting ready to begin a scene—a scene within a scene, if you will—at an exactly predetermined time. This self-consciously theatrical raising of the dramatic to the second power results from the presentation of characters who are well aware of experiencing life as a form of theater. Hence the special nature of Steinbeck's Europeans.

As the play moves through its first dozen lines, Dr. Winter observes that the invaders "hurry toward their destiny as though it would not wait. They push the rolling world along with their shoulders" (p. 277). This notion of the invaders as having the certitude of their own stature as men fated to rule over others becomes undercut, in the course of the play, by the contrary idea that such a "destiny" can be put to rout by another sort of men—men whose lives are concerned with the ordinary business of living unexceptional lives. Though he names neither the occupier nor the occupied by nationality, Steinbeck creates two camps of Europeans with the self-awareness that onstage characters traditionally, but unrealistically, possess. Thus they are characters seen precisely *as* characters, aware that they are playing roles in a drama for which they have already begun to rehearse. Small wonder, then, that they act and speak as "stagily" as they do.

This theatrical self-consciousness is adumbrated by such gestures of the invader as having their brass band play "beautiful and sentimental music in the town square while the townsmen, their mouths a little open and their eyes astonished, stood about listening to the music and staring at the gray-helmeted men who carried sub-machine guns in their arms" (p. 275). True, this is on the opening page and therefore not really part of the "play." But it nonetheless functions as part of the playwright's staging indications by giving us the mind-set of characters aware of putting on a performance, and others who as yet are simply "audience." By the time we are halfway through the play, however, the latter have begun to understand their roles, and that involves such resistance as that of young Alex—who is sentenced to death for violently resisting an order to work. When the youth admits to being afraid, the mayor assures him, "You will make the people one" (p. 313)—thus identifying the process of creation of the Steinbeckian "group-man" with the assumption of the implications of a role (in this case, going to one's death with the assurance that one's performance will move the audience appropriately). And how shall the performance—the execution—be carried out? This exchange takes place:

[Orden] said to the colonel, "I hope you know what you are doing."

Captain Loft gathered his papers and Lanser asked, "In the square, Captain?"

"Yes, in the square. It must be made public," Loft said.

And Orden said, "I hope you know."

"Man," said the colonel, "whether we know or not, it is what must be done." (pp. 313–14)

Shortly afterward, the execution can be heard taking place outside, and just as soon after, a shot is fired through the window, hitting Lanser (p. 314). Alex's "performance" has had the desired effect, eliciting action by a process that can be called organic. Meanwhile, the occupiers' sense of decorum has become disoriented; it has turned into rule following as mindless as the observance of Aristotelian unities by some modern playwright.

I have elsewhere described the process by which speech emerges out of situational need in Steinbeck's work generally by means of this same term, *organic*. I mean by this the way in which Steinbeck's characters discover who and what they are through moments of existential crisis, and then react to this discovery by producing language which is sometimes extraordinary, and always at least special. That concept is especially justified by the way in which the idea of "free men" is created to combat the notion of "herd men" in the final pages of *The Moon Is Down* (pp. 352–54).[4] But this process can be seen at work all the way through Steinbeck's succession of play-novellas, and it consistently involves the idea that self-identification (i.e., character development) means moving onto a new plane of language: means forsaking the realistic—and, heaven knows, the naturalistic—for the epiphanic. It accounts for the peculiarities of expression which now and then come—never without good reason—from a writer known for his ear for genuine (usually American) human speech. Essentially, it is a matter of characters suddenly seeming to take uncommon care with what they say and how they say it because all at once they are aware of the fact that people are *listening*.

And this process, which often involves a dogged search for the "right" phrase with which to express something, and then the almost musical repetition of that phrase—"a time-minded people" (p. 277); "a man of certain memories" (p. 314); "the flies have conquered the flypaper" (pp.

352–53)—leads to a kind of poeticization of the mundane, as if the materials of the everyday concerns of ordinary people could be marshaled to meet extraordinary needs just as the people themselves can be marshaled. By the same token, the character of the introductory material, which is simultaneously self-effacing and yet also given the function of dimensionality inducement assigned to the "intercalary" chapters of *The Grapes of Wrath*, also undergoes change. Chapter 5, which turns the story of the invaders onto a new, downward course, rises to a quasi-biblical level of narration: the rhetoric of foreordainment. "The days and weeks dragged on, and the months dragged on. The snow fell and melted and fell and melted and finally fell and stuck" (p. 314). Paragraphs and sentences are begun with the language of a bard telling out a national saga: "And there was death in the air" (p. 315); "And it did no good" (p. 315); "And the hatred was deep in the eyes of the people, beneath the surface" (p. 315); "Now it was that the conqueror was surrounded" (p. 315); "If he . . . ," "If he . . . ," "If he . . . ," (p. 315); "And the men thought always of home" (p. 315); "Then the soldiers read the news from home and from the other conquered countries, and the news was always good, and for a little while they believed it, and then after a while they did not believe it any more" (p. 316); "And they knew . . . ," " . . . either," " . . . either" (p. 316); "Thus it came about . . ." (p. 316). Thus, in the tones of one informing his readers that the word had gone out from Caesar Augustus, John Steinbeck raises the rhetorical ante of *The Moon Is Down*.

It goes without saying that a play-novella could be expected to be structured in terms of recognizable scenes, and in *The Moon Is Down* this is certainly true. That observation, however, does not preclude a brief discussion of Steinbeck's scenic sense from having some critical value. One might profitably compare this sense with that of another American novelist with a penchant, if not quite a flair, for the dramatic—Henry James. But if James remained, to his considerable pain, a failed playwright all his days, nevertheless, his way of building whole novels— particularly when the added inducement of serialization was present— out of a succession of major encounters exploited to the scenic hilt makes for interesting comparison with Steinbeck's notions of scene. In James, typically, the reader is given great blocks of dense preparatory prose to wade through before the dialogue is permitted to carry the drama along. Having accomplished so much by way of reader preparation beforehand, James is able to bring off extraordinarily nuanced effects with only a minimum of interpolated stage directions. But Steinbeck is more economical both as to preparatory material—which, as I have noted is of the summary-generalization sort—and scene itself, largely letting the exchange of dialogue take place without authorial indications as to the manner of delivery of the lines. Nuances are left to the actors or—in the case of the prose version—to the imaginations of the readers.

However, if Steinbeck's dialogue in *The Moon Is Down* is largely unadorned by suggestions as to style of delivery, the same cannot be said about stage *action*. Steinbeck was dramatist enough to realize that a play cannot consist simply of speech, with nothing to occupy the eye; consequently, there is plenty of stage business before and during exchanges of dialogue. And in a play that demonstrates Steinbeck's increasing tendency to philosophize, he was shrewd enough to accompany his characters' musings with a fair amount of almost melodramatic action. On the other hand, stage decorum is observed in a way that it is not in *Of Mice and Men:* Steinbeck has learned the value of both offstage action and imminent action, with both chapter 6 and chapter 8 concluding with violent events about to occur. Mayor Orden's reasoned acceptance of his own coming execution, which is forthcoming as the final curtain descends, is so stirring an evidence of the play's newly stated notion of the way "free men" produce their leaders (pp. 352–54) that Steinbeck's critics have paid considerable attention to it. But equally theatrical—chillingly so, considering the fact that two of the most appealing characters in the play, Molly and Lieutenant Tonder, are involved—is the ending of chapter 6. Molly, the widow of the executed Alex Morden, has been visited by Tonder earlier in the scene, when he declared his affection for her; and now, he has returned as promised and waits outside tapping at the door and calling to her. Molly is alone onstage:

> Molly went to the center lamp, and her burden was heavy on her. She looked down at the lamp. She looked at the table, and she saw the big scissors lying beside her knitting. She picked them up wonderingly by the blades. The blades slipped through her fingers until she held the long shears and she was holding them like a knife, and her eyes were horrified. She looked down into the lamp

and the light flooded up in her face. Slowly she raised the shears and placed them inside her dress.

The tapping continued on the door. She heard the voice calling to her. She leaned over the lamp for a moment and then suddenly she blew out the light. The room was dark except for a spot of red that came from the coal stove. She opened the door. Her voice was strained and sweet. She called, "I'm coming, Lieutenant, I'm coming!" (p. 335)

One notices in this passage Steinbeck's attention to detail of theatrical presentation: Molly's silent soliloquy is a sequence of action involving a decision that quickly hardens into a determination; the prop scissors turn into a lethal weapon; the face of the decision-maker is twice illuminated by the conveniently available table lamp; and then the room goes dark but for the lurid glow of the stove's red light—a device interestingly anticipatory of the ending of act 1 of Arthur Miller's *The Death of a Salesman*. And, to repeat, the violent act is left to the imagination of the audience, like the gunshot left unheard at the ending of Harold Pinter's *The Dumb Waiter*.

But the sheer theatricality of the ending of this scene is accompanied by a chilling realization of just what a hard doctrine Steinbeck is ramming home when Molly Morden picks up the shears. Molly has accepted a new role for which she would never have thought herself suited before the events of the occupation; she is prepared to murder perhaps the most humane of the occupying forces, the one who at the end of chapter 5 is seen changing from someone who intended to settle permanently in the occupied country to someone who merely wants to go home to a sane and domestic existence (p. 323). Indeed, it is Tonder who has just formulated the phrase that is to survive him, the one which presents the triumphs of the occupying army as "flies conquer the flypaper" (p. 323). John Steinbeck, in trying to wrestle his old doctrine of the group-man into a format that made sense within the situation of a world war initiated by inordinately successful group-men, has invented a new distinction between "free" and "herd" men that is cheering until one realizes that what he is showing is a process of deindividualization of character only partially condoned by the exigencies of war. The light that lights up a determined Molly Morden's face is the illumination provided by the surrender of the self to the power of isness—of what therefore must be. It is this light which, in *Burning Bright*, is seen burning the Self out of the All.

When Molly's presumptive Norway requires her services, therefore, she can pick up a weapon against any German, no matter how sympathetic a character he may be. The attacks upon Steinbeck for presenting credibly human Germans quite miss the point of how irrelevant Tonder's humaneness is in the final picture, for Steinbeck—himself going through a lengthy struggle to accept his own individuality, his own ego—is in *The Moon Is Down* advancing an almost biblical conception of the interests of an entire people as the ultimate source of overriding moral imperatives. The question of Tonder's niceness, in that context, becomes no more important—except, perhaps, to the audience—than the probability that this or that of the pharoah's soldiers was primarily a loving family man. There is, in other words, a coldness underneath the rhetoric of resistance in *The Moon Is Down* that ought to undercut the melodramatics of heroism for any thoughtful reader. John Steinbeck's fundamental vision of drama—as opposed to the one he usually displayed in fiction—was what most would term "tragic"—a matter of accepting with religious fervor the necessity of what has to be.

That brings us back, of course, to the matter of character—and, in this case, specifically European character. In other words, how convincing *are* Steinbeck's portrayals of people of whom his only knowledge, by and large, could have come from literature? And what of his setting—his "Europe"? It must be noted that when John Steinbeck wrote *The Moon Is Down*, his knowledge of Europe and things European was still so slight that he might as well have been at the outset of his career writing *Cup of Gold*, which opens in a Wales Steinbeck borrowed from his readings and his imagination. While no one should deny the creative artist the right to allow the free play of the imagination to invent what is not actually "known" as such, the process is, of course, a dangerous one. Steinbeck avoids the danger by making the assumption that people, for the most part, are the same wherever they live—their remaining differences being accounted for by circumstances such as geography or, in this case, the condition of being far from home in the role of member of an occupying army in a war of aggression. The character summaries at the beginning of chapter 2, referring to the German officers, make little use of the conventional stereotypical attributes of Germans beyond such details as the facts that certain men are "sentimental" or have "blond sisters" (p. 290). More important are the distinctions imposed by circumstance, which, though a matter of particulars, have the potential for appearance which is universal, such as: "In marching, in mobs, in football games, and in war, outlines become vague; real things become unreal and a fog creeps over the mind" (p. 291). Thus Steinbeck points to situations which result in behavioral patterns; but these are situations which might come into existence anywhere in the world.

In a theatrical presentation those character summaries would be useless anyway; character would have to be elicited from performance and from dialogue. Steinbeck makes no attempt to write in the cadences of a foreign language, as Hemingway did; for that matter, he saw no reason not to make use of ordinary Americanisms as *substitutes* for characterization when the latter is uncalled for—as in this exchange when the occupying forces observe dynamite being parachuted to the resistance forces: "The sergeant said, 'Careful! It's a time bomb.' 'It ain't big enough,' a soldier said. 'Well, don't go near it'" (p. 338). This unimportant bit of filler illustrates Steinbeck's employment, at one end of the character spectrum, of a standard dramatist's technique: at the bottom end of the military rank scheme, a slight gradation of level of expression accompanies the difference between private and sergeant.

But this is largely a philosophical play involving exchanges at the other end of the chain of command—among lieutenants and colonels, doctors and mayors. In other words, the language of educated men conveniently becomes the speech by which the play's central issue— the nature and origins of leadership in free and totalitarian societies—is presented and articulated. The issue is finally stated as being the difference between "herd men, followers of a leader," and "free men," for whom "Mayor is an idea [that] will escape arrest" (p. 353). In *The Moon Is Down*, then, character emerges from a dialogue that is midway between the ostensibly naturalistic speech of *Of Mice and Men* and the exalted rhetoric of *Burning Bright*. The reminiscence about the time when Mayor Orden, for his school graduation ceremonies, had recited the words attributed by Plato to Socrates as the latter prepared for death is a clever means by which to elevate still further the level of discourse of the play-novella: of setting it firmly on the track of being yet another chapter in the struggle of the West to hold onto its invention—democracy; and of reminding the audience that the Socratic mode of leadership involved the acceptance, not the seizure, of a role—of "acting the part of a good man" (p. 349). Thus *The Moon Is Down*, which began with preparation for the enactment of a scene within a scene, comes to its ending on a note of still-further-heightened theatricality: with a character who is an actor in a scene preparing to become an actor in another, final scene—and then to hand his part on to another actor.

When *The Moon Is Down* received its first New York, wartime production in 1942, the critics were lukewarm at best, and the author himself decided that the play had been "dull."[5] It was a year in which neither the Pulitzer Prize for Drama nor the New York Drama Critics' Circle Award was given. Even before the play had been finished—even before Pearl Harbor was bombed—Steinbeck was revising a last act he then termed "sour."[6] The author's doubts are clearly expressed in a letter to Toby Street dated November 25, 1941: "The play? It's about a little town invaded. It has no generalities, no ideals, no speeches, it's just about the way the people of a little town would feel if it were invaded. It isn't any country and there is no dialect and it's about how the invaders feel about it too. It's one of the first sensible things to be written about these things and I don't know whether it is any good or not."[7] As is customary with the letters of John Steinbeck—indeed, with those of many a writer—the tone here involves a mixture of sincerity and whistling in the dark. The play *does* have generalities, ideals, and speeches. If it didn't, it might not have been attended in 1942. The anonymity that the writer refers to is also present as well. Small wonder that American audiences, with as yet only the slightest familiarity with the experience of war, would not have taken to a play which made Germans appear human—ditto American critics. On the other hand, the play's success in countries which had indeed been occupied during World War II argues a most convincing paradox: John Steinbeck, in projecting characters who are not particularly European at all and developments which in the gloomiest days of World War II only an American—or an Englishman—might believe in, had managed to make a dramatic statement in the delineation of which European audiences could recognize the universal—and themselves. In doing so, they were unwittingly acknowledging the writer's view of how and why and when the world becomes a stage.

V Cannery Row

Peter Lisca

10 *Cannery Row:* Escape into the Counterculture

Between *The Grapes of Wrath* and *Cannery Row,* Steinbeck's next major work of fiction, came a period of five years during which he was occupied with a variety of writing. During the last two of these years this writing was directly related to America's involvement in World War II, ending with Steinbeck serving five months abroad as a war correspondent. The war experience left Steinbeck so depressed that he refused even to edit his dispatches for publication in book form, and they were not published until 1958 (*Once There Was a War*). Instead, in less than two months he produced *Cannery Row,* the first of three works of fiction written in quick succession, varying widely in materials and techniques but each exploring some reaction toward a world whose basic values had plunged it in turn from eleven years of severe economic depression into the massive aggression and destruction of a world war.

In *Cannery Row* (1945) this reaction is one of escape into a counterculture superficially reminiscent of *Tortilla Flat,* except that the earlier novel is a light, tongue-in-cheek affair, and the new novel—for all its humor—is a philosophically based and impassioned celebration of values directly opposed to the capitalist ethic dominant in Western society. Looking through "another peephole," Steinbeck discovers that what normally might be called "thieves, rascals . . . bums" may just as truly be described as "saints and angels and martyrs and holy men." For as Doc, the central character, expresses it, the traits leading to success in our society are frequently "greed, acquisitiveness, meanness," whereas

Previously published.

failure may be the result of "kindness, generosity, openness, honesty, understanding and feeling."

The book is short and episodic, made up of thirty-two little chapters totaling only 181 pages. The setting is the section of Monterey, California, characterized by its sardine canneries (Cannery Row), and the time is just before World War II. Its numerous and varied characters include Doc, the biologist who runs the one-man Western Biological Laboratory; Dora Flood, madam of the Bear Flag Restaurant (a whorehouse); Lee Chong, owner of a grocery store; Mack and the boys (Hazel, Eddie, Hughie, Jones), who live in a storage shed they call the Palace Flophouse and Grill; Gay, who lives with the boys or in the jail to escape his wife; Henri, an avant-garde painter; Mr. and Mrs. Malloy, who live in an abandoned boiler; Frankie, a retarded juvenile whom Doc befriends; and many others, some of whom appear only briefly. The book's narrative line is a very thin one, consisting of Cannery Row's two attempts to give a surprise party for Doc, whom they all admire. The first one turns out to be a glorious failure, resulting in the wrecking of the laboratory and ending before Doc even arrives. After a period of gloom, a second party is launched and proves a riotous success. The novel closes with Doc washing the dishes the following morning.

Cannery Row offers neither a detailed anatomy of society's "mangled craziness" nor a program for changing it. Rather, it brings into being a new world to replace the one that is in the process of self-destruction. It is a world not of whole cloth but of bits and pieces, varying in chronology, recollected in nostalgia, and lovingly assembled, like the patchwork quilt presented to Doc by the girls of Dora's whorehouse, or one of the fantastic collages done by Henri, the novel's eccentric artist. Thus, while one episode concerns the death of the American humorist Josh Billings (1885), in another, Model T Fords are in common use; while Henry follows "feverishly . . . in periodicals the latest Dadaist movements and schisms," Sam Malloy's historically contemporary Chalmers 1916 piston and connecting rod is valued as a rare antique; elsewhere in the book, the year 1937 is clearly referred to as in the past. In addition to this free intermingling of various time levels, there is also a haunting effect of timelessness, achieved in part by the relative lack of plot (movement) and in part by the recurrence of specific descriptions and acts. A mysterious old Chinaman goes down to the sea each evening at five thirty and returns each morning. The rhythmic flopping of the loose sole on his shoe, normally a very temporary condition, through its presumed continuance accentuates that timelessness. These two qualities of the novel's time sense—its blurring of chronology and the sharp recurring detail—are the very essence of homesickness, out of which Steinbeck said he wrote the book; his close friend Ed Ricketts, the original of Doc, described it as "an essay in loneliness." *Cannery Row* brings together again in the unchanging world of art those qualities of life that—hastened by the war—had passed never to return, and for which Steinbeck felt a deep nostalgia. In this respect the novel is firmly in the pastoral tradition.

In the novel's preface, addressing himself to the problem of setting down Cannery Row "alive," Steinbeck proposes an analogy that resonates through all aspects of the work, for as its time sense is in free flux, so also are its other qualities. His comparison of the writing of this book to capturing whole fragile and delicate sea worms extends to both content (stories/sea worms) and method or form ("let the stories crawl in by themselves"/"ooze by themselves"). And as the seawater in which the specimens are held has no shape except that imparted by its container, so the novel seems equally arbitrary in form. Only about half of the thirty-two chapters pick up the tenuous narrative thread. Alternating almost regularly with these are "the little inner chapters" (as Steinbeck once called them) that sometimes add to our knowledge of the main characters and sometimes introduce material of no causal relationship. Generally, however, all these inner chapters serve in some way as comment or contrast to the novel's major theme.

The openness and freedom of the novel's structure is a formal expression of those same qualities in the Cannery Row community itself, upon which no convention or authority imposes conformity or direction. It has instead the natural order of a biological organism, manifesting its own inner dynamics. The lines of interaction between individuals and even between institutions proliferate in all directions—Frankie and Doc, the laboratory and the whorehouse, the Chinese grocery store and the Palace Flophouse, the idealized women in Doc's poetry books (Petrarch's Laura, the girl in "Black Marigolds") and Dora's practical prostitutes. Those relationships normally expected to be exploitative or repressive are mutually beneficial—the jailor and Gay, McKinley the diver and the Prohibition agents and the bootlegger, a landowner and trespassing bums, the police and a riotous party, even the whorehouse

and the Ladies' Anti-Vice League. This rich variety of viable relationships is possible because all elements of the community share a quality
that is most explicit in Steinbeck's description of Mack and the boys.
He calls them "the Beauties, the Virtues, the Graces" because in a
world of greed and rapacity—"ruled by tigers with ulcers, rutted by
strictured bulls, scavenged by blind jackals," they "avoid the trap" of
ambition. To this imagery of maimed animals is opposed a version of
the Peaceable Kingdom, in which Mack and the boys "dine delicately
with the tigers, fondle the frantic heifers, and wrap up the crumbs to
feed the seagulls of Cannery Row." Their lack of material gain is not
seen as lack of ability. Doc is certain that these "bums" can "get money."
But "they just know the nature of things too well to be caught in that
wanting." To Hazel's observation that Mack could have been President
of the United States had he wanted to be, Jones replies, "What could he
do with it if he had it?"

The novel's informing spirit is the *Tao Teh Ching* of Lao-tzu, a Chinese
philosopher of the sixth century B.C. Like *Cannery Row*, the *Tao Teh Ching*
was written in a time of brutal war ("Period of the Fighting States") and,
in reaction to those conditions, presented a system of human values devoid of all those qualities that had brought on that war. It is interesting in
this connection to quote from the prefatory remarks of two well-known
editions of the *Tao* published just before *Cannery Row*:

> For Laotze's book . . . teaches the wisdom of appearing foolish,
> the success of appearing to fail, the strength of weakness . . . if I
> were asked what antidote could be found . . . to cure this conten-
> tious modern world of its inveterate belief in force and struggle for
> power, I would name this book. . . . [Lao-tzu] has the knack of
> making Hitler and other dreamers of world mastery appear foolish
> and ridiculous.
> (Lin Yutang, *The Wisdom of China and India* [1942])

> And the Western world might well temper its characteristic faults
> by taking Laotzu to heart. . . . "Laotzu is one of our chief weapons
> against tanks, artillery and bombs."
> (Witter Bynner, *The Way of Life* [1944])

That Steinbeck was familiar with Lao-tzu's little text of forty or so
pages is certain, and most probably he was familiar with it in the Lin

Yutang translation, although several others were also available. In *Journal of a Novel* (1951) he listed Lao-tzu along with Plato, Christ, and Buddha as "the great ones." Significantly, Ed Ricketts, to whom *Cannery Row* is dedicated, was much attracted to Taoism and refers to it several times in his letters and unpublished papers. In chapter 2 Steinbeck speculates that Lee Chong, who takes up most of the first chapter and with whose name (which is similar to that of Lao-tzu's famous disciple Chuangtse) that chapter begins, is "more than a Chinese grocer. He must be. Perhaps he is evil balanced and held suspended by good—an Asian planet held to its orbit by the pull of Lao-Tze and held away from Lao-Tze by the centrifugality of abacus and cash register. . . ." Doc himself sometimes reads aloud to Lee Chong in English from the poetry of Li Po, a figure associated with Taoism. In this context even the novel's ancient and mysterious Chinaman is suggestive.

Taoism rejects the desire for material goods, fame, power, and even the holding of fixed or strong opinions—all of which lead to violence. Instead, man is to cultivate simple physical enjoyments and the inner life. To be obscure is to be wise; to fail is to succeed; in human relationships force always defeats itself; even laws are a form of violence; the moral life is one of inaction.

These principles are generally visible throughout *Cannery Row*; frequently the consequences of their absence are illustrated in the "little inner chapters." In addition, however, much of the novel seems to exemplify specific passages in the *Tao*. Sometimes there is even a similarity of expression. Steinbeck writes in chapter 2: "The word is a symbol and a delight which sucks up men and scenes, trees, plants, factories, and Pekinese. Then the Thing becomes the Word and back to Thing again, but warped and woven into a fantastic pattern. The World sucks up Cannery Row, digests it and spews it out, and the Row has taken the shimmer of the green world and the sky-reflecting seas." Surely Steinbeck's meditation upon his own creative act is reminiscent of the Gospel according to Saint John, but its similarity to the very first passage of the *Tao Teh Ching* is even more striking:

> Existence is beyond the power of words
> To define:
> Terms may be used
> But are none of them absolute.

In the beginning of heaven and earth there were no words,
Words came out of the womb of matter;
And whether a man dispassionately
Sees to the core of life
Or passionately
Sees the surface,
The core and the surface
Are essentially the same,
Words making them seem different
Only to express appearance.
If name be needed, wonder names them both:
From wonder into wonder
Existence opens.
(Witter Bynner, *The Way of Life*)

There are other correspondences of statement between the two works. Steinbeck's "Virtues and Graces" live with "no money, no ambitions beyond food, drink and contentment" whereas most men "in their search for contentment destroy themselves and fall wearily short of their target." Lao-tzu says,

There is no greater curse than lack of contentment.
No greater sin than the desire for possession.
Therefore he who is contented with contentment shall
always be content.
(Lin Yutang, XLVI)

Steinbeck's "another peephole," through which Mack and the boys are seen in different perspective, may be a version of

Who understands Tao seems dull of comprehension;
Who is advanced in Tao seems to slip backward;
. . . Great character appears like insufficient;
Solid character appears like infirm.
(Lin Yutang, XLI)

When Mack and the boys will not even turn their heads to look at the Fourth of July parade because "they know what will be in the parade," they illustrate the Taoist principle that "Without stepping outside one's doors, / One can know what is happening in the world" (Lin Yutang, XLVII).

Doc himself clearly embodies the traits of a Taoist sage. He is free of all ambition. He is a consummate "wordless teacher" to the entire community. In listening seriously to Mack's schemes or to Henri's illusions, he illustrates the Taoist principle that by not believing people you turn them into liars. His involvement in the welfare of Cannery Row demonstrates that "the Sage is good at helping men"; his care and kindness toward Frankie shows that for the sage "there is no rejected (useless) person" (Lin Yutang, XXVII). In his study of a tide pool or even a stinkbug, he conforms to the Taoist precept that one should look to Nature to know oneself, one's real human nature. "He didn't need a clock. . . . He could feel a tide change in his sleep." He is at one with his total environment—including the whorehouse, Lee Chong's, the Palace Flophouse—and thus in communion with the harmonious balance of Tao. At the height of his birthday party, Doc is seated calmly on a table, cross-legged in the Oriental posture of meditation.

The Sage dwells in the world peacefully, harmoniously.
The people of the world are brought into a community of heart
and the Sage regards them all as his own children.
(Lin Yutang, XLIX)

The world into which *Cannery Row* escapes is not a perfect one; not everyone lives according to the *Tao*. There is a series of misfortunes on Cannery Row, caused seemingly by some vague natural force about which "there is no explaining." But there is little in *Cannery Row* of the kind of evil men bring upon themselves through "greed, acquisitiveness, meanness, egotism and self-interest"; or through the desire to impose one's own standards on others; or even a single standard on oneself. And these incidents serve as contrasts to the book's theme. The poet Wallace Stevens could have been quoting Lao-tzu in his well-known line, "A violent order is disorder"; and his corollary statement, "A great disorder is an order," could be the epigraph for *Cannery Row*. For Steinbeck's created world is characterized by its rich variety, its benevolent chaos: "Cannery Row is a poem, a stink, a grating noise, a quality of light, a tone, a habit, a nostalgia, a dream. . . . tin and iron and rust and splintered wood, chipped pavement and weedy lots and junk heaps, sardine canneries." The same rich variety is evident in all its parts: Lee Chong's grocery store, with its hodgepodge of every conceivable commodity ("but one," Dora's), in and out of season; the Carmel

River, which, though short, has a long and varied list of characteristics—"everything a river should have"; Doc's lab, with its scientific apparatus, double bed, phonograph, cookstove, poetry books, and lady visitors; Eddie's "wining" jugs, containing bourbon, wine, scotch, beer, and even grenadine mixed together; the great tide pool (a microcosm of "the cosmic Monterey") in which Doc collects his specimens and in which is found such a variety of life forms and modes of survival. All are patterns of the rich community of Cannery Row and of the novel itself—both its form and content.

In this light, Steinbeck's prefatory analogy of letting the stories ooze into the book by themselves, like delicate sea worms into a collecting jar, rather than forcing them into an order, becomes also a moral statement. (There is no formal order in the *Tao Teh Ching*, either.) Mack learns that the first party failed because "we forced her," and that the second will succeed if they just "let it happen." Steinbeck tells us that those celebrations that are "controlled and dominated" are "not parties at all but acts and demonstrations, about as spontaneous as peristalsis and as interesting as its end product." William, the first bouncer at Dora's Bear Flag Restaurant, commits suicide because, unlike Alfred, his successor, he tries to force himself on people and is rejected. Henri can love boats and be happy because he does not drive himself to the logical conclusion of finishing his boat and thus having to go out upon the water, which he fears. On the other hand, Mrs. Malloy is unhappy because she wants to do such things as "force" lace curtains upon the windowless boiler in which she lives. The ambitious wife of the landowner in the hilarious frog-hunting episode fails as a wife because she forces her compulsive neatness upon her husband. The hitchhiker is ejected from the car because he expects everyone to hold the same principles about drinking that he does. Doc knows he is a "free man" because he can indulge the rich variety of his inclinations without fear of contradictions—Bach and Debussy, *Faust* and "Black Marigolds"; even, and at the same time, Palestrina masses and sexual intercourse. In fact, he himself looks "half Christ, half satyr."

The twin themes of *Cannery Row*, then, around which the novel's characters and events casually but effectively arrange themselves, are the escape from Western material values—the necessity to "succeed" in the world—and the escape from Western activism—the necessity to impose order or direction. Like Lao-tzu, Steinbeck elaborates these two escapes into a system of "Virtues and Graces."

Robert S. Hughes, Jr.

11   "Some Philosophers in the Sun": Steinbeck's
        Cannery Row

Throughout his career John Steinbeck was frequently accused of being an amateur philosopher, of having no consistent philosophy, or worse, of sentimentalizing when he should have grounded his work in some accepted ideology.[1] Perhaps the best-known charge of this kind came from Arthur Mizener, who, just before Steinbeck received the Nobel Prize, attacked him for watering down his books with "tenth-rate philosophizing."[2] Thus critics have shown considerable interest in this facet of Steinbeck's writing, and many attempts have been made to reduce his varied thinking into a unified system or belief. To complicate matters for these critics, Steinbeck was also prolifically unorthodox in his religion. While Christian and other religious themes appear repeatedly in his writing, Steinbeck developed his own brand of religion, which has occasionally made the clergy cringe as well as bitterly complain that his view of the established churches is unfounded and unfair.[3] *Cannery Row* is especially pertinent to Steinbeck's religious and philosophical thought, since the narrative persona in the book so clearly advocates the unconventional morality to which these clergy—and many critics—have objected in a number of Steinbeck's works.

In this essay I isolate the two most important strands of Steinbeck's thinking in *Cannery Row*: the moral and the ecological. The moral orientation of the novel emerges from a blend of Christian, Taoist, pantheist, and transcendentalist thinking, conditioned by an underlying pragmatism. Working from this orientation, Steinbeck inverts conventional morality by denigrating middle-class values—especially prudery and materialism—and championing the simple pleasures of his *Cannery Row* dropouts, namely, companionship, ease, and sense gratification. Though these latter values may seem primitive or hedonistic, in Doc's eyes (and Doc stands at the moral center of the book) they represent enlightenment and the best hope for survival of the human species. Not everyone on the Row thrives as do those adhering to these unconventional values. Some less fortunate characters, who attempt to live by the American "success" ethic the book rejects, grow ill and perish. That these unfortunates appear frequently brings to mind the second philosophical strand in the novel: the ecological. Inspired by the tide pool—a microcosm of endless reproduction, decay, and death—Steinbeck draws an implicit comparison between marine animals and the human community of *Cannery Row.* Both the tide pool and the cannery street in Monterey have their own ecologies, and both are by turns "lovely" and "murderous."[4] Thus, notwithstanding the variety of human values represented by characters in the novel, Steinbeck frequently reminds us, in Jackson J. Benson's words, of the "biological basis for all life."[5]

While Steinbeck has been said to view his characters in the nonteleological mode—that is, objectively without moral projections of "good" or "bad"—in *Cannery Row* he makes rather obvious judgments about them. He fondly approves of bums, prostitutes, and pimps, yet harshly criticizes those typically considered virtuous in American society. Steinbeck offers as a positive alternative Mack and the boys, Lee Chong, Dora Flood, and Doc. Mack and his friends renounce the unhealthy ambition of their struggling contemporaries in favor of a life of indolence and natural appetites. Grocer Lee Chong, having inherited the wisdom of China and the pragmatism of America, puts people before profits and still manages to balance his accounts. Dora Flood, revered madam of the Bear Flag Restaurant, provides the male community with feminine companionship and sexual release, neither apparently supplied by the "respectable" ladies of Monterey. And Doc, a "fountain of philosophy and science and art" (p. 28), as well as the novel's hero, acts as a spokesman for the values the novel upholds, bringing together the moral and the ecological strands of Steinbeck's thinking.

To understand how Steinbeck develops these characters founded on the philosophy described above, we must look closely at three aspects of the novel: first, the Monterey waterfront setting, whose temperate climate and coastal economy influence the characters' way of life; second, Steinbeck's preface to *Cannery Row,* which furnishes the book's moral vantage point and ecological underpinnings; and finally, the principal characters themselves—Mack and the boys, Lee Chong, Dora Flood, and Doc—who become the incarnation of Steinbeck's philosophy in the novel.

Perhaps more than any other novel Steinbeck wrote, *Cannery Row* depends for its mood, atmosphere, and, ultimately, its philosophy on a particular place and time—an oceanfront street in Monterey during the early 1940s, with its "sardine canneries of corrugated iron, honky-tonks, restaurants, whore houses, and little crowded groceries, and laboratories and flophouses" (p. 1). Also central to the book is the teaming marine life in nearby tide pools where Doc observes and collects specimens. Though seasonal changes are nearly imperceptible, the novel apparently begins in early spring and culminates on October 28, the morning after the final party in Doc's lab. Rain, once or twice mentioned in the book, never seems to fall. There are no blustery winds off Monterey Bay, no dangerous high surf, no fog, no bitter cold, and, of course, no snow or ice. This temperate, dry climate results in what Edmund Wilson has called a "sun-soaked California atmosphere of laziness, naïvete, good nature, satisfaction in the pleasures of the senses and indifference to property rights."[6] Characters may live indoors or out, depending on their preferences, since the streets are safe from crime, except for the petty thievery of Mack and the boys.

The economy on the row seems as favorable as the sunny climate, with some tragic exceptions. Because of the "big sardine catch" reported in the book (p. 100), employment at the canneries runs high. Jobs are available to Mack and the boys anytime for the asking, Dora's Bear Flag Restaurant jumps with business day and night, Lee Chong's grocery appears comfortably prosperous, and Doc (whose livelihood does not depend on the canneries) is up to his ears in specimen orders at Western Biological. Despite these signs of prosperity, the times are not flush for everyone. The shadow of the Depression still lingers over the Row, especially in the more naturalistic interchapters. Horace Abbeville, Frances Almones, Joey's father, and others always make "just a fraction less" than they need, their money diminishing until these unlucky characters "just dr[y] up and bl[o]w away" (p. 63). Such economic tragedies have little effect, however, on the novel's more solvent inhabitants, as well as on the bums who seem to get by on their wits alone.

Thus both the climate and economy of the cannery street in Monterey seem ideally tailored for the fringe life-styles Steinbeck depicts in the novel. The locals of the row flourish in large part because of this friendly environment, whereas one imagines them faring not nearly so well in the harsher conditions they might encounter in Chicago, Detroit, or New York. Needing only an abandoned boiler or the shade of a cypress tree for their homes, these dropouts can afford to cultivate laziness and ease. Ultimately, their way of life, and hence their values, are predicated upon the ambience of Cannery Row. Without the row there could be no Mack or Henri or Mr. and Mrs. Sam Malloy or, for that matter, even Doc.

Besides describing the atmosphere of this unusual street, Steinbeck's preface to *Cannery Row* provides a key to its moral vantage point and ecological metaphor. The single most important word in the preface is "peephole." Steinbeck tells us that how we view the inhabitants of Cannery Row depends entirely upon our angle of vision. Through one peephole this unusual street seems to be inhabited by "whores, pimps, gamblers, and sons of bitches"; through another peephole, however, they become "saints and angels and martyrs and holy men" (p. 1). Although we can observe these characters from either perspective, Steinbeck chooses the second. Thus he sees as virtuous those we might commonly call immoral, and vice versa. In effect, Steinbeck has turned conventional morality upside down. Later, he speaks more specifically about this inversion of the "good" and the "bad," by further defining these two categories of people found on the Row: those who own and run the sardine industry, and those "locals" who live on the fringes of the canneries. The former Steinbeck likens to a "generation of trapped, poisoned, and trussed-up men" (p. 15), and he calls their female counterparts a "twisted and lascivious sisterhood of married spinsters" (p. 16). In these negative portrayals we see evidence of what Benson calls Steinbeck's "deep antagonism . . . toward respectability and 'proper' society."[7]

Steinbeck supports his inversion of conventional morality introduced in the preface with a modern paraphrase of Mark 8:36: "What can it profit a man to gain the whole world and to come to his property with a gastric ulcer, a blown prostate, and bifocals?" (p. 15). Yet, unlike the Christian Scriptures, *Cannery Row* seems to locate its deity on earth rather than within the heavens. Steinbeck suggests further that the book's principal characters, especially Mack and the boys, are the elect in this spiritual system. "Our Father who art in Nature . . . must have a great and overwhelming love for no-goods and blots-on-the-town and bums, and Mack and the boys. Virtues and graces and laziness and zest" (p. 15). Beyond these allusions to the New Testament (and echoes of pantheism and transcendentalism), Steinbeck's inversion of conventional values stems from the *Tao Teh Ching* of Lao-tzu, a Chinese philosopher of the sixth century B.C. whom Steinbeck mentions twice by name (p. 14). According to Peter Lisca, the *Tao Teh Ching*, like *Cannery Row*, was written "during a time of brutal war . . . and, in reaction to those conditions, presented a system of human values devoid of all those qualities which had brought on that war."[8] "Taoism rejects the desire for material goods, fame, power, and even fixed or strong opinions—all of which result in violence. Instead man is to cultivate simple physical enjoyments and the inner life. To be obscure is to be wise; to fail is to succeed. In human relations force defeats itself and laws are a form of violence. The moral is one of inaction."[9]

Steinbeck found in the *Tao Teh Ching* two themes "around which the novel's characters and events casually but effectively *arrange* themselves": one is the "escape from Western material values" and the other, the "escape from Western activism." Thus, Taoism's nonacquisitive, contemplative approach to life supports Steinbeck's inverted morality in the novel. And the Taoist goal of cultivating simple enjoyments and contentment is demonstrated by several Cannery Row dropouts, especially by Mack and his friends, who often manage to harmonize with the flow, rhythm, and pattern of things.[10]

Steinbeck concludes his preface to *Cannery Row* by suggesting that the book can be read, in Benson's words, as "an ecological parable."[11] Because the stories are fragile—like the delicate flatworms collectors find in tide pools along the coast—the episodes must be allowed to "ooze and crawl of their own" (p. 3) onto the pages of the novel. The tide pool, "lovely and murderous" (p. 31), is Steinbeck's foremost biological world. The sea bottom becomes "fantastic with hurrying, fighting, feeding, breeding animals" (p. 30). "The smells of life and richness of death and digestion, of decay and birth, burden the air" (p. 32). We are reminded constantly of the biological foundation of life, which no human being, no matter how "exalted," can escape.[12] The ecology of the great tide pool, then, becomes a metaphor for the human community of Cannery Row. Nearly all the characters resemble their tide pool cousins in being "parasites and commensals and predators," as Joseph Fontenrose has observed.[13] Mack and the boys are surely parasites; Lee Chong, Dora, and Doc behave like commensals; and the business magnates who destroy themselves and others in their pursuit of wealth are predators.[14]

By carrying this tide pool analogy one step further, we can discern both the "lovely" and the "murderous" aspects of *Cannery Row*. While Mack and the boys, Lee Chong, Dora, and Doc partake of primarily the "lovely" side of life, the "murderous" side is equally evident, especially among characters in the interchapters. Most of the deaths in the novel (the majority are suicides) emerge in these intercalary pieces. Warren French contends that in the interchapters Steinbeck depicts characters "caught helplessly in Naturalistic tragedies."[15] From a purely ecological standpoint, some characters, given their natural skills and intelligence, adapt successfully to their environment, while other characters, lacking these, do not. To summarize, by establishing in his preface the moral and ecological bases of life on Cannery Row, Steinbeck introduces the two central strands of his philosophy, which we will now further investigate by analyzing several of the most significant characters.

Why do Mack and the boys accommodate themselves so easily to life on Cannery Row, while several less-fortunate characters die? As we have seen, the Palace Flophouse boys pursue simple pleasures and contentment as advocated by Taoism; and, unwittingly following Christ's counsel in the New Testament, they live with fewer material goods than their contemporaries. Hence Frederick Bracher has observed that "Mack's real strength, like Thoreau's, comes from renunciation. . . . [M]ost of the things valued by the middle class—mechanical gadgets, security, cleanliness, prestige, comfort—Mack finds too expensive."[16] In other words, Mack and his friends enjoy a durable, single-sex community, free from the financial, legal, and emotional commitments of middle-class life. They are neither sick from having too much money nor despondent from having too little. Based on the inverted moral perspective of the novel, then, the Palace Flophouse boys live more enlightened lives than the "respectable" Monterey with whom Steinbeck compares them.

The boys' comfortable adaptation to life is illustrated by their frog-hunting expedition into the Carmel Valley. They camp by the "lovely" Carmel River (p. 77) on the sandy shore of a deep, green pool, stewing a chicken (a windfall from their trip) over an open fire, as "around them the evening crept in as delicately as music" (p. 83). Mack and his friends blend so harmoniously with their surroundings that Steinbeck uses the word "happy" (p. 78) to describe their encampment. During this frog-hunting scene, Mack and the boys demonstrate not only their adaptability but also their talent for relaxation. Steinbeck more than condones this talent; he becomes its active champion. While "respectable" Monterey condemns the Palace Flophouse boys for being loafers, we know that in *The Log from the Sea of Cortez* (1951) Steinbeck (along with Ed Ricketts) views loafing as a sign of wisdom and strong survival value. "Only in laziness can one achieve a state of contemplation which is a balancing of values, a weighting of oneself against the world and the world against itself. A busy man cannot find the time for such balancing. We do not think a lazy man can commit murders, nor great thefts, nor lead a mob. He would be more likely to think about it and laugh."[17]

Just as laziness fosters contemplation, according to Steinbeck and Ricketts, so too does alcohol provide innumerable benefits. In *The Log* Steinbeck and Ricketts argue that the "theory that alcohol is a poison" is "too blindly accepted." Actually "our race has a triumphant alcoholic history," they counter, in which liquor has served as an "anodyne, a warmer of the soul, a strengthener of muscle and spirit."[18] This philosophy—or at least its outward manifestation—certainly carries over into Cannery Row, where drinking is a universal pastime. Eddie's infamous wining jug provides a centerpiece in the Palace Flophouse. Dora's Bear Flag Restaurant, among other things, is a favorite watering hole. And Doc—admirer of eighth-century Chinese poet of inebriation Li Po (p. 28)—daily imbibes several quarts of beer. Thus Cannery Row has its own cult of alcohol which attributes considerable powers to its consumption. Mack, for example, peers into an empty whiskey glass "as though some holy message were written in the bottom" (p. 95). But just how many of the collateral benefits of drinking mentioned by Steinbeck and Ricketts the Palace Flophouse boys receive is difficult to tell.

Perhaps liquor promotes their laziness, whose advantages have been outlined above. One might also conclude that they drink simply because it makes them feel good or helps them forget.

Nonetheless, Ed Ricketts (the model for Doc in *Cannery Row*) believed that the real-life prototypes of Mack and the boys were "the Lotus Eaters of our era, successful in their resistance against the nervousness and angers and frustrations of our time." As Steinbeck explains in "About Ed Ricketts," "Ed regarded these men with the admiration he had for any animal, family, or species that was successful in survival and happiness factors." Ricketts contended that bums like Mack and his friends would "*deliver* our species from the enemies within and without which attack it" (italics mine).[19] Doc's most succinct statement about the Palace Flophouse boys comes when a "Black Gloom" has settled over them after their disastrous first party in Doc's lab (p. 146). In a conversation with Richard Frost, Doc calls Mack and his cohorts "true philosophers" and then repeats the inverted moral perspective introduced earlier in the book: "In a time when people tear themselves to pieces with ambition and nervousness and covetousness, they are relaxed. All of our so-called successful men are sick men, with bad stomachs, and bad souls, but Mack and the boys are healthy and curiously clean. They can do what they want. They can satisfy their appetites without calling them something else" (p. 149).

This glowing appraisal is tempered somewhat by Mack's earlier admission to Doc: "I been sorry all my life. . . . Ever'thing I done turned sour" (p. 137). Lewis Owens points out this darker side of the "flophouse castaways, a sad and less pleasing dimension of failure, rejection, and withdrawal." Owens argues that rather than adjusting well to life, Mack and his buddies represent severe maladjustment. "Mack is in retreat from the world outside of the Row; he has failed in love and in any kind of deep commitment and has come to hide out from further commitment on Cannery Row."[20] The Palace Flophouse boys nonetheless remain crucial to the novel's inverted morality. They renounce the greed and sickness of their time, refusing to sell their souls "to gain the whole world" (p. 151). That they may be viewed as mere hedonists, on the one hand, or as saviors of mankind, on the other, reflects the moral ambiguity of these intriguing characters.[21]

Helping Mack and the boys survive comfortably on the Row is their occasional reluctant benefactor, Lee Chong. Steinbeck associates the humane and astute Chinese grocer with Taoism, yet also with the "abacus and cash register" (p. 14). Thus Lee Chong combines Oriental inaction and contentment with Western striving for material prosperity. He is not avaricious, though "if one wanted to spend money, he was available" (p. 5). Lee never presses those who owe him money, yet he cuts off credit when the bill becomes too large. He is a realistic man in the details of business, yet sympathic in matters of the heart—"a hard man with a can of beans—a soft man with the bones of his grandfather" (p. 14). One of Lee's finest qualities is that he sees beyond his own immediate profit or loss. While a conventional grocer would hardly bargain with bums like Mack and the boys, Lee does so, often to his own apparent financial disadvantage. For example, when he reluctantly "rents" the old Horace Abbeville place to Mack and his friends, Lee has the foresight to know that although they will never pay rent, at least the building will not mysteriously go up in flames, as it might if he refuses them. In addition, he gains several steady customers in his store, the loss in rent being more than compensated for by money they spend and goods they don't steal. Thus Lee Chong belies the stereotypical business "success" (condemned through the inverted morality of the novel) by combining seemingly incompatible traits of character. He manages not only to remain healthy and prosperous but also to avoid destroying others on his way to financial security.

Across the lot from Lee Chong's lies Dora Flood's Bear Flag Restaurant—a "sporting house" of twelve girls shunned by the "twisted and lascivious sisterhood of married spinsters whose husbands respect the home but don't like it very much" (p. 16). Steinbeck hardly takes their dim view of the Bear Flag, characterizing it as a "sturdy, virtuous club" (p. 16), and Dora as honest, charitable, disciplined, and realistic. Due to Dora's managerial skill, sex rarely arouses jealousies between competing lovers or disrupts families. All relationships with Dora's girls are "clean-cut, efficient, and simple," according to Lisca, and "terminate on paying the two dollars."[22] Nonetheless, since the Bear Flag's business is against the law, Dora leads a "ticklish existence." She "must be twice as law abiding as anyone else" and "especially philanthropic." When it comes to charity, Dora's "dirty wages of sin lead the list of donations" (pp. 17–18). Thus, in Lisca's words, Dora's "contributions to the community are far in excess of the financial considerations expected of her."[23] She and her girls minister to the sick and needy, and during the depression Dora pays "grocery bills right and left for two years and nearly [goes] broke in the process" (p. 18). Steinbeck suggests, then, that the "respectable" matrons of Monterey society have nothing on Dora and her girls. If anything, the Bear Flag hookers are their moral superiors.

Steinbeck's frank acceptance of prostitution as an integral, even beneficial, part of the community reflects a correspondingly negative view of marriage. Skepticism about married life runs deep, as we learn from Mack and the boys' complaints about Gay, the only nonbachelor in their group. "You can't trust a married guy. No matter how much he hates his old lady why he'll go back to her" (p. 82). Mack argues that even though Gay's wife hits him while he's asleep, "when Gay's away from her three days, he gets it figured out that it's his fault and he goes back to make it up to her" (p. 82). This bleak conception of marriage is reinforced by the boys' evening with the captain in Carmel Valley, whose perpetually absent wife has been elected to the state assembly. "When the Legislature isn't in session, she's off making speeches," complains her husband (p. 93). The captain's later confession that his wife "ought to of been a man. If she was a man I wouldn't of married her" (p. 98), suggests that by pursuing her own career she has violated a sex-role taboo.

Thus marriage, and especially marriage to a professional woman, rates very low on the hierarchy of values in Cannery Row. The preferred role for a woman is a prostitute, or second best, a housewife, though "wife" is generally a pejorative term in the book. The most a woman can hope to achieve on the Row is to become a madam like Dora Flood. As Mack utters in timid awe of Dora, "Now there is one hell of a woman" (p. 158). Dora thus represents the novel's perspective on women, marriage, and sexuality. Just as the material values of the middle class are condemned through Mack and the boys, so too are its high-mindedness and prudery assaulted by Dora's example. Although Steinbeck gives us brief glimpses of three stable marriages in the book (the Frosts, Talbots, and Malloys), the wedded lives he implicitly attacks are those of "the city officials and prominent businessmen" who visit Dora's at "the rear entrance back by the tracks" (p. 101). Since their marriages seem to lack honest communication and fulfilling love (are their wives the "twisted and lascivious sisterhood of married spinsters"? [p. 16]), these dignitaries visit the brothel, while their spouses very likely become consumed in such community "causes" as closing Dora's down.

On the ocean side of the street, across from Dora's, stands Western Biological Laboratory, its back lot rising on pilings over the sea. Doc, the owner and operator of the lab, is the "fountain of philosophy and science and art" (p. 28) as well as the hero of *Cannery Row*. At one time or another every principal character visits Doc for advice; he is considered a resident medical doctor, veterinarian, psychiatrist, and sage. As Benson points out, "Doc is there and he cares, and everyone around him knows he cares."[24] Doc's living quarters in Western Biological suggest the catholicity of his tastes. Amid tanks of marine animals, cages of reptiles and rats, containers of "bugs and snails and spiders" (p. 25), and smells of formaline, menthol, chloroform, and ether (pp. 26–27), Doc possesses a library of "books of all kinds" (p. 27), a great phonograph on which he plays the music of Beethoven, Bach, and Benny Goodman, and reproductions of Leonardo, Picasso, Dali, and other artists. "He lived in a world of wonders, of excitement" (p. 29). As Lisca says, "In him all opposites are reconciled. He is both scientist and mystic, both calculating and tender, both learned and common, both intellectual and emotional, both classicist and romantic."[25]

Despite these admirable qualities, Doc is "lonely and set-apart" (p. 104). Although he associates freely with nearly everyone, he remains inexplicably separate even when "in the dear close contact with a girl" (p. 104). Speaking of Doc's model, Ed Ricketts, Richard Astro notes this isolation as one of "the inherent shortcomings of the marine biologist's complex philosophy of life."[26] And in "About Ed Ricketts," Steinbeck tells us, "there was a transcendent sadness in his life—something he missed or wanted, a searching that sometimes approached panic. . . . It was like a deep and endless nostalgia—a thirst and a passion for 'going home.'"[27] According to Owens, Doc similarly sacrifices "a fullness of experience to seek a wholeness of vision."[28]

The whole vision Ricketts sought adds an important dimension to the philosophy of *Cannery Row*. One facet of this vision is Ricketts's concept of nonteleological thinking, which, according to Benson, leads Doc to "a fundamental openness to perception" and an acceptance of "what is" by seeing "beyond both traditional or personal projections."[29] Hence Doc does not judge Mack and the boys as losers or no-goods or parasites. To him they are fascinating human organisms who have adapted intelligently to their environment. He is aware of their cleverness, their deceit, their misdirected kindness, and their cunning, yet he accepts them without condition. His high regard for Dora also testifies to his ability to see beyond conventional mores.

Another aspect of Ricketts's vision which bears on the novel is his "philosophy of breaking through," a kind of higher consciousness involving the connection of pictures seemingly unrelated (through ordinary perception) into a whole larger than the sum of its parts—"an integrative moment of living."[30] Such breaking through is induced by "deep participation" in "correspondences" (akin to those in New England transcendentalism) between the realms of nature and spirit. Doc experiences a "breaking through" in the La Jolla tide pools when he glimpses a black-haired girl drowned beneath the water, and her "face burn[s] into his picture memory" (p. 114). This startling yet gentle vision of death, according to Benson, gives Doc a "flash of insight," as evidenced by the high flute melody he imagines.[31] Doc's experience of breaking through, then, comprises an emotional climax in the book.

In sum, Doc acts as a spokesman for the values advanced in *Cannery Row*—values identical in many cases to those introduced earlier by Steinbeck and Ricketts in *The Sea of Cortez* (1941). Since Doc is a moral theoretician of sorts, as well as a biologist, he incorporates the moral and the ecological strands of the book's homespun philosophy. Thus he becomes the philosophical standard-bearer of this unusual oceanfront community. As the book's most important character, Doc is also the measure of all others.

In the introduction to this essay we saw that throughout his career Steinbeck was often attacked for inconsistent or incoherent "philosophizing." To conclude, then, let us consider the philosophy of *Cannery Row* in light of these criticisms, attempting to answer two related questions: (1) How consistent and logically valid is this philosophy? (2) How well do the two strands—the moral and the ecological—twine together into one coherent whole?

As we have seen, the two strands of the book's philosophy merge in *Cannery Row*'s hero, Doc. To test the consistency and validity of this philosophy, then, we might profitably review our analysis of him. What we discovered in Doc is an extraordinary human being whose powers of thinking and feeling are unusually well integrated. Recalling Lisca's appraisal, Doc is "both scientist and mystic, both calculating and tender, both learned and common, both intellectual and emotional, both classicist and romantic."[32] The dispiriting thing about this exceptional man, however, is the apparent void in his life. As we noted earlier, Steinbeck's eulogy on the real "Doc" in "About Ed Ricketts" reflects this void.[33] The something missing in Doc, and missing in other *Cannery Row* characters as well, is the recognition that from commitments of love come what Owens has called a "fullness of experience."[34] Such fullness might complete Doc as a person and supply a needed element in the novel's moral philosophy. Moreover, without the kind of bonds between men and women that engender families, the analogy Steinbeck makes between tide pool animals and the human community on the Row is invalid on biological grounds; the littoral ecology "of life and richness, of death and digestion, of decay and birth" (p. 32) has been lost in the transition from sea to land. Since sexuality in *Cannery Row* is the exclusive domain of the brothel, the novel omits the essential reproductive process of human life. Because of this lack of love commitments in the novel, both the moral and ecological bases of Steinbeck's thinking—though consistent and valid to a point—eventually break down.

Steinbeck often experienced difficulty trying to incorporate his moral and biological visions. Peter Lisca has even argued that Steinbeck's moral thinking eventually subsumed his biological, causing his artistic powers to decline.[35] His struggle to blend the two reflects the fact that even in life they are often at odds; the moral requirements for maintaining a stable human community often conflict with the individual's, or even the group's, biological urges and drives. Judging from such late works as *East of Eden* (1952) and *The Winter of Our Discontent* (1961), Steinbeck finally came to believe that the moral side of human life takes precedence over the biological. In *Cannery Row*, however, the influence of these two visions seem roughly equal, perhaps reflecting a turning point in Steinbeck's writing from one predominant view to the other. Though their balance is at times unstable, as we have seen, an intriguing philosophy results. Thus *Cannery Row* is ultimately a book about human values. And the values that emerge are just what we might expect from either prophets or bums. All depends upon which "peephole" we look through.

Jackson J. Benson

12   *Cannery Row* and Steinbeck as Spokesman for the
"Folk Tradition"

John Steinbeck wrote *Cannery Row* at about the midpoint of our involve-ment in World War II. It was an odd time to write a funny book. At first glance the novel appeared to be a return to the social comedy and light satire of *Tortilla Flat*, and that, following the heavy impact of *The Grapes of Wrath*, seemed to most reviewers a giant step backward. At second glance the novel had too much death and too much bitterness to be considered nothing more than light entertainment. But if not a comedy, what was it? A comedy turned sour? A mishmash of odds and ends? While on the one hand, the book has become a favorite among many Steinbeck readers and has turned Ed Ricketts into legend and Cannery Row itself into a mecca for tourists, on the other hand, the novel still baffles the critics. Relatively little has been written about it—two major articles, a handful of notes, and another half dozen or so chapters or parts of chapters in critical books. And those who have been obliged to write something about *Cannery Row* in the course of writing a book about Steinbeck's work more often than not have appeared to be at a loss for something to say.

One of the things that makes the book so attractive is the fact that it has been such a puzzle. Steinbeck himself added to the mystery of the book by indicating on several occasions that there was more to *Cannery Row* than the critics had been able to discover. Then he added to the confusion by suggesting several years later that the novel was a "nostal-gic thing" written as relaxation from the depression caused by his expe-riences as a war correspondent. This statement rings true, although I don't think it is the whole truth. *Cannery Row* is, and I'm sure was meant to be, many things. Among them, the novel was designed as a tribute to a man and to a friendship. That man, of course, was Ed Ricketts. While some who knew Ricketts have felt that he only vaguely resembled the Doc of *Cannery Row*, the very close resemblance between Doc and

Previously published.

Steinbeck's description of Ed in the biographical sketch "About Ed Ricketts" makes it clear that Doc was patterned after Steinbeck's vision of Ricketts. Ricketts was a most unusual man—thoughtful, talented, and perceptive, as well as very loving and accepting. Part of the strangeness of *Cannery Row* is due to Steinbeck's attempt to re-create the spirit of this man and place it at the center of the novel. Yes, strange, because he was unusual and because there are no literary antecedents for Doc except in Steinbeck's own work. With Doc, Steinbeck presents a very different kind of literary hero for our admiration, a man to be admired not so much for what he does, but for what he is. The novel is infused not with a sense of things to be done, but with a sense of being. Such a dominant mode in itself makes the novel remarkable.

But Steinbeck has hinted several times at some mystery at the heart of the novel, something beyond the characterization of Doc and beyond the comedy of Mack and the boys. The first hint came in an article on *The Wayward Bus* written by Toni Jackson Ricketts for a local Monterey magazine which was later picked up and anthologized in *Steinbeck and His Critics* (1957). [1] Plainly irritated with reviewers and critics who seem always to miss the point while reading Steinbeck and who are unable to see that "Steinbeck consciously writes on several levels," Toni Ricketts cites the ineptitude of the critical response to *Cannery Row* and then notes one pale exception: "A single critic, Malcolm Cowley, puzzled by an underlying sense of violence in the book, read it again more carefully and concluded that if *Cannery Row* was a cream-puff, it was a 'very poisoned cream-puff.' If Cowley had read it yet again, said Steinbeck, he would have found how *very* poisoned it was." [2]

Joining in the mischief, Peter Lisca, who had access to Steinbeck's letters to his publisher when he wrote *The Wide World of John Steinbeck* (1958), brought forward two more comments by the author about *Cannery Row*. In one letter Steinbeck notes that "no critic yet has stumbled on the design of the book," and in another letter he observes that "no critic has discovered the reason for those little inner chapters in *Cannery Row*." [3] Nearly two decades after these statements were made available to us, we are still wondering if there is not some secret structural design at the center of the novel that has remained undiscovered.

No magic key to the novel has been found, however, and the reason, I suspect, is that no key of the sort that critics are inclined to look for actually exists. I am relatively certain that the problem of interpreting *Cannery Row* depends upon adjusting our perspective rather than discovering an elaborate literary apparatus. The problem of perspective has been the historic difficulty of Steinbeck's work: he has never been obscure, but he has been different. His attitudes, philosophy, and even materials have been on occasion so foreign to both reviewers and generalist critics that not very many of them have caught on to what he was talking about. A classic case is Edmund Wilson, who was never able to penetrate Steinbeck's point of view and, as a result, dismissed it as trivial. Wilson enjoyed reading *Cannery Row* but thought that it was undermined by its sentimental philosophy.[4] As was often the case, Cowley was right and Wilson was wrong. Calling *Cannery Row* sentimental is like calling *Huckleberry Finn* a children's book.

Because this is a modest book that deliberately avoids elaborate structuring, it is a mistake to bring it into the context of the modern novel as defined by such works as Joyce's *Ulysses* or Faulkner's *The Sound and the Fury*. What these novels have in common beyond complex technique is a distinct literary quality—that is, they spring as much from literature as from life. I don't mean to suggest by this declaration that *Cannery Row*, by contrast, does not employ any literary devices or does not make use of any literary conventions. But I do want to suggest that it is not *primarily* ordered either by reference to other literature or by the overt imposition of a literary system or form. The real puzzle of *Cannery Row* lies not so much in the problem of finding some hidden literary system as in the problem of trying to understand the novel after one realizes that there is neither much literary stuffing to uncover nor any really substantial literary skeleton to compare and classify.

In order to begin to understand and appreciate *Cannery Row*, I think we must look beyond the neo-Joycean standards which have tended to dominate our perceptions in recent years to other, more illuminating analogies. The analogies that first come to mind are novels which have been shaped by the peculiar personalities of their authors. There is, for example, a kinship between Steinbeck's book and Sterne's *Tristram Shandy*. Both are episodic and have only a nominal structure; indeed, both are really "non-novels" in which nothing of any consequence happens. Both are eccentric and extremely self-conscious, and both have fun in conspiracy with and against the reader. Most important, perhaps, is that the essential effect of both books is totally dependent on the manner of the telling and on the perspective of the narrator. In this latter respect, it is also illuminating to think of *Cannery Row* in terms of *Remembrance of Things Past*, for there is again a certain similarity of perspective. What Steinbeck gives us is a re-creation of experiences remembered and transformed *into* and *by* words. *Cannery Row* is a poem—now—as he tells us in his preface. By means of words applied to sensation and impression recalled, Steinbeck, like Proust, presents a mixture of the ultrareal (the stink and the rust) and the real as modified by personality and emotion (Mack and boys, who become the Virtues and the Graces).

But beyond the narrative as shaped by personality, we should look for a more specific artistic and cultural context which forms the foundation for the value system implicitly expressed in *Cannery Row*. This artistic and cultural context comes into view as a result of a general comparison of John Steinbeck and Mark Twain and a more specific comparison of *Cannery Row* and *Huckleberry Finn*. I should qualify these comparisons at the outset by pointing out that I know of no direct biographical evidence to suggest that Twain was an influence on Steinbeck, although Steinbeck read widely as a youth and young man and, according to his family, probably read both *Tom Sawyer* and *Huckleberry Finn* relatively early in life. However, the issue here is not influence so much as the possibility that Steinbeck came out of the same cultural tradition as Twain and adopted, for whatever reasons, many of the same values and attitudes.

Steinbeck and Twain have displayed many of the same strengths and weaknesses as writers.[5] Both succeed essentially as stylists who, out of a Western American tradition, establish what can only be called a "folk" position in regard to the world they observe. The folk position is characterized by unpretentiousness, egalitarianism, common sense, and a close relationship to the earth. This point of view laughs at the airs of the Eastern snob and the city slicker. And although it deals occasionally with people from the middle class, more often it deals with the lower classes or with people who are essentially classless. Steinbeck's and Twain's characters gain distinction not by wealth or birth but by demonstrating strength of character, common sense, and the ability to handle practical problems. The ideal is the man of skill—the riverboat pilot or the auto mechanic. Both writers, in the Western tradition, concentrate on a masculine society. Neither deals much with romantic love, except to satirize it, and ideal love is most often achieved between men.

A persistent and major theme in Steinbeck and Twain is creeping gentility, the corrupting influence of civilization as propagated by women, Sunday schools, and respectable people. Both writers despise respectability, and both admire plain honesty and a concern for one's neighbor. All of this, of course, touches on one of the most prevalent thematic complexes in American literature—East versus West, innocence versus sophistication, the machine versus the garden—as exposed by such critics as R. W. B. Lewis, Leslie A. Fiedler, Leo Marx, and any number of literary and intellectual historians. Twain has been a major figure in the literary discussions of this thematic complex, and many critics have seen a direct line between James Fenimore Cooper's Natty Bumppo and Huck Finn (despite Twain's mockery of Cooper): Bumppo always moves out into the wilderness ahead of the encroachment by frontier settlements with their whiskey and restrictions, while Huck lights out "for the Territory ahead of the rest, because Aunt Sally she's going to adopt me and sivilize me, and I can't stand it." *Cannery Row*, in a sense, is the end of the road; the Row is on the beach of the Pacific Ocean—the last frontier, now decayed. It is Natty Bumppo's last stand.

It is my contention that Steinbeck has really taken Twain's place during the last few decades as the major spokesman for the "folk tradition." And the thematic complex I spoke of above finds its last major expression in his work. To trace this expression in any detail would require a book, but briefly note the importance of "Westering" in his work (and the interpretation, overdrawn but still valid, of *The Grapes of Wrath* as a "wagons West romance" by Bernard Bowron).[6] That Steinbeck has assumed this position is, I think, the essential basis for his popularity, as well as the reason for the antipathy expressed toward him by Eastern intellectual criticism.

There are a number of striking parallels between Twain's and Steinbeck's careers. Both were fascinated by medieval literature, in particular Malory's *Morte d'Arthur*, and both were fond of allegory, the tall tale, and travel literature. Both wrote a wide variety of things during their careers, moving from form to form; and both wrote a great many things of very dubious literary value. And despite a large output, both writers are known primarily for having written one major novel. However, almost everything they wrote, even their most important works, was deeply flawed in one way or another. Both in their heart of hearts were satirists—disillusioned romantic idealists. Twain and Steinbeck have been classified as "funnymen," yet each of them had at times a very black vision of man's nature. No two American writers have had a firmer sense of the ordinary man and of ordinary life, and both maintained the common touch even after they became rich and successful. Yet each moved to the East after becoming rich and successful, and while in the East, each became more and more pessimistic and moralistic in his work. Both were very fond of metaphysics and philosophical discourse, and both were notably unsuccessful at reaching any profound level of philosophical thought.

What ties *Cannery Row* to *Huckleberry Finn* is primarily the deep antagonism at the center of both novels toward respectability and "proper" society. Steinbeck's Monterey (the town itself above the Row), with its civilized corruption, takes roughly the same position as Twain's Mississippi shore, with its shabby values. Whenever Doc leaves the Row, he encounters hostility, hypocrisy, and greed. And whenever the town reaches in to touch the Row, hypocrisy and greed are expressed. Dora and her establishment, for example, are tolerated as long as she is more law-abiding than everyone else and as long as she gives several times more to charity than everyone else. In both novels nature is the cleansing agent, so that Huck can rid himself of the taint of civilization on the river, and Doc can renew his spirit by periodic immersions (feet only) in the Great Tide Pool.

One of the main qualities that ties Doc and Huck together is a fundamental honesty, but in each case the character finds he must abandon his honesty in the face of pressure from society. Huck must tell lies and disguise himself in order to protect Jim, while Doc found as a young man on a walking trip through the South that he could not simply say that he wanted to enjoy the countryside, but had to lie and say he was "doing it on a bet." When he finally decides to try out his beer milkshake, he finds he must invent "doctor's orders" to justify his whim to a suspicious waitress. Both Doc and Huck have a certain openness, even vulnerability, which makes them particularly appealing and which contrasts with the hard façades erected by the respectable people they encounter.

Huckleberry Finn and *Cannery Row* are primarily satiric in mode, episodic in structure (both the escape of Jim and the party for Doc are secondary to the material developed along the way), and range in emotional tenor from light humor at one end of the scale to horror and black satire at the other. The central satiric device in each novel is the confrontation between the good people outside of conventional society, whom society frowns upon as criminals or bums, and those people within society who have been corrupted by respectability and made humorless, inflexible, and blind, with little or no ability to enjoy life.

The two most common image groupings in the two novels are death and money—thus exposing those two pillars of frontier settlement life, violence and the "hard cash" mentality. A third pillar, loneliness, is only slightly exposed in Twain's novel in the separation of Jim from his family, but it is revealed in some detail in Steinbeck's book. Whereas greed is somewhat more frequently satirized in *Huckleberry Finn*, there are also instances in *Cannery Row:* for example, there is the man on the beach at La Jolla who can think only of the bounty paid for the discovery of a body, in the face of Doc's complex vision of beauty and death. Money is the tool by which civilization tries to enforce conformity in both novels. Huck rejects the fortune held for him by Judge Thatcher to take off for the territory, and throughout the novel he resists the temptation of the bounty put on Jim's head. Mack and the boys, in the Steinbeck novel, solve the problem of enforced behavior through petty theft, fits of work (usually through the kindness of Doc), and the reluctant cooperation of Lee Chong.

There are a number of other connections, but all are rather generalized; they arise out of the value system behind the novels rather than out of the specific materials of the novels themselves. Subject, technical point of view, and specific characterizations are all different, of course. The most important point, beyond the kinship of the values involved, that can be made by using *Huckleberry Finn* as an analogy to illuminate *Cannery Row* may be that both books are products of vital, likable personalities. And it is the personality of the author in each case, as it is reflected in the tone and vitality of the narration, that appears to be the main factor in making each novel successful.

The folk position that Steinbeck shares with Twain is, as we have seen, heavily infused with what have been called "frontier values" as well as the literary conventions which have evolved from those values. Some of these values, such as the evils of civilization, are endorsed by

Twain and Steinbeck. Some, such as the feud in *Huckleberry Finn*, are satirized, while others are the source of good fun. No one has paid much attention to the fun that Steinbeck gets from these values as they have been translated into the conventions of popular Western literature.

By changing the Row and its canneries to Dodge City and its stock-yards, the Row can be viewed as the very model of the main street in a town of the old West. Doc becomes the kindly, wise, and patient general practitioner. He is the "fountain of philosophy and science and art," the only educated man, the only professional among the frontier ruffians. Dora is, of course, the saloon owner and madam, a combination practical businesswoman and mother to the entire male community. And Lee Chong runs the town's general store, a store which stocks nearly anything anyone would want, but which tends to sell more whiskey, beer, and chewing gum than anything else. Even the kids, who haunt the store when they are not throwing rocks or taunting each other or strangers, have a ragtag, frontier-town quality.

Henri is the crazy old prospector who rummages around in vacant lots looking for boat parts and who, like his Western counterpart who would be at a loss if he ever did find gold, never wants to complete his boat. Mack and the boys could just as well be living in the bunkhouse on the B-Bar-B Ranch as in the Palace Flophouse; and it is a nice touch to have the ranch foreman, Mack, taking his men to round up cats rather than cattle, and wild frogs rather than wild horses. The tactics of stampeding the frogs from one end of the "valley" into a trap are familiar.

As usual, the settlers—in this case the Malloys—are ridiculous with their chintz curtains. Then there are the inevitable knock-down-drag-out fights (all in fun and made up in good fellowship later) and the community crisis (the flu). When there is a party, the main ingredients are steak and whiskey. That Steinbeck has these conventions in mind is certified in the ending of the sequel, *Sweet Thursday*, wherein Doc gets the girl (a reformed saloon girl, of course) and the two of them ride his bucking car off into the sunset.

Steinbeck's parody of the Western is not the "secret" of *Cannery Row;* it joins a number of other modes and themes which in various ways comment on man's relationship to nature. Adjacent to the Western, another aspect of the novel concerns its pastoral elements. The pastoral does not extend throughout the novel nearly as far as the Western parody, but a few elements are obviously present and appear to work together with the parody on the lighter side of the novel. The only long-standing major article about *Cannery Row* is one which develops the pastoral—Stanley Alexander's "*Cannery Row:* Steinbeck's Pastoral Poem."[7] Unfortunately, Alexander is caught in the trap that catches most critics at one time or another: he takes the pastoral material and pushes it too hard, trying to force the entire novel into his pattern on the basis of only a few pieces of evidence. The novel really only hints at the pastoral, and usually in an inverted way.

Alexander's first mistake, I think, is to bring William Empson's *Some Versions of Pastoral* to bear on *Cannery Row*, probably because he sees Steinbeck inaccurately as a Marxist. He refers to Empson's view that the pastoral is the "primary literary convention which reflects the characteristic class relations of western society," bringing "together in rural or even wilderness scenes representatives of (relatively) exalted social classes and (relatively) low social classes."[8] If we try to apply this to *Cannery Row*, we are in trouble already, for only one out of three criteria applies. We do not have a rural scene, nor do we have a representative, except by distant implication, of exalted social classes. (There are no wealthy Monterey citizens in the novel except by distant reference to the man who gains "the whole world" and comes "to his property with a gastric ulcer, a blown prostate, and bifocals" (p. 15).

Trying to put Doc into this role simply does not work. According to Alexander, the form of *Cannery Row* approximates the Renaissance pastoral because of Doc, who represents "the secure, educated, powerful class from which he comes 'down' to operate the Western Biological Laboratory."[9] Nonsense. No one could read "About Ed Ricketts" in *The Log* and think such a thing. (The language used in *The Log* to describe Ed is almost precisely the same language used to describe Doc in the novel—the model is extremely close to the fictional character.) However, if one wants to avoid the biographical fallacy, one only has to look at Doc's role in the novel. He is almost classless, an eccentric among other eccentrics and iconoclasts. True, Doc does bring the arts and sciences to the Row, as well as a certain wisdom. But these are presented as the peculiar facets of Doc's character, not the badges of class. He may be the intellectual who has dropped out and joined the counterculture, but he has not dropped out of wealth, power, and security.

Alexander gets closer to the real uses of the pastoral in the novel when he admits that the locale is "neither sylvan dale nor frontier ranch nor family farm; it is instead an industrial slum."[10] That may be putting it a bit strongly (for those who remember the Row in its heyday, it is difficult to think of as a "slum"), but we should keep in mind the fact that the Row is dominated by factories which house machines which cut up animals and stick them in metal cans, and that Mack and the boys have been finding shelter in the discarded pipes of the canneries. The fact that they can only exist on vacant lots and among the refuse of factories suggests what the sylvan dale has finally come to.

The setting suggests that this is the reversal of the pastoral, or the pastoral corrupted. Alexander seems to recognize this temporarily when he talks about Doc sharing the scene with "mock-pastoral bums and whores who in better days were swains and maids."[11] Indeed, if *Cannery Row* must be referred to as a pastoral, it surely should be called a "mock-pastoral," playing upon the original form as it does by reversing many of the pastoral conventions. And if we must refer to Empson, it would be more appropriate to consult his chapter on the mock-pastoral, which examines *The Beggar's Opera*.[12] While Mack and the boys may not have a great deal in common with Mac and his gang, surely Newgate with its rogues and whores is closer to the Row with its rogues and whores than the Renaissance's "another part of the forest" with its disguised nobility.

If Doc is not the disguised prince among peasants, who is he in the pastoral scheme? The most likely answer, it seems to me, is that he is the shepherd. Who or what are his sheep? Well, one possibility is that all the inhabitants of Cannery Row are his flock. Or he may be the shepherd of the sea animals. Doc, who is described by Steinbeck as having a face "half Christ and half satyr" (no doubt in part a private joke between Steinbeck and Ricketts), may be an exaggerated version of the swain who is traditionally thought of as half connected to humanity and half to nature. But I agree with Peter Lisca, who suggests that Doc can be seen as a sort of "local deity"[13] (not, again, that he is powerful so much as he is more accepting, wiser, and more concerned with the welfare of others than anyone else around him—that is, he is Christ-like). If he is meant to resemble a god, he would appear to resemble Pan, who was the god of the shepherds and patron god of the pastoral and who was half man, half goat. Doc is constantly connected with music throughout the novel, and in the most striking pastoral interlude in the book, he hears a "high thin piercingly sweet flute" as he experiences a vision of great beauty. Also like Pan, Doc is "always in love with one nymph, or another, but always rejected."[14] Since Pan eventually became the god of all nature for the Greeks, it is fitting that Doc represent him in the universe of Cannery Row, wherein, as described by Steinbeck, "Our Father" is in nature.

Northrop Frye has said that "the pastoral of popular modern literature is the Western story,"[15] which seems to imply that all that is needed for a pastoral is people in a rural setting with animals. Actually, the conventions of both the Western and the pastoral are more complex than that, and such a statement really does not mean much. Nevertheless, although the amount of overt pastoral material in the novel is meager, we can say that the mock-Western, which we reviewed earlier, and the mock-pastoral in *Cannery Row* form a kind of community of parodic commentary on man's changing perception of his relationship with nature.

VI   The Pearl

John H. Timmerman

13   The Shadow and the Pearl: Jungian Patterns in *The Pearl*

It is everyone's allotted fate to become conscious of and learn to deal with this shadow.—Carl Jung, "The Fight with the Shadow"

John Steinbeck prefaced *The Pearl* with an enigmatic supposition: "If this story is a parable. . . ." Then, as Steinbeck suggested as a conclusion to his premise, the reader is free to take his own meaning from it. Indeed, readers have. The novella has been read as an analogy to the medieval *Pearl* manuscript, as an analogy to the biblical parable of the pearl of great price, and as a parable of the human soul.[1] The more beguiling part of Steinbeck's supposition, however, lies in the last, easily overlooked, clause: "perhaps everyone takes his own meaning form it and reads his own life into it." The novella is very much about how one reads one's own life. In fact, it is very much a parable of self-discovery, and, as I will explore in this essay, it parallels the Jungian confrontation with the shadow of the unconscious, an ultimate act of reading one's own life.

Mention of the pearl story first occurs in *The Log from the Sea of Cortez*, when the *Western Flyer* put in at the port of La Paz—thus the original title of the story, "The Pearl of La Paz," as published in *Woman's Home Companion*.[2] In *The Sea of Cortez* the nugget of the story appears in the context of a reflection upon human greed and the worth of "true" things. After relating the local legend of the pearl story, Steinbeck observes: "This seems to be a true story, but it is so much like a parable that it almost can't be. This Indian boy is too heroic, too wise. He knows too much and acts on his knowledge. The story is probably true, but we don't believe it; it is far too reasonable to be true."[3] Here Steinbeck establishes his conception of both the legend and the story as he would tell it. The legend tells of a heroic man, one "too wise." This hero is quite unlike the human nature Steinbeck sought to capture in his art, for his aim as a writer was to seize the often unreasonable "human direction."

At the time Steinbeck had been, and would remain, considerably under the influence of Carl Jung's psychoanalytic theory in his understanding of the direction of human nature. Along with works such as *Morte d'Arthur*, Shakespeare's plays, Milton's *Paradise Lost*, and the Bible, the works of Jung also exercised a lifelong influence. Jackson Benson points out that by 1930 Steinbeck, with his interest in "the black and sluggish depths of people," had been reading Jung and had been influenced by him in composing *To a God Unknown* and "Murder and Full Noon," the latter a piece that Benson appropriately deems "Jungian-flavored mumbo jumbo." Benson writes: "Carol and Dook Sheffield both testify to the fact that it was indeed Jung that captured Steinbeck's interest, not Freud (whose theories, Carol recalls, he tended to reject). Aspects of Jungian theory, particularly the collective unconscious, found fertile ground in Steinbeck's previous interests in myth and evolutionary biology."[4]

Robert DeMott lists nine separate works by Jung in his catalog of Steinbeck's reading.[5] DeMott states that Steinbeck arrived at Jung's works independently of Edward Ricketts, but that his interest in Jung intensified through conversations with Ricketts during the early 1930s. The imprint of Jung is already noted in Steinbeck's early conception of the phalanx theory: "I find that . . . in folk lore and in unconscious psychology Jung . . . is headed in the same direction and the direction is toward my thesis."[6] Of *To a God Unknown* Steinbeck wrote: "This volume which simply attempts to show some sense of how the unconscious impinges and in some cases crosses into the conscious, was immediately branded mystical. It had never occurred to the critics that all the religious symbology in the world were children of the generalized unconscious" (*SLL*, p. 87). Increasingly, scholars have observed the effects of Jung's influence over the range of Steinbeck's novels.[7]

In no work, however, is the influence more clear and systematic than in *The Pearl*, a work heretofore virtually ignored in psychoanalytic terms. Here Jungian patterns extend beyond the probing of the unconscious, the "human direction" of the parable, but also shape the very architecture of the story itself, so that the imagery carefully parallels the disclosure about human nature.

The fundamental premise undergirding Jung's theory of the shadow is that the conscious and the unconscious are necessarily in conflict. Even when one adopts a stylized mask, what Jung calls the "persona," for the conscious part of one's nature—and such a mask is necessary because the conscious is the extraverted part of personality, that by which we meet others—the unconscious part of one's personality will afflict the mask: "The shadow personifies everything that the subject refuses to acknowledge about himself and yet is always thrusting itself upon him directly or indirectly."[8] The unconscious is undeniable, and psychological imbalance results from the effort of denial. To achieve psychological harmony one must confront the reality of one's unconscious.[9] This confrontation Jung describes as "the meeting with the shadow."

The shadow must first be understood, then, in distinction from the persona, for the customary, outward, social mask often precludes confrontation. The shadow hides those parts of our personality that are not socially acceptable; they are locked away, repressed, cast into psychological darkness. Yet they are a part of the whole human personality, and therefore the tension of Jung's dialectic: "A conflict of duty forces us to examine our conscience and thereby to discover the shadow."[10] The longer the unconscious is locked away, the more dangerous the confrontation becomes.

A curious ambivalence marks Jung's language regarding the shadow. The term appears in nearly every major treatise, so central is it to all his thinking. In "Depth Psychology" he speaks of the shadow as "the inferior side of the personality."[11] Elsewhere he describes it euphemistically as "a very bad fellow in ourselves."[12] He is loathe to call it an evil nature in humanity. Yet it undeniably represents the darker side of human nature by virtue of the fact that it stands opposed to socially acceptable norms for behavior. Indeed, at one level the shadow may be described as the individual's conflict with society itself—the tension between self and others, between personal aims and conventional directions for achieving those aims. Such seems to be the case when Jung writes:

One has any amount of subjective reactions, but it is not quite becoming to admit these things. . . . We do not like to look at the shadow-side of ourselves; therefore there are many people in our civilized society who have lost their shadow altogether, they have got rid of it. They are only two-dimensional; they have lost the third dimension, and with it they have usually lost the body. The body is a most doubtful friend because it produces things we do not like; there are too many things about the body which cannot be mentioned. The body is very often the personification of this shadow of the ego. Sometimes it forms the skeleton in the cupboard, and everybody naturally wants to get rid of such a thing.[13]

The shadow, then, represents certain things about ourselves that we lock in the closet of the unconscious lest they come into open conflict with social mores and the persona that deals with these mores.

Clearly, this general premise—an individual's conflict between the socially acceptable persona and unconscious desires—is reflected in Kino. Kino represents an extension of early character types in conflict with civilized social order. His predecessors wander through lonely passages of Steinbeck's fictional world, extending back to Henry Morgan fleeing his home for the high seas. They include the inhabitants of Steinbeck's xenophobic valleys in *The Pastures of Heaven* and *The Long Valley*. Tularecito's artistry clashes with Miss Martin's orderly authority. Elisa Allen sees the "bright direction" of her womanhood only to have the lid closed on that glimmer of possibility. Pat Humbert remains chained to his dead parents' rules. Peter Randall remains chained to his invisible harness. Each kicks against the expected, routine social norms; each is wounded in the effort. These predecessors include George and Lennie with their doomed dream in *Of Mice and Men*, and their terrible realization that society has no place for "the loneliest guys in the world." These predecessors include the Joads, trampling into the maw of the landowner and the grapes of wrath. They surely include Danny and the paisanos of *Tortilla Flat* and their Anglo counterparts of *Cannery Row*. It is a common pattern in Steinbeck's work, heightened and sharpened in *The Pearl*, where Kino's subjective self clashes dramatically with civilization.

At its most immediate, narrative level *The Pearl* details the explosive conflict of the civilized world, as Steinbeck uses that term in the Cannery Row trilogy to signify the aggressive power structure of society and the uncivilized, outcast minority. Kino and his small clan on the beach are roughly equivalent to the small clan on Cannery Row encroached on by the civilized world. Typifying the beach group are qualities of family ties, poverty, the dreams of a better life; qualities one observes in all of Steinbeck's outcast minority groups. Typifying the civilized world are the traits of hatred for the outcast, some degree of wealth and desire for more, and the ignoring of human need. Ever protective of its wealth and power, the civilized world becomes a devourer, a combine raking the lives of lesser creatures into its insatiable belly. After Coyotito is stung by the scoprion, the tiny beach group, seeking help, proceeds into town like a small morsel of food straying into the jaws of a predator. That is precisely the nature of civilization in Steinbeck's perception—it will devour all lesser objects. The town itself is presented in animalistic imagery: "A town is a thing like a colonial animal. A town has a nervous system and a head and shoulders and feet. A town is a thing separate from all other towns, so that there are no two towns alike. And a town has a whole emotion" (p. 32). Beyond the town, moreover, lies an ever-larger chain of predatory civilization. Behind the many hands of the pearl buyers lies one large hand that controls. While the doctor rejects the Indians, he dreams of Paris, which has rejected him. And beyond the sea, we are told, lie great cities which seem part of an ever-enlarging sphere. The image arises of a huge biological chain, its larger members preying constantly upon lesser members; and the smallest unit is comprised of the Indian people on the Gulf. Their confined little world of traditional innocence and naïvete is a fragile and susceptible prey. The tidal-flat imagery of *The Log from the Sea of Cortez* and the Cannery Row novels prevails here also: "Out in the estuary a tight woven school of small fishes glittered and broke water to escape a school of great fishes that drove in to eat them. And in the houses the people could hear the swish of the small ones and the bouncing splash of the great ones as the slaughter went on" (p. 47). The marine-biological image typifies the social order of Kino's larger community.

Not surprisingly, then, when Kino finds the pearl, he thinks of it first and foremost as a means to gain access to things of the civilized power structure, for just as the large organism preys upon the lesser, the smaller organism aspires toward the larger in an evolutionary spiral. One notices this tension particularly in Kino's reaction to the doctor of the village upon his first trip: "Kino felt weak and afraid and angry at the same time. Rage and terror went together. He could kill the doctor more rapidly than he could talk to him, for all the doctor's race spoke to all of Kino's race as though they were simply animals. And as Kino raised his right hand to the iron ring knocker in the gate, rage swelled in him, and the pounding music of the enemy beat in his ears, and his lips drew tight against his teeth—but with his left hand he reached to take off his hat" (pp. 15–16). The contrast between the animalistic antagonism—"his lips drew tight against his teeth"—and his trained deference to civilized niceties—"with his left hand he reached to take off his hat"—encapsulates the tension of the book. Thus the pearl initially represents for Kino the ability to aspire upward, to defeat the civilized power structure by acquiring its properties. The first effect of the pearl, then, is to trigger the unconscious desires of Kino in a conflict with civilized norms.

The conflict between persona and shadow, manifested socially as a conflict between the individual and social norms, represents the first stage of confrontation. As the tension intensifies, according to Jung, the individual is likely to project dreams of power over civilization. This signifies the arousal of the shadow, its effort to manifest itself. Jung describes this uncertain, early stage of confrontation as the "projection" of the unconscious upon the conscious personality. The individual, at this stage, is not fully aware of the work of the unconscious, sensing only a disquiet and an impulse for power over civilization: "The individual's feeling of weakness, indeed of non-existence, was thus compensated by the eruption of hitherto unknown desires for power. It was the revolt of the powerless, the insatiable greed of the 'have-nots.' By such devious means the unconscious compels man to become conscious of himself."[14] Jung states that one "tries to repress the inferior man in himself, not realizing that by so doing he forces the latter into revolt."[15] This tension between feelings of inferiority and a desire for power collides in the unconscious and emanates to the conscious through dreams.

The parallel action in Kino's dreams is clear. The reader notes four stages of his dreams as he stares into the pearl which is "the mirror of his soul": a socially proper marriage, socially proper clothes, a rifle, and an education for Coyotito. Each dream represents a stage of power acquisition as the unconscious reaches out in defiance.

Thus one finds the same conflict Jung outlines between the persona and the shadow, the extraverted and intraverted personalities, encapsulated in *The Pearl* in the conflict between Kino and the power structure of civilization. The drama of Jung's confrontation with the shadow penetrates the novella in a far more profound manner, however. The significance of *The Pearl*, the aesthetic quality which lifts it from propaganda to powerful fiction, inheres in its subtle complex of image patterns that are remarkably consistent with those employed by Jung to describe the meeting with the shadow. There are several levels to such imagery: the patterns of the trap and the narrow door, patterns of light and dark, animal patterns, and water patterns.

According to Jung, when one lives unaware of his shadow, that "dark side" of his personality becomes a trap for him. Avoiding a direct confrontation with the shadow, he trips over the threshold of the shadow into a trap it holds for him. The shadow will insist upon breaking out; it will impinge upon the conscious and its social mask. Jung describes the situation like this: "A man who is possessed by his shadow is always standing in his own light and falling into his own traps."[16] At other points Jung uses the imagery of a narrow door through which the shadow lures the conscious mind toward discovery.

The Pearl opens with a startling prefiguration. Kino sits upon the shore of the bay. Indolently he awaits the power of the rising sun. The world seems at peace. But, in a sudden juxtaposition, much like his description in *Cannery Row* of the frothy ocean giving way to brutal marine warfare beneath its surface, Steinbeck places a minute terror against the surface placidity. A microcosmic warfare rages against this setting in the ant lion's trap: "The ants were busy on the ground, big black ones with shiny bodies, and little dusty quick ants. Kino watched with the detachment of God while a dusty ant frantically tried to escape the sand trap an ant lion had dug for him" (p. 5). The image here is prefigurative. Kino's calm world is about to be irrevocably shattered. He will stumble into several traps: the doctor's trap when he poisons Coyotito so that he may obtain the pearl, the trap of the pearl buyers in the city, the trap of the flight to the mountains.

Kino does not direct this action; he is its victim. His flight, moreover, moves through increasingly threatening doors. At the doctor's door he raises his hand to the knob, half-defiantly, half-deferentially, his hat fumbled in his fingers, his rage rising to taut lips. The flight into the mountains winds through narrow corridors, past the "stone teeth" of sharp pinnacles as he staggers blindly into the maw of dark violence. The passage bears eerie parallels to Jung's description of confrontation: "The shadow is a tight passage, a narrow door, whose painful constriction no one is spared who goes down to the deep well. But one must learn to know oneself in order to know who one is. For what comes after the door is, surprisingly enough, a boundless expanse full of unprecedented uncertainty."[17]

Thus the initial confrontation with the shadow lies in a stumbling awareness, a tripping into traps that the shadow places, and the increasing tension between individual discovery and social conventions. This intensifies toward direct confrontation with the shadow, represented by Jung in a second pattern of imagery—the clash between light and darkness and their moral, symbolic equivalents of good and evil.

The very term "the shadow" suggests the halfway world between light and dark. The confrontation is a probing of the dark, because unknown, world of the unconscious: "We are now getting into deep waters because here we are coming into darkness. I will give you the name first: *the subjective components of conscious functions.*"[18] The unconscious personality, heretofore making itself known by the projected world of dreams, is now engaged; the darkness of the unknown side of human personality is breaking through to the light of knowledge.[19] It will always remain something of a mystery, of course, and therefore a shadow.

Jung claims to use "the shadow" to respond to the dogmatism of empirical psychology and to suggest the ambiguities of human personality.[20] It becomes apparent in his work, however, that light and dark also raise the implications of good and evil: "The shadow is a moral problem that challenges the whole ego-personality, for no one can become conscious of the shadow without considerable moral effort. To become conscious of it involves recognizing the dark aspects of the personality as present and real. This act is the essential condition for any kind of self-knowledge, and it therefore, as a rule, meets with considerable resistance."[21] He also argues that "there can be no doubt that man is, on the whole, less good than he imagines himself or wants to be. Everyone carries a shadow, and the less it is embodied in the individual's conscious life, the blacker and denser it is."[22] Generally, Jung prefers to speak of "ethical demands" rather than the more absolutist terms *good* and *evil*. The "evil" of the shadow should be understood in two ways. First, insofar as the unconscious lies in defiance of social norms, as we have observed, then according to those very norms it may be considered evil. Social conventions repress the energy of the shadow; thus, "if the repressed tendencies, the shadow as I call them, were obviously evil, there would be no problem whatever. But the shadow is merely somewhat inferior, primitive, unadapted, and awkward; not wholly bad."[23] Second, the shadow also represents evil in the threat of psychological imbalance fomented by the failure to recognize *and* confront the shadow: "It is quite within the bounds of possibility for a man to recognize the relative evil of his nature, but it is a rare and shattering experience for him to gaze into the face of absolute evil."[24] Only by this experience of direct confrontation, however, may the evil be overcome by means of integrating it into the conscious self. Too often people simply recognize their shadow and bury it deeper. This does not constitute genuine confrontation for Jung, since the aim of such is to harmonize the shadow into conscious life. Failure to do so, he points out, only drives the shadow deeper, where it gathers strength:

> What actually happens is that the conscious mind is then able to free itself from the fascination of evil and is no longer obliged to live it compulsively. The darkness and the evil have not gone up in smoke, they have merely withdrawn into the unconscious owing to loss of energy, where they remain unconscious so long as all is well with the conscious. But if the conscious should find itself in a critical or doubtful situation, then it soon becomes apparent that the shadow has not dissolved into nothing but is only waiting for a favourable opportunity to reappear.[25]

The light and dark imagery, for Jung, clearly suggests a moral conflict for the individual.

As with the struggle between individual characters and the large power bloc of civilization, light and dark imagery forms an aesthetic tapestry throughout Steinbeck's work. He developed the imagery most effectively, perhaps, in *East of Eden*. In the opening chapter the Salinas Valley is depicted as a place caught tensely between light and dark, life and death, good and evil. The thematic tension escalates between

Cathy Ames and her obsession with both physical and moral darkness, and Sam Hamilton with his love for physical and moral light. The light-dark imagery provides a basic aesthetic frame in *The Pearl* as well and, as in Jung's thinking, suggests a conflict of good and evil.

Steinbeck's novella begins in "near dark" that washes into golden morning, "a morning like other mornings and yet perfect among mornings" (p. 3). The crystal clarity is shattered when Coyotito is stung by the scorpion, and the following morning dawns in a haze: "Although the morning was young, the hazy mirage was up. The uncertain air that magnified some things and blotted out others hung over the whole Gulf so that all lights were unreal and vision could not be trusted; so that sea and land had the sharp clarities and vagueness of a dream" (p. 21). By the time the villagers journey into the town, the light has faded to be replaced by an oppressive blackness symbolic of the villagers' greed: "The news stirred up something infinitely black and evil in the town; the black distillate was like the scorpion" (pp. 34–35).

By chapter 5, after the open conflict in the town, the atmosphere has become opaque and dim. This time Kino "opened his eyes in the darkness." Only the pale light of the moon stabs the gloom. The shift from brightness to darkness and from clarity to obscurity is accompanied by a decisive shift in color emphasis, from the clear golds, yellows, and earth hues of green and brown that dominate the first chapter to more emotionally charged colors. In chapter 5 Kino's "brain was red with anger." Now the light which was formerly a source of joy becomes a threat: "Suddenly Kino was afraid. The light made him afraid. He remembered the man lying dead in the brush beside the path, and he took Juana by the arm and drew her into the shadow of a house away from the light, for light was danger to him" (p. 88). And the physical darkening in the novella is mirrored psychologically in Kino's own fear and uncertainty:

> In a few moments Juan Tomas came back with her. He lighted a candle and came to them where they crouched in a corner and he said, "Apolonia, see to the door, and do not let anyone enter." He was older, Juan Tomas, and he assumed the authority. "Now, my brother," he said.
>
> "I was attacked in the dark," said Kino. "And in the fight I have killed a man."

"Who?" asked Juan Tomas quickly.

"I do not know. It is all darkness—all darkness and the shape of darkness." (p. 89)

Such characters fumble in a morass of darkness. Kino, Juana, and Coyotito climb into the tenebrous and threatening mountains from which "the sun had passed." They head west, into the dying sunlight, and wander a maze of crooked chasms. Finally, it is "late in the golden afternoon" when Kino and Juana attempt to reclaim the light by hurling the pearl into the sea. As they walked toward the sea, "the sun was behind them and their long shadows stalked ahead, and they seemed to carry two towers of darkness with them" (p. 119). Only when the pearl disappears beneath the waves do we get a suggestion of renewed light: "And the pearl settled into the lovely green water and dropped toward the bottom. The waving branches of the algae called to it and beckoned to it. The lights on its surface were green and lovely. It settled down to the sand bottom among the fern-like plants. Above, the surface of the water was a green mirror" (p. 122).

The transition in imagery from the gentle familiarity of light to the fearsome dark is supported through increasingly predatory animal imagery. The corollary pattern is worth noting in this instance, for it is also one used frequently by Jung, who argues that the shadow "represents sublunary nature and in particular man's instinctual disposition, the 'flesh'—to use a Gnostic-Christian term—which has its roots in the animal kingdom. . . . By 'shadow' I mean the inferior personality, the lowest levels of which are indistinguishable from the instinctuality of an animal."[26] Again, in his "Answer to Job," Jung states that the "unconsciousness has an animal nature."[27]

In *The Pearl*, the setting at large is carefully established in animal imagery—the colonial organism, the devouring power of civilization, the doctor's regard for the Indians as so many insects—but the progress of the pearl's influence on Kino is also measured by his devolution into the animalistic. His very finding of the pearl, in fact, announces the transformation: "Kino's fist closed over the pearl and his emotion broke over him. He put back his head and howled. His eyes rolled up and he screamed and his body was rigid" (pp. 30–31). From that point on, the animal imagery steadily becomes more grim and feral, as a primitive hatred rises in Kino. It is impossible to list all the examples of animal imagery in the book, but the following illustrate the transformation of Kino revealed in animal imagery. When he went to sell the pearl, "Kino had grown tight and hard. He felt the creeping of fate, the circling of wolves, the hover of vultures" (p. 69). When Juana attempted to throw the pearl away, "Kino looked down at her and his teeth were bared. He hissed at her like a snake, and Juana stared at him with wide un-frightened eyes, like a sheep before the butcher" (p. 80). When attacked by robbers, "Kino moved sluggishly, arms and legs stirred like those of a crushed bug, and a thick muttering came from his mouth" (p. 84). When his canoe was destroyed, "he was an animal now, for hiding, for attacking, and he lived only to preserve himself and his family" (p. 86). When he fled the village, "some ancient thing stirred in Kino. Through his fear of dark and the devils that haunt the night, there came a rush of exhilaration; some animal thing was moving in him so that he was cautious and wary and dangerous; some ancient thing out of the past of his people was alive in him" (pp. 94–95). And finally, when pursued, "Kino edged like a slow lizard down the smooth rock shoulder," and "the song of the Family had become as fierce and sharp and feline as the snarl of a female puma" (pp. 114–15). The steps trace the reversion in Kino to the primitive and predatory; they also trace the confrontation with his own shadow.

The stages of Jung's theory discussed above represent approaches toward the shadow: the recognition of tension between the individual and society, between the unconscious and the conscious persona; the impingement of the unconscious upon the conscious imaged by traps and doorways; the growing awareness of the shadow figured in light and dark as well as animal imagery. The actual meeting with the shadow, however, provides one of the most startling parallels with *The Pearl*. Often overlooked or misunderstood in *The Pearl* is the crucial role of Juana. Her role precisely figures the discovery of the locus of the shadow in the anima.

Consider that Jungian theory has plunged us ever nearer the shadow itself. We stand, as it were, on the very edge of a lake, about to dive headlong into the depths of the unconscious. Indeed, it is very much like Kino's plunge into the ocean depths to find the pearl—his symbolic shadow soul, his unconscious. In his discussion of this perilous stage, Jung fuses two imagery patterns: animal and water. The plunge into the unconscious is very much like a plunge into the mysterious depths of the ocean.[28] The action discloses the primitive, bestial side of human personality: "The unconscious is commonly regarded as a sort of incapsulated fragment of our most personal and intimate life—something like what the Bible calls the 'heart' and considers the source of all evil thoughts. In the chambers of the heart dwell the wicked blood-spirits, swift anger and sensual weakness. . . . In this blind alley [one] is exposed to the attack of all ferocious beasts which the caverns of the psychic underworld are supposed to harbour."[29] The plunge into the unconscious, for Jung, is also a stripping away of the persona as one dives deep: "True, whoever looks into the mirror of the water will see first of all his own face. Whoever goes to himself risks a confrontation with himself. The mirror does not flatter, it faithfully shows whatever looks into it; namely, the face we never show to the world because we cover it with the *persona*, the mask of the actor. But the mirror lies behind the mask and shows the true face."[30]

In his theory of archetypes Jung extends his diving-into-water metaphor with the discovery of a fish. But, he writes, "they are waterbeings of a peculiar sort. Sometimes a nixie gets into the fisherman's net, a female, a half-human fish. . . . The nixie is an even more instinctive version of a magical feminine being whom I call the anima."[31] We now arrive at the heart of Jung's theory of both archetypes and the shadow, for this same anima which lies at the heart of the archetype also lies at the heart of the shadow. Each gender, in what Jung calls his syzygy theory, has an unconscious countergender: for the male the anima, for the female the animus.[32] It is this undisclosed part of the personality that makes known to the conscious part the presence of the shadow. It seems to be the governing power of the shadow. Like the shadow, the anima seems at times to be a complex of good and evil. In his "Psychological Approach to the Trinity," from "Psychology and Religion," where he adduces his quaternity theory, Jung holds that in the Christian tradition people have commonly associated the anima with the devil. This "other side" of male personality accounts for natural instincts, or the Pauline idea of "the flesh." Jung finds such labeling insufficient. Like the shadow itself, the anima is often considered evil simply because she represents the unknown, and because she often stands opposed to social conventions. Also like the shadow, the anima simply wants life: "She affords the most convincing reasons for not prying into the unconscious, an occupation that would break down our moral inhibitions and unleash forces that had better been left unconscious and undisturbed from society's point of view. As usual, there is something in what the anima says; for life in itself is not good only, it is also bad. Because the anima wants life, she wants both good and bad."[33] We note here that the anima is reluctant to expose herself but is also at once insistent upon her influence. The same reluctance-insistence, we shall see, marks Juana.

In one of his startling analyses of fairy tales in "The Phenomenology of the Spirit in Fairytales," Jung applies his shadow-anima theory, suggesting that the princess of the story is the anima riding, and possessing, a horse, which symbolizes the shadow.[34] We may conclude from his analysis that the anima is a governing agency of the shadow, and her task is to bring the shadow to full participatory life in the consciousness of the person. Thus the anima is a completion of personality, however threatening or socially contentious her emanation might be.

In this process the anima functions by questioning the conscious. While discussing the anima and animus jointly, Jung observes: "One of the most typical manifestations of both figures is what had long been called 'animosity.' The anima causes illogical moods, and the animus produces irritating platitudes and unreasonable opinions. Both are frequent dream-figures. As a rule they personify the unconscious and give it its peculiarly disagreeable or irritating character."[35] The anima questions the dreams or projections of the conscious self; her task is to query the mask of the persona. Jung describes her work as an unsettling countervoice to the conscious persona:

> The anima is a factor of the utmost importance in the psychology of a man wherever emotions and effects are at work. She intensifies, exaggerates, falsifies, and mythologizes all emotional relations with his work and with other people of both sexes. . . . When the anima is strongly constellated, she softens the man's character and makes him touchy, irritable, moody, jealous, vain, and unadjusted. He is then in a state of "discontent" and spreads discontent all around him. Sometimes the man's relationship to the woman who has caught his anima accounts for the existence of this syndrome.[36]

In the theory of the anima—the final discovery of the work of the shadow prompted by the questioning and directing power of the feminine side of a man—we find a psychological framework for understanding the nature of Juana. A qualification should be made, however. By no means does this argument suggest that Juana is nothing more than an unconscious voice in Kino's psyche. Indeed, her character is so full and complex that she stands quite independently as one of Steinbeck's major heroines. The argument does assert, however, that Juana's relationship with her husband in this narrative is remarkably like the relationship of the anima with the conscious personality in confrontation with the shadow and in the effort to establish psychological balance.

In the narrative plot of *The Pearl*, Juana incarnates many of the character traits that distinguish the inimitable Ma Joad. Both are the spiritual and physical nurturers of the family. While Juana works the corn for morning cakes, the family song lilts gaily about her. Like Ma Joad, Juana is also a woman of action. When the scorpion strikes Coyotito, it is Juana who rushes to his aid: "She put her lips down over the puncture and sucked hard and spat and sucked again while Coyotito screamed" (p. 8). And like Pa Joad, rendered helpless by the baffling power of the landowners in *The Grapes of Wrath*, here too Kino "hovered; he was helpless, he was in the way." Like Ma Joad at Weedpatch, ordering the family to go out to find work, Juana orders Kino to go to the village to find the doctor. Interestingly, and in violation of Indian custom, "Kino followed her" as she led the way into town. Here already one finds the prompting action of the anima; later she will follow Kino; at the conclusion they walk side by side.

One finds, then, familiar qualities of Steinbeck's heroines vested in Juana: spiritual and physical succor to the family, an ability to act forcefully and quickly, a dramatic ability for leadership in times of crisis. The test of Juana's character arises concomitantly with Kino's in the discovery of the pearl. This discovery initiates her psychological function as the anima, with clear stages marking her relationship with Kino in his confrontation with the shadow. In the early stage, from her traditional place in the family routine, Juana instigates and projects Kino's unconscious desires, much in accord with Jung's first stage of confrontation when the unconscious projects upon the persona. She forces him to brave the civilized world of the doctor. She urges Kino to open the oyster as he stares dumbfounded at its huge, fluted shell. In the last stage, Juana's power emerges openly as the threats to Kino increase. As Kino is plunged more deeply into self-confrontation, she becomes his guiding power.

In the early stages of the narrative, Juana functions as a kind of questioner of Kino's inmost being, much as Jung described the early, prompting activity of the anima. When Kino hides the pearl, Juana asks, "Who do you fear?" His response: "Everyone." In her questioning, Juana too seems a mirror of Kino's soul. She voices the first warnings to Kino that are also stirring in his unconscious. When they were attacked in the night, Juana's tension "boiled up to the surface." Her voice is pwoerful: "This thing is evil. . . . This pearl is like a sin! It will destroy us" (p. 54). With her prescient vision Juana declares, "It will destroy us all. . . . Even our son" (p. 55).

What prevents Kino from heeding her advice? His compulsion is to seize power over civilization: "This is our one chance. . . . Our son must go to school. He must break out of the pot that holds us in" (p. 54). His compulsion rages so powerfully that he ignores Juana's advice, which indeed ultimately proves to be true.

Kino advances, leading Juana, into the predatory world of the civilized power structure to sell his pearl. Thus he exposes himself. Thus he opens his shadow to the predators, and the effect is immediate: "But Kino had grown tight and hard. He felt the creeping of fate, the circling of wolves, the hover of vultures. He felt the evil coagulating about him, and he was helpless to protect himself" (p. 69). His only source of strength emanates from Juana: "He felt a little tugging at his back, and he turned and looked in Juana's eyes, and when he looked away he had renewed strength" (p. 70).

This feminine side of himself acquires strength and courage as Kino reels in the power struggle: "Juana watched him with worry, but she knew him and she knew she could help him best by being silent and by being near. And as though she too could hear the Song of Evil, she fought it, singing softly the melody of the family, of the safety and warmth and wholeness of the family. She held Coyotito in her arms and sang the song to him, to keep the evil out, and her voice was brave against the threat of the dark music" (p. 75). Taking the matter into her own hands, Juana tries to fling the pearl back into the sea. Twice she has shown Kino a better way. For the second time he rejects it: "Kino looked down at her and his teeth were bared. He hissed at her like a snake, and Juana stared at him with wide unfrightened eyes" (p. 50). Juana attempts to fling the pearl back into the sea because her goal, unlike Kino's, is clear and sure—the restoration of harmony: "All of the time Juana had been trying to rescue something of the old peace, of the time before the pearl" (p. 54). With the harmony so terribly disrupted, however, she will battle fiercely to restore it.

The flight into the stone-toothed mountains follows. The light and dark imagery intensifies. Kino is now afraid of the light. Moreover, deep unconscious voices, much like those urging Pepe in "Flight," urge them as they flee: "Some ancient thing stirred in Kino. Through his fear of dark and the devils that haunt the night, there came a rush of exhilaration; some animal thing was moving in him so that he was cautious and wary and dangerous; some ancient thing out of the past of his people was alive in him" (p. 95). During all this time, we should note, Juana is still the follower. Kino leads.

During the climactic battle in the mountains, however, Juana's steady voice and vision acquire strength and directive power. As Kino's interior struggle swirls in confusion, Juana's participation solidifies into rocklike adamancy. She will not be denied:

> She looked full into his eyes for a moment. "No," she said. "We go with you."
>
> "I can go faster alone," he said harshly. "You will put the little one in danger if you go with me."
>
> "No," said Juana.
>
> "You must. It is the wise thing and it is my wish," he said.
>
> "No," said Juana.
>
> He looked then for weakness in her face, for fear or irresolution, and there was none. Her eyes were very bright. He shrugged his shoulders helplessly then, but he had taken strength from her. When they moved on it was no longer panic flight. (p. 106)

Finally, Kino himself turns hunter. Several psychological implications occur. First, his "music" solidifies into Juana's family song—not the music of the pearl: "And Kino's own music was in his head, the music of the enemy, low and pulsing, nearly asleep. But the Song of the Family had become as fierce and sharp and feline as the snarl of a female puma. The family song was alive now and driving him down on the dark enemy" (p. 115). Significantly, the song has the snarl of "a female puma." Juana's power has empowered Kino. Second, the hunt tragically leads to Coyotito's death, a killing by Kino of a part of himself. His dreams, we recall, culminated in his vision for Coyotito. And the third implication is that Juana's anima moves clearly in the fore of Kino's consciousness, thereby restoring, to a degree, the shattered harmony.

After Coyotito's death, Kino and Juana returned to La Paz, but "they were not walking in single file, Kino ahead and Juana behind, as usual, but side by side" (p. 119). The long towers of darkness they carry represent Coyotito's death and the confrontation they have shared. They walk past the villagers. There was only one song in Kino's mind now—not the mad shrilling of the pearl, and no longer the diabolic song of evil, but "in Kino's ears the Song of the Family was as fierce as a cry. He was immune and terrible, and his song had become a battle cry" (p. 12). Thus they walk, back to the water's edge, back to the abyss of the primeval unconscious.

There, Kino studied the pearl: "He looked into its surface and it was gray and ulcerous. Evil faces peered from it into his eyes, and he saw the light of burning" (p. 121). And he handed it to Juana to throw into the sea. Why? In recognition that she has been correct, of course. But Juana, the anima, will not settle for some cheap victory in a power move here. She appropriately refused. This is Kino's task—the way to harmony between his conflict of conscious persona and unconscious desire lies in *his* throwing the pearl back. He did, and with that action the restoration of psychological harmony is sealed by the restoration of light imagery. Restored to its natural place on the ocean floor, the pearl is no longer a threat: "And the music of the pearl drifted to a whisper and disappeared" (p. 122).

One does well to be wary of influence studies upon authors. The creative act involves a constellation of aesthetic impulses coming to bear on the one original light of the artwork. This is a particularly sound caution with Steinbeck, whose primary impulse as a writer was character revelation through a carefully wrought story. That caution heeded, however, it would be remiss to neglect the formative influences upon the author's art making. In such a spirit, one is free to make certain observations about such influences.

One observes, then, a pattern of influence of Jungian theory upon the making of *The Pearl* that seems to transcend mere accident. Like Jung's idea of the initial conflict between the persona—the civilized mask—and the unconscious, we see Steinbeck's Kino caught in the same tension. Like Jung's figurative imagery to describe the confrontation with the shadow, we see Steinbeck employing remarkably similar imagery to frame Kino's confrontation with his unconscious desires. The major patterns include light and dark imagery and animal imagery, both intensifying dramatically with the approach to the dark side of the primitive human unconscious held by the shadow. We observe a subtle interweaving of minor patterns, particularly the projection by the shadow of images of traps and stumbling blocks. And finally, like the feminine anima of Jung's archetypal theory, which instigates and guides the discovery of the shadow, we observe Juana as the guiding, directing power in Kino's ordeal.

Michael J. Meyer

14   Precious Bane: Mining the Fool's Gold of *The Pearl*

Although John Steinbeck had several critical successes after *The Grapes of Wrath*, the publication of his novella *The Pearl* only served to increase the controversy over whether Steinbeck was indeed a significant realistic novelist or merely a didactic preacher who overindulged in melodrama, allegory, and sentimentalism. However, the extreme reactions seem to indicate the diversity of expectations of the critics rather than a valid analysis of Steinbeck's accomplishment in this novel. On the one hand, Warren French presents a thorough denunciation of the work and seems to argue that Steinbeck's allegory lacks both insight and intrinsic worth. Calling *The Pearl* a disappointment and a betrayal of Steinbeck's past work, French suggests that Steinbeck's decision to write grew out of purely monetary concerns and his desire to gain exposure to a wider audience.[1] More important, French contends that at the novel's end, Kino is a defeated man who serves as evidence that Steinbeck is no longer interested in "man's restlessness or enlightenment." Instead of a solution to Kino's problems, French argues that Steinbeck leaves the weak impression at the end of *The Pearl* that "all is forgiven and will be forgotten . . . simply throwing these questions in 'the lovely green water' with the pearl; a gesture of rejection at the end [that] satisfies the reader, who feels that, after all, the simple life is best."[2] His ultimate contention is that the novella shows a decline in Steinbeck's work, and in the final analysis it is merely a paste substitute rather than a valuable treasure.

Ironically, this negative viewpoint is countered by Howard Levant, whose usual reaction to Steinbeck, at least structurally, is very critical and negative. Surprisingly, however, Levant is an ardent defender of the novella, praising Steinbeck's ability to drive "an apparent simple narrative into the darkest areas of human awareness." Disagreeing with French, Levant sees the ending as an

> anthropomorphic form of penance, a ritual burial, an ejection of evil, a token of the return to the genuine life of the organism, shaded by the fact of death which no human act can alter. The resolution is ambiguous, then, like the rest of the parable, for it echoes our flawed humanity. . . . Which is to say that *The Pearl* is a triumph, a successful rendering of human experience in the round, in the most economical and intense of forms, without any surrender to the simplified or imposed patterns that mar the conclusions of such different novels as *Tortilla Flat* or *The Grapes of Wrath*.[3]

Besides Levant, however, no one has contended that there is a great deal of ambiguity in the novel or that its presence is a plus rather than a detrimental flaw. Instead, many critics have persisted in criticizing Steinbeck's didacticism and seeing only the black-and-white absolutes they expect in parables rather than the complex moral lesson that the author provides through his setting, characters, and symbols. In this lesson Steinbeck asserts that duality undergirds all of man's actions, and that intertwining good and evil are a part of each postlapsarian human.

Nevertheless, mankind generally wishes to deny such a frustrating state of being and pretend that it doesn't exist. Steinbeck illustrates this well in Kino and Juana, his protagonists, who reluctantly experience duality. These primitive natives undergo an initiation rite in the novel similar to what Adam and Eve experienced when they ate from the tree of knowledge of good and evil. This initiation destroys the couple's naïve concept of what man and the world are like and leaves them bereft but wiser in their knowledge of themselves and of their society. Their discovery dispels the illusions of the "good" that surrounds them but also frustrates them as they struggle to cope with a reality which almost always involves a paradoxical yoking of opposites.

The yoking of opposites is most obvious in Steinbeck's use of imagery in the novel to portray an intersecting dichotomy of good versus evil. In the novel, sights and sounds as well as symbols are used to compose a pattern of images that offer evidence of the morally ambiguous state that Kino and Juana must contend with.

The first major image Steinbeck uses is a traditional one: light versus darkness. Although several critics have noted that *The Pearl* begins with sunrise and ends in sunset, few have noted that neither the symbolic light nor the lack of it remains the dominant visual image. Instead, light and darkness mingle together to form gray areas where good and evil are inextricably mixed.

Consequently, the reader cannot surmise that the purity and goodness which begin the novel are destroyed and blackened by the sunset which ends the work. In fact, the light/dark imagery fluctuates between positive and negative connotations just as good and evil do. In addition, the sunrise which begins the day is accompanied by another "positive" image—the harmony of music, the Song of the Family. This sound image also persists in the novel, using another traditional presentation of good's conflict with evil: harmony versus disharmony. Through this image Steinbeck affirms that the beautiful music and its lyric melody, like the early morning, cannot be maintained without the eventual intrusion of discord and dark. As Steinbeck stated in a letter to his close friend Pascal Covici in January 1941: "It seems that two forces are necessary in man before he is a man. [He is] a product of all his filth and disease and meanness, his hunger and cruelty. Cure those and you would have not man but an entirely new species you wouldn't recognize and probably wouldn't like."[4]

Here Steinbeck seems to agree with philosopher David Bakan, who postulates that duality is essential to mankind when he states that "the most critical paradox that man must live with, is the possibility that all that is characteristically associated with evil is, in some way, intimately intertwined with good, the notion that the sins of mankind, sex, aggression and avarice, are related to the survival of mankind."[5] It is thus not surprising that Steinbeck's use of images becomes syncretic, merging together the various sides of objects and symbols and presenting both the positive and the negative simultaneously. For example, Steinbeck notes that the Song of the Family is quite flexible, and, even though it only has three notes, it possesses an endless variety of intervals (p. 4). Similarly, although the melody signifies safety, warmth, and wholeness for the couple, it is significant that sometimes the song rises to a sobbing or aching chord that catches in the throat. Ultimately the dual image will expand until the clash of different melodies will indicate Kino's despair at ever being able to achieve harmony in his world.

The merged images of dissonance and darkness continue to preempt the bright music of Juana and are depicted as a threatening song which emanates from a scorpion, Steinbeck's first symbol of the sin and evil which threaten every man. This scorpion and its song conspire against even the innocent tiny baby Coyotito. However, the fact that this scorpion is portrayed as a random evil which invades the couple's lives seems to indicate Steinbeck's belief that the dark side of man's soul is uncontrollable and will eventually attack even the most peaceful, innocent, and harmonious of lives. In short, once again the novel asserts that if a mixture of good and evil is essential to existence, attempts to see only one side of the human condition are futile.

However, Juana and Kino, as representatives of an innocent Adam and Eve in the garden, are unaccustomed to the darkness and disharmony that infiltrate human society. Up to this point their lives have been so sheltered that they mistakenly believe that evil exists only in obvious outside forces like the scorpion. Such a force can be smashed into paste by the human hand or foot, and definitely will be overcome in a matter of time. However, once the sting of the evil one touches the baby, his parents begin to discover that their analysis is mistaken and that the evil that the scorpion embodies is impossible to wipe out. Thus, although the physical scorpion is destroyed, it is evident that another springs up in the city of La Paz. Despite the promises of peace that its name suggests, the city provides still further duality as Steinbeck examines the "civilized" community and compares its evil with the scorpion while contrasting it with the goodness of Juana and Kino's primitive existence. As soon as the native couple enter the city seeking help, they begin to learn the lesson that the town does not contain the same warmth and wholeness of their small thatched hut. Moreover, they also note the absence of the moral absolutes that simplified their lives. In the city the evil darkness intermingles intangibly with the good light. It cannot be extracted by folk cures, religion, or ancient spells because it runs rampant among the so-called civilized people, whose avarice and jealousy destroy their potential for good.

For example, the doctor who is so essential to the cure of Coyotito is initially associated with the light of education and the blessing of good health. He is seen by the couple as a potential savior, but actually he is the epitome of evil. The ability to distinguish good from evil is thus seen as difficult, at best, and Steinbeck reinforces this dilemma by describing the fine line that separates the two opposites as a "hazy mirage." As Steinbeck describes nature in chapter 2 as poison fish hiding in eel grass and dogs and pigs who feed off the dead, even the positive qualities of the pure surroundings of Juana and Kino are seen as questionable and hiding unknowns. This, of course, parallels a similar uncertainty for Kino and Juana about what is good and what is evil.

Soon the couple will find that nothing is sure and solid, and that moral ambiguity is man's heritage. Yet most critics of *The Pearl* have persisted in looking for absolutes and defining the meaning of images within strict boundaries which ultimately did not hold up under close scrutiny. But Steinbeck's parable is not so easily resolved. Chapter 3 begins in brightness as good returns in the form of the great pearl which Kino discovers, the Pearl of the World, gigantic in size and shape. Although not all readers are aware of his literary allusion to the medieval poem also entitled "The Pearl," Steinbeck carefully suggests that even though the gem appears to offer salvation, it is yet another example of the intermixture of good and evil. Specifically, the initial description points out the irony of the pearl's development (p. 21). It was created because an irritant, a grain of sand, penetrated the oyster's shell and lodged within it. In this incident Steinbeck shows how negatives are at times strangely transformed into positives, and worthless grains of sand become priceless treasures as the oyster works to dispel or neutralize the invading grain, which may cause life-threatening problems.

Once again Steinbeck reintroduces and merges his imagery as the symbolic pearl, which is precious and beyond price, is associated with light. For example, it is "as perfect as the moon. It captured the light and gave it back in silver incandescence. It was as large as a sea-gull's egg. It was the greatest pearl in the world" (p. 25). Yet at the same time the author also uses his light image negatively to stress the moral ambiguity of the gem by stating that the treasure has a ghostly gleam and that Kino mistrusts his perceptions and wonders if the prize might be more illusion than reality.

Elsewhere Steinbeck returns to the music imagery, the Song of the Family, and joins it with the Song of the Pearl That Might Be. At this point the pearl tune is described as a countermelody that blends in with the dominant music, but later in the novel the Song of the Pearl will be associated with something infinitely evil as the narrator notes that "the essence of the pearl was mixed with the essence of men and a curious dark residue was precipitated . . . the schemes, the plans, . . . the lusts, the hungers and . . . he [Kino] became curiously every man's enemy" (pp. 29–30).[6]

Yet Juana and Kino are reluctant to acknowledge the duality they are confronting, for it seems as if their long-sought-for salvation has arrived. Warm and happy in their newfound success and good luck, they can only believe that the music of the family has merged with the music of the pearl so that each beautifies the other.

Influenced by this belief, Kino begins to dream of new values and goals, of the light, harmony, and good that the pearl can bring to his life. By seeing only the benefits that the pearl of great price can bring to him, he ignores the treasure's potential for evil, and, unfortunately, his "positive" desires for material goods and for health and education for his son create a negative force in his life. As pride and conceit over his ownership begin to dominate his life, he turns from his former kindly disposition into a man as ruthless and evil as any of the townspeople. A similar irony exists in the fact that although the pearl may solve Kino's problems, Steinbeck reiterates after its discovery that "the dark is almost in" (p. 35). Eventually the coming night becomes a threatening dark that will reveal the greed of Kino's neighbors as they try to steal the pearl from him, turning his dreams into nightmares.

The symbolic pearl is combined with the sight and sound images here as the music of evil suddenly returns to Kino's ears, signifying the duality of the townspeople and the church but also the duality of the gem itself. This music image is described as shrill, as opposed to the sweet music Kino formerly heard from the pearl. Kino, once so positive about his find, now wonders whether anyone or anything can be trusted; his simple naïvete is being systematically destroyed. Even the medicine prescribed by the doctor is questionable, as Kino cannot help but wonder whether the prescription itself is not evil masquerading as good and whether Coyotito's illness has been caused by the doctor in order to gain the pearl for himself. Such duplicity continues in the narration when the doctor arrives and denies having heard of Kino's good fortune, thus craftily causing Kino to betray the secret hiding place of the treasure.

The symbols of the scorpion and the pearl, once quite separate and opposite, are now strangely joined, and just as the neighbors were previously associated with the characteristics of the scorpion (p. 30), so Kino is associated with the pearl. He is no longer pure, but like the oyster is infected by the sands of mistrust and fear. Steinbeck describes the hardness growing over him, but what results for Kino is no treasure (p. 36). This hardness suggests not wealth but man's animal-like state, where faith and hope in goodness and light and harmony have disappeared as human traits. Soon Kino dreams of darkness, not only a darkness which blots out his own dreams for success but one that also denies the potential of Coyotito's future. Combining this depressing action with sound, Kino begins to recognize that every sound in the world is now an indicator of a dark thing. Kino is transformed into a raging beast, and suddenly the evil side of a primitive life-style is exposed. The formerly docile Kino, his very life now threatened, transforms into a wild animal whose one law is the dark violence of the jungle. Kino has grown in hatred, sin, and wrongdoing, and Steinbeck again suggests that he is similar to the evil part of the pearl: hard, cold, and unyielding.

Despite the use of the negative parallel, Kino still does not understand the concept of the duality of all things. The pearl is still seen as positive because it will provide for a good, the healing of the baby. Yet shortly thereafter, Steinbeck removes this motive as the poison appears to recede from Coyotito's body and it is no longer necessary to use the pearl to obtain the needed payment for the doctor's services. Now the dominant song of joy and happiness is drowned out by Kino's manic desire to keep the pearl at any price, even murder. His readiness to kill in order to keep the treasure leads to the first verbal recognition and admission of the gem's duality. Again an ironic twist is used as Juana, unlike her biblical counterpart Eve, is the first to see the dark elements in the pearl.

Yet despite his wife's warning, Kino persists in seeing only one side of the pearl, and consequently only one side of his human nature. He refuses to acknowledge how inextricably good is mixed with evil, light with darkness, and harmony with dissonance, nor does he see the pearl and the scorpion as similar. Indeed, the vague wavering of Kino's mind about the subject is suggested as the narrator pictures the pearl as "winking and glimmering in the light of the little candle, cozening Kino's brain with its beauty" (p. 51).

Later, when Kino's brother Juan Thomas tries to reason with him, he suggests the futility of trying to obtain a fair price from the pearl buyers in the town, where there is a further duplicity: a cheating monopoly of merchants who pose as agents of free enterprise but who are in fact defrauding their customers and controlling the prices in the pearl market for their own personal gain.

Nonetheless Kino persists in his refusal to listen to and recognize duality, still preferring to believe in a rigid code of good and evil which is applicable to all men, and not to just a select few. Such a code is not vague or hazy in nature but upright and constantly just and honest. Obviously this idealistic code is unattainable, and Kino's belief in it is destroyed when the pearl buyers assert that the pearl's size makes it only a curiosity—clumsy, undesirable, and of less worth.

This act of trickery infuriates Kino, and Steinbeck repeats his association with the pearl as Kino becomes tighter and harder rather than more pliable. As Todd Lieber notes, the pearl is "a complex talisman, containing Steinbeck's vision of man: it is a thing of great worth and beauty and promise, but it also appears cancerous and ugly; it evokes avarice and greed, but also generosity and kindness; it produces high and noble thoughts and ambition, but also theft and murder. Steinbeck had come to believe that good and evil were inseparable from being, intimately related parts of that which is."[7]

Lieber, however, fails to note Kino's intense identification with the talisman and how the evil of the pearl coagulates about its victim, entrapping him with its glistening yet deadly light. Consequently, Kino is as helpless in its throes as he is before the deceiving pearl buyers. Like the townspeople, his only solution is to lie to himself, for admitting the duplicity around him would force both Kino and his friends to acknowledge the lengthy amount of time that they have allowed themselves to be duped.

The dark music returns to Kino's life as he refuses the offer of monopoly for the Pearl of Great Price, but the evil melody is still countered and balanced by Juana's Song of the Family, which restores safety, warmth, and wholeness at least momentarily. However, shortly thereafter Juana restates her mistrust in the treasure: "Kino," she says, "the pearl is evil. Let us destroy it before it destroys us. Let us crush it between stones. Let us—let us throw it back in the sea where it belongs! Kino, it is evil, it is evil!!" (pp. 73–74).

Sadly, Kino again ignores the warning, this time asserting that the qualities of his masculinity—determination and ingenuity—will serve as proof against evil. What he fails to recognize is that the dark side of these qualities—stubbornness and craftiness—have also infiltrated his life. In order to attain the self-insight about moral ambiguity that he so desperately needs, Steinbeck forces Kino to face death itself. Nothing less than physical death is required to transcend or cope with his fallen nature. It is the price a person must pay to discover his true identity. Each one must give birth to himself, then die of the consequences. To be human is to know death.

Kino's ensuing fight with Juana emphasizes the separation, dissonance, and darkness in their relationship that have been caused by the questionable treasure. Kino becomes more domineering and greedy, and in a short while he is forced to commit murder as well as battery in order to retain the pearl. After this, the powers of evil seem to concentrate on an absolute destruction of Kino's life. In a way it is a punishment for his unwillingness to accept the ambiguous nature of the pearl and for his determination to see it as an absolute. The now-dominant dark force destroys Kino's canoe (his life source) and his brush home and eventually seeks even his life. As Kino reflects on the shifting nature of everything around him, he recognizes, like Conrad's Kurtz in *Heart of Darkness*, that "it is all darkness—all darkness and the shape of darkness" (p. 84). Yet, like Kurtz, he must pursue his life though it causes him misfortune, and he must seek his goals though they bring about his own destruction. His self-identification with duality is complete as he states, "The Pearl has become my soul. If I give it up, I shall lose my soul" (p. 87). Kino's life has been transformed; he is totally the opposite of what he was at the novel's beginning.

The only option for Juana and Kino now is flight, and like Adam and Eve they are evicted from their Eden into a hostile world complete with an unfriendly wind and cold, uncaring stars in a black sky. Like man's first parents, they mistrust one another, and the oneness of their marriage in the early chapters is replaced by separation and selfishness. Returning to the sight imagery, Steinbeck notes that the joy which was previously held in the light has been transformed into Kino's revelry in death and destruction and the ways of the dark. The sound image also returns: "the music of the pearl was triumphant in Kino's head and the quiet melody of the family underlay it" (p. 91). This positive picture is, of course, ironic, and it suggests that despite the bitter trials which his newfound wealth has brought, Kino still persists in his belief that the pearl's dual nature must be illusory. Though its evil glow burns in his eyes, he sees his bad luck as emanating from elsewhere than his treasure, and, ironically, he still seeks his vision in its surface.

When he once again consults the pearl's surface for answers, the magic crystal ball reveals that his own goals have been twisted and warped. The power of the rifle has become murder, the ecstasy of religious faith and commitment have become spouse abuse, and the value of an educated child has been transformed into illness and even death. As L. Marks notes, "The courageous and trusting Kino experiences for the first time in his life the emotions of defensive fear and suspicion, and in his blindness he courts destruction of all he values most. His vain struggle to protect the pearl brings about the loss of his home, a spiritual estrangement from his wife and the death of his son."[8]

Stubbornly Kino rejects the evil vision, but as he thrusts the pearl into his clothing, the sound images remind him that the Music of the Pearl has become sinister in his ears and is interwoven with the music of evil. At this point the novel again poses the premise that in order to overcome evil, man's duality must be acknowledged rather than hidden or ignored. Failure to do so only results in a hell on earth, and so it is for Kino.

As he and Juana flee desperately toward the mountains, they discover only Eliot's Waste Land—waterless desert covered with cacti and sharp rocks. This is a sharp contrast from the biblical promise "I will lift up my eyes to the hills from whence cometh my help" (Psalms 121:1), and it is yet another ironic reversal which suggests the duality that infects man's world. These hell-like surroundings encourage the dual musical image to return, and it is described as loud, hot, secret, and poisonous (p. 100). The symbols of the pearl (originally positive) and the scorpion (originally negative) are now joined as Kino's existence becomes that of all postlapsarian Adams. He is drawn simultaneously toward "good" and "evil," which often are intertwined and inseparable.

Kino instinctively heads for a cleft in a rock and the safety symbolized by caves, water, and valleys in Steinbeck's other fiction. But despite the family's arrival at a supposed place of protection, there is still the potential for death and destruction. Like the pearl, the water and the cave have two faces, and the reader senses that both may signal death and destruction rather than resurrection and new life. The reader is again drawn to Steinbeck's musical imagery as Kino fights for his life. Suddenly the Song of the Family, previously peaceful and harmonic, has been changed into a sharp battle cry. Ironically, in order to attain a good for himself and his family, Kino must again resort to evil: the dark deed of murder.

Eventually he succeeds in his rescue plans, but darkness is essential to his attempt, and his efforts are marred by the light of the moon. On the third try, however, he is successful in killing all three of the dark riders who have pursued them. But this apparent victory is short-lived as he discovers that a random shot has struck the top of Coyotito's head, killing him instantly. The sacrifice of the firstborn son, a recurring concern in at least three other Steinbeck novels, brings Kino to his senses even as it awakened Abraham, the Israelites in Egypt, and believers in Christ Jesus.

After Coyotito's death, Juana and Kino seem removed from the present, and they are transformed into archetypes. The narrator, however, emphasizes the positive rather than the negative side of the experience: "They had gone through pain and had come out on the other side; that there was almost a magical protection about them" (p. 80). Kino now has a new and more accurate vision of the pearl. "He looked into its surface and it was gray and ulcerous. Evil faces peered from it into his eyes, and he saw the light of burning. And in the surface he saw the frantic eyes of the man lying in the pool. And in the surface of the pearl he saw Coyotito lying in the little cave with the top of his head shot away. And the pearl was ugly; it was gray, like a malignant growth. And Kino heard the music of the pearl, distorted and insane" (p. 117).

With this knowledge the relationship of Juana and Kino is restored; both now possess a complete awareness of the pearl's double nature. This change is indicated by the fact that when they return to La Paz, they walk not in single file but side by side, and when Kino throws the pearl into the water, they remain side by side for a long time. This return to unity suggests a catharsis and redemption, a return from the valley of the shadow of death. In fact, as the novel draws to a close, it appears as if Kino and Juana have traveled full circle and found renewed unity even in the darkness. "The sun was behind them and their long shadows stalked ahead, and they seemed to carry two towers of darkness with them" (p. 115).

As the novel returns to its initial setting of mixed light and dark, Steinbeck indicates man's inescapable condition. In the final pages, Kino has matured; he has accepted the duality of all things. As Harry Morris points out, Kino and Juana are doubles of Everyman, who in his journey toward death discovers who he really is.

> The full significance of Kino's throwing the pearl back into the sea now becomes clear: the act represents the willingness to accept a third journey, the journey still to be made, the journey that any fictional character has still to make after his dream-vision allegory is over. . . . They must apply their new knowledge and win their way to eternal salvation, which can only come with their actual deaths. But his real triumph, his real gain, the heights to which he has risen rather than the depths to which he has slipped back is the immense knowledge he has gained of good and evil. This knowledge is the tool that he needs to help him on the final journey, the inescapable journey that Everyman must take.[9]

A sadder but wiser Kino now faces his former existence with knowledge and intuition. He will never be the same, and neither will the sensitive reader who has accompanied him on his journey. In fact, this reader will be forced, like the protagonist, to examine his soul and to deny the lack of moral absolutes. Perhaps he will even agree with Steinbeck that "if this story is a parable, perhaps everyone takes his own meaning from it and reads his own life into it."[10] Whatever that meaning, the careful crafting of imagery (sight, sound, and symbols) reveals that Steinbeck's novella is indeed a complex tale which not only possesses archetypal significance but which, when examined closely, offers a deep moral lesson to conscientious readers.

Roy S. Simmonds

15   Steinbeck's *The Pearl:* Legend, Film, Novel

The Pearl, on the surface one of the most simple—one might even say simplistic—stories Steinbeck ever wrote, has, as Louis Owens has pointed out, "generated more contradictory criticism than any other work by Steinbeck."[1] This divergence of critical opinion, however, rarely extends beyond the conflicting interpretations of the book's inner meaning. Most critics are agreed on its intrinsic literary worth. Howard Levant, for example, boldly asserts that "*The Pearl* is a success," while conceding that it does contain a "flaw."[2] Richard O'Connor has referred to it as "a short novel almost as perfect as a real pearl."[3] The Indian scholar Sunita Jain has called it "a model of economy,"[4] and Lester Jay Marks sees it as "a beautifully written parable."[5] Lawrence William Jones has written that, in his opinion, "this well-made parable exemplifies all that is best in the fabulist's art."[6] On the other hand, Warren French represents the dissenting view, recording that when it first appeared, *The Pearl* was a "disappointment" to Steinbeck's many admirers, and contending that rather than simply being flawed, "*The Pearl* proved to be paste."[7]

French's judgment, it must be said, seems to be a minority one, as the above quotes suggest. The book has proved over the years to be one of Steinbeck's most enduringly popular works, as well as one of the most widely read. It has become an all-time favorite among the set books of many a high school literature course, and certainly it is eminently suited to that particular role by virtue of its aforesaid simplicity of style, content, and language, not to mention its comparative brevity. In the readership stakes, *The Pearl* has enjoyed one distinct advantage over Steinbeck's other novels in that it is the only one to have achieved prebook publication in a popular glossy magazine, appearing in the December 1945 number of the *Woman's Home Companion* under the title "The Pearl of the World." It was not until November 1947, nine months after the publication of the novel *The Wayward Bus* (which immediately followed *The Pearl* in order of composition) that *The Pearl* was published between hard covers to tie in with the release of a film version of the story.

In any discusison of *The Pearl* it is imperative to bear in mind its genesis and the circumstances in which it was written. Steinbeck first heard the tale that was to become the germ of the book while he was engaged on a biological expedition with his great friend Edward F. Ricketts to the Gulf of California in March and April 1940. In *Sea of Cortez* (1941), an account of that expedition, Steinbeck retells the legend of an Indian boy of La Paz who discovers "a pearl of great size, an unbelievable pearl." The boy is astute enough to realize that this fabulous object can provide the means not only to enable him to satisfy all the desires and needs of the flesh in this life (by providing him with the wherewithal to give up work, to be drunk for as often and as long as he might wish, to take a wife and as many mistresses as he might covet), but also to ensure that in the afterlife he would be popped "out of Purgatory like a squeezed water-melon seed" (he would guarantee his own salvation by the purchase of sufficient masses during the remainder of his life). But he soon comes to realize that possessing the means of acquiring such joys is altogether a different matter from actually converting those means into the desired ends. When he approaches the pearl dealers with his treasure, they act concertedly to cheat him. When, angered by their greed and collective duplicity, he refuses to sell, he is attacked and hunted, until eventually he throws the pearl back into the sea from whence it came. By this action he makes himself "a free man again with his soul in danger and his food and shelter insecure." Steinbeck comments, "This seems to be a true story, but it is so much like a parable that it almost can't be. This Indian boy is too heroic, too wise. He knows too much and acts on his knowledge. In every way, he goes contrary to human direction. The story is probably true, but we don't believe it; it is far too reasonable to be true."[8]

The story obviously made a deep impression on Steinbeck, so much so that when he visited Mexico with his second wife, Gwyn, in January 1944, while still working on the novel *Cannery Row*, and received offers from various Mexican film companies to make a film there, he began turning over in his mind the possibility of a treatment based on the story he had heard in La Paz four years previously. By the time he and Gwyn returned to New York that spring, a deal had been struck and he had committed himself to making the film "in Lower California with an all-Mexican cast and director and money."⁹

Between the spring of 1940, when he first heard the story of the Indian boy and his pearl, and November 1944, when he began writing his own version of the legend, much had happened to Steinbeck. He had been divorced from his first wife, Carol, in 1942, and in the following year he married Gwyn, who was to give birth to his first child, Thom, in August 1944. Accredited by the U.S. War Department as an official war correspondent for the *New York Herald Tribune*, he had spent June through October 1943 reporting on the war in England, North Africa, and Italy. For a time he had been assigned to a special naval operations unit during its forays in the Tyrrhenian Sea, and had observed at unhealthily close quarters the bloodbath of the Salerno beachhead. When he returned to New York and his wife in late October or early November 1943, he was physically and emotionally exhausted. Even so, he had worked through to mid-December writing up the last of his war dispatches from the notes he had made while overseas. As soon as these were completed, he began work on *Cannery Row.*

Although the presence of death hangs ominously over both *Cannery Row* and *The Pearl*, it seems that Steinbeck was endeavoring to block out of his mind the terrible things he had witnessed in England and, more especially, in Italy. If he wrote *Cannery Row* as, so he thought, a piece of escapism, referring to it as "a silly book that is fun anyway,"¹⁰ then it would seem that he consciously planned to begin writing works which would express a more overtly moralistic view of life. To this end he began increasingly to turn his attention to the parable form. The story of the Indian boy and his pearl was, of course, tailor-made for Steinbeck's purpose, being simple and brief in plot and certainly explicating a moral truth. Perhaps even more to the point, it provided a ready-made structure on which to fashion the film scenario he had undertaken to write.

Steinbeck had been for some time fascinated by the cinema, recognizing it as not only an art form but also one of the most potent of mediums for disseminating ideas and spreading propaganda. In 1941 he wrote the scenario for a documentary film, *The Forgotten Village*, shot in Mexico by Herbert Kline, in which he attacked the superstition surrounding folk cures and extolled the virtues of modern scientific medicine. The following year he was approached by the U.S. Army Air Corps to make a film about the training of air crews, a project which was ultimately shelved. At the beginning of 1943 he wrote a story specifically for the movies, *Lifeboat*, which was to be directed by Alfred Hitchcock. This whole project turned out badly so far as Steinbeck was concerned, for when the film was released in 1944 he was angered and disgusted at the way in which his original story had been adapted and altered by subsequent screenwriters and by Hitchcock himself. *A Medal for Benny*, a film for which he wrote the screenplay in collaboration with his old friend Jack Wagner, went into production in late 1944. He was disturbed when he began receiving reports that again the studio was not keeping to the spirit of the original screenplay. After the debacle of *Lifeboat* and the anticipated debacle of *A Medal for Benny* (and his fears about the latter film were eventually to be realized), he must have welcomed the opportunity to work on a film treatment and screenplay over which he understood he would exercise tight control.

Obviously, the legend of the Indian boy and his pearl would not, as it stood, provide sufficient narrative content to support a full-length feature film. In fleshing out the basic story, Steinbeck transformed the character of the Indian boy into the poor fisherman, Kino, complete with common-law wife, Juana, a baby son, Coyotito, and a brother and sister-in-law. After discovering the great pearl, Kino's immediate thoughts are properly not of the carnal joys that now could be his. Instead, he contemplates the joys of paying for his union with Juana to be blessed in the eyes of God by marriage in the church, buying new clothes, acquiring a rifle, and sending his son to school to learn to read and write and do sums. Coyotito's knowledge, Kino predicts, will "make us free because he will know—he will know and through him we will know."[11] But in addition to changing the character and the status of the principal protagonist, Steinbeck also sensationalized the events following Kino's proud and angry rejection of the dealers' derisory monetary offer. Kino's canoe, the sole means of his livelihood, is smashed; his house is burned to the ground. Not only is he attacked and wounded and hunted, like the boy in the original legend, but he succeeds in killing four of his attackers and suffers the death of his baby son before he throws the pearl back into the sea.

Steinbeck wrote *The Pearl* during the period between late November 1944 and early February 1945 while Gwyn and he and their baby son were living in Monterey, California. According to his own account, he experienced a number of setbacks before he managed to complete the work. In a letter dated November 30, 1944, to his editor and friend Pascal Covici, he complained that he had embarked too hastily on the writing and had been obliged to discard the first day's output.[12] He encountered several "slumps," as he called them, during the period of composition. Even when he was within a week of finishing the work, he wrote to his agents: "I still don't know if it is any good or a mess but *I think it is certainly a good picture.*"[13] When the work was completed and his agents had expressed their approval, he again confessed: "Naturally I am very glad and frankly relieved that you like the Pearl. It was so full of experiments and I had no idea whether they would come off at all."[14] In an earlier letter he had described *The Pearl* as "a strange piece of work full of curious methods and figures. A folk tale I hope. A black-white story like a parable."[15]

The creative difficulties ostensibly experienced while writing *The Pearl* are not immediately apparent from an examination of the holograph manuscript in the John Steinbeck Library at Salinas.[16] Steinbeck was a marvelously instinctive, or natural, writer when his creative juices were flowing freely, as they seem to be here, and the manuscript gives the appearance of having been written at high speed.

The manuscript, unfortunately incomplete, consists of 68 foolscap sheets, the first 21 written in pencil, and the remainder in ink. The first page of the manuscript is headed: "Trial sheet to be thrown away." This seems to accord with Steinbeck's account in his November 30 letter to Covici of his initial dissatisfaction with the first day's work. On the other hand, it shows that he obviously had second thoughts, for the ensuing manuscript text is virtually identical (subject to later minor revisions of spelling, syntax, punctuation, and paragraphing) with the opening paragraphs of the published book. There are two lacunae in the manuscript—the first covering several pages of the printed text toward the end of chapter 3 and the beginning of chapter 4, the second a few lines at the beginning of chapter 5—and the manuscript breaks off just prior to Kino's attack on the three trackers. A single note relating to the fight sequence—"The barrel flame made a picture on his eyes"—is tacked on to the end of the manuscript text. As with the first page, the whole of the surviving manuscript text, suitably refined and paragraphed, is almost exactly as published.

Thus we can assume with some degree of confidence that the John Steinbeck Library manuscript, although undated, is the one on which Steinbeck worked from November 1944 through February 1945, and also that it is Steinbeck's original film treatment for *The Pearl*, written with the double intention of providing the film backers with a detailed concept of what the finished film would be like and of producing a narrative which could be published in its own right as a work of literature.

This was neither the first nor the last time that Steinbeck employed such a double-purpose technique in his writing. Both *Of Mice and Men* (1937) and *The Moon Is Down* (1942) were attempts "to write a novel that could be played from the lines, or a play that could be read."[17] He wrote a third of these "play-novelettes," *Burning Bright*, in 1950 before finally abandoning the form. While in 1937 he had considered the experimental *Of Mice and Men* "a failure," he also expressed the hope that if, "with greater care and experience," such an experiment "could go further than experiment and become a practiced, valid form, then it is not beyond contemplation that not only might the novel benefit by the discipline, the terseness of the drama, but the drama itself might achieve increased openness, freedom and versatility."[18]

As it transpired, *Of Mice and Men* was the only wholly successful manifestation of the play-novelette form, despite Steinbeck's professed doubts concerning that work. *The Moon Is Down*, as a novel, suffers from the stage conventions and limitations imposed on it, while *Burning Bright*, the least successful of the three, is generally considered to have been a disaster and Steinbeck's worst book, even though at the time of its publication Steinbeck still maintained that he considered the play-novelette to be "a legitimate form and one that can stand a great deal of exploration."[19] He continued to be unrepentant a month after *Burning Bright* was published to almost uniformly bad reviews, and he wrote a defiant reply to his critics, in the course of which he observed that

> if a writer likes to write, he will find satisfaction in endless experiments with his medium. He will improvise techniques, arrangements of scenes, rhythms of words, and rhythms of thought. He will constantly investigate and try combinations new to him, sometimes utilizing an old method for a new idea and vice versa. Some of his experiments will inevitably be unsuccessful but he

must try them anyway if his interest be alive. This experimentation is not criminal. Perhaps it is not even important, but it is necessary if the writer be not moribund.[20]

The Pearl was another of Steinbeck's experiments with form and technique, and he set out to write a "film-novelette" in exactly the same way and for the same reasons that he had experimented with the play-novelette form in *Of Mice and Men* and *The Moon Is Down*. Indeed, he had previously experimented with the film-novelette, although only in a tentative manner. The 244-page typescript of *Lifeboat* could quite easily be published in its own right as a novel, but in 1943, when he wrote it, Steinbeck had not mastered, as he was later to do in *Viva Zapata!* (released in 1952), film technique as a method of telling a story and creating atmosphere. The *Lifeboat* typescript is essentially a literary work, merely providing the story line for the projected film. *The Pearl* stands at a midway point, as it were, between *Lifeboat* and *Viva Zapata!* not only in time but also in terms of Steinbeck's development as a writer for the cinema. As Joseph J. Millichap has observed of *The Pearl:* "Steinbeck's prose in the novel often takes a cinematic point of view. Scenes are presented in terms of establishing shots, medium views, and close-ups. In particular, Steinbeck carefully examines the natural setting, often visually contrasting human behavior with natural phenomena."[21] The trouble is that as a novel, *The Pearl* suffers because the cinematic point of view is occasionally too intrusive.

Most of the action of the novel is seen through Kino's eyes, and almost the whole of the book's emotional thrust is expressed through Kino's simple and limited conscious thoughts. At the very beginning of the novel, for example, there is a description of Kino awakening in his hut in the morning. Kino's eyes become the camera lens through which the reader sees precisely what Kino sees, in the same way that the audience in the cinema sees precisely what the film's director wants it to see:

Kino's eyes opened, and he looked first at the lightening square which was the door and then he looked at the hanging box where Coyotito slept. And last he turned his head to Juana, his wife, who lay beside him on the mat, her blue head shawl over her nose and over her breasts and around the small of her back. Juana's eyes were open too. Kino could never remember seeing them closed when he awakened. Her dark eyes made little reflected stars. She was looking at him as she was always looking at him when he awakened.[22]

The Kino viewpoint is not, however, uniformly sustained throughout the book. There are occasions when intentional digressions are introduced—such as, to quote two examples, the scene in the doctor's bedroom in chapter 1 and the second paragraph of chapter 2, with its description of the tiny marine life of the beach—but there are those other occasions when Steinbeck slips awkwardly from the subjective viewpoint of Kino to an objective authorial viewpoint, as in the scene when the trackers and the horseman stop in the road opposite the spot where Kino is hiding:

> When the trackers came near, Kino could see only their legs and only the legs of the horse from under the fallen branch. He saw the dark horny feet of the men and their ragged white clothes, and he heard the creak of leather of the saddle and the clink of spurs. The trackers stopped at the swept place and studied it, and the horseman stopped. The horse flung his head up against the bit and the bit-roller clinked under his tongue and the horse snorted. Then the dark trackers turned and studied the horse and watched his ears.[23]

Although perfectly acceptable in cinematic terms, such an abrupt switch from subjective to objective viewpoint, when we have been conditioned to the idea that Kino's range of vision is severely restricted and he can see only the legs of the trackers and of the horse, is momentarily distracting and ruptures our complete identification with Kino, if not our continuing awareness and appreciation of his predicament.

While most of the cinematic techniques reflected in *The Pearl* are perfectly acceptable, and in some cases they work wonderfully well, the use of "theme music" as a means of pointing to a mood or emotion or to concentrate on a particular object does seem rather artificial on the page. The aural repetition of certain musical themes by way of background music is markedly more unobtrusive but more insidiously effective in registering on the subconscious of the individual members of a cinema audience than is the stark repetition of printed words on the eyes of the reader. In *The Pearl* we are introduced to the Song of the Family, the Song of Evil, the Song of the Enemy, the Song of the Pearl

That Might Be, the Song of the Undersea, and, of course, the music of the pearl itself. This use of "music" was an experimental device that Steinbeck had applied more subtly in *Cannery Row* during the episode when Doc discovers the drowned body of the beautiful young girl in the La Jolla tide pool and hears the "high thin piercingly sweet flute carrying a melody he could never remember."[24] It was a device that Steinbeck was to use again in the "tones" or "voices" that Doc hears within himself in *Sweet Thursday* (1954), the "sequel" to *Cannery Row*.

Despite these reservations, *The Pearl* works more successfully as a novel in its own right than does either *The Moon Is Down* or *Burning Bright*. The confinement to stage-setting interiors which bedevil those two books disappears in the far-ranging outdoor action of *The Pearl*. So from this point of view, at least, it can be argued that the cinematic form and the novel form are more readily compatible than the play and novel forms. Yet the freedom that Steinbeck enjoyed to open up the original basic story posed its own problems—problems he did not entirely solve. He weighed himself down with so much specific action, so much elaboration of character, not to mention metaphor and inner meaning, that the original simple story line became perilously overloaded.

The dispersal of stagecraft artificiality does not, however, ensure that a more realistic atmosphere will automatically pervade the work. We should bear in mind that Steinbeck consistently referred to *The Pearl* as a parable. If we attempt to consider the book solely as a work of realism, we find ourselves in immediate difficulties, for there is some justification in maintaining that Steinbeck failed to establish his characters in a completely believable set of circumstances. If one is to believe in the reality of the whole, one has to be able to believe in the reality of all, or most of, the component parts. In short, one has to believe that, against all odds, Coyotito would have survived the scorpion sting, that Kino could have so successfully and easily attacked and killed the three hired men sent to rob and murder him, and that one bullet fired more or less blindly toward the cave entrance from thirty feet or so below could have blown off the top of Coyotito's head as he lay under a blanket close against his mother's back.

Perhaps even more important from the realistic point of view, the principal problem that Steinbeck did not and could not solve was to reach a credible ending to the book. He was, of course, saddled with that ending, for it provides the whole raison d'être of the story. But what has been altered disastrously in Steinbeck's overelaborated version are the events leading up to the casting of the pearl back into the sea. In the legend, the Indian boy did not kill anyone. He had no wife or child, no boat, no house. Indeed, he had no identifiable position in the community. He existed conveniently as a single human being without family ties and without possessions. After he had been attacked and beaten and tortured, there was a simple logic to his gesture in throwing the pearl—the cause of all his troubles—back into the sea: he just wanted to be left alone to return to his old, uncomplicated, peaceful, if poverty-ridden, life. But as French has pointed out, in Steinbeck's version "too many loose ends remain unresolved."[25] Steinbeck has weighed Kino down with so many possessions at the beginning of the story, has established his position in the tiny fishing community so surely, that it becomes impossible for Kino, by the simple act of returning the pearl to the sea, to regain the dubious Eden of his former way of life. We cannot ignore the facts that his boat, his "bulwark against starvation,"[26] has been destroyed, his baby is dead, and his relationships with his wife and his brother and the other villagers have been radically and irretrievably altered by what has happened. In choosing to ignore Thomas Wolfe's edict that "you can't go home again," Steinbeck leaves his readers perplexed and unbelieving. The implication is that Steinbeck wants his readers to accept that this is a satisfactory, if not a happy, ending to the story, but as French has pointed out, it is no ending at all. We cannot believe that Kino would be content to return to the environment from which he thought he had escaped, nor can we believe that he would have been unreservedly welcomed back by those he had, in his briefly assumed position of superiority, been forced to leave behind in his obstinate search for wealth. And what of the three men he had killed? Are not the pearl dealers going to exact some sort of revenge, even if they cannot now get their hands on the pearl? It is surely significant that at the conclusion of the book, of all the things Kino desired when he first held the pearl in his hand, there is only one that he possesses: a rifle, a symbol of violence which he has acquired by violence. Kino will have to defend himself with it. There is more blood to be shed, ultimately Kino's own. The logical ending to the story is future tragedy and death.

It follows that if, after due consideration, we conclude that the book does not convince us as a work of realism, then we should be able to accept it as the parable Steinbeck says it is. Here, again, we face a problem. In its purest form, a fable or parable expresses a single moral truth. In *The Pearl* we have a multiplicity of possible moral truths or quasi-moral propositions; for example, in the words of Saint Matthew, "What is a man profited, if he shall gain the whole world, and lose his own soul?" (Steinbeck's original title for the story was, after all, "The Pearl of the World"); one should accept one's preordained social station in life and not presume to aspire above it; pride goes before a fall; greed is never rewarded; happiness cannot be obtained through material wealth, and so on. Again, because Steinbeck has so loaded the story with detail, with various examples of human behavior, any one of these conclusions, or any combination of them, can be regarded as equally valid. Steinbeck has left the reader with an open-endedness which is not only unsatisfactory on the realistic level but on the fabular level as well.

Steinbeck's own ambivalent attitude toward *The Pearl* is clearly expressed in the brief introductory note to the published book. "If this story is a parable," he suggests, "perhaps everyone takes his own meaning from it and reads his own life into it."[27] It is possible that Steinbeck consciously set out to make the work mean all things to all men. On the other hand, there could have been a confusion of intent in his mind, so that when the work was finished, as his letter to his agents implies, he felt that he had failed in what he had set out to do.

If Steinbeck did fail, he certainly failed not because *The Pearl* is too simple a work but because it is too complicated. In it he tried to encompass not only three quite distinctive narrative forms (cinematic, realistic, and fabular) but also an overwhelming preponderance of identifiable symbols, metaphors, and philosophies for so slight a story. Strong echoes of the Bible, Greek tragedy, and Faustian legend are all present in the manner of the telling. If Steinbeck has succeeded, as most critics would maintain, in creating a considerable work of art, it may have been by default. A work that can raise so many passions in its critics, generate so many contradictory interpretations, elicit so much praise for the beauty and clarity of its prose, and give immense pleasure to millions of discerning readers cannot be adjudged a failure.

If, as many critics assert, Steinbeck's decline as a writer can be dated from the completion of *The Grapes of Wrath* in 1939, we should remind ourselves that he was never content to stand still and rest on his laurels. He rejected moribundity and boldly continued to experiment with new forms and techniques. *The Pearl* was just another stage in his development as a writer. If some of the experiments can be viewed as failures, we should still applaud Steinbeck for his constant and dedicated search for those new forms and techniques with which to enrich the texture and to extend the frontiers of the novel. He never lost the courage to experiment, and if this was one of his greatest strengths—and, some would say, one of his greatest weaknesses—it cannot be denied that it was also the measure of a true artist.

VII Sweet Thursday

Charles R. Metzger

16 Steinbeck's Version of the Pastoral

Many critics of Steinbeck's work are victims of what psychologists refer to as "set." Having identified Steinbeck as one who has written occasionally in the naturalistic tradition, these critics have gone on to measure all of his work by the special standards of judgment which attend that particular tradition. Inasmuch as Steinbeck is a highly versatile writer, one conversant with a number of other traditions as well—with the elegaic, the epic, the romantic, the pastoral—these critics have found a good deal of his work unsatisfactory. They have dismissed as "not serious" a number of Steinbeck's more interesting works for the reason, apparently, that such works are not true to the type which is the measure of their set. *Sweet Thursday* is such a work. Viewed as a piece of naturalistic fiction, it is admittedly less than adequate. Yet it appears to be a very interesting, a very serious novel—when viewed in light of the pastoral tradition.

Anyone rereading *Sweet Thursday* with the pastoral tradition in mind can recognize immediately several of the major features discussed by William Empson in *Some Versions of the Pastoral*. Pervasive throughout *Sweet Thursday* is that aura of good feeling by which Empson characterizes the "old pastoral." It is a feeling which implies "a beautiful relation between the rich and poor," between the educated and the uneducated, the intelligent and the unintelligent. As Empson suggests, seeing these contrasting sorts of persons so presented enables the reader to think better of both. This good feeling and this beautiful relationship are

Previously published.

prepared in *Sweet Thursday* by the author's working out the pastoral theme of resolution, which is one of the principal features distinguishing the pastoral treatment of humble characters and incidents from naturalistic treatment. Writers operating within the naturalistic tradition usually concern themselves with the theme of conflict, worked out specifically in the defeat of the protagonist-victim who blunders into a situation from which he is unable to escape. Relationships between these naturalistic characters and their conditions in life tend to be treated simply. The not-too-bright protagonist falls into a trap and is destroyed. He may be aided by a weak friend, a strong enemy, fate, or by any combination of these. It is clear from the beginning, however, that there is no hope for the protagonist, his class, or his group, none, in some of the gloomier examples, for mankind.

In the pastoral, relations between apposite sets of characters and their conditions in life are not treated simply; resolution is never quite as simple as conflict. As Empson suggests, the pastoral writer's attitude is a complex one, and his approach to his material is sophisticated and for the most part aesthetic. (This, he demonstrates, is so in *A Midsummer Night's Dream* and in *Alice in Wonderland*.) The pastoral *can* be condescending, demonstrating in rude form the superior "attitude of the complex man toward the simple one," but seldom in the better examples. In *Sweet Thursday*, for instance, the relationships between the various sets of characters and their conditions are revealed not only in the reactions of the complex characters to their complex world (including their simpler companions in it) but in the reactions of the simpler characters to their world, including the complex characters they encounter in it. When the attitude of the author toward any particular class of characters becomes grossly condescending, it ceases also to be complex; the theme of resolution cannot develop properly, and we are not legitimately prepared to think as well of both groups as we might.

In *Sweet Thursday* the principal resolutions of conflict between contrasting characters and conditions show up ultimately as realizations dawning upon the reader in consequence of preparations made by the author in developing his characters and advancing his plot. These realizations may be summarized roughly as follows: (a) that it takes at one time or another both the complex man's view and the simple man's view, sometimes both of these views applied together, to deal adequately with exigent problems of human existence; (b) that to live a beautiful life—i.e., in the pastoral mode—it is necessary to be able to accept (without necessarily approving of them) many different points of view; and (c) that to do this is impossible without arriving at a properly generous emotional condition. Seldom in *Sweet Thursday* does either the complex man or the simple one become irritated and express hostile feelings toward persons and points of view which he finds foreign to his temperament and training (as men do habitually in real life). Steinbeck's attitude, like that of most of his characters, is essentially the expansive, the generous, the aesthetic attitude which Empson suggests as characteristic of the pastoral.

These principal qualities of the pastoral—(1) the aura of general good feeling, (2) the author's and the character's concern with resolving (if only temporarily) outstanding conflicts between different characters and conditions, and (3) the dominant presence of an expansive, generous attitude toward the unfamiliar, the perplexing, the uncouth—all are qualities which *can* appeal to the learned and the unlearned alike. But they are not qualities either in literature or in life which appeal to persons whose learning or whose ignorance is dominated by a restrictive or exclusive point of view. William Empson's *Some Versions of the Pastoral* provides an unusually fine guide to *Sweet Thursday* not only because it advances some very intelligent observations about the pastoral tradition but also because it demonstrates an attitude which is depressingly rare among the learned, yet one which is unusually rewarding when applied to consideration of a term or a tradition. Empson's attitude toward the pastoral is appropriately an expansive one. It is unusual for the reason that traditions and the terms connected with them are most often viewed restrictively, proscriptively. Selected examples tend to become classic. Ultimately, only the classic examples are judged to fit accepted definitions, and only accepted definitions are judged adequate to describe classic examples. The end result is that both the definitions and the examples are idealized to the point of removal from contemporary consideration, and thus the tradition languishes because it has become esoteric and for the most part meaningless.

Fortunately, all it takes to revive awareness of a decent tradition is a little thoughtful translation, and this has been Empson's service regarding the pastoral. In viewing the pastoral expansively, he has pointed up what appears ingenious only because we have allowed ourselves to become so obtuse—namely, that the pastoral has not died with the masque but has remained with us in alternate forms. As Empson suggests, the pastoral as form has maintained considerable flexibility, even though most discussions of the tradition deal with it crystallized in classic postures. Thus the form shows up in unsuspected places, such as the poesies of Wordsworth and Dodgson, where it is no less pastoral merely because of our inability to recognize its salient features.

Examining *Sweet Thursday* as a version of the pastoral provides exercise in the kind of translation necessary to perceive the range of that tradition. Immediately, certain obvious pastoral features pop into view. We are struck by the incorporation of the formal masque into the design of the plot. Fauna, one of the principal sponsors of the masquerade, is not only aware of its appropriateness in Cannery Row ("There's only two kinds of people in the world give a masquerade—people who got too much and people who ain't got nothing"), but she is also aware of the tradition. She sums it up for Mack succinctly:

> "There was a queen a long time ago and she was loaded. Didn't think nothing of paying a couple hundred bucks for a housedress. Got so many bracelets she couldn't bend her arms. You know what she done when she had a birthday or a hanging or something?"
> "Overalls," said Mack.
> "No, but you're close. Dressed like she was a milkmaid. They'd wash up a cow and the queen'd sit on a gold stool and take a whang at milking."

The theme that Fauna and Mack finally choose for the masquerade is stolen appropriately from Walt Disney's vernacular *Snow White and the Seven Dwarfs*.

The pursuit of pastoral features in *Sweet Thursday* returns us repeatedly to Empson's essay. A quotation from the "Jabberwocky," as well as a chapter on "The Great Roquet War" involving behavior as mad as any Alice ever encountered on a croquet court, suggests Empson on Dodgson's pastoral. Hazel's role as comic hero, his attempts to live up to the responsibility burdening one doomed to be President of the United States, leading him to an uncharacteristic insistence on being Prince Charming at the masquerade (out of regard for the dignity of the high office of the presidency)—these recall Empson's discussion of the comic plot in the pastoral.

As in the old pastoral, *Sweet Thursday* involves an intermingling of rustics with sophisticates, of rich with poor, and includes in or out of costume a cast of nymphs, satyrs, Bacchic characters, and an appropriately pastoral hero and heroine. The nymphs appear in Steinbeck's translation of the pastoral as whores. This transformation of nymph into whore is not particularly strange: the prostitute and the bitch appear more commonly in American fiction than in American life; they are idealized, mythical, exotic figures that have a position in the public mind about as closely related to the real thing as a hamadryad to a woodchopper's daughter. The satyrs appear generally as patrons of the Bear Flag, cast as sailors or as members of the Rattlesnake Club down from Salinas on a memorial visit. But the noblest of the satyrs are not members of a formal group; they include old Jay the millionaire, whose physical description might have been taken from the balding creatures that prance obscenely on classic vases; they also include Doc, who doesn't patronize the Bear Flag—whose nymphs come to him, wearing expensive, fashionably tailored clothes. The Bacchic crew is provided by the winos from the Palace Flophouse—Mack, Hazel, and the boys.

As pastoral hero Doc reflects faithfully the image our culture demands of the type. To serve as image of our better selves, he must be a scientist. But to function as pastoral hero he cannot be just any scientist; a rocket engineer, a theoretical physicist will not do. He must be an outdoor scientist, dealing with physical nature sympathetically—viewing the echinoderm as only the zoologist can who classifies himself as a vertebrate mammal; he must approach insight less by means of numbers than words, less by means of words than feelings; he must be conversant with the arts. As a scientist Doc must be objective, but as pastoral hero his objectivity cannot be the negative or restrictive sort which reduces everything to mathematical statement; it must be the positive, expansive sort that tries everything, including powdered chocolate on fried eggs. Doc must be Henry Thoreau's kind of scientist—one who sees, hears, feels better than other men, who is the most scientific because he is "the healthiest and friendliest man." He must in addition be openly hedonistic in a way that would appall Henry, but that makes Doc acceptable to Mack and the boys. As pastoral heroine, Suzy is appropriately a nymph, i.e., whore, yet chaste withal; she is appropriately unlearned, yet intelligent—appropriately ingenuous, yet honest with herself to a degree attained by few sophisticates.

Examining particular characters in *Sweet Thursday*, we become aware that the relationships between them are indeed not simple. Steinbeck presents in his pastoral not only a network of interpersonal relationships to stir the soul of a small-group sociologist, but in the process provides a dynamic catalog of human types and conditions which contribute through their proper connections to the kind of resolution that is the pastoral's principal function. This resolution can be viewed from two levels: from the level of plot development, and from the level of conceptual exposition—concerning the expression of attitudes toward human values, of attitudes toward life. At both levels in *Sweet Thursday* resolution is approached through character. At the plot level resolution is a mere, albeit complex, matter of problem solving: Mack and the boys have a problem (they think the Patrón owns the Palace Flophouse); Hazel has a problem (according to Fauna's casting of his horoscope he is doomed to become President of the United States, go to Washington, and eat oysters). Fauna has a problem (Suzy has no aptitude for the sporting profession she has drifted into); this is also Suzy's problem (she's too big in the bust, too narrow in the hips, too honest, too independent, not lazy enough to be a successful whore). Doc has a problem (he wants to write a paper but can't because he's lonesome—he also needs a microscope). Old Jay the millionaire has a problem: he wants to give his friend a microscope but feels he cannot afford it (gifts to friends are not tax deductible); the seer has a problem: he is unable to get a completely balanced diet from the sea (too much protein, insufficient carbohydrates—he steals candybars). Steinbeck deserves more than a little credit for plotting these problems so that nearly all of them are connected with a single resolving sequence of events.

At the conceptual level involving the expression and evaluation of attitudes toward life, Steinbeck avoids the gross pairing of character types and attitudes which makes some pastorals more artificial than artful. As Empson suggests, the pastoral by its very existence *implies* criticism—of society and its presiding attitudes. (A desire to mingle with rustics implies criticism of the court; assertion of an ideal relation between rich and poor suggests that such is rarely the case.) Yet often in the pastoral, criticism is not left to inference but is stated outright. In line with the complex treatment of materials in the pastoral, Steinbeck criticizes our society and its attitudes both directly and indirectly. Furthermore, he sets up his judgments of our various measures of value, of well or ill being (of richness and poverty, of learning and ignorance, of intelligence and stupidity) not in terms of single characters or opposing pairs of characters—not in terms of single or opposing views of richness, of erudition, or of intelligence, but in terms of many. The characters in *Sweet Thursday* are, for example, both rich and poor in many ways, and the resolution of conflicts inherent in the usual polar view of such matters comes largely from Steinbeck's suggesting that there are many ways of being rich and poor besides the grossly fiscal ones.

Steinbeck suggests ultimately that richness involves simply having something of value, and poverty involves wanting it. Things of value include money, education, intelligence, friendship, physical pleasure, comfort, and love. By these measures of value Doc is the richest character in *Sweet Thursday*. Although he hasn't a large income, he manages to get by; he is never so broke that he cannot buy beer. He is rich in learning; the sea is his storehouse and he knows where everything is located in it. He is intelligent (as he is learned) both officially and actually. "I am a reasonable man," says Doc, "a comparatively intelligent man—I.Q. one hundred and eighty-two, University of Chicago, Master's and Ph.D. An informed man in his own field and not ignorant in some other fields." He is richest of all in friends and in his attitude toward his friends. "Doc was never bored. He was beloved and preyed upon by his friends, and this contented him. For he remembered the words of Diamond Jim Brady who, when told his friends were making a sucker of him, remarked, 'It's fun to be a sucker—if you can afford it.' Doc could afford it. He had not the vanity which makes men try to be smart." Doc's richness is secured by his expansive, his pastoral attitude. The only persons with whom Doc does not relate are Joe Elegant and the citizens of Pacific Grove. This is not accidental. These persons are incapable of the pastoral attitude.

Old Jay the millionaire is rich in the obvious way, but even his obvious richness is qualified; Jay holds some claim to learning in his own right. He is not a member of the ignorant rich any more than the Seer is a member of the ignorant poor. Both the Seer and Jay relate to Doc through their erudition and their attitude. From the Seer we learn that the gonads of the male sea urchin taste sweet, the female sour; from him we hear a statement concerning richness that informs us about all three men. "Appetites are good things," says the Seer. "The more appetites a man has, the richer he is." Although the Seer appears poor in the obvious way, his poverty, like Jay's richness, is qualified. He is a man rich in wisdom and sunsets—rich because he is "happy without equipment" and so only superficially poor. Both Jay and the Seer understand Doc's one big area of poverty, presumably because they share it. The Seer says simply that some tasks cannot be accomplished alone, without love. Old Jay says it analogically: "I think you have violated something or withheld something from yourself—almost as though you were eating plenty but no Vitamin A. You aren't hungry, but you're starving." Maybe, he says to Doc, "you can't be wholly yourself because you've never given yourself wholly to someone else."

None of the important characters in *Sweet Thursday* is rich or poor merely in the obvious ways. Neither is any central character learned or ignorant in obvious ways only. Doc, Old Jay, and the Seer represent not only three varieties of richness but also three varieties of erudition. Indeed, everybody in *Sweet Thursday* is rich or poor, learned or ignorant, intelligent or stupid in various manners and degrees. Joe Elegant, Fauna, and the Patrón, for example, possess three kinds of learning that fill major gaps in the continuum suggested by Doc, Old Jay, and the Seer. The title of Joe Elegant's novel *The Pi Root of Oedipus* and the fact that it is not "intended for the masses" suggest the kind of closed-circuit erudition which he represents. His is the exclusive, the esoteric erudition. Joe sneers most of the time, smokes foreign cigarettes in a long holder, types his MS on green paper. His erudition is that of the constipated soul straining at being different. His is not the expansive but the exclusive, not the pastoral but the provincial attitude.

Fauna's erudition is of two kinds: the esoteric and the practical. Even at its most esoteric, Fauna's learning is social. Although full professorships have been won in medieval studies from casting the horoscopes of Canterbury Pilgrims, astrology remains most alive in Fauna's vernacular, its social, form. At the so-called practical level Fauna's learning deals in table manners, ladylike deportment—instruction to her charges in the graces that facilitate honorable retirement from the profession. In addition, Fauna possesses that fund of shrewdly won insights into "the angles on things" (call it social geometry) which is the cause of her success and of the Patrón's respect for her. Fauna and the Patrón share this learning of "the operator"—deriving from an innate ability to see relationships which makes the simplest fact of life a usable, storable, resuable tool. Theirs is the learning that runs a Midnight Mission on a paying basis, that raises and markets a bumper crop of marijuana in the ornamental gardens at the Plaza of Los Angeles.

Even as richness and poverty shade into kinds of learning and ignorance (and every character, even Doc, has ignorance to match his learning), so also do the varieties of learning and ignorance displayed in *Sweet Thursday* lead to a survey of intelligence and stupidity. Intelligence is defined in *Sweet Thursday* both directly and obliquely. We see it defined directly in terms of IQ, of erudition, of academic achievement, of ability to solve problems. Doc, Fauna, and Old Jay all score high, viewed in these terms. Often as not (in real life as in the novel), intelligence is judged obliquely or negatively in terms of degrees and kinds of stupidity. Stupidity in *Sweet Thursday* is most often presented as a form of poverty, i.e., as lack of insight. Steinbeck suggests a variety of causes for this lack. The simplest of these causes, inattention, is demonstrated initially by Hazel. It is matched by that hyperattention to everything but the obvious problem which temporarily debilitates Doc. Opposed to the selflessness of Hazel and the hyperobjectivity of Doc are the defensive egoism of Joe Elegant (which rejects as irrelevant all that does not contribute to making him "different") and the more openly aggressive smartness of the Patrón, the "smartness that cuts its own throat." Steinbeck's critique of intelligence measured negatively in terms of stupidity cannot be left without a word about his view of institutionalized stupidity. Old Jay discourses on it with special reference to the tax laws: "The only creative thing we have," he says, "is the individual, but the law doesn't permit me to give money to an individual. I must give it to a group, an organization—and the only thing a group has ever created is bookkeeping." Steinbeck suggests finally that all forms of poverty, of ignorance, of stupidity relate back ultimately to the restrictive attitudes of individual persons—nonpastoral, exclusive, parochial attitudes.

It is hardly necessary to point out that *Sweet Thursday* is a very witty book; but it may be rewarding to consider the degree to which Steinbeck's wit is appropriate to the pastoral form. The trope of the pastoral—the oxymoron—is also Steinbeck's major trope. Although the oxymoron does not always indicate a resolution of conflicting terms, ideas, or conditions, it never indicates less than some kind of balance, and this balance itself frequently provides foundation for resolution. It is important in this regard to consider Steinbeck's uses of the oxymoron at successive levels. Its simplest use is as a complex term. The name *Palace Flophouse* is a case in point. "Inspired by the glory of having a home, Hazel compounded the name of something he knew about and something he didn't, the known and the unknown, the homely and the exotic." Most of the homiletic statements made by various characters and by the author represent extensions of the trope. Fauna suggests to Suzy that the "best way in the world to defend yourself is to keep your dukes down." The Patrón knows "that the only person you can trust is an absolutely selfish person." This tropological approach becomes the basis in *Sweet Thursday* for presenting the complexities of character which make people (whether real or fictional) interesting. Old Jay is "so close to reality that he has completely lost touch with realism." The Patrón is so busy being smart that he never has time to become wise. He is a wistful idealist; somewhere he feels there is "a profession illegal enough to satisfy him morally and yet safe enough not to outrage his instinctive knowledge of the law of averages."

The trope of the pastoral contributes to the development of the action. It plots the structure of complex events. It is Hazel the moron (watching "life as a small boy watches a train go by—mouth open, breathing high and light, pleased, astonished, and a little confused") who finally figures out the solution to Doc's problem—and he does so using a version of Gallup's method. Most important of all, the oxymoron structures insight. Through the rhetorician's artifice we are prepared to face reality, to recognize, for example, that awareness of our self-deceptions is a mark of incipient intellectual honesty—that beauty is inseparable from ugliness, richness from poverty, learning from ignorance, intelligence from stupidity—that possibly the most effective way to criticize society is indirectly, according to the pastoral mode.

Clearly Steinbeck does more than apply traditional wit to the expression of traditional sentiment; he transcends both. His resolutions amount to more than the mere assertions of pastoral balance indicated by the oxymoron. They have structural as well as ornamental functions and prepare for considerations of richness, learning, and intelligence in terms of a kind of psychic completeness. Although the major characters in *Sweet Thursday* are all of them both rich and poor, learned and ignorant, intelligent and stupid in a variety of ways and degrees, no single character has achieved complete equilibrium; none has arrived at the ideal condition of complete self-realization (C. G. Jung calls it individuation) which constitutes the highest richness. (Doc, of course, approaches this condition.) It is a tribute to Steinbeck's wit that it goes beyond the oxymoron (the trope of the Palace Flophouse, the trope of the pastoral) to comment on this kind of completeness.

Steinbeck suggests that all of the conditions discussed in his novel—richness, poverty, learning, ignorance, intelligence, stupidity—lead the person who experiences them—when they are unmodified by compensating attitudes and insights—in the direction of social isolation; and the richer or poorer, or the more learned or more ignorant the person is, the more severe his isolation may become. Empson in discussing *Alice* refers to this isolation—specifically to the isolation which attends "the self-centered emotional life imposed by the detached intelligence." (He sounds as though he was talking about Doc.) Steinbeck suggests that this social isolation is not inevitable but may be avoided or at least mitigated. He does not suggest that isolation is bad per se any more than he does that socialization is unqualifiedly good. He indicates rather that the way to avoid too much isolation, the way to achieve a measure of psychic completeness, the way to achieve an acceptable relation with the rest of the world—in short, the way to achieve defensible richness—is by adopting some version of the pastoral attitude.

Louis Owens

17   Critics and Common Denominators: Steinbeck's *Sweet Thursday*

Chapter 31 of Steinbeck's *Sweet Thursday*, "The Thorny Path of Greatness," begins with this declaration: "When people change direction it is a rare one who does not spend the first half of his journey looking back over his shoulder." In *Sweet Thursday* Steinbeck is looking over his shoulder, for this slight novel, published in 1954—when Steinbeck had passed fifty and left behind the region of his birth and major fiction, married for a third and final time, and relocated on the East Coast—marks a major change in direction for John Steinbeck's life and work. With this bittersweet comedy Steinbeck said farewell to California, to Monterey, and to the pattern and direction of his life for half a century.

Understanding Steinbeck's movements between the writing of *Cannery Row* and *Sweet Thursday* can help us to understand this sundering of ties. In October 1944, immediately after he had completed *Cannery Row*, Steinbeck ended nearly two years of residence in New York by moving back to Monterey, the place of his youth, artistic maturation, and first successes. Before moving back, he wrote his lifelong friend Carlton Sheffield to say, "We are getting out—going back to Monterey. I've had a wonderful sense of going home, but just lately I'm a little scared. . . . There must have been a change in me and in everyone else."[1] Steinbeck's foreboding would prove prophetic. Within a few months of returning to Steinbeck country, he was writing to Pascal Covici to say, "There is no home coming nor any welcome. . . . This isn't my country any more. And it won't be until I am dead. It makes me very sad."[2] It was then that Steinbeck left Monterey and California for good, moving east to New York to finish out his life and career. Almost a decade later, Steinbeck country's rejection of Steinbeck would bear fruit in *Sweet Thursday*, a cathartic comedy written for the stage.

As always with Steinbeck's fiction, *Sweet Thursday* offers itself up to a reader in complex layers. The surface story, of course, is a romantic comedy, a work written explicitly for adaptation as a musical comedy by Rodgers and Hammerstein.[3] This is the superficial story of lonely Doc, the guy who needs a dame. In *Cannery Row*, Steinbeck's earlier novel about the scientist and the lost generation of the littoral, Doc was a "lonely and a set-apart man," the same anguished visionary found in Steinbeck's description of Ed Ricketts—the model for Doc—in the preface to *The Log from the Sea of Cortez*, a man isolated from his community through his quest for a nonteleological detachment. The Doc of *Cannery Row* suffered profoundly from the same incapacity for commitment to his fellow man found in Doc Burton of *In Dubious Battle* and, in a different but equally profound manner, in young Dr. Phillips of "The Snake." In *Sweet Thursday* Doc's loneliness returns, but much altered and much diluted. Now the quest for the "whole picture" that haunted the earlier Doc has vanished, and the unnameable yearning described in Steinbeck's portrait of Ed Ricketts in the preface to *The Log* has become a very understandable motivation in a lightweight love story. What Doc needs in *Sweet Thursday* is not a philosophical breakthrough but simply the love of a good woman. Suzy, the hooker of quintessential innocence, is the easy answer to Doc's angst.

To facilitate this simple reading of a previously complex character, the authorial voice—the implied author—of *Sweet Thursday* conveniently misremembers the Doc of *Cannery Row*, declaring that "before the war Doc had lived a benign and pleasant life" and "all in all, he had always been a fulfilled and contented man."[4] The complex, Christ-like sage of the earlier novel, with all of the despair of that novel's final scene, has become a simple man in a simple, sentimental world—precisely the material for a successful musical comedy.

Early in *Sweet Thursday* Steinbeck writes, "Change was everywhere. People were gone, or changed, and that was almost like being gone" (p. 2). Indeed, everything is changed or gone. Dora, the tender madam with a calculating heart in *Cannery Row*, has been replaced by her sister, Flora/Fauna, whose fairy-tale names fit neatly her role as proprietor of a finishing school for prospective brides which only the uncouth might mistake for a whorehouse. In *Sweet Thursday* Lee Chong has sailed away in what sounds amusingly like a quest for an easygoing grail and has been replaced by the comic, impotent villainy of Joseph and Mary Rivas. Mack, the painfully failed outcast of *Cannery Row*, has become a Latin-spouting, sententious bore whom the dropouts of the earlier novel would surely have stoned out of the Row upon the first "hoc sunt." Gay, the Saint Francis of the carburetor in the first novel, is very portentously dead in this sequel.

Sweet Thursday is not a "continuation" of *Cannery Row*, as Steinbeck once called it.[5] It is, as Warren French pointed out very early, a kind of potlatch, a selling out.[6] The sellout amounts to self-parody. In the course of this comedy Steinbeck parodies and casts off virtually all of the characters, symbols, and themes that dominate his fiction from *Cup of Gold* in 1929 through *East of Eden* in 1952. In this idyll the Christ figure, a sacrificial entity appearing throughout Steinbeck's writing in its manifold guises as Christ, hanged god, and fisher king, is drastically reduced, becoming "Mr. Deems," the giver-and-taker-away of roque courts whom the people of Pacific Grove sacrifice in effigy each year. "They make a celebration of it," Steinbeck writes, "dress up a life-like figure, and hang it from a pine tree. Later, they burn it" (p. 49). With the unmistakable allusion to *The Golden Bough*, this episode seems designed to deflate the figure of central significance in virtually everything Steinbeck had written to this point in his career. With Mr. Deems the heavy inheritance of *The Waste Land* is acknowledged and, for the moment at least, cast aside. That this novel is entitled *Sweet Thursday* suggests that Steinbeck has indeed shifted the terrain of his fiction to the day *before* Good Friday, to that part of our mythic history free of the burden of the Christian sacrifice, free of that weight of responsibility. Even Arthur, the lost moral center of *Tortilla Flat* and a type of Christ, is parodied in *Sweet Thursday* in the form of Gay, dead in a foreign war, leaving behind his canopied bed as an ironic siege perilous: "No one had ever been allowed to sit or sleep in Gay's bed. He might return one day, the boys thought, even though he was reported dead, and his Army insurance paid" (p. 167).

The list of deflations is extensive. The sea, that dark pool of unconscious from which the woman of "The Snake" looms to threaten Dr. Phillips, the medium from which arises the vision of a drowned Ophelia in *Cannery Row,* and the darkly Jungian night-sea of *Once There Was a War,* has lost its force in *Sweet Thursday.* The levels of consciousness in conflict within Doc now merely point him toward romantic love à la Suzy. The Palace Flophouse castaways—Mack and the boys—are concerned about proper apparel for a party. Even the novel's novelist, Joe Elegant, offers a coy parody of Steinbeck himself. The effeminate Elegant, posturing as he explains myth and symbol and polishes his novel, *The Pi Root of Oedipus,* may call to mind a young Truman Capote,[7] but he sounds even more suspiciously like a reverse image of Steinbeck himself, the writer so obsessed throughout his career with myth and symbol, and the author who, in a 1954 letter, spoke of a "projected book" of his own entitled "Pi root."[8] The bull's-eye Joe Elegant paints on Hazel's bare bottom suggests rather neatly Steinbeck's targeting of all of his characters in this deconstruction of *Cannery Row.*

Underlying this lighthearted sellout is a reliance not upon the Christian mythology and Arthurian romance prevalent in Steinbeck's writing but instead upon fairy tale. From Flora/Fauna's name to Suzy's "love apples" dress and the whole fairy godmother shebang of the would-be betrothal party (complete with wood nymphs), this musical-comedy novel recalls the world of Snow White rather than that of Malory's fisher king. This fairy-tale world may well be a realm of dark undercurrents, as Bruno Bettelheim's *The Uses of Enchantment* suggests, but in the case of this novel it is also one of magic and happy endings.

Sweet Thursday offers a pair of metaphors for Steinbeck's method in this novel. The first is that of Cannery Row reflected through a pinhole in Fauna's windowshade:

> The playful sun picked up the doings of Cannery Row, pushed them through the pinhole, turned them upside down, and projected them in full color on the wall of Fauna's bedroom. Wide Ida waddled across the wall upside down. . . . And a little later, Doc, weary, feet over his head, walked along the wallpaper carrying a quart of beer that would have spilled if it had not been an illusion. At first Fauna tried to go back to sleep, but she was afraid she might miss something. It was the little colored ghost of upside-down Doc that drew her from her couch. (p. 113)

Drawing the reader's attention to the novel as illusion, Steinbeck attempts here to undercut any reading of *Sweet Thursday* as mimetic realism. The cartoon Doc of this work is indeed the "little colored ghost" of the Doc from *Cannery Row*, just as the entire world of that novel—a "poisoned cream puff" in Malcolm Cowley's perceptive words—is turned upside down here. From the twin "peepholes" of *Cannery Row*, with their implied shifting of vision "from the tide pool to the stars," our vision in *Sweet Thursday* has contracted to a pinhole perspective of a comic stage.

And while one of the controlling metaphors of *Cannery Row* was the microscope through which Doc looked too deeply, the parallel metaphor in *Sweet Thursday* is the telescope which Mack and the boys present to Doc in all their splendid ignorance. Microscopes focus downward and inward, illuminating flaws; telescopes bring us closer to the heavens, gazing blissfully with empyreal vision. *Cannery Row* showed the poison in the cream puff; *Sweet Thursday* illuminates only the pastry.

Why did Steinbeck write such a book? An obvious answer is that he did it for the stage, and poisoned pastries don't go over well as musical comedies. That his vision had shifted from the deadly battle of the tide pool to the empyrean of Hollywood is suggested in a letter he wrote to Henry Fonda, star of the film version of *The Grapes of Wrath*, declaring, "You will remember also that when I was writing *Sweet Thursday* I had you always in mind as the prototype of Doc."[9] Another, more significant reason is that this is a watershed, a shifting of course, a satirical retrospective and attempt to cut himself free of the burden of California and Steinbeck country. The series of failed parties for Doc which culminates in the one successful gift giving at the end of *Sweet Thursday* may even reflect Steinbeck's feeling that the previous attempts to delve into the character of his closest friend and greatest influence—attempts registered in "The Snake," *In Dubious Battle*, *Cannery Row*, and *Burning Bright*—were inevitable failures given the complexity of Ed Ricketts. *Sweet Thursday* then becomes the one "successful" and final ceremony for Doc/Ed Ricketts, a kind of poignant and romantic farewell to Ricketts (who had died in 1948) and to that phase of Steinbeck's life and career.

On still another level, *Sweet Thursday* is an investigation into the role of the artist as author, a convincingly appropriate process of self-reflection for a writer involved in the kind of monumental mid-life changes Steinbeck was going through. Certainly Doc is another version of Ed Ricketts, Steinbeck's marine biologist friend, teacher, business partner in Pacific Biological, and favorite subject. Just as certainly, the Doc of *Sweet Thursday* bears a resemblance to John Steinbeck. Doc's writing method of buying legal pads and two dozen pencils, and laying out the sharpened pencils before beginning his day's work, is very nearly identical to Steinbeck's own method described with obsessive detail in *Journal of a Novel* (Viking Press, 1969). Doc's making and studying of the "little world" of the octopus tank suggests strongly the fiction-making process of the author, just as Doc's declared goal calls to mind the role of the artist: "I want to take everything I've seen and thought and learned and reduce them and relate them and refine them until I have something of meaning, something of use" (p. 62). Doc's removal from "real" life also suggests Steinbeck's concern for the effect of an artist's detachment from his subject.[10]

Mack's role in the novel may indicate still more sharply a kind of self-consciousness operating in *Sweet Thursday*. In the published prologue to the novel Mack is carefully established in the role of critic: "One night Mack lay back on his bed in the Palace Flophouse and he said, 'I ain't never been satisfied with that book *Cannery Row*. I would of went about it different. . . . I guess I'm just a critic.'" That Mack has indeed become a critic is amply illustrated by the alteration in his speech between *Cannery Row* and *Sweet Thursday*. While in the former novel Mack was a deep thinker upon matters of pleasure and survival, his speech was that of a social dropout and Flophouse habitué. In *Sweet*

Thursday, with his Latin flippancies and proclivity for spouting frag-ments of verse, Mack has become painfully literary and rather pom-pous. This is not the sorry Mack of *Cannery Row*—the complex outcast who sought refuge from the American Dream near the sea's edge. This is a musical-comedy Mack for whose critical approval the novel is offered. By thus characterizing Mack and drawing attention in the prologue to the critic, Steinbeck is attempting to make it very clear that this novel is a departure, the first Steinbeck novel written explicitly with the intention of pleasing the popular audience and critic. The message is, essentially, "I know what I'm doing."

That Steinbeck was thinking very explicitly of those critics who had consistently cried foul at his previous serious works is made even more clear in a variant introduction to an earlier draft of the novel. This introduction, entitled "Mack's Contribution," is worth quoting here in its entirety, for it is strikingly different from the published prologue:

A number of years ago when the book called *Cannery Row* was issued, it caused only a mild disturbance among the people it had set out to chronicle. In the main the complaints were that the story was not told right or that the best story was left out. There were some favorable reviews of the book, but as usual the good notices were forgotten in the rage against bad notices.

What infuriated the people of Cannery row was the reference to them by the unfriendly reviewers as "bums" or "derelicts" or "dwellers on the fringes of society."

Now Mack and the boys didn't think they were "the fringes of society." Mack went to the library and brought the reviews down to the Palace Flophouse where he read them to the boys, and the maddest of all was Hazel. Now Hazel hadn't read either the book or the notices. There is some question as to whether Hazel ever read anything, but Hazel got so mad when he heard the notices that Mack had to soothe him.

"I've give it a lot of thought," Mack said. "You just take it easy, Hazel. There's good critics and bad ones. The good critics like you."

"The sons-of-bitches," said Hazel. "I ain't no bum. Why, hell, my uncle was a deputy sheriff."

"Didn't he get sent up for running liquor?" Mack asked.

"That was after," said Hazel. "He figured he knew the angles."

"Well, I've laid out a lot of time on critics," said Mack. "Some of them don't listen while they read, I guess. They say like, 'over-ambitious,' or 'romantic,' or 'naturalistic doggavation.' And then there's one that writes for *Time* magazine. He says everything is a great book but it fails. Now what the hell does that mean?"

"The sons-of-bitches," said Hazel. "They got no right to call me a fringe."

Mack went on, "All of a sudden I began to understand critics. Hazel, if you understand things, why they're all right. You can even like them."

"Not me," said Hazel.

"You never understood nothing," said Mack. "Them critics I'm talking about are kind of like Hazel here," he said to the others. "Suppose I want to say something so that everybody will get it? I try it out on Hazel, because I figure that if Hazel gets it a two-headed calf will get it. Maybe that's how they pick critics, like cattleguards to the lowest possible denominator—"

"They said we're bums, they said we're fringes!" Hazel broke in.

"Now you calm down," said Mack. "It's only natural for critics to think society's made up of critics." He turned to Eddie and Whitey. "If I was to tell Hazel there was a bunch of guys that don't do nothing but read books and then quick write notes about them, why, Hazel would say, 'What a bunch of bums!'"

"What a bunch of bums!" said Hazel.

"You see," Mack continued, "Hazel thinks he's society too. So do I, so does everybody. I happen to think a critic leads a kind of screwy, warmed-over life. But I'm a lazy-fair kind of guy. I say, critics got a right to live."

"Why?" said Hazel.

"You got me there," said Mack. "I'll study it out and I'll tell you. But understand, I don't want you to get the idea I'm satisfied with this *Cannery Row* book. I guess everybody's a critic. If I was doing it I would of went about it different."

"You wouldn't of went nowhere," said Whitey. "Leave it lay, Mack."

So Mack left it lay. They all did. The war came along and turned

Cannery row upside down just as it did every place else. After the war was over, it took a number of years for people to drift back. Some like Gay never made it by reason of death, and some like Hughie and Jones just didn't show up. But the ranks were filled by newcomers and pretty soon they were old-timers. A new Whitey moved in so that the old Whitey had to be called Whitey No. 1 to separate him from Whitey No. 2.[11]

Much more direct than the published prologue, this introduction provides a more obvious indication of Steinbeck's attitude in writing *Sweet Thursday*. Frustrated by critics' repeated failures to penetrate the complex layers of his previous works, and the resultant myopic dismissals by critics such as the reviewers for *Time*, Steinbeck recognized an opportunity to make his feelings known. What better device than a novel designed for staging as a musical comedy? Steinbeck, rather heavy-handedly in this unpublished introduction and more subtly in the published prologue, is making it clear that on one level, at least, he is giving critics what they seem bent on finding regardless: a one-dimensional story aimed at the lowest common denominator. That critics would miss the self-parody, the profound cutting away from the past, and the analysis of the artist's role would be a given from Steinbeck's point of view, for his popular critics had missed all such subtleties in the past.

Sweet Thursday is, as has often been claimed, Steinbeck's most obvious throw-away novel. Within it he is throwing away a great deal. It is, on the one hand, an affectionate farewell to the waste land (which would not provide a central structure for a Steinbeck novel again until *The Winter of Our Discontent* in 1961), and it is also a farewell to Ed Ricketts and to the entire region that had formed Steinbeck's best fiction. It is looking back on what it meant to be the author of what had gone before, an examination of the artist's role. It is an ironic offering to the critic. It is also a romantic comedy. Collectively, these elements turn a throwaway into a tour de force.

Richard Astro

18   Steinbeck's Bittersweet Thursday

John Steinbeck, author of over a dozen novels, three play-novelettes, numerous short stories, four full-length travelogues, and a host of other short works of nonfiction, is now dead. In general, the critical appraisal of his work is that he wrote one great book (*The Grapes of Wrath*), two or three good ones (*Tortilla Flat*, *Cannery Row*, and *Of Mice and Men*), and many bad ones. Indeed, almost without exception, Steinbeck's critics have condemned all of his writings since the mid-1940s, charging that they are contrived, hastily written, and best forgotten.

For the most part, this harsh critical evaluation of Steinbeck's most recent writings is valid; for Steinbeck's novels, short stories, and nonfiction works written during the past two decades lack both the wide thematic range and the stylistic adroitness of his greatest novels. Interestingly enough, however, these critics have singled out *Sweet Thursday* for particular condemnation, a work they regard as a weak, sentimental comedy which degrades the fictional materials which in *Cannery Row* helped to establish Steinbeck's reputation as a significant novelist.[1] Indeed, Warren French calls *Sweet Thursday* "a tired book,"[2] and Brendan Gill cites the novel as evidence to support his claim that Steinbeck's "talent diminishes from book to book."[3]

Steinbeck consistently rejected this sort of critical charge that demanded that each of his novels conform to a set thematic or structural format established in his earlier works. "Since by the process of writing a book I have outgrown that book," he notes in "Critics, Critics, Burning Bright," "I have not written two books alike. Where would be the interest in that?"[4]

Despite the critical disenchantment with Steinbeck's alleged inconsistency and so-called lack of pattern, his body of work contains what Emerson points to in "Self-Reliance" with his splendid metaphor of the best ship following a "zigzag line of a hundred tacks," which when seen from "a sufficient distance," straightens itself out; beneath the variety,

Previously published.

the lack of pattern, there is a harmonious agreement which occurs with a little height of thought.[5]

In Steinbeck's California novels, this pattern, this straightened line that resolves all zigzags, involves the thematic representation of a single era in American culture in which the earlier novels portray the infancy and development to maturity of a society which emphasizes human brotherhood and advocates man's kinship to and identification with the processes of nature and the human struggle for method, direction, and dignity, and in which the later works describe its gradual decay and eventual death. And in this context, *Sweet Thursday* serves as the climactic and bitter lament of the death of an era that Steinbeck revered and loved: it demonstrates how the demands of a new age have usurped and redirected those people and things from the past which they have not been able to destroy.

To be sure, on the surface *Sweet Thursday* is a sentimental novel. The crucial point in this regard, however, is the source of this obvious sentimentality, which, upon closer inspection, seems to reside less in the author himself than in his characters. In other words, in this novel, unlike in *Cannery Row*, Steinbeck seems to stand at a distance from the characters; and he shows how, in an age in which all the older forms of meaning and direction have been destroyed, they seek refuge in what they (and not Steinbeck) regard as a bit of harmless sentiment. *Sweet Thursday* is thus an ironic novel, for beneath the apparent jocularity and the characters' sentimentality is Steinbeck's disturbing picture of defeat, of frustration toward a world that has either consumed or annihilated the people and the type of existence the novelist loved most.

For one thing, *Sweet Thursday* is not merely a sequel to *Cannery Row*, for beyond the superficial similarities of setting and character is Steinbeck's obvious redefinition of the role nature (a crucial factor in the thematic designs of many Steinbeck novels) plays in the makeup of the setting and in the perceptions of the characters.[6] Even a cursory reading of *Sweet Thursday* reveals that Steinbeck is not nearly so preoccupied with nature and natural phenomena in this book as in *Cannery Row*. Absent are the marvelous descriptions of the Carmel River and the California coastline near La Jolla. There is but brief mention of the Great Tide Pool which is described so vividly in the earlier novel. And absent also are the wonderful depictions of natural life inside the Western Biological Laboratory, which in their intensity heightened the character of Doc (the leading character in both novels) as a man and scientist in *Cannery Row* and which, by their absence, diminish him in *Sweet Thursday*.[7] In fact, throughout the novel there is not a single paragraph and hardly a sentence devoted to the type of description of nature and natural life for which Steinbeck had such a major talent.

Perhaps even more revealing than the paucity of nature description in *Sweet Thursday* is the obvious dearth of interest, at times bordering on disdain, that Doc demonstrates toward the marine specimens that he collects and preserves. Described in *Cannery Row* as a marine biologist who loves his work in the tide pools and whose knowledge of these pools is intimate and complete, Doc now seems listless and indifferent toward his work. As Lisca points out, Doc is "no longer capable of sustained attention required for his work. He takes every excuse to malinger and is genuinely relieved when his specimens die."[8]

Doc malingers because of a gnawing feeling of discontent with himself which occasions him to question his basic sense of purpose in life: "The end of life is now not so terribly far away—you can see it the way you see the finish line when you come into the stretch—and your mind says, 'Have I worked enough? Have I eaten enough? Have I loved enough?' All of these, of course, are the foundation of man's greatest curse, and perhaps his greatest glory. 'What has my life meant so far, and what can it mean in the time left to me?' "[9]

Doc still goes out to the Great Tide Pool, but he is no longer enchanted by what impressed him in *Cannery Row* as "a fabulous place" where "the smells of life and richness, of death and digestion, of decay and birth, burden the air" (pp. 17–18). For now, as he works among the rocks in the tide pool, Doc's thoughts are elsewhere:

And sometimes, starting to turn over a rock in the Great Tide Pool—a rock under which he knew there would be a community of frantic animals—he would drop the rock back in place and stand, hands on hips, looking off to sea, where the round clouds piled up white with pink and black edges. And he would be thinking, What am I thinking? What do I want? Where do I want to go? There would be wonder in him, and a little impatience, as though he stood outside and looked in on himself through a glass shell. (p. 18)

At the heart of Doc's growing dissatisfaction with himself and underlying all of his self-questioning is his deep-seated and all-consuming loneliness and feeling of isolation, so that while in *Cannery Row* Doc was as complete a man as could be found in any Steinbeck novel, in *Sweet Thursday* he seems almost divided into thirds. Moreover, only one-third of him (and the most superficial, at that) finds any satisfaction in the natural marine phenomena which consumed him so entirely in the earlier novel:

> And there would be three voices singing in him, all singing together. The top voice of his thinking mind would sing, "What lovely little particles, neither plant nor animal (plankton) but somehow both—the reservoir of all the life in the world, the base supply of food for everyone." . . . The lower voice of this feeling mind would be singing, "What are you looking for, little man? Is it yourself you're trying to identify? Are you looking at little things to avoid big things?" And the third voice, which came from his marrow, would sing, "Lonesome! Lonesome! What good is it?" (p. 15)

Formerly a holistic marine biologist endowed with both an understanding and acceptance of the natural patterns of life which enabled him to regard all forms of life with sensitivity, Doc's interest in his work has now become wholly perfunctory.

In short, Doc's methodical attitude toward his work shows that he has become what, in *The Log from the Sea of Cortez*, a narrative about Steinbeck's leisurely marine collecting expedition to the Gulf of California with his close friend Ed Ricketts (the real-life prototype of the character of Doc), the novelist refers to as a "dry-ball," one of those scientists who "are the embalmers of the field, the picklers who see only the preserved form of life without any of its principle."[10]

> He [Doc] picked up a pencil and wrote, "The observed specimens were twenty small octopi taken in the inter-tidal zone near the town of La Jolla. Specimens were placed in a large aquarium under conditions as nearly approximating their natural habitat as possible. Sea water was continuously filtered and replaced every twenty-four hours. Animals from a typical ecological community were introduced, together with sand, rock and algae taken from the collecting point. Small crustaceans were supplied. In spite of precautions, five individuals died within one week." (p. 29)

In *The Log*, Steinbeck ridicules the scientific specialist whose interest in nature is not holistic and whose scientific endeavors are limited to detailed and highly pedantic investigations of a rare biological specimen which "may be of individual interest, but he is unlikely to be of much consequence in any ecological picture" (p. 216). Steinbeck does not mention any specific examples of this type of scientific pursuit, but had he written *The Log* thirteen years later, he could well have pointed to Doc's proposed paper on "Symptoms in Some Cephalopods Approximating Apoplexy." In *The Log*, Steinbeck stated that "the true biologist deals with life, with teeming, boisterous life, and learns something from it, learns that the first rule of life is living," and that the true scientist "must proliferate in all directions" (p. 29), but the Doc of *Sweet Thursday* really cares little about his specimens and barely proliferates at all.

Although Doc's faltering interest in the tide pools might easily be construed as proof of his (or Steinbeck's) diminishing concern with the search for a meaningful purpose in life, Steinbeck subtly demonstrates that Doc still attempts to fathom the great mysteries of the universe, despite the fact that his efforts are futile. When Doc tells a very bored young lady about his virtually meaningless observations of apoplexy in octopi, her rather caustic suggestion that perhaps he should study human apoplexy momentarily rekindles his quest for greater knowledge and understanding. Steinbeck notes that "a flame was lighted in Doc."

> The flame of conception seems to flare and go out leaving man shaken, and at once happy and afraid. There's plenty of precedent of course. Everyone knows about Newton's apple. Charles Darwin said his *Origin of Species* flashed complete in one second, and he spent the rest of his life backing it up; and the theory of relativity occurred to Einstein in the time it takes to clap your hands. This is the greatest mystery of the human mind—the inductive leap. Everything falls into place, irrelevancies relate, dissonance becomes harmony, and nonsense wears a crown of meaning. (p. 17)

Unlike Darwin, however, Doc invests little effort "backing it up"; very little "falls into place," and dissonance never turns to harmony. "I want to take everything I've seen and thought and learned and reduce them and relate them and refine them until I have something of meaning, something of use. And I can't seem to do it" (p. 47).

Steinbeck portrays Doc as unable to make the inductive leap to an understanding of the whole which the novelist demands of his greatest characters (Joseph Wayne in *To a God Unknown*, Jim Casy in *The Grapes of Wrath*, and the Doc of *Cannery Row*), and the new Doc, finding nothing of lasting worth in the tide pools or even in apoplectic octopi, now rechannels his search for meaning toward new and, for Steinbeck, wholly unacceptable goals. In short, the Doc of *Sweet Thursday* is a new man living, as I will show, in a new world, and Steinbeck's depiction of Doc's lapsing interest in his work and in his growing inability to reduce and relate experience into something of greater meaning seems to represent the novelist's lament of the destiny of the good man in a sadly altered world.

Eventually, and with some help from the seer and Joe Elegant, an unpublished novelist who writes books on green paper with green type and whom Charles Metzger accurately describes as "a constipated soul,"[11] Doc feels that only romantic love can provide a possible avenue to meaning in the world. Told by the seer that "there are things a man can't do alone. I wouldn't think of trying anything so big without . . . without love" (pp. 47–48), and following Joe Elegant's advice that "he needs love. He needs understanding" (p. 145), Doc gradually emerges from beneath a welter of contradictory and ambivalent feelings toward Suzy, the reluctant and sensitive whore from Fauna's Bear Flag Café. He proposes to her, and the novel ends with Doc and Suzy driving out of Monterey on a collecting expedition to La Jolla, with the reader knowing that Doc has already "collected" the only "specimen" he really cares about any more.

Doc's insistence that he can be whole only with Suzy clearly shows that his shifting interests from the tide pools to a reformed whore has resulted in his drastic redefinition of the very essence of wholeness. In short, Doc has been transformed from the ecologically oriented marine biologist of *Cannery Row* into a more self-directed individual who has ended his search to discern the universal whole in nature, since he believes that by marrying Suzy his quest for meaning will be complete.

Doc's solipsism is further implied by the important thematic role Steinbeck assigns to the mystic seer in *Sweet Thursday*, a character who seems a latter-day version of the old man in *To a God Unknown* whom Joseph and Thomas Wayne found at a coastal retreat proffering daily ritual sacrifices to the sun. But while the seer in *Sweet Thursday* retains this ritual feeling for the sun, the ultimate meaning of the feeling has been transformed from possessing an identification with nature in *To a God Unknown* ("In the moment, I am the sun. . . . I burn through the beast, am the sun. I burn in the death"),[12] to the seer's highly selfish insistence in *Sweet Thursday* that the sun depends upon him: "I have to go to the sunset now. I've come to the point where I don't think it can go down without me. That makes me seem needed" (p. 47).

The seer is not, as Metzger suggests, an admirable Steinbeck character, "a man rich in wisdom and sunsets—rich because he is 'happy without equipment,'"[13] but rather an idle dreamer who has visions of mermaids, steals candy bars for nourishment (wisdom and sunsets are not enough), and who, as Lisca suggests, has shifted the ground of his metaphysics "from mystic concepts of the unity of all life to the doctrine of romantic love, which he prescribes for Doc."[14]

Moreover, and this Lisca fails to note, Doc's reaction to the seer is far different from Joseph Wayne's response to the old man in *To a God Unknown*. Doc is obviously impressed by the seer and ultimately heeds his advice about romantic love, but Joseph Wayne could not accept the old man's doctrines ("'His secret was for him,' he [Joseph] said. 'It won't work for me'" [p. 178]). In other words, Joseph discards a slightly demented seer's way of life in order to save the land (Joseph's version of the whole), while Doc, desperately seeking a new type of salvation, swallows the theories of an utter buffoon in order to save himself (Doc's version of the whole).

It is not enough simply to note the absence of descriptive detail in *Sweet Thursday* or to lay bare Steinbeck's portrayal of Doc as a "dry-ball" and solipsistic scientist in order to show Steinbeck's attitude about nature's faltering ability to provide man with meaning in the modern world. For before Steinbeck's alteration of Doc's character can be linked with the novelist's changed picture of the world, it seems necessary to examine both the reasons for this shift in character and to investigate his portrayal of "the new Monterey."

Most Steinbeck critics, with varying degrees of emphasis,[15] seem to agree that a major reason for *Sweet Thursday*'s failure as a significant work of fiction is Steinbeck's use of the codes of traditional morality, in the course of which Steinbeck degrades the Doc of *Cannery Row*. As Lisca notes, Steinbeck either tries "to destroy or desecrate his former mask," or, having sacrificed everything to his new thematic intentions, he loses touch with "the original vital purpose of his mask or *persona* and is unaware of the violence done to the figure of Doc."[16]

In spite of this general assumption of Steinbeck's concern with conventional morality, it is indeed difficult (and certainly painful) to conclude that in *Sweet Thursday* Steinbeck deliberately set out to demean the actions of a heroic character based on the life of his closest personal friend, whom he had praised so heartily only three years before in "About Ed Ricketts," a short piece which tells of his close friendship with Ricketts and serves as an introduction to the Compass edition of *The Log from the Sea of Cortez*. Rather, it appears that Steinbeck has merely come to recognize the futility of an inherently decent and intrinsically charming way of life, one which has become perhaps impossible in a self-oriented and wholly materialistic society. Moreover, Steinbeck's transformation of Doc from a holistic marine biologist and genuine lover of nature into a lonely and lovelorn sentimentalist seems a most bitter comment on the tragic destiny of the heroic figure living in a thoroughly unheroic age.[17]

Sweet Thursday does not, as Watt maintains, lack the "poison" or the sharp "cutting edge" of *Cannery Row*,[18] nor is it, as Edward Weeks claims, a novel of "good clean fun."[19] For beneath the apparent goodwill is a serious and pervasive undertone of regret and despair. A close examination of the text of the work reveals a substantial amount of significant evidence which verifies this hypothesis.

First of all, it must be noted that Doc's change between *Cannery Row* and *Sweet Thursday* has been accompanied by as great if not greater change in the basic character of the Row itself, which is no longer the center of the teeming and boisterous life of Monterey it was in the earlier novel. "The canneries themselves fought the war by getting the limit taken off fish and catching them all. It was done for patriotic reasons, but that didn't bring the fish back. . . . The pearl-gray canneries of corrugated iron were silent and a pacing watchman was their only life. The street that once roared with trucks was quiet and empty" (p. 1). A new era has been born on the Row; and in describing its inception, Steinbeck, in a vitally important passage, satirically suggests that the entire natural order has been upset and overturned and the natural life of the past age mutated or utterly destroyed.

> Looking back, you can usually find the moment of the birth of a new era, whereas, when it happened, it was hooked on to the tail of another.
>
> There were prodigies and portents that winter and spring, but you never notice such things until afterward. On Mount Toro the snow came down as far as Pine Canyon on one side and Jamesburg on the other. A six-legged calf was born in Carmel Valley. A cloud drifting in formed the letters O-N in the sky over Monterey. Mushrooms grew out of the concrete floor of the basement of the Methodist Church. Old Mr. Roletti, at the age of ninety-three, developed senile satyriasis and had to be forcibly restrained from chasing high-school girls. The spring was cold and the rains came late. Vellela in their purple billions sailed into Monterey Bay and were cast up on the beaches, where they died. Killer whales attacked the sea lions near Seal Rocks and murdered a great number of them. . . . And last, but far from least, the Sherman rose developed a carnation bud. (p. 12)

The fish are lying dead on the beaches; the desert is coming. "Everything is changed, Doc, everything," says Mack, one of several Monterey vagabonds who live off Doc's kind heart, and Doc's portentous answer, "Maybe I'm changed too," simply reflects the dismay of a man who has returned (from the war) to a moldy laboratory ("dust and mildew covered everything") and to an empty and diseased Cannery Row.

Again by way of comparison, Steinbeck wrote in *Cannery Row* that "the word is a symbol and a delight which sucks up men and scenes, trees, plants, factories, and Pekinese" into "a fantastic pattern" that converts chaos into cosmos.[20] In that novel, "the word" makes Lee Chong more than a Chinese grocer; it transforms Mack and the boys from shiftless vagabonds into "the Virtues, the Graces, the Beauties," children of "Our Father who art in nature"; and it makes the Great Tide Pool a repository of limitless forms of marine life and a symbolic manifestation of the universal whole.

In *Sweet Thursday*, however, Steinbeck ironically alters his symbols.

"The word" still exists, but it illuminates nothing. The Great Tide Pool has become lifeless and uninteresting, Mack and the boys are vagabonds again who wield baseball bats in the name of romantic love, and Lee Chong has left the Row altogether to seek a fresher world in the yet untainted South Sea islands.[21] Hence, Joe Elegant tells Hazel, another vagabond, that the old symbols can no longer furnish man with meaning and insight into life; that even Doc's paper (itself a more modern symbol than the word of *Cannery Row*) is now inadequate: "The symbol is the paper he wants to write, but that in itself has impurities. . . . His symbol is false" (p. 145). Unfortunately, however, the symbol the shortsighted Joe proposes to substitute for the paper is not "the word" but romantic love, which offers Doc a good deal of sentiment instead of the key to the meaning of life he once sought in the tide pools.

Additional verification of Steinbeck's underlying despair in the novel is apparent when considering the central doctrine of romantic love. Lisca, Watt, and Metzger argue that it is Steinbeck's solution to Doc's problem; in reality, however, the romantic love solution is not advanced by the author but by those characters in *Sweet Thursday* whom he consistently ridicules and seems to dislike. It is advanced by the crackpot seer and by Old Jingleballicks, whom Steinbeck parodies as a symbol of modern philanthropic waste, a fictional edition of an individual who, in "About Ed Ricketts," Steinbeck noted was one of the few people Ricketts did not like.[22] Moreover, the romantic love solution to Doc's problems is proposed by Joe Elegant, the author of moody books filled with "dark rooms" of "cryptic wallpaper" and "decaying dreams."[23] It is these men—none of whom appear in the word-ordered cosmos of *Cannery Row*—who instigate and champion Doc's venture with Suzy; it is they who turn Doc's outward-looking eyes inward; it is Jingleballicks who arranges for him to leave the Row altogether; it is, in short, they who literally hurl the cosmos of Cannery Row into chaos. Doc, beset by a host of faulty advisers, acts less in *Sweet Thursday* than he is acted upon. Rendered nearly helpless by the decayed world of the new Cannery Row, Doc is no longer Steinbeck's fictional persona, but merely his ironic victim, and his fate seems indeed less tragic than pathetic.

In his analysis of the role of Doc in the conclusion of *Sweet Thursday*, Metzger examines Steinbeck's use of the pastoral in terms of Empson's definition of that form in *Some Versions of Pastoral*, and he reflects that Steinbeck's novel climaxes in "good feeling" with "a beautiful relationship" which is occasioned by "the author's working out of the pastoral theme of resolution."[24] This resolution, says Metzger, is the romantic union between Suzy and Doc, the pastoral hero, whom the critic insists "sees, hears, feels better than other men," and is the "most scientific because he is 'the healthiest and friendliest man.' "[25]

It seems apparent that Metzger has his Steinbeck confused, for the Doc he is speaking of is the Doc of *Cannery Row,* not the Doc of *Sweet Thursday.* More important, however, when *Sweet Thursday* is evaluated in terms of Empson's doctrine of the pastoral resolution of conflict, there is, properly speaking, no pastoral resolution at all. For the only reconciliation that occurs in the novel is between a lost and desperate man and a senseless, decaying world. And surely this is not the type of resolution Empson had in mind when he wrote *Some Versions of Pastoral.*

Steinbeck portrayed a defeated, lonely, and, in the end, pathetically sentimental Doc only three years after he praised Doc's nonfictional prototype in a genuinely sensitive eulogy ("About Ed Ricketts") that was thematically consistent with *Cannery Row* and *The Log from the Sea of Cortez.* The *Sweet Thursday* portrayal of Doc thus represents the conclusion of a definite stage in Steinbeck's writing. The stage began over twenty years earlier with *To a God Unknown* and *The Pastures of Heaven,* when a young and inspired novelist championed a world of nature and the natural life and then created (in *The Grapes of Wrath, Of Mice and Men,* and *Cannery Row*) characters to people that world. In *Sweet Thursday,* however, this era has ended with the defeat of both the world and its greatest hero.

Although Steinbeck wrote four more full-length books, he never wrote another novel set in his native state. Moreover, the most recent Steinbeck (since *Sweet Thursday*) is no more the Steinbeck of *The Log from the Sea of Cortez* or *Cannery Row* than Doc, the husband and university researcher, is the Doc of the Great Tide Pool.

In short, Doc's demise is a mildly analogous fictional representation of a similar process that took place in the rest of Steinbeck's writing. (In "About Ed Ricketts" Steinbeck says, "it really wasn't Ed who died, but a large and important part of oneself" [p. xiii]). As *Sweet Thursday* ends, Doc and Steinbeck part company, forever. Doc and Suzy head south for La Jolla while Steinbeck turns east toward New York and Paris; all three, as Doc implies about himself as he and Suzy leave the Row, looking neither up nor down, but simply looking.

Steinbeck's last two novels, *The Short Reign of Pippin IV* (1957) and *The Winter of Our Discontent* (1960), lack his intensely honest observations of human nature. Moreover, in these works as well as in his most recent longer works of nonfiction, *Travels with Charley in Search of America* (1962) and *America and Americans* (1966), the genuinely simple and objectively clear and forceful prose idiom that characterizes his best writing almost totally disappears. Faced with the problem of finding something of meaning in a world which has destroyed or hopelessly mutated nearly everything he once valued most, Steinbeck plunges into the confines of traditional morality in a futile attempt to kindle new creative lights. Unfortunately, however, the vapid and inconsequential manner in which he deals with his new thematic material in these works indicates that the best that can be said about his efforts is that they show that his intense desire to find meaning in an increasingly hostile world persisted until the end of his career.

Nevertheless, John Steinbeck's stature as a significant novelist should not be minimized. For despite the many structural and thematic limitations of his latest works, and over and above the fact that much of his political material (which cemented his fame in *In Dubious Battle* and *The Grapes of Wrath*) is worn and somewhat obsolete, Steinbeck's best works contain a moving and certainly lasting statement of the nobility of the natural man who lives the simple, uncomplicated, and yet intensely meaningful natural life. Hence, while *Sweet Thursday* is not a great novel compared to *The Grapes of Wrath* or *Of Mice and Men*, it is an important one. For, by ironic implication, it portrays the destruction or mutation of all of those simple human virtues which Steinbeck admired most.

VIII Burning Bright

Carroll Britch and Clifford Lewis

---

19 *Burning Bright:* The Shining of Joe Saul

> And we are put on earth a little space,
> > That we may learn to bear the beams of love.
> —William Blake

The play-novelette *Burning Bright* (1950) is disclaimed by most Steinbeck scholars as either too abstract in conception or too contrived in style to read well. John Steinbeck himself dubbed the stage version "a flop"; nonetheless, the work remains a "daring piece of writing,"[1] and is surprisingly contemporary in its concept of surrogate parenting. But all is not new. The statement the plot makes concerning talking out problems as a means of healing is a well-established Steinbeck motif; so too is the emphasis on biological truth and the consequences to those who cannot make adjustments to the necessities of changing times.

A major question raised in *Burning Bright*, and in previous works such as *In Dubious Battle*, *Of Mice and Men*, and *The Grapes of Wrath*, is whether people can overcome traditional thought patterns, often unconscious ones, and so avoid their doom. In the works cited above, the answer is ambiguous. More than a few characters in those works share a heavy strain of pragmatism, i.e., judgment of the value of an action by its results. The exception to that is *In Dubious Battle*, where ideology, more than results, is the problem. The heart of the issue to be explored in *Burning Bright*, a story Steinbeck called "highly moral,"[2] is whether a man should be duped into begetting a child for another man, and upon asserting his biological claim, should be killed for a greater good. On a figurative level it is the id, or destructive part of one man, that is sacrificed so that another may prosper, in Steinbeck's definition as "father to all children."[3]

In broad outline the story goes as follows: Joe Saul, who is sterile, wants a child to carry on the family legacy. His wife seduces Victor, Joe's assistant, and becomes pregnant. Then she and a family friend, Ed, conspire to rid the world of Victor. With Victor's death, Joe Saul takes the child as his own. The story line draws its inspiration from an emotional crisis John Steinbeck suffered in 1948 when his wife Gwyn divorced him. Gwyn claimed (falsely) that his second child, John, was not his. Although John knew she was a pathological liar, her claim worried him a great deal and played a large part in his breakdown. His recovery may well have been dependent on the same kind of acceptance that finally comes to Joe Saul—which is a kind of rejection of ego. For therapeutic purposes Steinbeck left New York City for the privacy of his family cottage in Pacific Grove, California. Later detailed in *East of Eden* (New York: Viking Press, 1952) and *Journal of a Novel* (New York: Viking Press, 1969), Steinbeck's attempt at self-healing may be traced as well through a cascade of letters written to his friend and editor, Pascal Covici, who may have been a model for Friend Ed, guardian angel to Joe Saul. Ed Ricketts, who had been killed in an accident in 1948, may also have been a model. A letter to Covici reveals Steinbeck's unhappiness. "I still get the panic aloneness but I can work that out by thinking what it is. And it is simply the breaking of a habit which was painful in itself but we hold onto habits even when we don't like them. A very senseless species. There is no future in us I am afraid."[4] Two years later, in *Burning Bright*, Steinbeck saw the possibility of a future.

In Joe Saul (whose initials—but not necessarily whose ways—are the author's), John Steinbeck presents a character who feels "alone" and who is unaware that loved ones share his grief over having no children. Happily, when Joe recognizes the care others extend to him, he manages for a time at least to overcome his self-centeredness and to join the wider human race in the best way he knows how. Joe Saul is not the only character in *Burning Bright* whom Steinbeck draws from life. In *East of Eden* he uses Gwyn Steinbeck as the model for Cathy. But before that, he used her as the first wife of Joe Saul, also named Cathy.

Significantly, the Cathy of *Burning Bright* died some three years before Joe Saul's marriage to the beautiful and young Mordeen. In the drama Cathy is but a memory. In bringing new life to Joe Saul, Mordeen is modeled after Elaine Scott, whom Steinbeck married in 1950. Elaine brought to the marriage a daughter, Waverly. It is possible that Steinbeck's uncertainty about his true relationship to Waverly influenced the way he characterized Joe's attitude toward biological offspring. Of Elaine's relationship there is no uncertainty, for both the dedication, which reads, "To, for, and because of Elaine," and the text of *Burning Bright* testify to the contributions Elaine made to his life and art.

In creating the play-novelette, questions of art were at the forefront in Steinbeck's mind. He informed journalist Harvey Breit that he intended "to lift the theatre above the realistic."[5] He meant it. No one could describe the settings of Joe Saul's Everyman journey as realistic. The tent, farm, boat, and hospital settings—framed by poetic diction and allegorical allusions, and defined more by the characters' states of mind than by the trappings of place—are expressionistic in style, designed to reveal interior states rather than to mimic surfaces. Nevertheless, the settings function in much the same way as those presented, for instance, in *The Grapes of Wrath*. There, the rented farms as well as the lives are sterile, and the baby is born dead; the Joads journey by car rather than by boat, but the California they encounter at journey's end holds much of the same meaning as the urban port where the Sauls end their old life to begin as a new family; and although Ma Joad finds herself in a barn to begin anew and Mordeen in a hospital, both places serve as a nursery and as the threshold to renewed spirit. In the barn Rose of Sharon assumes the role of universal mother; at the hospital Joe Saul proclaims himself the universal father. The shorter and more cryptic play-novelette cannot succeed in developing character or charting ideas as well as the epic novel, yet each investigates the suffering in human terms brought about by the demise of cultural heritage.

In order to survive the death of old ways, the Joads and Sauls rely on a deep-rooted pragmatism. As Steinbeck creations, they are not alone in that. In the author's manuscript for *Lifeboat* (1943), a captured German naval officer is rescued by the very people his submarine had torpedoed. When those survivors learn that the German is steering them to another German vessel and their death, they elect to throw him back into the sea. In *Of Mice and Men*, the innocent but destructive Lennie keeps George's dream of living off the land alive. However, when it becomes clear that a mob will tear Lennie to pieces for having killed a woman, George spares Lennie—and likely himself as well—by putting a bullet in the back of Lennie's neck. Given the ethics of warfare, the survivors of *Lifeboat* will more than likely go on living without guilt. But given the sensitivity of a George or a Joe Saul, life after homicide will surely carry with it the sting of misgivings and sweat of nightmares. Happiness has its price.

The gift of a future for our "senseless species" that was beyond Steinbeck's vision in 1948 was even more remote in 1934, when he wrote *In Dubious Battle*. A modernized version of Milton's *Paradise Lost*, *In Dubious Battle* is in turn updated through the allusions Steinbeck makes to the cosmos of William Blake in shaping the plot of *Burning Bright*. In alluding to Milton and Blake, Steinbeck leads his audience to think upon the problem of good and evil, but through his treatment he narrows the problem to that of love and hate, to the passions which shape lives as they are humanly lived. Doc Burton of *In Dubious Battle* is the philosophical cousin of Friend Ed in *Burning Bright*. Doc explains to a Communist party official why social reforms do not address the underlying causes of social problems: "Man has engaged in a blind and fearful struggle out of a past he can't remember, into a future he can't foresee and understand. And man has met and defeated every obstacle, every enemy except one. He cannot win over himself. . . . Psychologists say a man's self-love is balanced neatly with self-hate. Mankind must be the same. We fight ourselves and we win only by killing every man."[6]

In balance and out, self-love and self-hate reappear in the respective figures of Friend Ed and Victor, and, as attributes, in the character of Joe Saul himself. In a crucial scene with Mordeen, when Victor has the choice of tempering his pride so as to live among men, he cannot win over himself, and so he is doomed. Joe Saul chooses otherwise and explains himself in figurative language: "our ugly little species, weak and ugly, torn with insanities, violent and quarrelsome [is still alive]. . . . I've walked into some kind of hell and out. The spark continues. . . . survived even the self-murdering instinct."[7]

Convinced that economic inequality was the problem, no one listens to Doc Burton's psychological critique—certainly not the young Jim Nolan, who, like Victor, suffers from an inability to develop warm human relationships. A difference is that Nolan has the illusion that he serves the party and the good of mankind when he actually benefits only himself. Victor has no such inclinations: He lives for victory over others to serve himself. Each dies at the hand of someone else, one willingly, the other ignominiously. Nolan's martyrdom helps no one. But Victor's murder clears the way for another of "our ugly little species" to glow— briefly anyway—with the "spark" of love.

Thus the theme we shall examine in *Burning Bright* is not so much the abstract one of good and evil as the human problem of hate and love. Steinbeck's fiction reveals that the struggle for a full life calls for sacrifices and even death. Mordeen sacrifices her wifely integrity, or at least the traditional view of such, to produce an offspring for her husband. And Joe Saul gives up his excessive pride in and craving for a biological heir to accept another man's child as his responsibility.

Like a medieval morality play, *Burning Bright* is fashioned from a soul-struggle plot. In creating a story where the characters exist as both themselves and as attributes of one another in the balancing act of becoming whole, and where what happens might happen to anyone, Steinbeck borrowed *Everyman*, from the medieval morality play, as his working title.[8] To amplify his point that in modern times it is not God who summons man for an accounting but man himself, Steinbeck has lifted outright from the fifteenth-century morality play the figures of Cousin (Will), Strength (Victor), Knowledge and Fellowship (Friend Ed), and the Doctor (Zorn). The nature and function of those figures vary but slightly from the original, although Victor features as well as the qualities of ignorance and selfishness. Steinbeck has updated the figure of Everyman, ostensibly Joe Saul, by sketching him in word and deed as little different from those about him. Indeed, in that Strength, Knowledge, and Will are *attributes* of Everyman as well as, in the allegorical sense, autonomous figures, a considered reference to them is most helpful in comprehending Victor, Friend Ed, and Cousin Will in terms of Joe Saul himself. To that end Steinbeck has not only paraphrased some telling dialogue but has duplicated as well the order in which the relevant allegorical figures exit from Everyman's life.

Less than a year before the opening action of *Burning Bright*, Cousin Will "missed the net" (p. 20), and so left Joe Saul with no living relatives to support his belief that bloodline wisdom is the one and only true thing in life to count on. Mocking that belief, the Cousin of Everyman

exits with the line "I will deceive you in your most need."[9] With the
demise of his cousin, Joe Saul loses the will to face the truth of himself,
not to mention that of those he counts on. Victor is the next to depart.
Like Strength, who calls Everyman "a fool to complain" and says, "Go
thrust thee into the ground!" (p. 231, l. 824), Victor exists with both the
attitude that Joe Saul's "constant talk about blood and family" is foolish
and with the threat that he will surely tell Joe Saul about the child,
which, if carried out, would have the same effect as the curse Strength
hurls at "old" Everyman. But with the loss of Strength comes the gain
of Knowledge. For Joe Saul, knowledge comes in two forms: (1) the
scientific fact that his sperm is dead, and (2) the insight expressed by the
Doctor in *Everyman* to "forsake Pride, for he deceiveth you in the end"
(p. 233, l. 904), and intensified by Friend Ed with the words "You crush
loveliness on the rocks of your stinking pride" (p. 98), said just after
Victor is killed. Joe Saul learns. Hence, in a fundamental way the
action of the plot is Joe Saul's passing from ignorance to knowledge in
recognizing and accepting the energy of life, or the "gift of love" (p. 97),
which Mordeen and Child symbolize. Accompanying him on his passage is the wrath and pain and ultimate joy peculiar to a triumphant
struggle with a troubled soul, and from which the metaphor of "fearful
symmetry" draws much of its force.

From the outset of action in the dressing tent, Steinbeck cues the
reader-audience to regard Joe Saul as a man whose interior life is at odds
with the straight face he paints on to show the world or to comfort
himself. Joe Saul painfully feels it is his duty to pass on the inherited
knowledge of his bloodline. Worse, until the end of scene 1, act 3, he
(not to mention his well-meaning wife Mordeen and Friend Ed) con-
spires to mask the secret of his "bitter seed" from those about him, and
from himself most of all. To accept his sterility and to recognize the
folly of his insistence on producing a genetic heir, Joe Saul needs help.
Yet the show-business atmosphere of the circus where he stars as a
trapeze artist seems to act in league with Mordeen and Friend Ed to
encourage him to hide from himself the awful truth of his infertility.
His cavelike[10] tent with walls stained brown and green and gray with
mildew, with only "prickles of sun" to light the "black dobe earth" (p.
17), is an emblem of man's primitive stage in the evolutionary process.

Nearly fifty, he disguises his age with liquid "dark hair dye" (p. 18).
Makeup is a requirement of his profession. However, at this stage of his

development, the powder Joe Saul dabs on his slightly pock-marked face is as necessary to his positive self-image as the like would be to any man in the street who worries about projecting an aura of youth and virility. At the close of act 1, when he—drunk—sees his unmade-up face in the large trunk-lid mirror, he reacts in much the same way as Poe's William Wilson does to his "own image . . . features all pale and dabbed in blood" by slamming the lid shut and breaking the mirror. On the gesture rides the tacit confession that his show of virility is all surface, that he cannot give Mordeen a child, and that, most disquieting of all, he cannot by himself reconcile his traditional notions of manhood with the biological fact of his dead seed. He falls asleep. And Friend Ed steals in to keep "vigil over Joe Saul" (p. 50), in effect, to serve as a reflector for what light remains in Joe Saul's soul and as a guide to his gathering up and acting through its positive energy.

Joe's dim realization of his part in a childless marriage has not happened with the suddenness of breaking glass. His first wife, Cathy, died childless, and for three years he has been married to Mordeen. He admits his sterility to himself, and says as much to Friend Ed by calling himself a victim of "some dark kind of curse" (p. 24). Even when fully made up and costumed in the image of male potency, he is not truly comforted. His nervous, "flexing hands" (p. 19) telegraph the message to himself as well as to Friend Ed that disguising the problem will not solve it. Yet, rightly or wrongly, Friend Ed in care and tenderness is as bent on keeping the "secret" secret as Joe. "Don't make him know [he is] a sterile man," he warns Mordeen, for "his self-contempt will settle over him, and you will never be able ever to find him again in his gray misery" (p. 41). Yet he tries to get Joe Saul to face his problem, to "let it out" and "go to doctors" for a possible solution—all without mentioning the issue of fertility by name. Shortly after that admonition, he apologizes to Joe Saul for suggesting that he might be too old to father a child (p. 25). In short, Friend Ed handles Joe Saul in the way any good friend or psychological counselor would. His approach is summed up in the line "I think I know your sickness but you will have to say it first, Joe Saul" (p. 21). It takes Joe Saul the better part of three acts "to say it," and until he does, Friend Ed functions less as an autonomous character than as a projection of the interior ambivalence of Joe Saul himself.

Indeed, from the first, Steinbeck makes it clear in numerous instances (of which we shall cite but a few) that he has created Friend Ed in the image of Joe Saul, and, contrary to the thought of one critic, not as God.[11] To establish the human but polymorphic identity of Friend Ed, the author costumes him and paints his face in a manner which mimics the essential features of Joe Saul; the "white face" and "white suit" of Friend Ed in act 1 is the "surgical mask" and "white tunic" of the transformed Joe Saul in the final scene of act 3; in the "Farm" and "Sea" acts, both are dressed in blue; and, most telling of all, the "astonishment" and "perplexity" (p. 18) on Friend Ed's clown face mirrors the "perplexed stare" (p. 28) of Joe Saul when he upbraids Victor for carelessness. And in act 3, scene 2, Steinbeck uses a word trick which appeals to the ear to merge the figure of Friend Ed into Joe Saul's. In white mask and tunic, Joe Saul enters the hospital recovery room where Mordeen awakens from "drugged unconsciousness." The narrator identifies him only as "He" (p. 103). But Mordeen addresses him as if he was Friend Ed, uttering, "Friend Ed, I wanted . . . him to have his child." Joe Saul responds, "He is here—and resting." The remainder of the speech clarifies that *he* refers to the child. But the ambiguity caused by the use of that pronoun is deliberate. For just before her "Friend Ed" line, Mordeen whispered, "Victor dead," to which Joe Saul replied, "No, Mordeen, not dead—here and alive, always." And there too the narrator refers to the masked man only as "He." Happily, the ambiguity does not obscure but rather articulates the identity of Joe Saul, and the argument of the plot as well.

Victor and Friend Ed are, respectively, manifestations of the selfish and selfless aspects of Joe Saul's soul—and each in the other manifests the "fearful symmetry" of humankind in general. Although perhaps less obviously than with Friend Ed, Steinbeck uses the person of Victor to reveal a side of Joe Saul which Joe Saul himself so little realizes that he makes no attempt to disguise it, and that is, as Friend Ed points out, his "twisted sense of importance" (p. 97). In his self-centered lust for progeny, Joe hardly acknowledges the biological connection between Mordeen and the baby she is to have, never refers to it as "hers," celebrates her pregnancy with the words "my immortality is preserved" (p. 62), and goes to buy her a gift[12] with the proclamation "My joy requires a symbol" (p. 66). Although cushioned by a deeply felt affection, his attitude is like that of Victor, who says, "I *cannot* . . . stand by like a cuckolded goat and see my woman and child in Joe Saul's arms" (p. 88).

In "white T-shirt and bandaged wrist" (p. 28), and without costume or makeup, Victor stands as the potent male and primal youth that Joe Saul in his passion for immortality would like to be but cannot be, pose how he may. Both men have unusually black eyes. More often than not, both wear a characteristic face of either anger to the extreme of rage or of sorrow to the extreme of suffering. Both brag about their ancestors. And here too there is cause for envy: all in Joe Saul's family are dead, while Victor's four grandparents are still alive. They both account for bad fortune with the line "[it] might have happened to anybody" (p. 28), which Joe Saul utters as solace for his sterility but which Victor blurts out as reason for the carelessness that led to his sprained wrist. As metaphor, Victor's sprain carries the same meaning as Joe's spastic hands: mortal beings are vulnerable in both body and soul.

Blake's pronouncement in "The Marriage of Heaven and Hell": "Man has no body distinct from his Soul; for that call'd Body is a portion of Soul discern'd by the five Senses," sums up the allegorical symmetry which Victor and Joe, as complementary forces, represent in concrete form. To emphasize that human condition, Steinbeck casts Victor as Joe's partner in the circus ring, where without Victor's participation the show does not go on. Although Joe works by both instinct and technical training and Victor by technical training alone, in the ring they perform as equals. But from there on, and with Mordeen pregnant, Victor, the very picture of "muscle and strength" (p. 29), becomes subordinate, holding at best a position as Joe's helper, until he dies at the hands of Ed. In the time frame of Victor's death, Joe witnesses his own "dead seed" at Zorn's office. In accepting that blow to his pride, it becomes possible for him to hear out Friend Ed and to free himself from the "unfortunate *choice* [our emphasis] . . . to mis-see, to mis-hear . . . [and from] the "self-centered chaos of childhood" (p. 33) which trapped Victor. Victor never learns how to love. Mordeen makes an effort to teach him by defining her love for Joe Saul to him: "There are very few great Anythings in the world. In work and art and emotion—the great is very rare. And I have one of the great and beautiful" (p. 36). Victor responds with insults, and Mordeen serves a warning: "I want to tell you this. . . . I will do anything—anything—anything to bring content to him" (pp. 36–37). His response is to assault her in an effort to obtain a kiss. Friend Ed witnesses this and delivers a warning: "it wouldn't be good for Joe Saul to kill you—not good for Joe Saul . . .

he'd carry a sourness all his life. You're not worth that much to him or to me" (p. 38). But Victor is given another chance by Mordeen. After Friend Ed and she agree that Joe Saul could not accept his sterility and still love her, Mordeen indicates to him she intends to become pregnant. Perhaps she wants his seed. He refuses any commitment. When Victor returns, Mordeen tries using a parable about sharing to show how Victor can be accepted into the circus family. "I felt good when I could give something so frantically needed, and I was not lonely anymore" (p. 46). Unfortunately, Victor can only respond, "What's your story about?" In response to her oblique appeal for a mutual gift to Joe Saul, "Victor went past understanding, went into triumph" (p. 47). Having failed to reach his mind or to touch his heart, she tricks Victor into impregnating her so that she can save Joe Saul. At act's end, Victor's diminutive character has been established.

No one in this story of selfishness and love is unblemished. Friend Ed and Mordeen are driven to give life to Joe Saul's wishes for a child at whatever cost. Victor's and Joe's goals are selfish ones. In going after what they want, few holds are barred. Victor, out of pride in his youth, performs the sexual act with Mordeen; Mordeen uses Victor's lust as a means to carry a child for Joe Saul. Hence, because Victor's intentions were self-serving, Mordeen refused to acknowledge the child as Victor's, but instead saw it as the product of her act of will, her sacrifice, and so hers to bestow upon her husband. Nor does she inform her husband of what she has done.

Yet it is through Joe Saul that Victor discovers Mordeen's pregnancy. Strengthened by some whiskey, for reasons he does not understand he demands that she acknowledge the child to be his. "I've got lots of girls in trouble so I know *I'm* all right—this is the first one that will be born. Don't you think I have some feeling for my own blood?" (p. 69). When force fails, he appeals to her compassion by throwing himself on the floor at her feet. She consoles him as a mother might a hurt child, advising "Poor Victor" that when he is "open" and "capable" of returning love, love will come to him (p. 71). "In pity" for his loneliness she strokes his forehead in a maternal gesture, and he "put his cheek down on her knees" (p. 72) to plead that she come away with him to be his love. His appeal to her is one of the most beautiful and heartfelt in American fiction.[13] Steinbeck composed it in the counterpoint rhythm of "moving life" in the passing seasons, where "summer ends . . . and the arrowing wild ducks are driving to the south . . . [and] the white drifts [are] curving down to the silver ice . . . as the earth rolls . . . [and Mordeen's] bearing is nearly done" (pp. 72–74). Unfortunately, the dialogue in the work never attains this eloquence. In the duet, Victor's language of love is far more convincing than Joe Saul's paltry declaration: "See—I am harsh breathing like a boy. I'm full of you" (p. 27). And that is as it should be. For when Joe Saul sounds his sterile phrases, they tell of the deadness within. But when Victor declares to Mordeen, "I love you. And it's not like anything I have ever known" (p. 71), the open simplicity of his phrasing tells of new life within, of a joy in feeling that lovemaking is more than sex.

Mordeen responds to Victor's moving proclamation by sizing up his character with, "I wish you could find the *strength* [our emphasis] to go away." She adds a warning, "It's Joe Saul's child. . . . I threaten you, Victor." Threatened and unwanted, his feeble reply is of helplessness: "Mordeen, I love you. I cannot go away" (p. 74). However, Victor does struggle against this baneful love. He almost leaves. He does not know that if he leaves, as Mordeen states, the heart will heal itself, that when one goal is unachievable, man finds another to replace it. Friend Ed goes to the heart of Victor's problem . . . he "is young, and that's a brooding time" (p. 80). Acquiring emotional control is his challenge.

But Victor does not go away, and in the last act he attempts to kidnap Mordeen. No wooing here. He is "crazy. . . . And maybe I will go crazier" (p. 87). His "hysteria" grows, and he threatens to tell Joe Saul all, not caring that it will, as Mordeen says, "destroy three people for the sake of one" (p. 88). Mordeen offers an alternative. She admits that she has been selfish in her love for Joe, but "would try to open the family" and make him part of it. Her broadened view of family life is beyond his vision, and she realizes he has no room for compromise when he says, "You don't have a choice. Get a coat" (p. 91).

Steinbeck, it seems to us, has in fact given Mordeen a choice: to remain and observe the consequences of what Victor tells Joe. But that she will not do. Apparently she agrees with Victor that she would have to live with Joe's hatred of wife and child. She finds that as unacceptable as Victor does her offer of family love and friendship. Victor, Mordeen rationalizes, has elected to die. Survival of her "world" has become the issue. And like the Nazi in *Lifeboat*, Victor is hit and tossed into the sea. But there is no war here to justify killing. Legally, a man has been killed;

pragmatically, witnesses plead self-defense in an attempted kidnapping; and morally, the work argues that humanity has been served.

Who is the responsible party? Mordeen would have done it because she originally assumed responsibility for the pregnancy: "I did it all by myself. . . . What I have started I will finish" (p. 92). However, Friend Ed takes command, saying, before "I wouldn't take the responsibility. Now I will" (p. 92). Responsibility for the course of human action is the matter at hand. It appears that he should have been the one to provide Joe Saul with a child. When he hits Victor and throws him overboard, he does not see himself as judge or jury—Victor has done that for him. He is, as Victor saw him before, "an executioner . . . judging where to put the rope" (p. 65). Saul never learns of Victor's watery grave. And that gives the happy ending of the old-fashioned love triangle a modern twist.

Until his desperate efforts to kidnap Mordeen, Victor has not even threatened to inform Joe about Mordeen—out of fear, it must be acknowledged—but has tried to leave the group. Joe Saul, who knows very little of Victor's constant threats to Mordeen, says that "Victor's all right." Of course he is not. Even after Victor's death, Mordeen and Ed concur that "he was not evil" (p. 93). Selfish, ignorant, undisciplined, and ultimately "crazy" from his unreciprocated love, Victor succumbs to his limitations. Not evil but excessive pride, lack of will and vision, and an unwillingness to sacrifice something dear are qualities that leave him lonely and, finally, that summon him to his death.

To dampen the moral question implicit in the justification of Victor's death, Steinbeck relies on the mixed-identity trick of blurring the image of Victor with Joe Saul. Simply put, to Mordeen, at least, Victor is but Joe's lower body. More generally, in the tradition of allegory, Victor is Strength—in this instance a false version of it. And, yes, as an agent of action, Victor is himself. But fecund though he is, he is also in image and meaning a projection of the negative energy Joe Saul generates and suffers up until the child is born. Steinbeck illustrates: with the onset of Mordeen's labor pains, Victor's "hands won't be quiet" (p. 87); back at the barn Mordeen saw Joe Saul's "face hovering" over her, not Victor's (p. 70); and at the farm and on the boat, whenever she calls out to Joe Saul for comfort, Victor appears to give distress. In brief, Victor *is* what Joe Saul *acts* like until that aspect of him dies or—better—is submerged in the joy of the new birth. Without Victor, Joe Saul's "self-murdering instinct" (p. 105) would lack clear expression, and his emergence from "an insanity" (p. 104), or Victor's "craziness," would lack force.

Alike in their belief that fertility is the statement of manhood, Victor differs from Joe Saul in how he performs the sex act—and for that we have Mordeen's word. She tells Friend Ed straight out that in bed, Joe Saul is "gentle and fierce and—wonderful" (p. 40). Much to his dismay, she tells Victor that Joe makes love in a way that is "most beautiful and filled with energy, like milk," but that in spite of the pride Victor has in "technique," his lovemaking leaves her cold, for it lacks the one "ingredient" which Joe possesses, i.e., "affection" (p. 35). Mordeen's measuring the worth of man by his capacity to give affection as opposed to his fitness to procreate serves not only to distinguish her husband from his surrogate but also to illuminate the nature of the tiger and the lamb, or the "fearful symmetry" of Blake, which Steinbeck borrows as a working metaphor to define the nature of the total Self and humankind in general. Further, in highlighting sex as the act which reveals the total Self, Steinbeck brings Blake's abstraction about the indivisibility of the Body and Soul down to earth, and explains in a stroke why Friend Ed's comparison of the "shrunken sperm" with a "sick soul" (p. 98) tears Joe Saul apart: biologically flawed, Joe Saul simply does not feel whole. The converse is true of his wife, surrogate, and mentor: feeling whole, they brood little, and when moved to act, they do so with unflinching resolve. Understandably, then, if the reader regards Joe Saul as an entity, as a character with no organic ties to Victor and Friend Ed, his speeches will seem rhetorical and his manner a bore.[14]

But for a few outbursts of joyful exuberance at the annunciation of the child and its birth, what Joe Saul does mostly is to flood the stage with self-pitying complaints about his mortality, the demise of blood wisdom, and the thinness of book knowledge. Perhaps he was conceived too much in the light of Blake or after the wisdom of Blake's "The Book of Thel." Whether or not Steinbeck wanted him to, Joe Saul sounds very much like the virgin Thel who complains constantly that she will die without "use," and that although she is a "shining woman," she will too soon fade away from her "shining lot." Joe Saul echoes her lament: "My line . . . is dead. And I am only waiting a little while and then I die" (p. 96). When Thel visits her own grave site, a voice asks, "Why cannot the ear be closed to its own destruction?" When Joe Saul mourns his dead sperm, Friend Ed tells him to "stop mauling yourself" (p. 56). "We live not for ourselves" is the lesson taught Thel; have "the generosity to receive" Mordeen's gift of "love and beauty" (pp. 97–99) is Ed's sermon to Joe. Yet despite his penchant for self-torture, Joe Saul carries within the potential of self-redemption, externalized in the figure of Friend Ed. First, though, Joe Saul must subdue his rage. Victor's rage becomes Joe Saul's when Joe returns from the doctor's office to the boat, "legs apart" and looking "hard with rage" (p. 93), as if he were about to do a bloody deed. Indeed, he threatens to kill both Victor and Mordeen, who retreats to a corner to escape this mad Othello. Again Friend Ed intercedes for Mordeen. At first, when asked what is wrong, Joe Saul lies by saying, "I'm a sick man. . . . I have a bad heart" (p. 92). Metaphorically, he has had a bad heart all along and has indeed been sick with pride, with self-love. But his visit to the doctor required a great effort of will—even if done out of pride—and he expresses that and his newly realized independence from Friend Ed, saying, "I went all by myself. No one asked me to go!" (p. 93), as if announcing to the world that he has finally arrived as a force to be reckoned with. There Steinbeck employs the now familiar wordplay trick to tie Joe's display of will to the murder of Victor; that is, he has Joe echo Friend Ed's remarks to Mordeen: "I wouldn't take the responsibility. Now I will" (p. 92).

Unlike Fellowship in *Everyman*, who makes a show of loyalty by saying, "But and thou will murder, or any man kill, In that I will help thee with good will" (p. 215, l. 281) Friend Ed, seemingly unsolicited, does the job. Indeed, in both friendship and knowledge, Ed meets the supreme test. When Joe pleads, "For God's sake, don't leave me alone. . . . It's a new, an unknown road. I don't know that I can find it alone," Friend Ed replies with great wisdom, "You'll never find it any other way" (pp. 99–100). In every significant respect Ed has followed the medieval model of the Knowledge who swears to Everyman: "I will not from hence depart [until] I see where ye shall become" (p. 332, l. 864). His job done, Friend Ed, like some kind of spirit of Christmas, disappears at midnight. On the run, he may never again share the company of his friend, Joe Saul. No doubt he will find someone of equal stature to guide. Whether he will eventually suffer guilt for having killed a man in the name of friendship only he can know. But if it comes to that, he will likely find comfort in his children, the twins. Ed has left Joe at a crossroads, heading along a "new, unknown road," where darkness would overtake him were he to continue on in his self-centered way. But he chances, instead, the other-directed route to self-esteem and into Mordeen's new "world" where he might outstrip the dark, and shine. This modern Saul, like his biblical namesake, has witnessed a blinding light on the road to Damascus. Not the vision of Jesus *or* Savior but the miracle of love confronts him. From persecutor to proselytizer, Joe Saul's discovery is the miracle of life beyond the self. The message now is not that of genetic determinants but of free will and responsible choices. He discovers, as do Jim Casy and Tom Joad, that individual survival demands a concern for the community; the recognition of social and individual interdependence is but a little spark lighting and darkness of Joe Saul's pathway.

Like Victor and Friend Ed, whom Joe Saul embodies, the places of *Burning Bright* represent evolutionary stages of what Steinbeck suggests is technological development. However, in terms of both the species and the individual, the nature of that development is morally ambiguous. For example, Joe proclaims that the species is more important than the individual, but does so in a private hospital "cell" which, as cited earlier, is "cut off from every world." On the face of it, the clinical sterility of the place begs the question of just what is progress, and seems to answer, if the "impersonal" (p. 103) is the mark of progress, who needs it. The room cries out for some human touch. Although he is masked and gowned in white, Joe's voice lends some humanity to the place. His presence suggests that it is the passion of the individual, and not the achievements of the technological collective, that really counts. True, the microscope revealed a painful but necessary truth to Joe, and drugs, even if not entirely necessary, eased the pain of Mordeen's birthing. But nothing of science has shown Joe and Mordeen how to live. Through acts of will they won themselves a family, of which Joe Saul finds himself the head.

Through the familiar imagery of husband, wife, and child, Steinbeck signals that the family Joe inherits is a very traditional one, a private unit, a tribal cell—not at all communal—whose main concern is and always has been its own welfare and survival. The plot argues, then, that in the evolutionary process the idea of the family has not changed, and that the instinct to make a family is perhaps the one saving grace of any civilization: past or present, primitive or technological.

But Joe's self-proclaimed role as universal father, although wonderful in spirit, posits an ideal hardly shared and, if so, rarely practiced by any in the reading or theatergoing public; consequently, it plays as a pipe dream. The "white . . . silent . . . box" (p. 103) where Mordeen lies in a "gray ether cloud" (p. 102) appears, in texture at least, as a gauzy world of dreams. That Steinbeck has his protagonist reach out in the ethereal fog to hang the hope of the race on some sort of metaphysical "shining" is a trick which allows the author's voice to be heard without destroying the integrity of the protagonist as a self-motivated character. The hospital scene is the epilogue of *Burning Bright*. And as would be expected by the conventions of a morality play, Joe Saul delivers there his inspired message of universal fatherhood. Joe Saul is not a blatant mouthpiece like, say, the wife of Willy Loman in *Death of a Salesman*, who proclaims in the epilogue that Willy "deserves respect because he was a human being." For one thing, the dreamy atmosphere of the hospital room distances Joe from a direct relationship with the reader or spectator, and so dampens the sermonizing qualities of his speech. For another, the words of his speech, "every man is father to all children," translate immediately into the action he takes of accepting Victor's child as his own. In short, the message Joe delivers for all to hear is the best possible advice for him to follow—if he is to find happiness with Mordeen.

The epilogue completes as well his portrait of the protagonist in tones foreshadowed in act 1. The surgical mask Joe Saul wears to announce the "shining" is in effect no different from the "masks" his ancestors wore when they were mimetic "gods" of healing (p. 23). His kind of sickness does not require that he go "crooked for fits and spastic for poison" (p. 22). However, it will be recalled that back at the circus Joe's hands were spastic, and that Friend Ed prescribed "talk" as the remedy for Joe Saul's trouble, "Else it will grow with poisoned fingers like a cancer in your mind" (p. 24). Joe listened. And now, dressed as a doctor, or perhaps some sort of priest, Joe practices the art of sympathetic participation with the healing powers of positive thinking: he attempts to heal his wounded ego by submerging it in the impersonal name of Everyone, and, as added medicine, he wears the mask to mark his would-be facelessness. Not everyone will find a cure in Joe's brand of medicine, but from all appearances it seems to work for him.

In his journey over land and sea Joe has been alienated by a discovery nearly as shocking as that of his sexual infertility. Here in the port city he finds himself cut off from even a vestige of the familial world, where know-how was passed down by word of mouth and work was done "right" by human hands which neither knew "how" nor "why" (p. 55). He is lost to recent history and, as well, to the ancient history of genetic pride. Consequently, in order to root himself in a history which might need—hence humanize—his existence, he assumes the role as a particular father to a particular boy and fills a position in life that predates even the most ancient of professions, and which all recognize as worthy and good. With son at hand, Joe has come to feel humanly whole, and, if words speak, he likes the man he has become. Steinbeck marks the occasion by having him tear off the mask to reveal to Mordeen the "shining face and eyes" of Joe Saul (p. 106), husband, as well as father to the child she bore.

Lest the audience take the unmasking scene as Steinbeck's way of stating that *Burning Bright* is, after all, a work of psychological realism written to air the personal struggle of one Joe Saul, whatever the relevance of that struggle to people in general, he double-casts him as Joseph, old husband to young Mary, mother of Jesus. Mordeen delivers in the Christmas season. What with her lying at center in "a high hospital bed," and Joe clad in a tunic looking "down at the muffled bundle that lay beside her" (p. 103), they make a tableau in the image of the Holy Family in a crèche. (A crèche, by the way, is a kind of hospital.) And like Joseph in Matthew 1:18–24, does not Joe Saul name the child? And when he learned that Mordeen got pregnant by another, did he not, like Joseph, threaten to break with his wife, until Friend Ed, a kind of angel, advised him to accept? Mordeen is no virgin, and the child is not Christ. But to a man who is sterile, becoming a father is a kind of miracle. Steinbeck does not stop at the birth. He pushes Joe Saul even further into the mystery of the Christ story—to the Transfiguration in Matthew 17:1–5, where, like Jesus, whose "face was shining" and whose "clothes were dazzling white," Joe Saul not only "gives light" but echoes as well the "voice from the cloud" that said, "This is my own dear Son, with whom I am pleased—listen to him!" with the words: "Here he lies sleeping, to teach me . . . *I love my son*" (pp. 105–6). Joe Saul is not God. But he is certainly inspired by the spirit which Christians try to follow. Born again through the gift of the child, he may indeed find redemption and rid himself—or the Friend Ed in him—of the mark of Cain.

Indeed, there is hope. The male child may grow up to increase the species. The thought of the child growing up carries an awful irony, however: He may turn out more like Victor, his blood father, than like Joe Saul, and so begin anew a violent cycle in the struggle for selfhood. Then, too, the logic of universal fatherhood carries with it the conclusion that as Joe Saul replaced Victor as father, so too can Joe Saul be replaced. Hence Steinbeck raises two major questions: (1) Just what makes up a family? and (2) What kind of a world would it be without the likes of Joe Saul? In answer to the first he clearly demonstrates that what makes man and woman and child a family is sacrifice and love and, when the unit is threatened, violence. The character of Joe Saul himself answers the second, for he is, after all, an affectionate and well-meaning man, and he has in him more the milk of Mordeen and the light of Friend Ed than the darkness of Victor. And although he balances on a high wire of moral illusions—i.e., possibly blind to the price Victor, Friend Ed, and Mordeen pay for his happiness—he is above all a survivor. In a *New York Times* interview Steinbeck explains, "I believe basically that the human species is *inextinguishable*. The human is always under all sorts of pressures, natural and political. But nothing has ever annihilated him. There is always a bobbing up of the spirit. Take this guy [Joe Saul]. He can't have a kid so he finds some other way."[15]

Written during the Cold War, it is easy to imagine that Steinbeck had in mind the annihilation of the world by nuclear fire when he settled on the title *Burning Bright*. The age seemed to call out for another Bethlehem. To argue the hopeful possibility, he created an Everyman who shines.

Mimi Reisel Gladstein

20 Straining for Profundity: Steinbeck's *Burning Bright* and *Sweet Thursday*

Sequels did not work well for John Steinbeck. In 1937 he published his first venture into a new form which he identified as the play-novelette. The experiment succeeded beyond his expectations. *Of Mice and Men*, whose original title was *Something that Happened*, elicited critical plaudits for its manifestation in three media. The novel was both a best-seller and a Book-of-the-Month Club selection. As a play it won the New York Drama Critics' Circle Award; the movie was a powerful and faithful adaptation of the novel.[1] *Of Mice and Men* is a tight, well-structured tale in which symbolism and philosophical content are sufficiently submerged in a straightforward story about itinerant laborers in the Salinas Valley. Steinbeck's subsequent attempts to duplicate the play-novelette form in no way equaled their predecessor. *The Moon Is Down* played to mixed reviews, while the critical reaction to *Burning Bright* was near-universal antagonism.

In a similar vein, Steinbeck was unable to duplicate his success with writing humorously about his friend Ed Ricketts and the quixotic denizens of Old Ocean View Avenue, among whom he spent some productive and enjoyable years during the early part of the depression. *Cannery Row*, which transported Doc, Mack, the boys, and the assorted whores and characters of the row into the world of literary stardom, was followed by *Sweet Thursday*, which is usually listed among Steinbeck's least-valued works. It may be significant that when Hollywood finally got around to making the movie, they combined the two works, calling the film *Cannery Row* even though the main story line came from *Sweet Thursday*. Hollywood took advantage of the positive name recognition of *Cannery Row* while at the same time catering to the mass-audience appeal embodied in the love story that is at the heart of *Sweet Thursday*. Heavily sentimental and soppily romantic, *Sweet Thursday*, on page and screen, is quintessential Hollywood fare.

Why was Steinbeck unable to duplicate his initial successes? What happened between Steinbeck's earlier works and their follow-ups that negatively affected the outcome? Answers are as various as the writers who suggest them. Commenting on what he saw as a general decline in the quality of Steinbeck's work after *The Grapes of Wrath*, Brian St. Pierre suggests that when Steinbeck left California, he uprooted himself from both his native soil and his richest source material, thus losing contact with a necessary nutrient for his writing.[2] Jackson Benson notes that after the success of *The Grapes of Wrath*, Steinbeck's editors were less likely to be critical. The early 1940s also marked the end of two important relationships which had strongly affected Steinbeck's early writing. The divorce from Carol deprived Steinbeck of her strong editorial influence. Though his relationship with Ed Ricketts remained strong, the physical distance between them affected its essential nature. Conversations with Ed had provided catalytic intellectual stimulation. Benson explains that, unlike his earlier works, some of these later works were written quickly and partly by dictation. *The Moon Is Down*, his first novel after *The Grapes of Wrath*, was one of the first works that did not have Carol's careful editing.[3] Explanations vary, but the general consensus is that Steinbeck's best work was written before 1945.

In this respect Steinbeck does not differ from a number of his illustrious colleagues. Like Steinbeck in his early works, most of the significant writers of Steinbeck's generation wrote about object, fact, and person, and rejected abstractions of all kinds. They were wary of statements of theme, relying on the reader to abstract the meaning from the language and sequence of events. However, as they grew older and achieved recognition, their work changed. Floyd C. Watkins posits the theory that "the general movement from objectiveness to abstraction, from the flesh to the word, is apparent in almost every major writer of the twentieth century."[4] Moreover, Watkins contends that as these writers moved toward abstraction and subjectivity, it had a detrimental effect on their writing. Watkins's book is an exploration of how that movement affected the works of Eliot, Hemingway, and Faulkner, whom he characterizes as the most notable American winners of the Nobel Prize. Steinbeck was the next American to win the prize after Hemingway, and the pattern that Watkins established for Eliot, Hemingway, and Faulkner is apparent also in Steinbeck's works. He, no less than the American Nobel Prize winners who preceded him, moved from the terse, concrete objectivity of *Of Mice and Men* and the honest inarticulateness of the Joads to the mouthy platitudes of *Burning Bright* and the soupy subjectivity of *Sweet Thursday*. He moved from the authorial restraint which is part of the genius of *The Red Pony* to the indulgence of Fieldingesque intrusions that pepper *East of Eden*. The inferiority of such works as *Burning Bright* and *Sweet Thursday* compared to their predecessors is in large part due to this movement from flesh to word, from objectivity to subjectivity. It is that movement and what I will call straining for profundity, that damage the later works. By "straining for profundity" I mean that in works such as *Burning Bright* and *Sweet Thursday* Steinbeck had either lost faith in himself or in the reader to the extent that, rather than allowing profundity to accrue from the particulars of situation and character, he was impelled to *tell* us what it all means.

Steinbeck's logorrhea is evident in both works, but it is less offensive in *Sweet Thursday*, which, after all, has few pretensions to deep meaning. It is a slight thing, not meant to weigh much heavier than necessary to hold the musical-comedy stage.[5] At that it was barely successful. *Pipe Dream*, the musical-comedy version of *Sweet Thursday*, ranks at the bottom of the list of Rodgers and Hammerstein musicals. *Burning Bright*, on the other hand, beginning with its allusive title, is a work as serious in intent as its precursor, *Of Mice and Men*.

The ambitious nature of Steinbeck's purpose as he set out to write his third play-novelette is evidenced by the initial title. Seeing himself as working in the tradition of the classical morality play, he referred to his early drafts as *Everyman*. The original *Everyman* is unambiguously allegorical. Its setting is eternal, its characters personifications, and its plot symbolical. Steinbeck's version attempts a setting in keeping with its allegorical purpose. A letter to Toby Street identifies the period as "completely timeless and placeless."[6] The three acts are set at "The Circus," "The Farm," and "The Sea" in another attempt to give his play universal and profound implications. Though Steinbeck obviously meant the interchangeable settings to indicate that the characters in his story represent entertainers, farmers, and/or sailors, three of the most ancient and traditional professions, the effect is not necessarily achieved. Because of the unified and linear plot, the use of multiple settings can be confusing. The characters in act 1 could easily be circus entertainers who winter at their farm in act 2. Their move to the sea in act 3 is harder to explain, but as circus people are traditionally nomadic, not inexplicable. Since the plot line follows what appear to be the same characters with the same problem through all three acts, the use of multiple settings to suggest the universality of situation seems contrived and forced, calling attention to itself as technique. Nor is the need for this purposeful abstraction clear.

There is little ambiguity about the setting for *Of Mice and Men*. Though the time is not mentioned, the geographical location is. The action takes place "south of Soledad," first in a thicket and then in a bunkhouse. Yet this geographic specificity does little to tie Steinbeck's play to a particular time or place. The play could be set in any countryside, at any farm. While we know that the play was written in the 1930s and probably refers to the situation of migrant workers in either the 1920s or 1930s, there is little in the play itself to date it. The problems of migrant workers are still with us a half century later. It is even a problem that Europe and America share. Crooks is segregated because he is black, but a change of race or nationality could still explain such division from fellow workers. A 1974 revival in which James Earl Jones played Lennie was heralded because of the "fresh resonance" of the racially integrated casting. Stefan Kanfer saw the interdependence of blacks and whites in this play as more tragic and poignant than the racial mix of the original.[7] Steinbeck's universality inheres in his themes of the loneliness of the dispossessed and the warmth of brotherhood. He does not need the contrivance of symbolically universal settings.

Another indication in *Burning Bright* of Steinbeck's lack of trust in his reader's or audience's ability to discern for themselves the significance of his characters' purposes or functions is seen in the name of one of the major characters, Friend Ed. The theme of strong male bonding is a recurrent one in Steinbeck's works of the 1930s. Besides George and Lennie, whose relationship is so close that it has been suggested that they represent two aspects of one human being, there are Mac and Jim, Tom Joad and Jim Casy, Danny and Pilon, to name a few. Jim Casy is the only one whose name provides a veiled clue to his behavior, and that clue is only in his initials. The naming of all other characters trusts the reader to discern the import of the relationships from the particulars of plot and action. In *Burning Bright* Steinbeck names each character's purpose, thus detracting from both the character's dramatic viability and the audience's pleasure. If Steinbeck wanted to provide a strong clue to the function of the second male lead in *Burning Bright* without laying it out for the audience, he could have done it in any number of ways; for example, he might have named him Jonathan, utilizing the biblical allusion. Instead, he chose the heavy-handed technique of calling him Friend Ed.

Friendship is an important theme in *Burning Bright*, as it is in many of Steinbeck's best works. Joe Saul and Friend Ed's relationship is one of equals, unlike Lennie and George's. After Joe Saul has shown his antipathy to Mrs. Molloy's natural pride in her son Tom and does some flexing of hands and swinging of feet, Friend Ed identifies Joe Saul's behavior as "nervy." "That's a new thing you're doing there," he says. "That's a nervy thing" (*BB*, p. 21). Obviously, they are close enough that Friend Ed feels free to comment on and probe Joe Saul's behavior. Still, although their closeness has been made obvious in the preceding dialogue and actions, Steinbeck has Friend Ed articulate the terms of their relationship in a subsequent question, "Do I have the friend-right to ask a question, Joe Saul?" (*BB*, p. 23). In *Of Mice and Men* George does not name his relationship to Lennie, nor does he feel called upon to name Lennie's peculiar behavior. He immediately knows that Lennie is hiding a mouse in his pocket when they get to the thicket. He can see from Lennie's wet shoes that he has retrieved it after George threw it away across the stream. George has his antennae tuned to Lennie's behavior and can sense trouble before it starts. The audience/reader intuits the depth of the relationship from what is heard and seen. Although George often hollers at Lennie, his behavior shows his caring. His harsh language is in opposition to his sensitivity, an opposition which increases the dramatic effectiveness of their interaction. It is only after the closeness of the relationship has already become evident that George explains to Slim his deep sense of responsibility for Lennie.

The language of *Burning Bright* is another area in which Steinbeck strains too hard for added import. In some cases he is poetically successful. Friend Ed compares Joe Saul's tension to "putting an itch in the air around you like a cloud of gnats in a hot evening" (*BB*, p. 22). Joe Saul and Friend Ed probably lack formal education, as they are circus people, a group which has traditionally avoided public institutions. Like country people, their language is often appropriately colorful and naturally metaphoric. However, Steinbeck mixes a kind of colloquial level of usage with a stilted syntax, probably meant to give the language a poetical tone. Thus "I see it coming on you" is followed by "It's not a thing of surprise to me" (*BB*, p. 21). Opting for poetic diction gives the writer certain leeway in the use of language. Steinbeck takes full advantage of his options. He creates hyphenated words to express emotions for which the language obviously doesn't have either specific enough or dramatic enough equivalents. Some examples are the words "wife-loss" and "friend-right" as well as the oxymoron "screaming silently" to convey the experience of inarticulate rage. The technique is not uniformly effective, although my reaction to it is not as negative as L. A.

G. Strong's, who caustically asked, "Have I, I wonder, the admirer-right to tell Mr. Steinbeck that this trick has set me screaming silently in my reader-loss?"[8]

Another area in which the comparison between the two play-novelettes *Of Mice and Men* and *Burning Bright* is relevant is in their handling of a similar moral issue. Each play involves a murder in a climactic situation. In both cases Steinbeck wants us to see the murder as an act of love. The profundity of the situation derives from that issue. Its works in *Of Mice and Men;* in *Burning Bright* it strains credulity. George's killing of Lennie, with its myriad symbolic implications, is part of a pattern of inevitability. From the beginning of the story, as Lennie kills first the mouse, then the puppy, then Curley's wife, all because of his desire to touch something soft, to achieve through his sense of touch a feeling of security, Steinbeck prepares the reader for Lennie's destruction of the dream of land ownership, the personification of security for all landless people. Not only is Lennie's end foreshadowed, but before he is killed, he kills. There is a sense of balance and retribution. George can be absolved of killing Lennie because Lennie is also a murderer. While it might be argued that Lennie's mental incapacity makes him legally not responsible, the situation in the play suggests that the issue will never come to trial. The audience/reader is made to understand that Curley will not wait for judicial justice. He means to shoot Lennie in the stomach, to gut-shoot him, in order to cause the most possible pain. Lennie is no match for Curley. Steinbeck has already prepared us for Lennie's lack of response to violence against self; he does not hit Curley, although Curley is pummeling him in the bunkhouse scene which ends book 1. George's responsibility to save Lennie from either the kind of incarceration where they will "strap him down and put him in a cage" or Curley, who plans to "shoot the guts outa that big bastard," is foreshadowed when Candy remarks that he should have shot his old and infirm dog himself rather than allowing Carlson to do it. George even uses the same Luger that Carlson used to kill the old dog.

But while George's killing of Lennie is carefully foreshadowed and sufficiently justified, the same cannot be said for the murder in *Burning Bright*. Victor may not be an admirable character, but he has killed no one. The only threat he makes is to tell the truth. Victor, who has been used as a stud by Mordeen, is killed because he wants to claim his child, because he threatens to tell Joe Saul that the child Mordeen is about to bear is his. Mordeen, who has committed adultery in order to fulfill Joe Saul's dream of having children, is ready to add the sin of murder to the adultery. She gets a knife out of its sheath in order to kill Victor. At this point Friend Ed, who squeamishly avoided endorsing her plan of adultery in an earlier act, shows no scruples about committing murder. It is a change of heart for which there is little foreshadowing or preparation. Still, it is a change of heart which might have been more palatable to the audience if Steinbeck had not felt it necessary to have Friend Ed tell us about it.

In act 1 when Mordeen tries to include Friend Ed in her plans, asking him to help her choose the least wrong of three possibilities, Friend Ed demurs, "I don't know. I tell you I will not advise you. I will not offer my responsibility" (*BB*, p. 60). Mordeen allows that perhaps she has "put too much strain on friendship" (*BB*, p. 61). She refuses to name her plan to Ed, assuring him, "If I am wrong about anything it will be *my* wrongness, and you need not think it or touch it" (*BB*, p. 61). However, by act 3, Friend Ed, seeing Mordeen with Victor, is ready to get involved. This he *tells* Mordeen, and he does so in front of Victor. "Once I wouldn't help you. I wouldn't take the responsibility. Now I will" (*BB*, p. 137). Friend Ed and Mordeen argue in Victor's presence about who is going to finish what Mordeen started, and the audience is then expected to believe that Victor understands none of this and is ready to follow Friend Ed on deck like a lamb to the slaughter. After "the crunching blow, the expelled moaning cry, and in a moment the little splash," Friend Ed returns. The only indication of any remorse on either part is Mordeen's acknowledgment that Victor was neither bad nor evil. Later, Friend Ed dismisses the murder by telling Joe Saul, "Forget Victor. Victor is not here" (*BB*, p. 141). Ironically, he then condemns himself out of his own mouth by telling Joe Saul, who is raging against Victor, "Stop it. . . . Don't blame Victor" (*BB*, p. 141). If, in the words of his murderers, Victor is neither bad nor evil nor to blame, how are we, the readers, to accept this murder?

To make the murder even less acceptable, it turns out to have been unnecessary because Joe Saul has found out that he is sterile anyway. As he ranges between anger and acceptance, Friend Ed helps him come to the realization that he can still love the child, that his particular seed is no more important than any other seed, that it is his knowledge and pride and warmth that Joe Saul can transmit, not just his bloodline that he can pass on to a child. After the child is born, the theme of the play, as articulated by Joe Saul, is "that every man is father to all children and every child must have all men as father" (*BB*, p. 158). This theme makes the murder of Victor abhorrent in terms of the message the play is transmitting, creating further problems for the reader/audience. Steinbeck means us to sympathize with Friend Ed and Mordeen because they committed this crime out of their love for Joe Saul. Still, if we are to accept the philosophy the play propounds, that "it is the race, the species that must go staggering on," then their precipitous killing of a member of that species is unjustified. By the terms of the play's philosophy, it is life that is precious, not the individual ego.

Burning Bright suffers not only from moral ambiguity but from Steinbeck's necessity to name things. We are too often told and too little shown. He would have done well to have heeded the words of Addie Bundren, Faulkner's language-mistrusting matriarch in *As I Lay Dying:* "words dont ever fit even what they are trying to say at."[9] Just as Anse Bundren is unable to violate Addie's aloneness because he is a word man rather than a deed man, so the characters in *Burning Bright* fail to impinge upon our consciousness because of their tendency to speak their emotions rather than show them.

If there is a character in the play-novelette who is initially believable it is Victor, and his realistic language is part of the reason. His character represents the life force; in the allegory he is the one who impregnates, creates life. Ironically, in this celebration of the race's survival, it is the life force which is snuffed out. As Victor's touch of reality and therefore lifelikeness is canceled, so is the effectiveness of the play. The story reads like a metaphor for canceling realism. Perhaps that is why it wouldn't play. As Steinbeck himself pointed out, it lacked that certain something, that magic of the theater. What reads does not necessarily play. Like Addie's words that rise up into the dead flat air, so the words spoken by the unrealistic characters flatten and fall. Because Joe Saul, Friend Ed, and Mordeen all speak the abstract language of their "timeless and placeless" world, their theatrical reality is often at odds with that of Victor. Victor's early lines have some punch and power. He expresses his rejection of words. When Mordeen changes her attitude toward him, he asks, "did you dig down through your pile of sticky words and find out that they were only words, when you needed hard and young action?" (p. 64). In the first act, his language, harsh and defensive, bespeaks his lack of sensitivity, his lovelessness. He tells Mordeen, "I came in to tell you once and finally what I think of the crap you were shoveling around." Mordeen, as she weaves her web of entrapment for him, tries to communicate to him through story. Victor sees through what she is doing, telling her, "What do you want me to get from it: Your stories are loaded, Mordeen" (*BB*, p. 67). As even Victor, who is meant to represent physicality with little sensitivity, does not need it explained to him, the reader might have been spared Mordeen's explanation that her speech was "about making you feel welcome. And I thought that if you would help me, when I need help, it might be good rich thing for both of us" (*BB*, p. 67).

The ensuing scene between Victor and Mordeen is illustrative of Steinbeck's insistence on telling us the emotions of the characters rather than allowing those emotions to reveal themselves through the dialogue. It is a poor technique for something which is meant to be dramatic rather than discursive. One longs for the first scene of *Of Mice and Men*, where Lennie's mental incapacity and the relationship between Lennie and George are made obvious through the dialogue. But in *Burning Bright* Steinbeck prefaces Victor's lines with such explanations as "his truculence was going out of him and in spite of himself a jauntiness crept in" (*BB*, p. 67). As Mordeen appeals to him to understand her need for his complicity, Steinbeck explains to the reader that "Victor went past understanding, went into triumph" (*BB*, p. 68). This reading is obvious from Victor's subsequent dialogue. As Mordeen forces herself to this act which is abhorrent to her, as we have already learned in her previous interchange with Friend Ed, Steinbeck explains to us again that "Mordeen's eyes veiled with pain, and she withdrew a little into herself," turning toward Victor, "her throat was tight, but she had made her decision" (*BB*, p. 69). Such descriptions smack of melodrama more than morality play.

In act 2 when Joe Saul learns that Mordeen is pregnant, he is overcome, casting about for some appropriate means of celebration. Friend Ed makes the mundane suggestion that they might have a party, that he'll bring ice cream and whiskey and kill a turkey. All of this is appropriately festive, without straining credulity. Any circus person, farmer, or sailor might celebrate thus. The turkey has the connotations of Thanksgiving. But Joe Saul responds to his realistic suggestion in an apoplexy of metaphoric wordiness. "I see myself and myself's torment whirling away out of range of sight and feeling—torment in blood and heart that the line, a preciousness carried and shielded through the stormy millennia, is snapped, the product discontinued, the stamen mildewed" (*BB*, p. 87). The murky images and unstructured thought pattern are reminiscent of some Faulknerian character's stream-of-consciousness reaction. As the author's description of the inner working of the mind, this might be acceptable; as words to be spoken out loud in response to the suggestion of having a party, they strain the audience's and/or reader's patience.

Learning of Mordeen's pregnancy fills Joe Saul with such joy that he wants to go out and buy Mordeen a present. He spills out his need to bring her "a beauty thing," "a red flaring ruby of thanks" (*BB*, p. 98). Again, Steinbeck does not trust his reader to understand why Joe Saul needs to do this thing, so he has Joe Saul articulate it: "My joy requires a symbol" (*BB*, p. 98). Therein lies much of the problem with the whole play. Not only does Steinbeck test our endurance with strained metaphoric and abstract language, but having chosen to use the metaphors and abstractions, he still feels impelled to explain to us what they all mean. Word replaces flesh, and the reader/audience is left with empty abstraction.

Burning Bright's theme of universal parenthood is appealing, if not convincing. Perhaps because of his personal stake in the issue, Steinbeck was unable to maintain adequate objective distance from his subject.[10] He was dealing with a weighty subject, and he may not have been convinced that his characters were substantial enough to carry the burden of his theme.

If this explanation works for *Burning Bright*, it does little to explain the presence of similar faults in *Sweet Thursday*, which is obviously not a work dealing with heavy issues. Unlike *Burning Bright*, which is weighted down with its need to be profound, *Sweet Thursday* floats lightly along in terms of the fantasy it is meant to be, thudding down only occasionally when Steinbeck leaves his fairy-tale realm to indulge his need to preach. As he explained in a letter to Elizabeth R. Otis, to whom the book is dedicated, the book is light and gay and astringent, but "it may even say some good things."[11] When it is light, when it is gay, and even when it is, at times, astringent, it works well, and at least the language of the characters is consistent with their occupations and education. Its problems develop from its author's need to "say some good things."

Cannery Row is grounded in a specific locale. Its characters are modeled on real people. Still, its purpose is larger than nostalgia or whimsy. It is, as Malcolm Cowley pointed out, "a poisoned cream puff."[12] The poison is in its cynical yet loving depiction of human beings, particularly in its send-up of middle-class morality. Benson is on target when he describes *Cannery Row* as a work as complex as its writer, "funny and deadly serious at the same time, sentimental and coldly deterministic, loving and satirical, lyrical and yet very precise."[13] At its best, *Sweet Thursday* projects some of the same complexities; however, it is often not at its best. One of the main problems with *Sweet Thursday* derives from Steinbeck's decision to resort to the most conventional of all plot patterns: boy meets girl, boy loses girl, boy gets girl back, and they ride off into the sunset to honeymoon in a tide pool. It is a love story which panders to one of the most cherished of Hollywood-nurtured fantasies, the one about the poor and uneducated girl who captures the heart of the rich and respected physicist, the servant girl who marries the lord of the manor, the story that answers the question "Can a girl from a little mining town in the West find happiness as the wife of England's richest, most handsome lord?"[14] It is as conventional and sentimental a plot as any on the morning soaps.

Much of the pleasure of reading *Cannery Row* proceeds from its lack of conventionality. Its Beauties, Virtues, and Graces are bums, winos, and the refuse of society. Even its hero behaves according to his own sense of values. He easily accepts one and all, even tipping his hat to dogs. *Cannery Row* is a masculine preserve. Such women as inhabit it are there to provide the men with sexual release on a businesslike basis. Romantic love is singularly absent from Steinbeck's best works. Women are scarce and their presence perfunctory.[15] The addition of Suzy, the whore who is not really a whore, to the cast of characters of the row, is indicative of the problem with *Sweet Thursday*.

Unlike the other characters on the row, Suzy has no model in reality. Although there were whores who worked on Cannery Row who later married either customers or men they met on their days off, Ed Ricketts neither married one nor had a significant relationship with one.[16] Nor is it likely that Suzy is modeled on one of these women, as they tended to hide their former profession when they married, and Suzy and Doc plan to stay right there on the row. Suzy is too obviously a symbol, a contrived character whose reality intrudes on rather than grows organically out of plot structure. In case we don't understand what Suzy is meant to symbolize, Steinbeck underlines it for us.

Joe Elegant, Steinbeck's satirical portrait of an effeminate aspiring novelist, tells Suzy that she would not understand the novel he is writing. Suzy remonstrates, "Then what good is it?" Elegant responds, "It isn't intended for the mass." Susie acknowledges, "I'm the mass, huh? I guess you got something there" (*ST*, p. 83). The main problem with this novel is ironically encapsulated in the scene between Suzy and Joe Elegant. The character of Joe Elegant is a satire of pretentious and affected writers. Both the title of this novel, *The Pi Root of Oedipus*, and its plot poke fun at strained symbolism. Steinbeck looks down on writers who write in some pseudo-profound and mannered style; their's are works meant for critics rather than readers. Joe Elegant looks down on Suzy and the general public, not expecting them to understand the complexity of his novel. Still, he offers to read Suzy some of his work, and when she retorts that he had said she wouldn't understand it, he offers, "I'll explain it as I go along" (*ST*, p. 83). This is obviously not the way literature should be read, and Steinbeck justifiably satirizes Joe Elegant and writers of his ilk. Still, in terms of his own writing, he is behaving toward the reader in a manner parallel to Joe Elegant's. He is explaining it as he goes along.

Joe Elegant is not the only character who "tells" us that Suzy represents humankind. Doc also sees her in generic terms. When he observes her living conditions in the boiler he exclaims, "My God, what a brave thing is the human!" (*ST*, p. 248). Steinbeck means the reader to see Suzy not only as the masses but as that unconquerable spirit of humanity, that which will not only endure but prevail, to echo Faulkner's Nobel Prize speech. But rather than allowing readers to fashion their own responses to Suzy's remarkable accomplishments in leaving prostitution, letting her dyed hair grow out, resuscitating business at the Golden Poppy, and setting up housekeeping in a boiler, Steinbeck has Doc, the University of Chicago Ph.D., compare Suzy's accomplishments to Bach's. Suzy turns out to be more admirable than Bach because "old Bach had his talent and his family and his friends. And what has Suzy got? Absolutely nothing in the world but guts" (*ST*, p.

245). Doc continues his hyperbole by claiming that Suzy has taken on an atomic world with a slingshot. The metaphor does not hold true. Nothing in *Sweet Thursday* even hints at the high technology or psychological trauma of an atomic world. Still, the point is not whether or not the metaphor is an appropriate one, but the fact that Steinbeck is here, more obviously than in most other places in the novel, straining for profundity. Suzy's personal battle to make herself worthy of Doc is hardly the equivalent of taking on the atomic world with a slingshot, and it certainly strains credulity if the reader is expected to respond, as Doc does, that "if she doesn't win there's no point in living any more" (*ST*, p. 246). The import here is too studiedly planted in the text; it does not develop organically from character or situation.

It is difficult to assess the blame for the inferiority of both *Burning Bright* and *Sweet Thursday*. Perhaps Steinbeck, reacting to his disappointment that critics did not respond to the subtleties of earlier works, felt the necessity for overt explanation. Maybe his fame created a self-consciousness, a need to be "literary." His characterizations certainly suffer when they are developed whole cloth out of abstraction rather than by his earlier method of basing them, in part, on real human beings. I do not want to fall into the trap of judging Steinbeck as a realist or a naturalist when obviously he meant to be something else. Nor do I wish to begrudge him his right to change styles, to experiment, to try a new genre. Still, the two works are not new experiments; they are in some ways sequels to earlier works. If *Burning Bright* is not a sequel in the usual sense, it is a repetition of a previously successful methodology. *Sweet Thursday* is a proper sequel. Still, neither is in the same class as its predecessor. In Steinbeck's most successful works, he is able to work on many levels at the same time. *Grapes of Wrath*, *Of Mice and Men*, *Tortilla Flat*, *The Red Pony*, and *Cannery Row* all operate at symbolic, mythic, and archetypal levels while at once being earthy, philosophical, realistic, biological, and even naturalistic. The multiple levels do not intrude upon each other. A large part of the success of Steinbeck's greatest works is tied to the surface, or realistic, level, which only appears opaque. The language of his characters, be they paisanos or Okies, is a close approximation of reality, or if it isn't, it convinces the reader that it is. In Steinbeck's greatest works, what is left unsaid is often more important than what is said. In those works he does not make anti-climactic, and often unnecessary, statements about actions in which the emotional meaning has already been made patently clear. But most of all, in his greatest works such universal truths and profound insights as are to be gained by the reader accrue from character and action and are not the result of obvious authorial manipulation. Both *Burning Bright* and *Sweet Thursday* retain much of the excellence that makes reading even poor Steinbeck an enjoyable experience. Still, both often suffer from Steinbeck's obvious desire to be profound, in the former case, and, in the latter, from his need to "say some good things."

IX The Short Reign of Pippin IV

Louis Owens

21 Steinbeck's "Deep Dissembler": *The Short Reign of Pippin IV*

As with other Steinbeck works, critics have long been divided concerning the merits of John Steinbeck's late novella *The Short Reign of Pippin IV*. Even critics usually inclined to praise Steinbeck have labeled this work "tasteless,"[1] "sapless and languid,"[2] or evidence of Steinbeck's "surrender of artistic integrity."[3] At least one critic has complained that the satire on French politics in this novel is tastelessly buffoonish and that the reform program outlined by Steinbeck through the character of Pippin is unnecessary because "France already has had this sort of legislation for many years."[4] Conversely, other critics have called this little book Steinbeck's "wittiest satire," his "most effective novel in a decade,"[5] and a "charming miscellany of satirical and witty comment" displaying a "stunning" range of style.[6]

The problem critics have consistently faced with *Pippin IV* seems to be that this is a humorous novel, a satire following closely on the heels of Steinbeck's previous "funny" book, *Sweet Thursday*, and yet this satire becomes a little too bleak. Howard Levant summarizes this position nicely, if unconvincingly, declaring that "just so far as Steinbeck drops out of a tonal and thematic absurdity into seriousness, just so far the novel fails to maintain its delicate, associational structure."[7] For Levant, the novel fails because of its "indeterminate intention."[8] The problem, as a number of critics have seen it, seems to be that Steinbeck may have been uncertain as to precisely what he was creating in this novel, an uncertainty of intention that results in a blurring of effect. Looked at in this way, *Pippin* appears to be a funny book that grew inadvertently too serious. Levant, again, sums up this position: "Pippin's will to institute the good life is a more serious matter than the bulk of the novel's comic dance . . . can sustain."9

It is my contention that although *The Short Reign of Pippin IV* will always remain one of Steinbeck's minor works, its balance of easy laughter and dark criticism is neither inadvertent nor indeterminate, and although Steinbeck may have had a great deal of fun composing this novel,10 he intended it from the beginning to be a rather black critique not of France and French politics but of America and American politics. That France had no need for the reforms Pippin proposes is a moot point, for throughout this novel Steinbeck's thoughts are very specifically on America. *The Short Reign of Pippin IV* is, I believe, Steinbeck's successful practice run for his grim investigation of the American conscience in his final novel, *The Winter of Our Discontent*.

A key to this reading of *Pippin* may be found in the novel's opening paragraphs. Following his invariable technique, Steinbeck begins the story by firmly fixing his protagonist in place. Pippin Heristal lives at "Number One Avenue de Marigny in Paris," above "stables, very elegant with carved marble mangers"—appropriate quarters for a noble, yet Christ-like, savior. Furthermore, Steinbeck tells us that the house "was built as the Paris headquarters of the Knights of St. John." That Pippin is associated with the Knights of Saint John, the Knights Hospitallers, is important, just as in *The Winter of Our Discontent* it will be important that Ethan Allen Hawley, the fallen descendant of American freebooters, will be associated with the more militant Knights Templar by way of his Templar's hat with its yellowed plume.

The Knights of Saint John, the Hospitallers, were in medieval times an order devoted to charity by caring for the ill and unfortunate. The increasing secularization and growing wealth of the order, however, led to threats in 1236 by Pope Gregory IX to excommunicate both the Hospitallers and the Templars and to a papal bull inveighing against the scandalous lives of the Knights of Saint John. It was the French Revolution that finally proved fatal to the Knights of Saint John, when the grand master of the order sided too conspicuously with the losing cause. With the establishment of the republic, the Hospitallers' vast holdings in France were confiscated. One of the surviving orders of Saint John, however, was the Prussian Johanniterorden, in which members were required both to be of noble birth and to belong to the Evangelical church. The cross worn by this order is of white-enameled gold with four black eagles between the arms. Pippin is, as he reminds his Uncle Charlie, of German blood, and he certainly exhibits evangelical zeal in his crusade to save his country from itself. Late in the novel Steinbeck inserts a subtle reminder of the Knights of Saint John when Sister Hyacinthe, Pippin's adviser and friend, appears to Pippin as a great black bird. And in keeping with the link to the Knights of Saint John, it is fitting that Sister Hyacinthe play a major advisory role in the novel, for unlike the militant Knights Templar, the Hospitallers welcomed the participation of women in their order. Pippin's Avenue de Marigny address further highlights Pippin's links to the Hospitallers and the tumultuous political history of France, for the name of this avenue echoes that of Enguerrand de Marigny, the royal chamberlain and principal minister of finance to Philip IV of France, the monarch primarily responsible for the destruction of the Templars and the transfer of Templar wealth to the Hospitallers.[11]

With his rather subtle linking of Pippin to the Knights of Saint John, Steinbeck is, from the first paragraph of the novel, carefully associating Pippin with an older system of moral values that fell into ruin and finally obscurity. The order's decline in France with the rise of the French Republic parallels the fate of Pippin's noble antecedents. That Pippin, a nobleman of Germanic heritage who inhabits the old headquarters of the Hospitallers, should care very purely for the fallen, morally diseased France suggests in Pippin a rebirth, or purification, of the old moral order. That at the end of the novel Pippin's reign should end with the creation of a new French Republic underscores a kind of cleansing, renewing cycle. Pippin's role as mock king, long ago pointed out by Joseph Fontenrose, fits this cycle perfectly.[12] Sister Hyacinthe, whose name calls to mind Hyacinthus, the Greek symbol of sacrifice leading to rebirth, as well as the "hyacinth girl" of *The Waste Land*, is the fitting adviser for such a king.

From the first pages of *Pippin IV* America comes in for a far more severe lambasting than does France. American materialism has its ingenuous exponent in Tod Johnson, whom Steinbeck describes ironically as "the ideal American young man."[13] It is Tod who dreams up the idea of selling French titles to American oil millionaires. Tod represents a no-nonsense belief in the American buck. He is an Eisenhower-era version of Henry James's Christopher Newman, of Mark Twain's

Yankee; he is a product of American consumerism, a seller of honor, himself the perfect American product who will sweep Pippin's daughter Clotilde off to Hollywood and more illusion. It is also Tod who declares fervently that "the first function of business is to create the demand and the second is to fulfill it" (*Pippin*, p. 99), a declaration Steinbeck would echo harshly almost a decade later in *America and Americans:* "We manufacture things we do not need and try by false and vicious advertising to create a feeling of need for them."[14]

When Uncle Charlie tells the story of the millionaires tricked through their own greed and dishonesty into buying forgeries of the Mona Lisa, Tod wonders naïvely why the king is upset at the story. "He is sensitive," Uncle Charlie explains, and Pippin adds, "I believe that all men are honest where they are disinterested. . . . It seems to me reprehensible to search out areas of weakness and to exploit them" (*Pippin*, p. 101). Tod's acute response, suggestive of Steinbeck's feelings about American politics in the 1950s, is, "Aren't you going to have some difficulty being king, sir?" (*Pippin*, p. 101). It is also Tod who explains U.S. government: "You might say we have two governments, kind of overlapping. First we have the elected government. It's Democratic or Republican, doesn't make much difference, and then there's corporation government" (*Pippin*, p. 115). To Steinbeck, who as early as 1944 was working for Democratic candidate FDR, and who continued to work hard for Adlai Stevenson and later Democratic leaders, it certainly mattered whether government was Democratic or Republican. Finally, Tod anticipates the canker at the bitter heart of Ethan Allen Hawley's New Baytown in *The Winter of Our Discontent* when he defines the central question, not simply in business but apparently in life, as: "What have you got to sell and who is going to buy and have they got the money?" (*Pippin*, p. 121). When Tod proposes to sell French titles to Texas millionaires, the king says flatly, "That isn't right." Tod replies in all innocence, "What do you mean, right?" (*Pippin*, p. 122). Tod is a deformed product of American materialism, the ideal young man who has lost all sense of the kind of ethics Pippin wants to reassert. The corruption of American politics is further underscored when Tod says approvingly, "If those oil and cattle boys can rig the tax laws and the utilities laws, they aren't going to have any trouble with a little old law against titles" (*Pippin*, p. 123). Pippin replies, "How about simple honesty, simple logic?" And Tod says flatly, "That has never worked" (*Pippin*, p. 124).

The true antagonists of this novel are Tod Johnson and Pippin Heristal, the ironically ideal American and the idealist monarch. In these two characters Steinbeck opposes new and old values in the forms of America and Europe in a work masquerading only lightly as a critique of modern France.

America's naïve rapaciousness is highlighted even more sharply in this novel in the character of Willie Chitling, the movie producer who "built the entire bar in his ranch house at Palm Springs with the furniture, paneling, and thirteenth-century altar from the chapel of the Chateau Vieilleculotte" (*Pippin*, p. 21). And the empty values predominant in American life are further underscored by Uncle Charlie's recommendation that Pippin hire an American advertising agency to run the kingdom for him, declaring, "If such a company can merchandise a president and a political party, why not a king?" (*Pippin*, p. 64). As Uncle Charlie becomes more excited about this possibility, he exclaims abruptly, "Do you have a dog?" Underlying this apparent non sequitur is very likely Uncle Charlie's (and Steinbeck's) remembrance of the famous Checkers speech in which Richard Nixon pulled America's heartstrings and got himself out of a tight spot with the aid of his household pet. According to Steinbeck's biographer, Jackson Benson, Steinbeck saw Richard Nixon as the single greatest threat to American democracy (*TA*, p. 836), and of Nixon, Steinbeck once wrote, "He has so few principles that he would even do a good thing if it suited his needs" (*TA*, p. 861). In 1960, in a letter to close friend and fellow Nixonphobe Adlai Stevenson, Steinbeck would compare Nixon to Richard III, quoting at length: "He was close and secret, a deep dissembler, lowly of countenance, arrogant of heart, outwardly companionable when he inwardly hated, not letting to kiss . . . whom he thought to kill; despiteous and cruel, not for evil will always, but after ambition and either for surety or increase of his estate." Nixon would bring about his own downfall, Steinbeck prophesied, declaring, "Perhaps it is an accident that the names are the same—but the theme of Richard III will prove prophetic" (*TA*, p. 878). It is surely a painful awareness of the political cynicism Steinbeck saw in both Nixon and Joseph McCarthy that informs the dark side of *The Short Reign of Pippin IV*, and just as surely when Steinbeck chose his title for *The Winter of Our Discontent* from the play featuring literature's most famous deep dissembler, he was thinking of Nixon.

In *Pippin IV* Uncle Charlie discovers eventually that the American advertising companies are all too busy to take on the king's case: "19— was a monster year for American advertising. BBD & O was up to its ears rewriting the Constitution of the United States and at the same time marketing a new golf-mobile with pontoons" (*Pippin*, p. 72). Again, in this Madison Avenue sellout of Jeffersonian democracy Steinbeck is taking a shot at the Eisenhower propensity for conducting national policy on the golf course, the same propensity darkly spoofed in Robert Coover's later satire on this era, his 1977 novel *The Public Burning* (Viking Press). Warren French directed us toward this point some years ago when he declared, "Although the criticism is ostensibly of France, much of it clearly applies to the smugly complacent United States of the Eisenhower years."[15]

Steinbeck's correspondence during this period indicates that as he worked on this penultimate novel his thoughts were never far from the oppressive political scene in the United States, as McCarthyism gained ground and began to damange and destroy lives. By April 1956, while finishing *Pippin IV*, Steinbeck had already made arrangements to report as a journalist on both the Democratic and Republican national conventions, and in July of that year, thinking of the Democratic Convention in Chicago, Steinbeck wrote to James S. Pope to say, "Working furiously on my French History and there's just a . . . chance I may finish it before Chicago."[16] In November of that same year he wrote to his agent, Elizabeth Otis, to say, "I've finished now the Short Reign. . . . There's a great unease about it at Viking, but there's unease all over and maybe one thing transmits to another" (*Letters*, p. 541). Earlier, in June 1954, as he was involved with the initial work on *Pippin IV*, Steinbeck had written to Elizabeth Otis from Paris to say,

> With something of a shock I realize that I have written about nothing current for a very long time. . . . It has occurred to me that we may be so confused about the present that we avoid it because it is not clear to us. But why should that be a deterrent? If this is a time of confusion, then that should be the subject of a good writer if he is to set down his time. I must think about this. I wonder whether this might not be the reason there are so few good mss coming from the young writers. If it were so then it would be valid to inspect the scene for its salients, its character tendencies,

its uncertainties, its probable effects on the future in terms of character making and warping of people now growing up. (*TA*, 758–59)

And in October 1954 he had written to Otis to declare, "There is one thing I want to do. When I get home I want to sort of clear my mind and then do some work I have laid out but then about the late spring I want to take a drive through the middle west and the south and listen to what the country is about now. I have been cut off for a very long time and I think it would be a valuable thing for me to do. . . . And it isn't politics so much as the whole pattern. I have lost track of it I think" (*TA*, p. 767). The work he has laid out is, of course, the writing of *The Short Reign of Pippin IV*, a novel about moral uncertainties, about character making and the warping of young people such as Clotilde and Tod Johnson. And as these letters make clear, before, during, and after the writing of *Pippin IV* Steinbeck's thoughts were unmistakably focused not upon France and Europe but upon America, and particularly American politics.

Early in 1954 Steinbeck had written to American playwright Arthur Miller about his fears concerning the damage the House Committee on Un-American Activities was doing (*TA*, p. 746), and in June 1957 he published in *Esquire* a defense of Miller, who had been cited for contempt of Congress for his refusal to testify before the committee. In this article Steinbeck wrote

Law, to survive, must be moral. To force personal immorality on a man, to wound his private virtue, undermines his public virtue. If the Committee frightens me enough, it is even possible that I may make up things to satisfy the questioners. This has been known to happen. A law which is immoral does not survive and a government which condones or fosters immorality is truly in clear and present danger. . . .

The men in Congress must be conscious of their terrible choice. Their legal right is clearly established, but should they not think of their moral responsibility also? In their attempts to save the nation from attack, they could well undermine the deep personal morality which is the nation's final defense. The Congress is truly on trial along with Arthur Miller. (*TA*, p. 812)

Even earlier, in the fall of 1953, Steinbeck had written a piece entitled "If This Be Treason" as a response to the threat of McCarthyism (*TA*, p. 748).

America and the relation between private and public morality were quite obviously much on Steinbeck's mind as he planned and wrote *The Short Reign of Pippin IV*, and it is precisely America and this relationship that the novel is about. France provides a foil, a satirical device reminiscent of Swift's Lilliput but almost equally transparent. The genial comedy of the novel never darkens to the shade of Swift's Juvenalian satire, but there can be no doubt that Steinbeck's intention from the first lines was to question a kind of undue conceit of material sufficiency in America, a line of questioning that gave rise very directly to Steinbeck's next, and last, novel, *The Winter of Our Discontent*, a work in which public immorality is the seemingly irresistible destroyer of private virtue.

That Steinbeck's thoughts were moving in the direction of his last novel as he worked on *Pippin* is further indicated by a letter to Elizabeth Otis, dated February 1956, in which he mentions a short story he has just written, "How Mr. Hogan Robbed a Bank," and simultaneously speaks of an early version of *Pippin* tentatively entitled *All Your Houses*. "Mr. Hogan," as Steinbeck referred to the story, would, of course, later be expanded into the American jeremiad entitled *The Winter of Our Discontent* (*TA*, pp. 784–85).

In *The Short Reign of Pippin IV* Steinbeck stages a ritual purification in the form of seemingly light satire. The old government must fall to be replaced by a new one. In the interim Pippin, the mock king, rules as a scapegoat and reminder of older, more lasting values resilient enough to confront the threat posed by American materialism. In the end, Pippin's daughter is carried away to Hollywood—the lotus land of material dreaming—by the enemy, Tod Johnson; but through his sacrifices, Pippin has made a strong attempt to inject morality back into the government of his land.

In 1959, two years after the publication of *Pippin* and two years before the appearance of *Winter*, Steinbeck had written that "immorality is what is destroying us, public immorality. The failure of man toward men, the selfishness that puts making a buck more important than the common weal" (*TA*, p. 858). *The Short Reign of Pippin IV* is an illumination of this failure, a prodding of the American conscience aimed not at the quixotic politics of France but squarely at the dangerous combination of complacent materialism and cynical opportunism Steinbeck saw in the era of Eisenhower. That the rather too-gentle didacticism of this novella was insufficient for Steinbeck himself is attested to by the fact that from *Pippin* he would go on to *The Winter of Our Discontent*, a much darker and more explicit attempt to awaken Americans to the dangers of self-delusion and moral decay. Later still, in *America and Americans* Steinbeck would decry Americans' loss of purpose and direction, declaring that his countrymen were "poisoned with things," and that increasingly "we lose our feeling of wrong." "Why are we," he asked in that work, "on this verge of moral and hence nervous collapse?"[17] *The Short Reign of Pippin IV* represents an attempt to ask and answer the same question, a question asked again in *The Winter of Our Discontent* and still again in *America and Americans*.

Howard Levant

---

22 The Narrative Structure of *The Short Reign of Pippin IV*

John Steinbeck was fifty-five in 1957 when *The Short Reign of Pippin IV*[1] was published. Nevertheless, the book is essentially a youthful effort, a charming miscellany of satirical and witty comment on things-as-they-are, strung out along a consciously artificial plot line. Only the easy and certain technique and the virtuosity of the technique denote the author's artistic maturity. In fact, in its miscellaneous aspect, *The Short Reign of Pippin IV* is a further extension of Steinbeck's commitment, most evident in *East of Eden*, to an exaggerated kind of panoramic structure, the result of an extreme version of "is" thinking. The firmly articulated plot line recalls *Sweet Thursday* but reaches beyond it by holding together the otherwise fragmentary episodes.

The consequences of a restoration of monarchy in France in 1957 refer to mankind at large, but the basic idea is a fantasy that invites a possibility rather than a literal fact. Fairyland becomes the fact of the

Previously published.

political chaos of the Fourth Republic—an exaggerated mirror of fantasy which men are capable of inventing—and extends into the virtues of kingship.[2] Cannery Row can seem to be a more immediate fairyland.[3] Finally, the fantasy rests on distance; Frenchmen are stranger (in Henry James's sense) than Americans. The materials of the fantasy can be entirely contemporary, the stuff of today's newspaper; and so they are.

As in *Sweet Thursday*, Steinbeck is completely aware of the impression he wishes to create and of the proper technical means to achieve his end. It is no accident that *The Short Reign of Pippin IV* is subtitled *A Fabrication*. The subtitle refers to the structure—the miscellaneous range of the episodes—as obviously as to the royal fantasy. If anything, the highly fabricated plot emphasizes the artificial quality of the dramatic structure, thus drawing attention to the entertainingly panoramic miscellany of episodes. A note on the cover of the paperback edition is an accurate measure of the range of the episodes, which exceeds anything Steinbeck had attempted previously: "John Steinbeck's hilarious and affectionate spoof on French politics, Texas millionaires, teen-age girl novelists, sex, and other human frailties."[4]

The association of an extremely panoramic structure with the rigidity of an exceedingly artificial plot line continues and extends the novelistic formula of *East of Eden*, to the benefit of the comic spirit. The association of structures permits Steinbeck to range through any subject, in any manner, as he pleases, while the satire and wit relate to the dramatic structure, the plot line of a restoration of French monarchy. As in *Sweet Thursday*, this controlled freedom invests Steinbeck's familiar themes, techniques, and devices with a cheerful, refreshing ease.

The defect in this procedure is that, at worst, the materials are topical (the French crisis and the vogue of the girl novelist have passed or taken new forms), and the structure loses force through its inherent diffuseness, which extends to incoherence. Still, within the range of Steinbeck's work, *Sweet Thursday* and *The Short Reign of Pippin IV* are better than *Burning Bright*, at the opposite extreme. In fact, each of these extremes is a "fabrication," but one is charming and the other is merely rigid. The difference does not seem to lie in the extent of Steinbeck's commitment to theory, since both types are theory-ridden, but in the relative harmony (or association, as the case may be) between structure and materials that each type of novel makes possible for Steinbeck.

The plot is reductively lucid, as in *Sweet Thursday*, and it develops similarly through a series of major and minor parallels. While Pippin, an amateur astronomer and codiscoverer of the Elysée comet, is recording an unexpected cosmic shower, the hopelessly fragmented political parties—there are forty-two—decide through their leaders to restore the monarchy. Literally, stars fall on Pippin. The detailed political squabbling includes some of Steinbeck's funniest writing. The Communists, Socialists, Christian Atheists, Christian Christians, Left and Right Centrists, and the Non-Tax-Payers' League determine to support kingship "for different reasons and for reasons beneficial to" themselves, and the ten royalist factions, after deadlocking, agree to recommend "the holy blood of Charlemagne," that is, Pippin, who alone is unaware of the fuss, lost in his delighted observation of the cosmic shower.[5]

Reactions permit a development of character. Pippin tries to find Uncle Charlie—Charles Martel, a genteel dealer in "unsigned paintings," other "art and bric-a-brac," and loans—for advice "in matters spiritual and temporal"; he turns to his daughter's touring American suitor, Tod Johnson, son of the Egg King of Petaluma, California, for advice in handling power.[6] Pippin's solidly bourgeois wife, Marie, turns for womanly consolation to her school friend, Sister Hyacinthe, a former nude dancer at the Folies Bergère who took holy orders because her feet hurt; in due course, Sister Hyacinthe advises Pippin with deep understanding. These paralleled advisers are "placed" swiftly, but in some amusing depth. The thinnest character is Pippin's daughter, Clotilde, a twenty-year-old in revolt "against everything she could think of."[7] Clotilde is useful to the author because the theme of youthful rebellion allows Steinbeck to parody several tendencies of the time without much concern for internal consistency. Clotilde wrote a novel, *Adieu Ma Vie*, at fourteen, toured Europe and America in the wake of the novel's success as a film, introduced American teenage clothes into France ("blue jeans, saddle oxfords, and a man's shirt"), and at sixteen and a half entered politics by joining the Communist party but encountered a priest during a strike and became inspired with religious zeal.[8] In spite of this shotgun characterization, Clotilde's function within the plot is clear. She justifies the presence of Tod Johnson, a more important and unified character.

The presentation of these characters is choreographic rather than realistic, and their balanced, lucid relationship is centered by a mutual reference to Pippin's obsessive problem of what to *do*, as a king, to promote the good life of France. The theme of the good life is familiar in Steinbeck's work, but its comic reduction conflicts with its finally serious relevance to society when Pippin attempts to alter the social order. Hence there is a distraction in the constant humor of gratuitous juxtaposition—the astronomer become king, the nude become a nun, and the daughter become everything. *The Short Reign of Pippin IV* is more plainly a victim of its episodic humor than *Sweet Thursday* because it is ultimately a serious commentary on "a mad world, my masters," not merely a "pure entertainment." The aesthetic problem lies not in the youthfully callow banter but in the indeterminate intention of the fiction. Just so far as Steinbeck drops out of a tonal and thematic absurdity into seriousness, just so far the novel fails to maintain its delicate, associational structure.

The problem is uncomfortably visible in Steinbeck's handling of certain characters, where there is a recall, through an inversion of type, of earlier Steinbeckian characters. Pippin is much like the early Doc, a scientist dedicated to seeking absolute truth and to doing good; now he is the comfortable bourgeois whom Steinbeck handles roughly in the earlier work. Marie is a kind and really efficient bourgeoise, bound to her domestic economy. Marie could be turned easily into Helen Van Deventer in *The Pastures of Heaven*, Mrs. Morales in *Tortilla Flat*, the puritanical lady in *Cannery Row*, and even Bernice Pritchard in *The Wayward Bus*. Clotilde is not unlike Steinbeck's unformed adolescents, such relatively unsympathetic characters as Rose of Sharon in *The Grapes of Wrath*, Norma in *The Wayward Bus*, and even Curley's wife in *Of Mice and Men*, but Clotilde is plainly a harmless, charming butterfly, rescued from utter futility by Tod Johnson. At least Uncle Charlie is true to type—as a sophisticated version of Mack in *Cannery Row* and (to an extent) *Sweet Thursday*—since he knows and uses "the world" but remains uncorrupted. Sister Hyacinthe is less obvious than Uncle Charlie but as true to type. She is the good whore or love goddess transformed into a Catholic nun; she is not unlike the clever, soft-hearted madams— Dora in *Cannery Row* and Fauna in *Sweet Thursday*—or such wise creatures of love as Camille in *The Wayward Bus* and Suzy in *Sweet Thursday*, or, even further back, the shyly pleasant and virginal mother, Lisa, of *In Dubious Battle*. Tod Johnson is the only consequential persona who is not an inverted or direct echo of an earlier Steinbeck character, perhaps because Johnson represents a class Steinbeck had not dealt with to much extent in earlier work.

Steinbeck's inversion or recall of earlier characters is not the point at issue, however, since any author must be free to do as he wishes. The point is that Steinbeck handles these characters strictly for whatever comedy can be extracted from their behavior. This use creates a comedy of inversion, which undercuts Pippin's ultimate and serious effort to refashion France so the nation may enjoy the good life.

The novel exhibits the author's considerable technical skill and range, as in the polished alternation of Pippin's private and public life, the interchapters (in effect) which concern Clotilde or the old man in charge of the statues, the inserted brief narratives of political maneuver, or the puzzlement of the city dog in the country (assuming a strange, biological determinism), the internal monologues in Steinbeck's own voice, the determined play on names, and the constant, ironic juxtapositions in large and small matters (the king's motor scooter, or the company that realizes a small fortune by selling miniature guillotines at the coronation). The range of style is also stunning, for it includes some literal French, some American slang transposed into French idiom, many epigrammatic phrases which convey the sense of ordinary French idiom, some literal American slang, and Steinbeck's relaxed, colloquial diction. Yet this talent in details does not transpose adequately from a royal fantasy into the serious proposals Pippin offers to the nation at the conclusion of the novel. Otherwise, as an end in itself, the fantasy is as delightful, as apt, and as narrowly conceived as the sentimental *Sweet Thursday*, which preceded it.

The narrative sequence exemplifies these difficulties. With its focus on Pippin's adventures, the novel consists of five unnumbered sections (each introduced by a drawing), extending from thirty to fifty pages. Each section details Pippin's growing consciousness of what he is bound to attempt to accomplish through the power of kingship. This thematic development thrusts against the plot line, or the absurdity of the situation.

The first section opens with several expository pages on the theme of the felicity and privacy (equated terms) of Pippin and his family. As usual, a formal essay introduces the characters, but brevity and wit reduce the customary flatness of the introduction, and an ironic juxtaposing (always related to plot line) provides the essential momentary interest. The introduction occupies only five pages. The family lives in a converted coach house, rented from "a noble French family," which is seen only formally and by accident.[9] The irony enforces a happy anonymity. In the end, after being deposed, Pippin returns to that anonymity; no one is the wiser. Pippin is "fifty-four, lean, handsome, and healthy," his passion the "celestial hobby" of astronomy.[10] Aside from the irony of royal blood investigating the rigid (feudal?) sequence of the heavens, Pippin's age, person, and scientific bent suggest that he is (like Juan Chicoy in *The Wayward Bus*) something of a god of the machine. (This section is prefaced by a breezy drawing of a star-studded telescope which is surrounded by tools and posed against a moving heaven—suggesting Pippin's role and its comic guise. *The Wayward Bus* has a cover drawing of Juan's gods and penates—to call attention to that novel's heavier symbolism.) Astronomy, with its overtone of a certain mysticism, is an interest that lifts Pippin above Steinbeck's Americans who know and love machines (Tom Joad, Juan Chicoy) without blurring the relationship; Pippin's budget is limited and his celestial photographs are published in *Match*. More sophisticated as well as simpler than the earlier Doc, Pippin is a broadly civilized intellect: "He knew German, Italian, and English. He had a scholarly interest in progressive jazz, and he loved the cartoons in *Punch*. . . . He knew and liked Cole Porter, Ludwig Bemelmans, and, until a few years before, had known sixty percent of the Harmonica Rascals. He had once shaken hands with Louis Armstrong and addressed him as Cher Maître Satchmo, to which the master replied, 'You frogs ape me.'"[11] His modest, constant income from "the very best of a holding once great" in the wine country assures him the means to indulge in all of the intellectual joys, "carefully selected plays, concerts, and ballet . . . a good social club and three learned societies . . . books as he needed them," and the status of a "respected amateur" astronomer.[12] Pippin is in all ways a gentleman and one of Steinbeck's most attractive versions of the humanistic scientist. His suggestively associative name confirms Pippin's royalty and humanity.[13]

In Marie's character Steinbeck extols French virtues that can be American vices. Marie's domestic concerns have puritanical overtones in other Steinbeck contexts; here, they are admirable, and Marie's solidity is not unlike Ma Joad's. For example, Steinbeck uses juxtaposition to alter a possibly bad quality into an excellence, sentence by sentence, in these four typical sentences:

[Marie] was a good wife and a good manager who knew her province and stayed in it. She was buxom and pleasant and under other circumstances might have taken her place at the bar of a very good small restaurant. Like most Frenchwomen of her class, she hated waste and heretics, considering the latter a waste of good heavenly material. She admired her husband without trying to understand him and had a degree of friendship with him which is not found in those marriages where passionate love sets torch to peace of mind.[14]

If the second and fourth sentences are cut, Marie is not unlike Steinbeck's most hateful American women—middle-class and puritanical in values. But combined with the other details, the quick, inclusive, comic portrait establishes the feel of pleasant economy combined with civilized formality which Steinbeck considers a French virtue. The portrait is an obvious contrast, then, with some unattractive elements in American life.

Similarly, Steinbeck emphasizes what is most favorable in Clotilde's character—her silliness is childish (hence charming) rather than destructive, as in a sequence of adjectives describing her: "intense, violent, pretty, and overweight."[15] Omit the low comedy of "overweight," reverse the sequence, and one has a fearsome description of an American female, possibly of the college variety. With the details arranged as they are, the effect is disarming.

In all, the tonal control of the brief introduction sets the dominant impression of an orderly and pleasant universe, somewhat mad but most deeply rational, as expressed by the naturally witty people who inhabit it. Pippin's subsequent adventures strain the fabric of this fictional universe, but never to the breaking point. The good life, which Pippin knows, and the better life, which he can imagine out of his goodness, absorb the insane power relationships outside of Pippin's private sphere. He fails in the effort to refashion France, but his effort has its effect.

The remainder of the first section foreshadows much of this effort and failure. Pippin's extremely formal argument with Marie suggests the extreme civilization of French manners, which permit the concurrent political crux to end, in all logic, with a restoration of the monarchy and the election of Pippin to the throne. Pippin's argument with Marie over the purchase of a better camera relates equally to the politics of the moment, for Pippin wants "to stop the fiery missiles in their flight."[16] As a further parallel, the current premier, M. Rumorgue, is really a plant expert, far more willing to work on his peculiar "feeling" thesis than at politics. Clearly, these people are more civilized than political; that is an aspect of their insane politics. Steinbeck deepens the point by a dancelike parallelism. Uncle Charlie advises Pippin to encourage Marie's guilt, just as Sister Hyacinthe advises Marie. The private wholeness of the family is restored through conflicting and somewhat cynical advice; even Clotilde's screen test has its place in that order. The private "sound and fury" which is worked out through cross-purposes is paralleled by the fantastic, formal maneuvering of the politicians, which ends in the creation of a throne and the selection of Pippin as monarch. The clutter of parties is logical; the dance movement echoes the party lists and the various reasons which convince everyone that a monarchy is necessary. The specific French context supports the political nonsense, and the classical tradition of comedy supports the designed contrivances of parallelism. The basic conception demands the slashing effect of high comedy, but many of Steinbeck's humorous touches are in the key of low comedy; the disproportion between intention and execution is a failure of artistic choice.

Pippin's will to institute the good life is a more serious matter than the bulk of the novel's comic dance of parallelism and juxtaposition can sustain. The shift is wild, as though the king of fairyland were reported to favor the fair-trade law and the minimum wage. Steinbeck must not have felt that aesthetic shock, since there is no transition from the low comedy of grotesque humor to Pippin's moral earnestness.

This essential division deepens in the succeeding sections of the novel. Thus Steinbeck ranges at will from satire to low comedy in the juxtapositions of section 2. Satire inspirits the comment that the coronation is "a triumph of disorder" because no American advertising agency can find the time to manage the affair: "BBD & O was up to its ears rewriting the Constitution of the United States and at the same time marketing a new golf-mobile with pontoons. Riker, Dunlap, Hodgson, and Fellows would have taken the French job in the fall, but could not pull its key people off promotion of Nudent, the dentrifice which grows teeth."[17] The wonderfully juxtaposed coronation march is closer to low comedy in its genial representation of past and present: "First came the state carriages of the Great Peers, decorated with gold leaf and tumbling angels; then a battery of heavy artillery drawn by tractors; then a company of crossbowmen in slashed doublets and plumed hats; then a regiment of dragoons with burnished breastplates; then a group of heavy tanks and weapon-carriers, followed by the Noble Youth in full armor. A battalion of paratroopers followed, armed with submachine guns."[18] As high comedy, Pippin grows bored with the procession, props up his royal robes in the carriage, and disappears in the crowd; no one detects the "prop" during the march.[19]

These several kinds of comedy are panoramic in their detail. The delightful scattering does not fuse into a whole, or with Pippin's moral earnestness. The association of structures works fairly well in *Sweet Thursday*, but the miscellaneous comedy, the series of details in the manner of "is" thinking, linked to the dramatic structure of the artificial plot, is served inadequately in this more complex novel. Steinbeck seems to recognize and welcome the result, since increasingly the comic detail occupies one corner of the novel, and Pippin's search for effective power to institute the good life occupies another corner.

Clearly, by the third, or middle, section, the comic detail tends to be panoramic and the materials concerning Pippin's search for power tend to be dramatic. The detail is mainly by the side, while Pippin's adventures dovetail with the development of the plot.

Comic juxtaposition includes placing the perfect bourgeoise, Marie, in "that gigantic old dustbox Versailles," among the bums who are the real nobility; and the appearance of Sister Hyacinthe, released to Versailles by her order to provide Marie with gossip "upon recognition of certain advantages which might accrue" to the order as well as "satisfaction" for a good deed.[20] These materials are framed, on the one side, by the "era of good feeling" of the political parties ("Christian Christians saw the churches full. Christian Atheists saw them empty"), and, on the other, by Tod Johnson's practical hint that titles might be sold in Texas and Beverly Hills to finance the retirement of the French nobility.[21] At the center, through conversations with Uncle Charlie, Tod, Clotilde, and especially Sister Hyacinthe, Pippin clarifies his basic desires for the nation on the principle that "people are good—just as long as they can be."[22] Sister Hyacinthe is the primary catalyst of the elements in Pippin's developing idea of kingship. She recognizes the danger of mere pride, yet concludes earthily, "You are a good man, Sire, and a good man draws women as cheese draws mice."[23] Pippin's primary adviser is Tod Johnson (through his father's questions), the pragmatic businessman. Tod observes that a government must have something to sell; Pippin suggests "perhaps peace, order—perhaps progress, happiness," or the good life.[24] Tod recommends a corporate organization, the socialism of business, and a firm grip on authority. In short, Tod understands power and Pippin's compulsion to do good, but he shows Pippin a course of action that no Frenchman can envisage in a context of Uncle Charlie's fearful cynicism, Clotilde's anger, and Sister Hyacinthe's resignation.

The division between comic detail and plot is intensely continued in section 4. Comedy is mostly restricted to the opening frame of juxtaposed hits. The "little cloud," like a similar device in *Cannery Row*, introduces mainly serious matters.[25] The parable of a city dog recovering a sense of the past, once free in the country, illuminates Pippin's awareness of a role to play. Several visits to a Wordsworthian old man clarify his resolve. Sister Hyacinthe's mysterious faith in love sets off Uncle Charlie's brutal realism. The smoothly lucid progression, joining the parabolic freedom, the old man's sense of duty, and Sister Hyacinthe's faith that only love is the source of goodness and good deeds, puts down Uncle Charlie's worldly realism. As an association, Pippin *acts* for the first time, on his second visit to the old man, by entering the fight with the toughs. That private, releasing act moves Pippin to determine to act as a public figure for the good of the entire country: "——by God, I'll do it!"[26] Pippin determines to play the sacrificial Christ role, and Sister Hyacinthe confirms the rightness of that choice by praising it: "I have read your remarks to the convention. They were bold remarks, Sire. Yes, I imagine that you have failed, you personally, but I wonder whether your words have failed. I remember another who failed—whose words we live by."[27] Steinbeck identifies other men with Christ in other novels (Jim Casy, Juan Chicoy), in part through initials. Here, the frank identification requires proof through action, not through a device. Steinbeck gains clarity through directness—at some cost, it should be noted, to the novel's structural integrity.

A final event pulls together the plot, since the comedy has been lost. Still wet from the fight (he had been tossed into the moat) and hot with a conviction to act, Pippin returns to the palace, bursts in on Marie, and makes love to her. This event recalls Mr. Pritchard's gesture, but it is more fortunate. Marie does not show Mrs. Pritchard's bitchy reactions. Pippin's lovemaking is his second positive act, denoting his willingness to perform in accord with his conscience.

Some absurd or comic detail is scattered about, such as Pippin's habit of going into the country on a motor scooter, his crown replaced by a crash helmet, or the "elderly nobleman who spoke earnestly and loudly in Gothic type into Charles's ear," but this kind of detail tends to be associated with the development of the plot more consistently here than in the earlier sections.[28] A formal pattern of opposites governs the comic touches. Pippin is told, for example, that his speech to the convention that will adopt the Code Pippin must be restricted to patriotic generalizations, but he nevertheless orders the convention to undertake a program of economic reform. A low-comedy detail is fitted carefully into this pattern of opposites, for as Pippin turns away from the convention, which is in a state of shock, he is revealed as a silly figure, to the relief of the audience:

> An open-mouthed page was standing on the edge of his purple and ermine-collared cape. It ripped from his shoulders and fell to the floor, exposing the row of safety pins up the back of his tunic, and the baggy crotch of the trousers flopping between his knees. Strain in children and adults opens two avenues of relief—laughter or tears—and either is equally accessible. The safety pins did it. Beginning with a snigger in the front benches, it spread to giggles, and then to hysteric laughter. . . . Thus they channeled the shock the king's message had given them, the shock and the terror and their own deep sense of guilt.[29]

The twelve final words indicate Steinbeck's purpose and reveal the rationale for the completely appropriate comic strategy. After all, Pippin is not in fact a Christ, nor is his message a religious insight. He is a modern saint, perhaps, in the sense that he has an orderly, humanistic, scientific mind. He had studied the problems thoroughly; his evident interest in the truth is the cause of the cloud that prefigures the ultimate horror in the audience. So, in not being a Christ, a heroic persona of sacrificial dignity, Pippin must be the fool. His sad calm and his safe, anonymous return to the converted coach house (where Marie has

preceded him) is a metaphor of the acceptance of merely human limitations, of the best one can do in an imperfect universe.

So these comic details are structural in their support of the satiric
plot. The governing principle is that Pippin's humiliating public display—his speech as well as the accident that follows it—is really the
only way in which Pippin can act. As a framing detail before the
speech, the convention committee insists on wearing court dress and
forces Pippin to wear an especially badly fitting costume. The old
Socialist, "Honnete Jean Veauvache, now Comte des Quatre Chats,"
explains why in an essay speech which concludes on this key point:
"And if to this assembly should come the king, dressed in a two-button
suit and a Sulka tie, carrying his papers in a briefcase, I shudder to think
of the reaction. Indeed I feel that such a king would be laughed out of
office."[30] "A venerable Academician" underlines the suggested threat:
"The king may not permit himself to be ridiculous."[31] Again, as another framing detail, Pippin consults with Uncle Charlie, who is ready
to fly the country in expectation of the address and who repeats the
point in somewhat racier language: "When a pawn tries to do the work
of government—then the pawn is a fool."[32] In a sense, Pippin is
laughed out of office, since he does permit himself to *seem* (but not to *be*)
ridiculous, and he plays the fool by intent as well as by accident. If he is
somewhat a victim—of birth as of accident—assuredly he wills the
speech of reason and goodness which is his true downfall. His comic
exit assumes that he will not be harmed for truthfulness, essentially
because the nation is mindlessly forgetful and rational in equal parts.
Hence, after the confrontations which clarify these points, Pippin
simply goes home to become again (even to the gendarme called out by
the rioting) no more than the private citizen. Of course, with French
prudence, Pippin takes the precaution beforehand of secreting his motor scooter; he does not need it for flight, only for a return to the
converted coach house; and it runs out of gas. The conclusion is that the
clown is allowed everything and forgiven everything.

Several conclusions are in order. First, *The Short Reign of Pippin IV* is
in genre a roman à clef, whose parts separate into superficial comic hits
and serious essays on the good life. The aesthetic result is a novelistic
wabble—a delightful comedy of the times and a serious tract for the
times. Second, because the two intentions do not fuse, the novel lacks
structural unity. As comedy, the novel accepts the condemnation that

Steinbeck applied to *L'Affaire Lettuceburg:* "And this book is fairly clever, has skillful passages, but tricks and jokes."[33] As a serious work, the novel depends heavily on the essay, the set speech, the authorial comment. The sharp detail of "is" thinking degenerates into relatively isolated hits; an externalized plot provides an otherwise unobtainable narrative lucidity; instead of a dramatic structure conceived as a sequence of actions, as in Steinbeck's most impressive work, pure statement carries the burden of the events, recalling the play-novelette theory and the allegorical signs that crop up repeatedly in the ambitious longer fiction which Steinbeck produced in the period after 1940. Third, the mix of these various tendencies and devices does not seem to cause Steinbeck misgivings. Completely relaxed, he indulges what he knows. The consequent aesthetic mess is clearly intentional. No further development seems possible along the line of misguided novelistic theory as exemplified by *The Short Reign of Pippin IV*.

X Overview

Robert E. Morsberger

23   Steinbeck and the Stage

John Steinbeck may be said to have invented what he calls a "new form—the play-novelette."[1] From the time of *Frankenstein* on, a great many novels have been adapted to the stage with varying degrees of success, though seldom successfully by the novelist himself. Henry James, who always aspired to be a playwright, wrote unsuccessful adaptations of *Daisy Miller* and *The American* in which he violated the integrity of his novels by altering their tragic endings to happy ones. James also adapted two failed plays into the moderately successful novels *The Other House* and *The Outcry*. Other novelists have written plays, and some playwrights have written novels. What is unique about Steinbeck's play-novelettes is that he conceived of them simultaneously in both forms. Of the three works that he so conceived, the first, *Of Mice and Men*, was an outstanding success in both genres; the second, *The Moon Is Down*, was a moderately successful novel and a moderately unsuccessful play; and the third, *Burning Bright*, a failure in both forms, is generally considered Steinbeck's poorest work. What may concern the literary critic and historian is the ways in which conceiving of a work simultaneously as a short novel and a play affected its writing in each genre.

In his introduction to the Bantam edition of *Burning Bright*, Steinbeck explained the rationale by which he undertook his three play-novelettes. Claiming to find it difficult to read plays and considering the limited number of theatergoers who might see even a successful play, he considered that the novelette version would find a larger audience. His second reason was to provide the director, producer, and performers more descriptive and interpretive detail than the terse stage directions in an acting copy of a play. The novelette, he thought, provides the author's intention more fully (*BB*, pp. 1–2). Conversely, the discipline of the theater forces the novelist to be clear and concise. Despite the downward curve of his success with the play-novelette, Steinbeck found the combination "highly rewarding. It gives a play a wide chance of being read and a piece of fiction a chance of being played without the usual revision" (*BB*, p. 3).

After completing *In Dubious Battle*, Steinbeck announced to his agents, "I'm doing a play now. I don't know what will come of it. If I can do it well enough it will be a good play. I mean the theme is swell." *Of Mice and Men* was published as a novel before Steinbeck undertook a dramatization of it, but apparently he wrote it in such a way that it could easily be turned into a play, for in 1936, while the work was in progress, he told George Albee, "It is a tricky little thing designed to teach me to write for the theatre."[2] At this time Steinbeck had had comparatively little exposure to the stage and to theater people, but in his best work he wrote some of the best working-class dialogue in American literature, and episodes from some novels read almost like scenes from a play. Accordingly, in 1937 director Herman Shumlin invited him to write a dramatization of *In Dubious Battle*.[3] Wisely, Steinbeck declined, for despite its numerous dramatic episodes, the novel is too sprawling for the stage. In any case, he was concentrating on *Of Mice and Men*. Before he could do his own adaptation, he agreed to let a labor drama group in San Francisco, the Theatre Union, mount its own staging to inaugurate its new Green Street Theatre in North Beach. When its president, Wellman Farley, told Steinbeck he wanted to put on plays about current local history, Steinbeck presented him a manuscript of the not-yet-published novel.[4] The Theatre Union dramatization opened on May 21 and and ran on Friday and Saturday nights for sixteen performances.[5] Reviewing it in the *San Francisco Chronicle*, John Hobart found that it "follows the novel closely; the dialogue has been lifted straight from the book and transferred to the stage with hardly a single change."[6] Although in his introduction to *Burning Bright*, thirteen years later, Steinbeck claimed that his short novels "can be played simply by lifting out the dialogue" (*BB*, p. 1), Hobart found that "since Steinbeck was writing primarily for readers the result is a play that seems slightly ill at ease in the theatre."[7]

Likewise, Margaret Shedd found that the Theatre Union version "does no more than block in the tantalizing outlines, with too much sentimental detail of rabbits and murders and with gaping omissions."[8] She concluded that *Of Mice and Men* is certainly not a great play, although just as certainly it has in it the raw material of one.[9] Steinbeck himself admitted that when he undertook to do his own dramatization for experienced theater people, he had to do extensive rewriting.[10]

Of Mice and Men attracted several playwrights, but Annie Laurie Williams, of Steinbeck's agents McIntosh and Otis, recommended the novel to Beatrice Kaufman, wife of George S. Kaufman, who became enthusiastic, writing to Steinbeck that the novel "drops almost naturally into play form and no one knows that better than you" (*SLL*, p. 136). Though his own plays had been chiefly comedies, often in collaboration with Moss Hart, Kaufman was eager to direct *Of Mice and Men* and encouraged Steinbeck to dramatize his novel. When Steinbeck showed his adaptation to Kaufman, the veteran playwright knew it needed work. Accordingly, he brought Steinbeck to his farm in Bucks County, Pennsylvania, where they spent an intense week in which the novelist revised the script under Kaufman's guidance (*SLL*, p. 141). Kaufman felt that "it is only the second act that seems to me to need fresh invention. You have the two natural scenes for it—the bunkhouse and the negro's room, but I think the girl should come into both these scenes, and that the fight between Lennie and Curley, which will climax Act 2, must be over the girl. I think the girl should have a scene with Lennie before the scene in which he kills her. The girl, I think, should be drawn more fully; she is the motivating force of the whole thing and should loom larger" (*SLL*, p. 136).

Essentially, Steinbeck followed these suggestions in revising his script. The dialogue in act 1 follows the first two chapters of the novel almost verbatim; even the stage directions are usually verbatim from the novel's descriptive and narrative details. Of necessity Steinbeck had to omit some descriptive passages that could not be staged, particularly the novel's opening four pages and the sentimental description of Slim on page 61. Of course the language salvaged from the novel for stage directions and character descriptions would not be heard by the audience, but reading the opening scenes is essentially the same experience as reading the first two chapters. However, on her first appearance, in the second scene, Curley's wife gets a bit more dialogue in the play: "I'm just lookin' for somebody to talk to. Don't you never jus' want to talk to somebody?"[11] The addition of just these two sentences makes her a bit more sympathetic. After she leaves, her perfume lingers. "God Almighty, did you smell that stink she's got on?" George asks. "I can still smell her. Don't have to see *her* to know she's around."[12] Thus, in the next scene, before the fight with Lennie, Steinbeck adds the detail of having Curley sniff her perfume and swear she was there.

Again, just before Curley's appearance and the fight, act 2, scene 1, gives Curley's wife three additional speeches, which go further in making her sympathetic, more a victim than a provoker. In the novel she does not appear in this scene at all. In the play, after agreeing to include Candy as a partner in the farm, George adds the line, "You know, seems to me I can almost smell that carnation stuff that god-damn tart dumps on herself," whereupon Curley's wife enters and says angrily, "Who you callin' a tart! I come from a nice home. I was brung up by nice people. Nobody never got to me before I was married. I was straight. I tell you I was good. *(A little plaintively.)* I was. *(Angrily again.)* You know Curley. You know he wouldn't stay with me if he wasn't sure. . . . You got no right to call me a tart."

When George responds by asking her why she is always hanging around guys when she has a husband, she replies, pleadingly, "Sure I got a man. He ain't never home. I got nobody to talk to. I got nobody to be with. Think I can just sit home and do nothin' but cook for Curley? I want to see somebody. Just see 'em an' talk to 'em. There ain't no women. I can't walk to town. And Curley don't take me to no dances now. I tell you I jus' want to talk to somebody."

When George replies by asking why she gives men the eye, she answers sadly, "I just wanta be nice."[13] Then, hearing Curley and Slim approach, she disappears.

Considering the impact she makes, it is surprising to consider how brief a role Curley's wife has in the novel. Prior to the chapter when Lennie kills her, she has only two brief appearances, one for 2 pages, another for 9. In chapter 5 she has 10 more pages, for a total of 19 pages out of 186. Probably the role seems larger because Curley and the others frequently talk about her. But in the play and film versions the enlarged role earns the actress supporting star billing. Again, further changes make her more sympathetic in the play. When she interrupts Candy, Crooks, and Lennie in Crooks's room, in the novel she threatens to have Crooks lynched by lying that he made advances to her. The play cuts this unsympathetic passage and instead has George come into the scene and argue with her. At the end, as she is about to leave, she speaks to Lennie with "a note of affection in her voice" as she realizes it was he who ruined her husband's hand, and she says to him, "Well . . . maybe you're dumb like they say . . . an' maybe . . . you're the only guy on the ranch with guts. *(She puts her hand on Lennie's shoulder. He looks up in her face and a smile grows on his face. She strokes his shoulder.)* You're a nice fella."[14] This, of course, leads more naturally to the brief intimacy between them in the barn.

In the barn scene, the play adds another detail, bringing her more naturally there by having her hide with a packed suitcase, prepared to run away. Thus, when she tells Lennie about her dream of becoming a movie star, the novel's "I coulda" is changed to "I'm gonna," and her unexpected death at the moment of her supposed liberation becomes even more poignant.

The final scene of the play cuts several passages from the novel; it omits Lennie's fantasy conversations with Aunt Clara and with a gigantic rabbit, and it ends with the gunshot that kills Lennie, omitting the following anticlimactic dialogue when the lynch mob and Slim reappear.

All in all, these changes, plus a few other minor ones, tighten the dramatic structure and impact of the work. Steinbeck modestly said that Kaufman deserved most of the credit, but all the dialogue is Steinbeck's, and at least 80 percent of it comes verbatim from the novel. Kaufman deserves credit for advising Steinbeck to enlarge the role of Curley's wife; it is not clear which of them decided to make her more sympathetic.

Otherwise, Kaufman's chief contribution was as director. Kaufman was considering Victor McLaglen for the crucial role of Lennie but decided it might be better not to have to put up with star temperament, though star names were helpful for the box office *(SLL, p. 137)*. Accordingly, he cast Wallace Ford and Broderick Crawford, then comparative unknowns, as George and Lennie. Will Geer played Slim, and Claire Luce was Curley's wife.

Before rehearsals began, Steinbeck met with the staff, said that everything seemed to be in such good hands that he was not needed, and departed for California. Accordingly, much to Kaufman's chagrin, the author was in Los Gatos when the play opened in New York on November 23, 1937, at the Music Box (*SLL*, p. 141). He kept in touch by phone and was gratified to learn that the reviews ranged from enthusiastic to ecstatic. Brooks Atkinson called it "a masterpiece of the New York stage."[15] Recalling that Steinbeck was known to have written the novel "with the stage in mind," Atkinson found that "the economy of the story, the unity of the mood, the simple force of the characters, the tang of the dialogue are compactly dramatic, and *Of Mice and Men* is not theatre at second hand. . . . To be technical about it, *Of Mice and Men* is a perfect work of art."[16] The play ran for 207 performances in New York and won the New York Drama Critics' Circle Award as best play of the year, beating *Our Town* by a vote of twelve to four. In presenting the award, the critics praised the play "for its direct force and perception in handling a theme genuinely rooted in American life."[17] Later, more hostile critics would accuse Steinbeck of sentimentality, but in 1937, what impressed critics was, in George Jean Nathan's words, the play's "unabashed realism," its "beautifully honest . . . scrutiny of speech, act, emotion, and character."[18] Indeed, the realism in both action and language then seemed so raw that some viewers left the theater in indignation, and *Of Mice and Men* has never since ceased to be attacked by puritanical and right-wing censors.

George Jean Nathan predicted that the play could never be filmed, that the movies would never "dare to risk such things intact," since its language and subject matter would get it shot down by the Hays office and would "bring down the wrath of every women's club in the land."[19] But in 1939 Hal Roach brought out a brilliant film version, directed by Lewis Milestone, with music by Aaron Copland and memorable performances by Burgess Meredith (who became a lifelong friend of Steinbeck) and Lon Chaney, Jr., as George and Lennie. Eugene Solow's script was faithful to the novel and play, and the film has become a classic. Since then, there have been two highly acclaimed television versions.

In 1958 Ira J. Bilowit and Wilson Lehr adapted *Of Mice and Men* into a musical play, with lyrics by Bilowit and music by Alfred Brooks. It played briefly off Broadway but fared poorly. Louis Calta judged that while "Mr. Steinbeck's drama still remains a work of substance and power," the score lacked "the necessary passion, grandeur and breadth."[20] An operatic version by Carlisle Floyd fared no better in

1970; when it was revived in San Francisco in 1974, music critic Martin Bernheimer judged that the simple eloquence of Steinbeck's language sounds "stilted, silly and artificial when blown up for grand operatic treatment."[21]

But the play seems to go on forever. It continues to be revived frequently and widely and has attained the stature of a dramatic classic.

Royalties from *Of Mice and Men* enabled the Steinbecks to make their first trip to Europe, visiting Denmark, Sweden, Finland, and Russia. Though they did not get to Norway, Steinbeck got a feeling for Scandinavia. When they learned from two fellow travelers that May 17 was Norwegian Independence Day, they became "a kind of auxiliary Norwegians"; "spiritually we felt Norwegian."[22] Thus Steinbeck was outraged when the Nazis invaded and occupied Norway. Even before our entrance into the Second World War, Steinbeck became involved with resistance movements, associating with refugees from occupied countries who were trying to aid underground movements back home. His imagination also became occupied with the role of Quislings and collaborators and with punitive acts by the Nazis against resistance activities.[23] Accordingly, when William J. Donovan, head of Agency Coordinator of Information (which later became the Office of Strategic Services), asked Steinbeck to write a work that would lend support to resistance movements, he was more than ready to oblige. Considering that "each separate people had to learn an identical lesson, each for itself and starting from scratch," he decided that "if I could write the experiences of the occupied . . . such an account might even be a blueprint, setting forth what might be expected and what could be done about it" ("Reflections," p. 3).

He began the work as a play, at first set in an American town to show, as in Sinclair Lewis's novel (which was also staged) *It Can't Happen Here*, that it can happen here. But when he submitted this version to the Foreign Information Service for approval, it was rejected on the grounds that even a fictional story of our possible defeat and occupation could damage morale.[24] In the 1980s films like *Red Dawn* and *Amerika* dramatized such a story, but the idea was unacceptable during wartime. Outraged, Steinbeck's friends in the resistance groups urged him to change the setting to an occupied country. "The book might hurt American morale, they said, but it would be very good for the morale of the resistance men" ("Reflections," p. 3). Consequently, Steinbeck "placed the story in an unnamed country, cold and stern like Norway, cunning and implacable like Denmark, reasonable like France. The names of people in the book I made as international as I could. I did not even call the Germans Germans but simply invaders" ("Reflections," p. 3). Nevertheless, from the fact that the invaders are fighting England and Russia, there is no doubt as to their identity. The play might be set in any country, but the novel version, with far more detail about weather and terrain, is clearly set in Norway.

Steinbeck wrote to Webster F. Street, on November 25, 1941, "The play? It's just about the way the people of a little town would feel if it were invaded. It isn't any country and there is no dialect and it's about how the invaders feel about it too. It's one of the first sensible things to be written about these things and I don't know whether it is any good or not" (*SLL*, p. 237). He completed the play on December 7, the day Pearl Harbor was bombed, and entitled it *The Moon Is Down*. Then, working with intense concentration, he rewrote it as a novel, which was rushed into print by March 1942. For his first book after *The Grapes of Wrath*, expectations ran high; the Book-of-the-Month Club ordered 200,000 copies, and prepublication orders exceeded those of *Grapes* by two to one (*SLL*, p. 242).

The play opened on April 8 in New York at the Martin Beck Theatre, under the direction of Chester Erskin, with Otto Kruger as Colonel Lanser, Ralph Morgan as Mayor Orden, Whitford Kane as Dr. Winter, and William Eythe as Lieutenant Tonder. Again, expectations ran high. Steinbeck wrote to Street on opening night that "a curious kind of wave of excitement is going through theatrical New York. I never saw anything like it. I think the publicity has been so great that the critics will crack down on the play" (*SLL*, p. 243). Steinbeck was prophetic, for two days later he wrote to Street that the reviews "are almost uniformly bad. Furthermore, they are almost entirely right. They don't really know what bothered them about the play, but I do. It was dull. For some reason, probably because of my writing, it didn't come over the footlights. In spite of that it will probably run for several months. It is too bad it isn't better. I don't know why the words don't come through" (*SLL*, p. 244). Later, he apparently changed his mind, for he wrote to Street, "Oddly, the play goes on to crowded houses in spite of the critics. The critics have all stopped being critics and have turned propagandists. They are judging what should be told the people, what is good for the people to know. And the people are doing a better job than the critics" (*SLL*, p. 245).

What critics of both play and novel objected to was Steinbeck's treatment of the Nazis as human beings, lonely and homesick, rather than the cartoon monsters of propaganda, and to what they considered his overly optimistic vision of Nazi defeat. Nevertheless, the novel went on to sell nearly a million copies in its first year.[25] According to Burns Mantle, the novel "caused as startling an explosion of superlatives in book review circles as any work of the year,"[26] yet James Thurber (then irritable from undergoing a series of eye operations) and Dorothy Thompson were savagely hostile, and a lively controversy ensued. Over the years, received opinion from the critical establishment is that *The Moon Is Down* is a negligible work, the beginning of Steinbeck's alleged decline. In 1958, in a sweeping condemnation of Steinbeck's entire canon, Alfred Kazin complained of "banal propaganda" in *The Moon Is Down*,[27] and in 1962 Stanley Edgar Hyman wrote that the novel made him lose interest in Steinbeck's work because of what he perceived as a shift in the author's "social commitment."[28] But such dogma needs to be constantly reexamined. Certainly *Moon* is not in the same league as *The Grapes of Wrath*. It was not intended to be. Steinbeck wrote it more or less on assignment—quickly—and it accomplished what it set out to do. The resistance movements applauded the book, and the underground circulated mimeographed copies.[29] One can even argue that it is the best World War II novel written during the war. As a play, it is certainly better than Hemingway's *The Fifth Column*, and the novel is arguably superior to his *Across the River and into the Trees*. If there is not the richness of character, language, and setting found in the best of Steinbeck's 1930s work, the writing is nevertheless clear, workmanlike, and free from the sometimes stylized, pretentious language that flaws *Burning Bright* and parts of *East of Eden*. As a piece of theater, the work is well constructed, with each of the play's eight scenes and the novel's corresponding eight chapters building to a dramatic climax.

One factor that critics have overlooked is how early in the war Steinbeck wrote *The Moon Is Down*. When he was working on it, we were not yet in the war. He completed the manuscript of the play on Pearl Harbor Day. When the novel and play appeared in the spring of 1942, the Axis powers still seemed to be winning everywhere. Yet

Steinbeck predicted, with almost prophetic insight, the nature of the ultimate defeat. There is considerable subtlety in his portrayal of the supposed conquerors, still nominally in command, acknowledging that in essence they have already been defeated. Scene/chapter 5 is especially skillful, as Steinbeck shows the members of the occupying force terrified by "death in the air, hovering and waiting"; by the stubborn sabotage, occasional assassinations, and the cold, sullen hatred that has isolated them; by their inability to relax, to let down their guard for a moment; by the irresistibly growing nervous tension, aggravated by loneliness and homesickness; by their suspicion that everywhere else where there is officially proclaimed victory the same sense of hopeless futility prevails; by the awareness that the conquered will kill them all if given the chance, and that retaliation brings not submission but only more relentless hatred.

By any objective reckoning *The Moon Is Down* is unqualifiedly against the Nazis. Where Steinbeck deserves credit, in fact, is in his realization that not all members of the Wehrmacht were intrinsically savage, that some of them may have been basically decent people who were deluded by their own propaganda or forced by military discipline to do things that they too found revolting. Thus Colonel Lanser resembles Melville's Captain Vere, who, though he loves Billy Budd, nevertheless executes him in compliance with military law. Lanser is much the same way. A superficially civilized man, he wants to minimize bloodshed; he hopes to accomplish his assignment of working the coal mines without resistance, but when the resistance comes, he retaliates by reprisals, by starving the families of miners who do not cooperate, and by taking and killing hostages. Richard Lockridge's complaint in the *New York Sun* that Steinbeck's invaders are "more sinned against than sinning"[30] is wholly inaccurate, taking Lanser and his officers at their own estimate. Lanser may consider himself a man of goodwill, like Captain Vere, but his actions condemn him. He realizes, as Lieutenant Tonder has earlier suggested, that the Leader is a madman, that the orders from the capital to shoot more and more hostages only deepen the hatred and resistance. Ultimately his best hope is to minimize the casualties during the inevitable retreat, but though he has no faith in his orders, he says that they are clear and that he will carry them out "no matter what they are."[31] Likewise, in condemning Billy Budd, Captain Vere says that it is not he who condemns but martial law. "For that law and the rigor of it, we are not responsible. Our vowed responsibility is in this: That however pitilessly that law may operate, we nevertheless adhere to it and administer it."[32] The defense of "just following orders" is that of all perpetrators of war crimes, from Henry Wirz to Adolf Eichmann, and it will not pass muster. As Thoreau observes, when the laws are unjust, it is the just person's duty to disobey them and to go to prison if necessary. Nevertheless, Steinbeck's portrait of Lanser and his fellow officers is far subtler than those in wartime movies. Certainly innumerable Nazis running the slave labor and death camps were capable of the most ghastly cruelty (though the worst had not yet happened in 1941, when Steinbeck wrote *The Moon Is Down*), but with his belief that people are not "very different in essentials" ("Reflections," p. 3), Steinbeck realized that even the Nazis were also human beings.

Among them there is considerable variety. Captain Loft is an impatient martinet; Major Hunter is a mathematician devoted chiefly to the intricacies of engineering; Captain Bentick is an imitation of an English squire; Lieutenant Prackle is a "snot-nosed" undergraduate; and Lieutenant Tonder is "a bitter poet" (*Moon*, pp. 44, 46). Some of them carry out their unsavory mission enthusiastically, some reluctantly, some with indifference. But there is no question that the invasion is evil, that what the invaders do, regardless of their various attitudes, is brutal and murderous. When Colonel Lanser urges Mayor Orden to collaborate in the execution of Alex Morden for killing a soldier, Orden responds that he will do so only if Lanser will execute his soldiers who murdered six townsmen on the day of the invasion. There is also no question that the invaders will ultimately be defeated. Nowhere does Steinbeck offer comfort to the Nazis. Such qualified sympathy as he shows is for decent individuals like Lieutenant Tonder, caught up in the tragedy of history; they too are victims of the Nazi horror.

From our perspective this is clear enough, but during 1942, when the Allies still seemed to be losing, hysterical war fever caused some to label Steinbeck's humane approach at best as sentimental, at worst as close to treasonable. This may be one reason why the play ran in New York for only nine weeks.[33]

Another reason, however, may be that the play, though written first, is not as good as the novel. For one thing, Steinbeck did not have the benefit of George S. Kaufman's professional advice. For another, the novel benefits considerably from the addition of passages that could not be staged and that enrich the book's texture. Each chapter begins with several pages of narrative that fill in the background, relate offstage actions, set the mood, describe the grim Nordic weather, and give a sense of geography and community missing in the play. Sometimes the additional material is only a page or two, but several times it is a third of a chapter. It is much more than simply fleshed-out stage directions. In these narrative portions we see the patrols on the streets, get a sense of the sullen hatred that surrounds them, feel the bleak wintry isolation, and learn details of the initial invasion and the subsequent acts of resistance. Steinbeck opens up the action and expands the scene, which in the play is confined to the mayor's palace for seven of the eight scenes, plus one at Molly Morden's house. The sense of community, so important to Steinbeck's thesis, is largely missing in the play, which is confined to the dialogue of the invading officers, the mayor and his household, and Molly and Alex Morden, but Steinbeck provides it in the additional pages of his novel. He also provides additional irony in his descriptions of setting and character, and the detailed analysis of the Nazi officers in chapter 2 adds considerably to the complexity of their portraits.

Most of the dialogue is identical in both versions. But since the novel, though written after the play, was published before the play was staged, there are small changes in the latter, perhaps worked out during rehearsal. Some of them sharpen and clarify an issue. In the penultimate scene the play adds about a page of dialogue not in the novel, and here the loss is the novel's. Probably Steinbeck wrote the passage after the novel was already in print. In it, debating with the Quisling Corell, Lanser asks, "Have you ever thought that one execution makes a hundred active enemies where we have passive enemies? Even patriotism is not as sharp as personal hurt, personal loss. A dead brother, a dead father—that really arms an enemy." He goes on to observe, "I know we have failed—I knew we would before we started. The thing the Leader wanted to do cannot be done."

CORELL *(excitedly):* What is this? What do you say?
LANSER *(quietly):* Oh! Don't worry. I will go about it as though it could be done and do a better job than the zealots could. And when the tide turns, I may save a few lives, from knowing how to retreat.
CORELL: They shouldn't have sent a man like you here!

LANSER: Don't worry—as long as we can hold, we will hold. I can act quite apart from my knowledge. I will shoot the Mayor. *(His voice grows hard.)* i will not break the rules. I will shoot the doctor. I will help tear and burn the world.[34]

Despite the superiority of the novel, the play is workmanlike, and after its two months on Broadway it had a successful road show, with Conrad Nagel replacing Otto Kruger as Colonel Lanser. Despite its comparatively brief New York run and generally unfavorable reviews, *The Moon Is Down* came in second in the New York Drama Critics' voting for the best play of the year, getting two votes to four for *In Time to Come*, by Howard Koch and John Huston; however, eleven critics voted to give no award that year.

The 1943 film version fared considerably better. Nunnally Johnson, who had written the script for *The Grapes of Wrath*, did the scenario and also produced the film. While keeping Steinbeck's plot and using much of the dialogue verbatim, he opened up the action, dramatizing episodes that occur offstage in the play and novel, with the result that the Nazis seem harsher, while we get more of a sense of the community's resistance. Steinbeck applauded the results, writing to Johnson, "There is no question that pictures are a better medium for this story than the stage ever was. It was impossible to bring the whole countryside and the feeling of it onto the stage, with the result that the audience saw only one side of the picture."[35]

Despite the play version's lukewarm and sometimes hostile reception in America, it did exceptionally well in Europe. Early in 1943 the play was a smash hit in London and Stockholm. As for the novel, Steinbeck noted that "the little book was smuggled into the occupied countries. It was copied, mimeographed, printed on hand presses in cellars, and I have seen a copy laboriously hand written on scrap paper and tied together with twine. The Germans did not consider it unrealistic optimism. They made it a capital crime to possess it, and sadly to my knowledge this sentence was carried out a number of times. It seemed that the closer it got to action, the less romantic it seemed" ("Reflections," p. 3). The king of Norway decorated Steinbeck for the support that both novel and play gave to the resistance movement.[36] Initially, the Russians were disappointed, thinking that Steinbeck showed too much compassion for the Germans.[37] But while Steinbeck was in

Moscow in 1963 as a cultural ambassador, the play was revived there, to favorable reviews in TASS.[38]

In the United States, the play has not been revived since its 1943 road show, nor is it likely to be, but the novel remains in print and deserves not only rereading but reevaluation. Perhaps it has fewer aesthetic and intellectual complexities than fiction and drama by authors more beloved of graduate schools, but it certainly made more of a difference in real life; and while not a major work, it is intellectually and aesthetically respectable enough. In Steinbeck's canon, it is important for an examination of his ongoing concern with the nature of leadership and of group man, which he dealt with from *Cup of Gold* through *In Dubious Battle*, "The Leader of the People," *The Grapes of Wrath*, and *Viva Zapata!* Mayor Orden, the authentic leader, is responsive to the will of the people, and when he is killed, more leaders will rise up spontaneously, whereas Colonel Lanser obeys orders even when he disagrees with them, and his Leader (or Führer) does not lead but betrays his people, who in blindly following him show the conduct of herd men, as contrasted to the invaded community, where the resistance movement demonstrates genuine communal action.

In 1947 Steinbeck started another play-novella, based upon a suggestion by Burgess Meredith, who had been invited to do a play for Dublin's Abbey Theatre, that he might dramatize a modern Joan of Arc who warns us against the atomic bomb.[39] Intrigued with the possibility of writing a play for the Abbey Theatre, Steinbeck worked on *The Last Joan* during the first months of 1947, aiming for a summer run in Dublin. But by April, after trying numerous approaches, none of which worked, he admitted to Frank Loesser, "I have finally faced it. The play is no good and I have thrown it away and have so warned Buzzy Meredith. It just didn't come off."[40] The unpublished manuscript has not been preserved. The basic idea, though it excited Meredith and Steinbeck at first, seems quite untheatrical; it might make a jeremiad, but it is hard to think how it could have been embodied in either a play or a novel.

In the late 1940s Steinbeck worked on several screenplays—*The Pearl*, *The Red Pony*, and *Viva Zapata!*—but he did not return to playwriting until 1949, when he wrote to Elaine Scott, whom he was to marry a year later, that he was working on a play entitled *Everyman* (*SLL*, pp. 380–81). Eventually retitled *Burning Bright*, this was Steinbeck's third play-novelette. The plot deals with a middle-aged man named Joe Saul, who is obsessed with the need to carry on his family line by having a child but fears he is sterile. Out of a deep compassion and love for him, his wife, Mordeen, gets herself impregnated by Joe Saul's apprentice, Victor, hoping to pass the child off as her husband's. When he discovers the truth, he must learn "that every man is father to all children and every child must have all men as father. This child is not a little piece of private property, registered and fenced and separated. Mordeen, this is The Child. I love The Child. I love our child. Mordeen, *I love my son.*"[41] "My Christ! it's a dramatic thing," he wrote to Elaine Scott (*SLL*, pp. 380–81). Conceiving of the work, like the medieval *Everyman*, as " a morality play, completely timeless and placeless" (*SLL*, pp. 661–62), Steinbeck tried to give the story universality by the experiment of having the characters as circus people in act 1, farm people in act 2, and seafarers in act 3, while retaining their names and relationships.

The work proceeded rapidly. Steinbeck wrote the play first and then novelized it. By February 1950 the novel was already in production at the Viking Press, for Steinbeck wrote to Pascal Covici that he had just made some minor changes in the play and was sending them over; "since they will be in the play, it is just as well if they are in the book too."[42] By the middle of the summer he complained to Covici, "There is one disadvantage to the play-novel form. The novel has to go to press and stay that way but little changes take place in the play right up to opening night" (*SLL*, pp. 404–5). One major change that had just taken place was the title; Steinbeck had favored *In the Forests of the Night*, but Richard Rodgers and Oscar Hammerstein, who were producing the play, thought the title too long and literary and suggested *Burning Bright*. Though the new title had no connotations for Steinbeck, he went along with it.

Despite his enthusiasm, he might have seen storm clouds gathering, for in late August he wrote to Webster F. Street that the short novel version had been "turned down by every magazine in the country. The Book Clubs would not touch it. . . . This is a highly moral story and they are afraid of it. It also gives me reason to believe that I am not writing crap. Indeed I think it might start a new trend in the theatre." He was convinced that "it's a good play, strong and simple and basic with no smartness. It will either strike with a smash or not go at all."[43]

To his friend Bo Beskow he wrote that *Burning Bright* would go into rehearsal on September 5, 1950, and a second play a month later; but this second play, whatever it was, failed to materialize (*SLL*, p. 402). Instead, several days after *Burning Bright* opened in Boston on October 2, Steinbeck found himself rewriting the second act. On October 6 he wrote to Annie Laurie Williams, "I think we have a tight and dramatic second act now but I'll know more when I see it tonight. They have practically chained me by the leg to the hotel radiator." The next day he reported to her that the show was better than ever and that the company were all "very much heartened. All of us are determined to bring in a good show. And now I think we really are going to." He added that "many people may not like it but those who do love it passionately and feel that it is somehow theirs. Katharine Cornell who came to the opening told me that this was one of the very few times she wished she were younger. 'If I were 20 or even 10 years younger,' she said, 'you couldn't keep me out of it.' Lillian Gish called me and told me not to change a line" (*SLL*, pp. 411–12).

So much for great expectations. On October 18 the play opened in New York at the Broadhurst Theatre, and thirteen performances later, it closed. There were two favorable reviews, one mixed one, and the rest were devastating. High praise went to Jo Mielziner's sets and to the performances by Barbara Bel Geddes as Mordeen, Kent Smith as Joe Saul, Howard Da Silva as Friend Ed, and Martin Brooks as Victor; the hostility was directed at the play itself. To Eugene Solow, Steinbeck wrote, "The critics murdered us. . . . I wish you could have seen the play because it is a good play. I think it will do well in Europe where people are neither afraid of the theme nor the language. The sterility theme may have had something to do with the violence of the criticism" (*SLL*, p. 412). To Jack and Max Wagner he reported, "It got the shit kicked out of it. It was a good piece of work and a lot of people are pretty mad at the critics for destroying it" (*SLL*, pp. 413–14). He was puzzled that knowledgeable theater people like Guthrie McClintic, Rodgers and Hammerstein, and others could have been so wrong in their positive assessment of the play, but at last he conceded, "It was not a good play. It was a hell of a good piece of writing but it lacked the curious thing no one has ever defined which makes a play quite different from every-thing else in the world. . . . This thing read wonderfully but it just did not play. . . . I had the best possible production, the best direction and sets that would break your heart they were so wonderful" (*SLL*, pp. 413–14).

Not only is it not a good play, it is far from being "a hell of a good piece of writing." For *Burning Bright*, Steinbeck attempted a literary rather than a vernacular style, but instead of seeming poetic, it seems merely stilted, abstract, self-conscious, and pretentious. Steinbeck observed that "the universal, mildly poetic language seemed to enrage" the critics (*SLL*, p. 412). For one thing, there are few contractions, and the characters always address each other in a formal way; Joe Saul is always Joe Saul, never Joe; Friend Ed is always Friend Ed, never just Ed, and exchanges like "Did you hear about that, Friend Ed? . . . Well, you can't blame her, Joe Saul," ring false (*BB Acting*, p. 6). So do such lines as "Mordeen is tenderness. Mordeen is fire. She puts loveliness around her like a light so that everyone near her shines a little in reflection," to which Friend Ed responds, "What a good thing to say! What a sweet thing to hear!" (*BB Acting*, p. 7). Lines like "Oh, very yes" sound gushy. Brooks Atkinson faulted such phrases as "strong in your wife-loss," "I am harsh-breathing," and "do I have the friend-right to ask a question" as sounding too formalistic and allegorical.[44] One reviewer, in a pastiche of the play's style, asked, "Have I, I wonder, the admirer-right to tell Mr. Steinbeck that this trick has me screaming silently in my reader-loss?"[45]

One of Steinbeck's great strengths as a writer, and what made *Of Mice and Men* work as a play and *The Grapes of Wrath* as a film, is his use of pithy vernacular speech; one can argue that he writes the best dialogue for working people of anyone in American literature. When he abandons the vernacular for a consciously literary, abstract, and metaphorical language, the results are usually disastrous. Steinbeck's attempts at poetic language have all of the effusiveness of Marchbanks's poetasting in Bernard Shaw's *Candida*. Sometimes there are striking metaphors, but overall the effect is embarrassing.

In addition, the plot is contrived and predictable, resembling a combination of *Desire Under the Elms* and *Strange Interlude*. Men may long for children and fear sterility, but Friend Ed's suggestion of adoption is far more sensible than the surreptitious surrogate parenting and Friend Ed's murdering Victor to keep Joe Saul from discovering the truth.

Even more contrived is Joe Saul's getting a medical examination as a gift to his unborn child and discovering during the exam that his sperm is dead.

It is the play that is dead, and Steinbeck's venting his frustration in an article entitled "Critics, Critics Burning Bright," in which he faulted audiences for prudery and for snickering at a taboo subject and blamed critics for their failure to accept the play's language, did not bring it back to life. "This language did not intend to sound like ordinary speech, but rather by rhythm, sound and image to give the clearest and best expression of what I wanted to say."[46] Steinbeck made the meaning of his drama almost painfully clear, but his characters, with their abstract speeches, sound more like philosophers than circus people, farmers, and seafarers. The language does not work; it lacks the genuine poetry of *Murder in the Cathedral* and *Under Milk Wood* and instead of seeming universal, it seems merely archaic and pseudoliterary.

Nevertheless, Boston's drama critic Elliott Norton found *Burning Bright* to be "one of the stimulating and challenging dramas of the season, curious and arresting in its form, affirmative in its philosophy of life, beautifully acted," and John Chapman judged that "Mr. Steinbeck's intentions were artistic and honorable, but his drama could not be taken as seriously as it should have been."[47]

The Viking Press published hardcover editions of the dramatic versions of *Of Mice and Men* and *The Moon Is Down* but failed to do so for *Burning Bright*. The only published version, long out of print, is the acting copy of the Dramatists' Play Service. The novel, however, remains in print. For the most part it reproduces the play verbatim, turning the stage directions and descriptions of character into narrative and descriptive passages, sometimes amplified in the novel. Subtitled *A Play in Story Form*, the novel is even divided into three acts rather than chapters. The main changes are in the final scene in the hospital, where Steinbeck adds about one-third more dialogue. Joe Saul has his face covered by a surgical mask, and in the novel Mordeen asks him, "Where is your face? What's happened to your face, Joe Saul?" He answers, "It's not important. Just a face. The eyes, the nose, the shape of chin—I thought they were worth preserving because they were mine. It is not so. It is the race, the species that must go staggering on" (*BB*, p. 129). At the end she says, "It is very dark. Turn up the light. Let me have light. I cannot see your face." Joe Saul responds, "'Light,' he said. 'You want light? I will give you light.' He tore the mask from his face, and his face was shining and his eyes were shining" (*BB*, p. 130).

Despite the failure of *Burning Bright*, Steinbeck remained friends with its producers, Richard Rodgers and Oscar Hammerstein II, who were to write and produce his last theatrical venture, *Pipe Dream*. Its genesis was Steinbeck's proposal to dramatize *Cannery Row*. At the same time he discussed with composer Frank Loesser the idea of turning *Of Mice and Men* into a musical.[48] By the fall of 1952 he had changed his plans and was now considering adapting *Cannery Row* into a musical with a score by Loesser. But the adaptation was not working, and Steinbeck decided instead to write a new story with the same setting and some of the same characters. As producer Ernest Martin explained it, "The story of *Cannery Row* per se wouldn't make a show. It needed more. So we asked John to see if he could develop for us the basis of a musical play . . . based on the characters of the Row, built around the character of Doc. . . . The form that we had in mind was to be a story about Doc and some woman" (*SLL*, p. 459). Steinbeck started out writing a libretto but gave up and concluded that he would do better to turn the project into a novel and then adapt it or have someone else adapt it to the stage.[49] In a similar way, when asked to write a screenplay for Alfred Hitchcock about the Merchant Marine in World War II, Steinbeck had written a novel, which Jo Swerling then adapted into the scenario that Hitchcock filmed.

Using the working title *Bear Flag*, Steinbeck aimed the novel in progress for a musical comedy adaptation. By now Rodgers and Hammerstein had replaced Frank Loesser, and as Steinbeck completed sections of his first draft, he mailed them to Hammerstein, who was taken with the story and characters, though Rodgers worried about whether they could get away with showing a house of prostitution and having the heroine a working prostitute. Rodgers warned his collaborator that they must be careful.[50] As it turned out, this concern and caution would be fatal to the show.

The novel was published in 1954 as *Sweet Thursday*, and Hammerstein, having persuaded Rodgers to do the score, began his adaptation. To play Doc, everyone wanted Henry Fonda, to whom Steinbeck wrote, "I keep your face and figure in my mind as I write." Fonda would have made a fine Doc in a nonmusical version, but as he told producers Feuer and Martin, "Boys, I can't sing for shit." Though he was persuaded to take singing lessons for the better part of a year, Fonda's singing remained "just terrible."[51] Instead, the part went to William Johnson, with Judy Tyler as Suzy. To play Fauna, the earthy madam of the Bear Flag brothel, Rodgers and Hammerstein picked grand opera diva Helen Traubel, who turned out to be fatally miscast, her grand opera voice and manner totally out of style with both the character she was playing and with the other performers.

Aside from the miscasting of Traubel, most of the flaws came from Hammerstein's book and lyrics. Rodgers and Hammerstein had always written wholesome "family" shows. But *Sweet Thursday*, though its bums are idealized, its whores have hearts of gold, and its madam is, as Hammerstein told Traubel, "wholesome," has an underlying toughness. Though Steinbeck described the book to Elizabeth Otis as "light and gay," he also called it "astringent" (*SLL*, p. 472), and it is that astringency that is missing in Hammerstein's adaptation. Hammerstein's first draft followed Steinbeck closely, using much actual dialogue from the novel, but as he continued to revise the work, he cleaned up the script, in Traubel's words, "to the point of innocuousness . . . as scene after scene became emasculated."[52] Steinbeck was dismayed and wrote lengthy memos to Hammerstein, giving detailed suggestions for restoring what he called the work's "guts." Mainly he objected to Hammerstein's altering the initial cause of Doc's discontent and basing it on his first meeting with Suzy, to a lack of clarity about Doc's character, and to the way in which Hammerstein evaded the fact that Suzy was working as a prostitute. The libretto cuts her background of having been made pregnant and abandoned at sixteen, of her having lost the baby and been jailed for vagrancy. Hammerstein uses extreme circumlocution and euphemism in his treatment of the Bear Flag and even more so in his treatment of Suzy, so that it is never clear that she is a working prostitute; instead, she may merely be a roomer at what his lyrics call the "happiest house on the block," a "little blue heaven" which "is friendly and foolish and gay" (*Pipe Dream*, p. 103). By this evasion Hammerstein removed the essence of Doc's rejection of Suzy, of her reason for reform, and of the pain that causes her to reject him as well as the happiness that she finds in taking control of her life.

The novel's Suzy is not just the stereotyped prostitute with a heart of gold; it is her toughness and integrity more than her prettiness and gentleness (under Fauna's coaching) that appeal to Doc. Doc admires the truth, in no matter how rough a guise, and he finds a truth in Suzy. The scenes between them have a tension because each is trying to hang on to integrity; they quarrel because they are as much alike as they are different. Doc may have an IQ of 182 and a Ph.D. from the University of Chicago, but he cannot condescend to Suzy; he must approach her as an equal. The musical sentimentalizes their relationship into a fairly routine love story. Steinbeck complained of this and wrote to Hammerstein that his version had no tension or drama because Doc and Suzy have been reduced to "two immature people who are piqued at each other." Steinbeck urged Hammerstein to finally bring "into the open, but wide open," the conflict caused by Suzy's being a working prostitute, arguing that he would thereby solve the show's great weakness and raise it "to a high level. You will have also overcome the most universal and consistent criticism we have had, that the show sidesteps, hesitates, mish-mashes and never faces its theme. . . . If this is not done, I can neither believe nor take *Pipe Dream* seriously."[53]

According to his associates, Hammerstein was a bit of a prude, and he ignored Steinbeck's memos. Rodgers and Hammerstein's shows generally have a wholesomeness that sometimes descends to the saccharine, and that is in any case all wrong for Cannery Row, which Steinbeck called "a poem, a stink, a grating noise, a quality of light, a tone, a habit, a nostalgia, a dream."[54] In the hands of Rodgers and Hammerstein, the stink and grating noise have been eliminated, and what remains is chiefly the nostalgia.

In consequence, when it opened in New York at the Shubert on November 30, 1955, critics were disappointed, calling it "RH negative."[55] John Chapman found it dull much of the time, perhaps because "Hammerstein and Rodgers are too gentlemanly to be dealing with Steinbeck's sleazy and raffish denizens."[56] Rodgers agreed, conceding that "we weren't as well acquainted as we might have been with bums, drifters and happy houses of prostitution."[57] Though the show played for a respectable 246 performances, it had the shortest run of any Rodgers and Hammerstein production and lost money.

How well does *Pipe Dream* hold up when read? It is agreeable enough but bland, and compared to the novel, it is quite thin. One thing missing is Steinbeck's authorial voice, which provides much of the novel's unexpected yet deadpan humor. Instead of the subtleties of Steinbeck's style, we have Hammerstein's all-purpose dialect, which he uses indiscriminately for Oklahoma, the New England of *Carousel*, and California's Cannery Row; it consists mainly of having people say "feller" (contrast to Steinbeck's "fella") and "winder." Also missing is the "hooptedoodle" that provides the narrative with texture. Hammerstein is unable to get into the minds of the characters, and so we miss a great deal of their substance, together with more humor. There is none of the novel's opening sense of the aftermath of World War II, no sense of what Cannery Row has been and of the background of its characters, without which they don't make a great deal of sense. Many characters are missing altogether; there is no Old Jingleballicks, no Joe Elegant, no Seer, no Wide Ida, no Ella, no Becky, and the comically corrupt Joseph and Mary Rivas, with his con-man rapacity, has been reduced to "Joe (the Mexican)," little more than a name. The only attempt Hammerstein makes to present Steinbeck's inversion of conventional values is a song, "A Lopsided Bus," in which the boys challenge the strait-laced Puritan work ethic and sing,

> We hop on our lopsided bus
> And chase another day
> As happy as candles that shine on a cake,
> As gay as the bells on a sleigh! (*Pipe Dream*, p. 50)

We do not get the ecology of Cannery Row, and the closest we get to the ecology of the natural world is Doc's saying that "everything is connected" and singing about starfish, buzzards, and armadillos, with the refrain, "It takes all kinds of people to make up a world" (*Pipe Dream*, pp. 20–21). Rodgers's show tunes replace Doc's recordings of Gregorian chants, the masses of William Byrd, Bach's fugues, and Mozart's *Don Giovanni*. The lyrics are sometimes clever and occasionally romantic, but both songs and book have much less raffishness than the novel. No one even drinks Old Tennis Shoes. Doc, Mack and the boys, and even Fauna and the girls would be dismayed.

What, then, is the final score for Steinbeck on stage? One hit, two runs, and one error. One out of four does not sound too great, but such a judgment is too facile. Though only a moderate success or a mild failure on stage, depending upon one's method of reckoning, *The Moon Is Down* did accomplish its aim of helping resistance movements in Axis-occupied Europe and ran successfully overseas, and the novel, though a minor work, deserves an honorable place in Steinbeck's canon. *Burning Bright* remains a failure both as play and novel, but it deserves some credit as a flawed experiment and is certainly no worse than such experiments by Eugene O'Neill as *Lazarus Laughed* and *Dynamo*. *Pipe Dream* is inconsequential, but working on a musical sequel to *Cannery Row* resulted in *Sweet Thursday*, which, despite some sentimentality, such as passing Suzy off as Snow White, has much choice humor and "hooptedoodle" and is arguably Steinbeck's best novel of the 1950s. Thus, writing a work simultaneously as a novel and a play produced positive dividends. One does not ordinarily think of Steinbeck as a playwright, but *Of Mice and Men* has become an enduring classic of the American stage, one of the ten best plays written in America. That is no small accomplishment.

Notes

2 Nonteleological Thinking in *Tortilla Flat*

1 Howard S. Levant, *The Novels of John Steinbeck* (Columbia: University of Missouri Press, 1974), p. 59.

2 Howard S. Levant, *"Tortilla Flat:* The Shape of John Steinbeck's Career," *PMLA* 85 (1970): 1088–89.

3 Edwin Berry Burgum, "The Sensibility of John Steinbeck," in *Steinbeck and His Critics: A Record of Twenty-five Years*, ed. Ernest W. Tedlock, Jr., and C. V. Wicker (Albuquerque: University of New Mexico Press, 1957), p. 107.

4 John Steinbeck, *Tortilla Flat* (New York: Covici-Friede, 1935), p. 11. All further references to this work in the text use this edition.

5 Burgum, pp. 106–7.

6 Frederick Bracher, "Steinbeck and the Biological View of Man," in *Steinbeck and His Critics: A Record of Twenty-five Years*, ed. Ernest W. Tedlock, Jr., and C. V. Wicker (Albuquerque: University of New Mexico Press, 1957), p. 194.

3 Historical Introduction

1 "Mice, Men, and Mr. Steinbeck," *New York Times*, December 5, 1937, quoted in Jackson J. Benson, *The True Adventures of John Steinbeck, Writer* (New York: Viking Press, 1984), p. 364.

2 Steinbeck's college roommate, Carlton Sheffield, gives an account of Steinbeck's experience on the ranch in his introduction to *Letters to Elizabeth: A Selection of Letters from John Steinbeck to Elizabeth Otis*, ed. Florian Shasky and Susan F. Riggs (San Francisco: Book Club of California, 1978).

3 John E. Steinback [*sic*], "Fingers of Cloud: A Satire on College Protervity," *Stanford Spectator* (February 1924).

4 John Steinbeck to Claire Luce, 1938, from *Steinbeck: A Life in Letters*, ed. Elaine Steinbeck and Robert Wallsten (New York: Viking Press, 1975), pp. 154–55.

5 "Mice, Men, and Mr. Steinbeck." Jackson Benson suggests Steinbeck may have been putting on a "wild west" act for reporters.

6 Letter to Louis Paul, February 1936, in *Life in Letters*, p. 120.

7 Postcard to Louis Paul, undated, in *Life in Letters*, pp. 123–24.

8 Letter to Elizabeth Otis, Stanford University Library, Department of Special Collections.

9 Letter to Elizabeth Otis, April 15, 1936, Stanford Department of Special Collections.

10   Letter to Elizabeth Otis, May 27, 1936, Stanford Department of Special Collections.
11   Letter to George Albee, 1936, in *Life in Letters*, p. 132.
12   February 27, 1937, review.
13   February 27, 1937, review.
14   Quoted in *Life in Letters*, p. 136.
15   Joseph R. Millichap, *Steinbeck and Film* (New York: Ungar, 1983), p. 13.
16   Frank S. Warnke in *Opera News Review*, March 14, 1970.
17   Warren French, *John Steinbeck* (New York: Twayne Publishers, Inc., 1961), p. 74.
18   James D. Hart, *The Oxford Companion to American Literature* (New York: Oxford University Press, 1941), pp. 722–23.
19   Margaret Marshall, quoted in Peter Lisca, *The Wide World of John Steinbeck* (New Brunswick: Rutgers University Press, 1958), p. 5.
20   Edmund Wilson, *The Boys in the Back Room: Notes on California Novelists* (San Francisco: Colt Press, 1941), pp. 41–43.
21   Jackson J. Benson, "Hemingway the Hunter and Steinbeck the Farmer," *Michigan Quarterly Review* 24, no. 3 (Summer 1985): 452–53.
22   Lisca, *Wide World*, pp. 134–36.
23   Wilson, *The Boys in the Back Room*.
24   So described by Steinbeck in a letter to George and Anne, January 11, 1937, in *Life in Letters*, pp. 133–34.

4   Parable of the Curse of Cain

1   Frederic I. Carpenter, along with several others, calls *Of Mice and Men* a tragedy. See "John Steinbeck: American Dreamer," in *Steinbeck and His Critics*, ed. E. W. Tedlock, Jr., and C. V. Wicker (Albuquerque: University of New Mexico Press, 1957), p. 76 (referred to hereinafter as Tedlock and Wicker). Warren French calls *Of Mice and Men* a "dark comedy" in *John Steinbeck* (New Haven, Conn.: College and University Press, 1961), p. 76. French also pushes the thesis of the novella's descent from Arthurian legend; see p. 73. Joseph Fontenrose says, "*Of Mice and Men* has no recognizable mythical pattern," in *John Steinbeck, An Introduction and Interpretation* (New York: Barnes and Noble, 1963), p. 59. The political theories of *Of Mice and Men* are quoted from Edwin Berry Burgum and Stanley Edgar Hymen, pp. 109 and 159, respectively, in Tedlock and Wicker. Sociological points are stressed by French in *John Steinbeck*, p. 77. Freeman Champney says *Of Mice and Men* is "little other" than the theme of "every man [*sic*] kills the thing he loves" (in Tedlock and Wicker, p. 140). The "pleasures often oppose and thwart our schemes" thesis is in Fontenrose, p. 57. "The nonmorality of Nature" is the interpretation of Burton Rascoe, p. 65, Tedlock and Wicker. The quotations from Beach and Kazin, respectively, are in Tedlock and Wicker, p. 90; and *On Native Grounds* (New York: Doubleday, 1956), pp. 309–10.
2   The quotation is in Tedlock and Wicker, p. 307.

3   One of Steinbeck's critics unconsciously confirms this discouraging thesis when he says, "Steinbeck represents George as being closely attached to Lennie. But George's feeling is not convincing because it is not that of most men in real life" (Woodburn O. Ross in Tedlock and Wicker, p. 175). To Mr. Ross we might reply, with John Steinbeck, *tant pis!* This is the same outlook that provides the context for the tragedy of George and Lennie!

4   First appearance suggests that Steinbeck might be guilty of antifeminist sentiment by his use of the Hemingwayesque "Men Without Women" theme: "Everything was fine with us boys until that trouble-making female came along," etc. Curley's wife, however, is presented as the victim of the same impulses as the men in the story; she too is impelled out of loneliness to seek company, and she too is the victim of a dream: "Coulda been in the movies, an' had nice clothes," etc. With this emphasis Steinbeck includes Curley's wife in the problems and striving of all men who inherit the curse of Cain. In any case, though she does in fact have trouble-making propensities, she is no worse in this respect than her husband and overall is unquestionably a more sympathetic character than Curley.

5   Obviously Steinbeck faced a problem in his portrait of Lennie as a sympathetic though dangerous moron who has great difficulty in keeping his hands off women. (Compare William Faulkner's treatment of Benjy in *The Sound and the Fury.*) The author's entire emphasis would have been thrown off balance if Lennie had attacked Curley's wife (or the girl in Weed) in some gross and lascivious manner. Clearly, if he were prone to this sort of behavior George would not be traveling with him in the first place. Lennie must be as he is— powerful and potentially dangerous, but essentially childlike and innocent—for other reasons as well. His condition lends emphasis to the basic idea of general aloneness of men; if Lennie were normally intelligent, he would most likely be busy pursuing his own interests. Finally, the basic innocence of Lennie's sensual impulses reinforces Steinbeck's critique-of-Hebrew-Christian-morality theme by making the point that there is nothing evil, per se, in man's natural sensuality.

6   All my quotations from *Of Mice and Men* are taken from *The Portable Steinbeck*, selected by Pascal Covici (New York: Viking Press, 1960), pp. 227–323.

7   See Joseph Fontenrose, *John Steinbeck*, p. 60; and Edward Wagenknecht, *Cavalcade of the American Novel* (New York: Henry Holt, 1958), p. 446.

6   The Red Pony as Story Cycle and Film

1   A particularly noteworthy example of an author's changing an earlier novelette while preparing a film version is provided by the two forms of Alan Sillitoe's *The Loneliness of the Long-Distance Runner*. See Warren French, "Fiction vs. Film 1960–1985," in *Contemporary American Fiction*, ed. Malcolm Bradbury and Sigmund Ro (London: Edward Arnold, 1987), pp. 106–21.

2   Forrest L. Ingram, *Representative Short Story Cycles of the Twentieth Century* (The Hague: Mouton, 1971), p. 13.

3   See Warren French, *John Steinbeck*, 2d ed. rev. (Boston: Twayne, 1975), pp. 62–68, for the detailed explication from which the brief quotations in this summary are taken.

4   Steinbeck made his only appearance in a commercial film as a commentator linking film versions of five stories by O. Henry in *O. Henry's Full House* (1952). While this film explored the possibilities of making a feature film by combining a number of short subjects, the group chosen for this film did not constitute a thematically linked cycle, so that the only continuity was provided by Steinbeck's unpretentious commentaries.

5   That Steinbeck did view the story cycle and film as initiation stories is evident, however, from a proposed introduction to Copland's *Red Pony Suite*, derived from his background music for the film. In 1964 Copland asked the aging Steinbeck if he would be willing to write an introduction that could be read at performances of the suite at children's concerts. Steinbeck responded enthusiastically with an apparently unpublished "Narration," about three hundred words in length, a copy of which has been located in the Annie Laurie Williams Collection at the Rare Book and Manuscript Library, Butler Library, Columbia University, along with a correspondence between Steinbeck and Copland concerning it. In the "Narration" Steinbeck describes a boy whose experiences are recalled by the suite, who ends up a man as a result of passing through the experiences. Copland felt that the narration was not suited for children, but Steinbeck did not wish to revise it. (Annie Laurie Williams handled permissions for Steinbeck's agents, MacIntosh and Otis.)

6   Frye's theories were propounded long after Steinbeck's composition. The point is, however, that Frye might have used Steinbeck's work with traditional classics in formulating his theories, for they are based upon the same archetypal experiences. Steinbeck was aware of the mythic implications of his tales, for in the "Narration" mentioned in n. 5 above he writes, "into the ever-morning and the ever-present, comes the intimation of other mornings and the knowledge that the path has been travelled before, that the little boy is not a fresh created uniqueness in the Universe."

7   The article summarized here appears as "John Steinbeck and American Literature," *San Jose Studies* 13, no. 2 (Spring 1987): 35–48. The quoted passages are from Northrop Frye, "The Archetypes of Literature," *Kenyon Review* 13 (1951): 104–5.

8   While it may be difficult to contemplate juvenile Jody Tiflin as the kind of mythical figure that Northrop Frye describes as "partly the sun, partly vegetative fertility and partly a god or archetypal human being," ("The Archetypes of Literature," p. 104), Jody in "The Promise" dreams of being such a figure, and Steinbeck was intrigued in other novels like *To a God Unknown* and *Tortilla Flat* with characters who either played gods or challenged the gods.

9   All references to the completed film are based on a commercial videotape, presumably made from the master print in the Republic Studios archive and distributed under the Republic brand name by the present holder of the studio's copyrights. I have not been able to compare this tape with a release

print of the film, but the visuals and dialogue differ somewhat from the "estimating script" that Aaron Copland used in preparing the soundtrack for the film and which is now in the Rare Books Room at Dartmouth College Library.

10 Joseph Millichap, *Steinbeck and Film* (New York: Ungar, 1983), p. 121.

11 Steinbeck's narration, which was delivered for the film by Burgess Meredith, who had starred in Lewis Milestone's film version of *Of Mice and Men*, was published with many stills from the film in *The Forgotten Village* (New York: Viking Press, 1941).

12 Elaine Steinbeck and Robert Wallsten, eds., *Steinbeck: A Life in Letters* (New York: Viking Press, 1975), pp. 195–96.

13 Jackson J. Benson, *The True Adventures of John Steinbeck, Writer* (New York: Viking Press, 1984), p. 472.

14 Ibid., p. 453.

15 Ibid., p. 481.

16 Steinbeck apparently did not think too highly of the finished film. In a letter to Aaron Copland in July 1964 he expressed the hope that it could stay locked away in a bank vault.

17 Robert Morsberger, ed., *Viva Zapata! The Original Screenplay*, by John Steinbeck (New York: Viking Press, 1975), p. 131.

18 *The Red Pony* has been dramatized a second time as a television film by Robert Totten in 1973, starring Steinbeck's good friend Henry Fonda as the father and Maureen O'Hara as the mother. Although this first made-for-television adaptation of a Steinbeck work won a Peabody Award for outstanding television drama, it is entirely unsatisfactory as an adaptation of Steinbeck's work, principally because Totten eliminated the key character of Billy Buck, Jody's mentor, in order to enlarge Henry Fonda's role. As fine an actor as Fonda was, he was too old when the film was made to be convincing as the father of a pre-teenager. Since Steinbeck, who had died in 1968, had no connection with this production, it cannot be considered in any way representative of his work, but only as a subversion of his intentions. See Millichap, *Steinbeck and Film*, pp. 167–68, for a longer discussion of this production, which he concludes "really has little to do with Steinbeck's *The Red Pony*."

7 A Study in Narrative Technique

1 John Steinbeck, *The Long Valley* (New York: Viking Press, 1938). All later page references are to this edition. Several parts of *The Red Pony* were published during the winter of 1933.

8 Dr. Winter's Dramatic Functions

1 John Steinbeck, *The Moon Is Down* (New York: Viking Press, 1942). All quotations are from this text and identified hereinafter parenthetically.

2 Steinbeck, "My Short Novels," *Wings* 26 (October 1952): 7–8.

3 Steinbeck, *East of Eden* (New York: Viking Press, 1952), p. 132.

4 "Steinbeck's Nobel Prize Acceptance Speech," in *Nobel Prize Library: William*

Faulkner, Eugene O'Neill, and John Steinbeck (New York: Alexis Gregory, 1971), p. 206.

9 Steinbeck's "European" Play-Novella

1 For reasons of convenience I am using the novella text of *The Moon Is Down* published in *The Short Novels of John Steinbeck* (New York: Viking Press, 1953). All parenthesized page citations are to this edition.

2 See my "Ritual Murders in Steinbeck's Dramas," *Steinbeck Quarterly* 11, nos. 3–4 (Summer–Fall 1975): 72–76.

3 Recently Tetsumaro Hayashi contributed a volume of essays on this single work, noting not only the Shakespearean affinities of *The Moon Is Down* but also studying the dramatic function of a single character, Dr. Winter (see chapter 8 in this volume). Thanks to his lead, it has become evident that there is even more left to say. See Tetsumaro Hayashi, *Steinbeck's World War II Fiction; "The Moon Is Down": Three Explications* (Muncie, Ind.: Steinbeck Research Institute, 1986).

4 See my "Steinbeck as Dramatist," in *John Steinbeck: From Salinas to the World*, ed. Shigeharu Yano et al. (Tokyo: Gaku Shobo Press, 1986), pp. 13–23.

5 *Steinbeck: A Life in Letters*, ed. Elaine Steinbeck and Robert Wallsten (New York: Viking Press, 1975), p. 244.

6 *A Life*, p. 235.

7 *A Life*, p. 237.

11 Philosophers in the Sun

Title quotation from F. O. Matthiessen, "Some Philosophers in the Sun: John Steinbeck's Novel *Cannery Row* Is a Tale of Lovable Bums in Monterey," *New York Times Book Review*, December 31, 1944, p. 1.

1 See Jackson J. Benson, "Through A Political Glass, Darkly: The Example of John Steinbeck," *Studies in American Fiction* 12 (Spring, 1984): 44–59.

2 Arthur Mizener, "Does a Moral Vision of the Thirties Deserve a Nobel Prize?" *New York Times Book Review*, December 9, 1962, p. 44.

3 See John S. Kennedy, "John Steinbeck: Life Affirmed and Dissolved," in *Steinbeck and His Critics: A Record of Twenty-five Years*, ed. Ernest W. Tedlock, Jr., and C. V. Wicker (Albuquerque: University of New Mexico Press, 1957).

4 John Steinbeck, *Cannery Row* (New York: Viking Press, 1945), p. 31. All subsequent references in the text are to this first edition.

5 Jackson J. Benson, "John Steinbeck's *Cannery Row:* A Reconsideration," *Western American Literature* 12 (May 1977): 24.

6 Edmund Wilson, "John Steinbeck's Newest Novel and James Joyce's First," *New Yorker* 20 (January 6, 1945): 62.

7 Benson, "John Steinbeck's *Cannery Row*," p. 17.

8 Peter Lisca, "*Cannery Row* and the *Tao Teh Ching*," *San Jose Studies* 1 (November 1975): 23–24. See also chapter 10 in this volume.

9 Ibid., p. 24.

10 Ibid., p. 27.

11 Benson, "John Steinbeck's *Cannery Row*," p. 25.

12 Ibid., p. 24.
13 Joseph Fontenrose, *John Steinbeck: An Introduction and Interpretation* (New York: Barnes and Noble, 1963), p. 106.
14 Benson, "John Steinbeck's *Cannery Row*," p. 26.
15 Warren French, *John Steinbeck*, 2d ed. rev. (Boston: Twayne, 1975), p. 127.
16 Frederick Bracher, "Steinbeck's Biological View of Man," in *Steinbeck and His Critics*, p. 193.
17 John Steinbeck, *The Log from the Sea of Cortez* (New York: Viking Press, 1951), p. 193.
18 Ibid., p. 199.
19 Ibid., p. xxxiii.
20 Louis Owens, *John Steinbeck's Re-Vision of America* (Athens: University of Georgia Press, 1985), p. 184.
21 Owens, p. 184; Steinbeck, *The Log*, p. xxxiii.
22 Peter Lisca, *The Wide World of John Steinbeck* (New Brunswick, N.J.: Rutgers University Press, 1958), p. 204.
23 Ibid., p. 203.
24 Benson, "John Steinbeck's *Cannery Row*," p. 30.
25 Lisca, *Wide World*, p. 215.
26 Richard Astro, *John Steinbeck and Edward F. Ricketts: The Shaping of a Novelist* (Minneapolis: University of Minnesota Press, 1973), p. 159.
27 Steinbeck, *The Log*, p. liii.
28 Owens, pp. 189–90.
29 Benson, "John Steinbeck's *Cannery Row*," p. 36.
30 Ibid., pp. 31–32.
31 Ibid., pp. 32–33.
32 Lisca, *Wide World*, p. 215.
33 Steinbeck, *The Log*, p. liii.
34 Owens, pp. 189–90.
35 Peter Lisca, "Steinbeck's Image of Man and His Decline as a Writer," *Modern Fiction Studies* 11 (Spring 1965): 3–10.

12 Steinbeck as Spokesman for the "Folk Tradition"

1 Antonia Seixas (pen name for Toni Jackson Ricketts), "John Steinbeck and the Non-teleological Bus," *What's Doing on the Monterey Peninsula* (March 1947); rpt. in *Steinbeck and His Critics*, ed. E. W. Tedlock, Jr., and C. V. Wicker (Albuquerque: University of New Mexico Press, 1957), pp. 275–80.
2 Ibid., p. 276.
3 Peter Lisca, *The Wide World of John Steinbeck* (New Brunswick, N.J.: Rutgers University Press, 1958), p. 208.
4 "John Steinbeck's Newest Novel and James Joyce's First," *New Yorker* 20 (January 6, 1945): 62.
5 Another comparison of Steinbeck and Twain (which deals, I hasten to add, with material different from my comparison here) can be found in Sidney J. Krause's "Steinbeck and Mark Twain," *Steinbeck Quarterly* 6 (Fall 1973): 104–11.

6 "*The Grapes of Wrath:* A 'Wagons West' Romance," *Colorado Quarterly* 3 (Summer 1954): 84–91; rpt. in *A Companion to "The Grapes of Wrath,"* ed. Warren French (New York: Viking Press, 1963), pp. 208–16.
7 *Western American Literature* 2 (1968): 281–95; rpt. in *Steinbeck: A Collection of Critical Essays,* ed. Robert Murray Davis (Englewood Cliffs, N.J.: Prentice-Hall, 1972), pp. 135–48. Page references are to the reprinted version.
8 Ibid., pp. 135–36.
9 Ibid., p. 137.
10 Ibid., p. 141.
11 Ibid.
12 *Some Versions of Pastoral* (Norfolk, Conn.: New Directions, 1960), pp. 185–240.
13 Lisca, *Wide World of John Steinbeck,* p. 212.
14 Edith Hamilton, *Mythology* (New York: New American Library, 1953), p. 40.
15 Northrop Frye, *Anatomy of Criticism* (New York: Atheneum, 1969), p. 43.

13 The Shadow and the Pearl

1 John Steinbeck, *The Pearl* (New York: Viking Press, 1947). Quotations cited parenthetically are from this edition. For some of the varied readings of *The Pearl,* see Harry Morris, "The Pearl: Realism and Allegory," *English Journal* 52 (October 1963): 487–95, 505; Peter Lisca, *John Steinbeck: Nature and Myth* (New York: Crowell, 1978); and chapter 7 of my *The Fiction of John Steinbeck: The Aesthetics of the Road Taken* (Norman: University of Oklahoma Press, 1986).
2 The manuscript, "The Pearl of La Paz," was written during 1944–45 and was completed by February 1945. It was first published in the December 1945 issue of *Woman's Home Companion* under the title "Pearl of the World." It was released by Viking Press in November 1947.
3 John Steinbeck, *The Log from the Sea of Cortez* (New York: Viking Press, 1951), p. 103.
4 Jackson J. Benson, *The True Adventures of John Steinbeck, Writer* (New York: Viking Press, 1984), p. 207.
5 Robert J. DeMott, *Steinbeck's Reading: A Catalogue of Books Owned and Borrowed* (New York: Garland, 1984), pp. 62–63.
6 Ibid., p. 63. In several other letters Steinbeck mentioned the influence of Jung on his phalanx theory. For example, to George Albee he wrote: "Now in the unconscious of the man unit there is a keying mechanism. Jung calls it the third person" (*Steinbeck: A Life in Letters,* ed. Elaine Steinbeck and Robert Wallsten [New York: Viking Press, 1975], p. 80). (Further quotations from *Steinbeck: A Life in Letters* will be cited parenthetically as *SLL.*) At other times the language Steinbeck used for the phalanx is markedly Jungian. To Carlton Sheffield he wrote, "The greatest group unit, that is the whole race, has qualities which the individual lacks entirely. It remembers a time when the moon was close, when the tides were terrific. . . . It remembers every step of its climb from the single cell to the human" (*SLL,* p. 75). In a letter to Carl Wilhelmson from the same time (1933), Steinbeck wrote of his own understanding of realism as a probing of individual consciousness, the forces that move men to actions: "There are

streams in man more profound and dark and strong than the libido of Freud. Jung's libido is closer but still inadequate" (*SLL*, p. 87).

7 See Clifford L. Lewis, "Jungian Psychology and the Artistic Design of John Steinbeck," *Steinbeck Quarterly* 10 (Summer–Fall 1977): 89–97; Robert De-Mott, "Toward a Redefinition of *To A God Unknown*," *Windsor Review* 8 (1973): 34–53; Charles E. May, "Myth and Mystery in Steinbeck's 'The Snake': A Jungian View," *Criticism* 15 (1973): 322–35; Donald Stone, "Steinbeck, Jung, and *The Winter of Our Discontent*," *Steinbeck Quarterly* 11 (Summer–Fall 1978): 87–96.

8 Carl Jung, "Archetypes of the Collective Unconscious," *AION*, vol. 9, pt. 1, *The Collected Works of Carl Jung*, trans. R. F. C. Hull (London: Routledge and Kegan Paul, Bollingen edition, 1960), pp. 284–85. Although some discussion of the shadow appears in nearly all of Jung's work, the key analyses appear in several works directly relating to the topic.

9 It should be noted that *harmony* is an often used but slightly misleading term in Jung's psychology. It suggests an easy equilibrium which can never be fully attained and which exists as an ideal. Moreover, the term lessens the jarring psychological action of the meeting with one's shadow. *Balance*, by recognition of and confrontation with the unconscious, is a preferable term that suggests the full impact of the weight of the unconscious upon an individual's life.

10 Jung, "Depth Psychology and a New Ethic," *AION*, vol. 18, p. 620.

11 Ibid., p. 484.

12 Jung, "The Symbolic Life," *AION*, vol. 18, p. 280.

13 Jung, "The Tavistock Lectures," *AION*, vol. 18, p. 23.

14 Jung, "The Fight with the Shadow," *AION*, vol. 10, pp. 222–23.

15 Jung, "Psychology and Religion," *AION*, vol. 11, p. 79.

16 Jung, "Archetypes of the Collective Unconscious," *AION*, vol. 9, pt. 1, p. 123. (References from this lengthy study include the chapter subheadings "Concerning the Archetypes and the Anima Concept," "The Phenomenology of Fairy Tales," and "The Psychology of the Trickster Figure.")

17 Ibid., p. 21.

18 Jung, "Lectures," p. 22. See also "The Structures and Dynamics of Self," *AION*, vol. 9, pt. 2, where Jung writes: "Anyone who identifies with the daylight half of his psychic life will therefore declare the dreams of the night to be null and void, notwithstanding that the night is as long as the day and that all consciousness is manifestly founded on unconsciousness, is rooted in it and every night is extinguished in it" (p. 30).

19 In "Archetypes" Jung points out that "the 'projection' is not really appropriate, for nothing has been cast out of the psyche; rather, the psyche has attained its present complexity by a series of acts of injection" (p. 25).

20 In "Psychology and Religion" Jung writes: "Empirical psychology loved, until recently, to explain the 'unconscious' as mere absence of consciousness—the term indicates as much—just as shadow is an absence of light" (p. 84).

21 Jung, "The Shadow," *AION*, vol. 9, pt. 2, p. 8.

22 Jung, "Psychology and Religion," p. 76.

23   Ibid., p. 78.

24   Jung, "The Shadow," p. 10.

25   Jung, "Archetypes," p. 266.

26   Jung, "The Structure and Dynamics of the Self," *AION*, vol. 9, pt. 2, pp. 233–34.

27   Jung, "Answer to Job," *AION*, vol. 11, p. 383.

28   The water imagery used here by Jung has its correlation in Steinbeck. In *The Log from the Sea of Cortez* Steinbeck uses water imagery for humanity's archetypal consciousness: "For the ocean, deep and black in the depths, is like the low dark levels of our minds in which the dream symbols incubate" (p. 31). Also, "there is tied up to the most primitive and racial or collective instinct a rhythm sense of 'memory' which affects everything and which in the past was probably more potent than it is now. It would at least be more plausible to attribute these profound effects to devastating and instinct-searing tidal influences active during the formative times of the early race history of organisms" (p. 33). The pattern is revisited in *The Winter of Our Discontent* when Hawley crawls into his cave by the ocean in his personal confrontation with his shadow.

29   Jung, "Archetypes," p. 20.

30   Ibid., p. 20. Jung goes on to describe this stripping-away process as a confrontation with one's unconscious nature: "This confrontation is the first test of courage on the inner way, a test sufficient to frighten off most people, for the meeting with ourselves belongs to the more unpleasant things that can be avoided so long as we can project everything negative into the environment. But if we are able to see our own shadow and can bear knowing about it, then a small part of the problem has already been solved: we have at least brought up the personal unconscious. The shadow is a living part of the personality and therefore wants to live with it in some form. It cannot be argued out of existence or rationalized into harmlessness. This problem is exceedingly difficult, because it not only challenges the whole man, but reminds him at the same time of his helplessness and ineffectuality" (pp. 20–21). Although not within the domain of this study, one might observe the striking similarities between this passage and Steinbeck's theory of teleological versus nonteleological thinking set forth in *The Log from the Sea of Cortez*.

31   Jung, "Archetypes," pp. 24–25.

32   As might be expected, Jung's emphasis upon the feminine anima has aroused some concern among feminist critics. One of the most ambitious revisionist efforts occurs in *Feminist Archetypal Theory: Interdisciplinary Re-Visions of Jungian Thought*, ed. Estella Lauter and Carol Schreier Rupprecht (Knoxville: University of Tennessee Press, 1985). The stated purpose of the collection of essays is "to reformulate key Jungian concepts to reflect women's experiences more accurately" (p. 3). Is this really necessary? Clearly, Jung distinguished between anima and animus, the female counterpart in the male and the male counterpart in the female. Yet the majority of his concern—in fact his almost exclusive concern—is with the anima. The value of these essays lies in the acknowledgment that "Jung's psychology does give us a workable view of the unconscious.

Jung's understanding of the unconscious is positive and creative in many respects" (p. 37). And the authors are correct in their belief that Jung's analysis of gender is, nonetheless, incomplete and deserves refinement.

33 Jung, "Archetypes," p. 28.
34 Jung writes, "She has taken possession of the inferior half of the hero's personality. She has caught him on his weak side, as so often happens in ordinary life, for where one is weak one needs support and completion" ("Archetypes," p. 245).
35 Jung, "Psychology and Religion," p. 30.
36 Jung, "Archetypes," pp. 70–71.

14 Precious Bane

1 Warren French, *John Steinbeck* (New York: Twayne, 1961), p. 137.
2 Ibid., p. 142.
3 Howard Levant, *The Novels of John Steinbeck: A Critical Study* (Columbia: University of Missouri Press, 1974), pp. 195–97.
4 Elaine Steinbeck and Robert Wallsten, eds., *Steinbeck: A Life in Letters* (New York: Viking Press, 1975), p. 221.
5 David Bakan, *The Duality of Human Existence* (Chicago: Rand McNally, 1966), p. 37.
6 John Steinbeck, *The Pearl* (New York: Viking Press, 1945). Parenthetical page citations refer to the Bantam Pathfinder edition; New York: Bantam Books, 1963.
7 Todd Lieber, "Talismanic Patterns in the Novels of John Steinbeck," *American Literature* 44 (1972): 262–75.
8 Lester Jay Marks, *Thematic Design in the Novels of John Steinbeck* (The Hague: Mouton, 1969), p. 106.
9 Harry Morris, "The Pearl: Realism and Allegory," in *Steinbeck and His Critics: A Record of Twenty-five Years*, ed. E. W. Tedlock, Jr., and C. V. Wicker (Albuquerque: University of New Mexico Press, 1957), p. 160.
10 Steinbeck, *The Pearl*, preface.

15 *The Pearl*: Legend, Film, Novel

1 Louis Owens, *John Steinbeck's Re-Vision of America* (Athens: University of Georgia Press, 1985), p. 35.
2 Howard Levant, *The Novels of John Steinbeck* (Columbia: University of Missouri Press, 1974), p. 205.
3 Richard O'Connor, *John Steinbeck* (New York: McGraw-Hill, 1970), p. 94.
4 Sunita Jain, *Steinbeck's Concept of Man* (New Delhi: New Statesman, 1979), p. 78.
5 Lester Jay Marks, *Thematic Design in the Novels of John Steinbeck* (The Hague: Mouton, 1969), p. 106.
6 Lawrence William Jones, *John Steinbeck as Fabulist*, ed. Marston LaFrance (Muncie, Ind.: Steinbeck Monograph Series, no. 3, 1973), p. 22.
7 Warren French, *John Steinbeck* (New York: Twayne, 1961), pp. 137, 142.

8 John Steinbeck, *Sea of Cortez* (New York: Viking Press, 1941), pp. 102, 103.
9 *Steinbeck: A Life in Letters*, ed. Elaine Steinbeck and Robert Wallsten (New York: Viking Press, 1975), p. 269.
10 Ibid.
11 John Steinbeck, *The Pearl* (New York: Viking Press, 1947), p. 38.
12 Thomas Fensch, *Steinbeck and Covici: The Story of a Friendship* (Middlebury, Vt.: Paul S. Ericksson, 1979), p. 37.
13 Letter, John Steinbeck to Mildred Lyman, January 27, 1945, Stanford University (my italics).
14 Letter, John Steinbeck to Elizabeth R. Otis, May 3, 1945, in *Life in Letters*, p. 281.
15 Letter, John Steinbeck to Lyman and Otis, January 22, 1945, Stanford University.
16 I am grateful to John Gross, director of the John Steinbeck Library, Salinas, and to the estate of John Steinbeck for providing me with a xerox copy of the manuscript for the purposes of this paper.
17 John Steinbeck. "The novel might benefit by the discipline, the terseness of the drama. The drama might achieve increased openness, freedom and versatility." *Stage* 15 (January 1938): 50–51.
18 Ibid.
19 John Steinbeck, *Burning Bright* (New York: Viking Press, 1950), p. 13.
20 John Steinbeck, "Critics, Critics, Burning Bright," *Saturday Review* 33 (November 11, 1950): 20–21.
21 Joseph R. Millichap, *Steinbeck and Film* (New York: Ungar, 1983), p. 97.
22 *The Pearl*, p. [3].
23 Ibid., pp. 101–2.
24 John Steinbeck, *Cannery Row* (New York: Viking Press, 1945), p. 115.
25 Warren French, *John Steinbeck*, rev. ed. (Boston: Twayne, 1975), p. 129.
26 *The Pearl*, p. 22.
27 Ibid., p. [2].

17 Critics and Common Denominators
1 *Steinbeck: A Life in Letters*, ed. Elaine Steinbeck and Robert Wallsten (New York: Viking Press, 1975), p. 272.
2 *Life in Letters*, pp. 280–81.
3 Peter Lisca, *The Wide World of John Steinbeck* (New Brunswick, N.J.: Rutgers University Press, 1958), pp. 276–77.
4 Steinbeck, *Sweet Thursday* (New York: Viking Press, 1954; New York: Bantam Books, 1956), p. 17. Subsequent references are to the Bantam edition and are cited by page number within the text.
5 *Life in Letters*, p. 474.
6 Warren French, *John Steinbeck*, 2d ed. rev. (Boston: Twayne, 1975), p. 156.
7 French, p. 159.
8 *Life in Letters*, p. 759.
9 *Life in Letters*, p. 603.

10   An interesting discussion of Steinbeck's sense of the artist's isolation is in Arthur L. Simpson, Jr., "'The White Quail': A Portrait of an Artist," in *A Study Guide to Steinbeck's "The Long Valley"*, ed. Tetsumaro Hayashi (Ann Arbor: Pierian Press, 1976), pp. 11–15.

11   Steinbeck, *Sweet Thursday*, unrevised proof in the John Steinbeck Collection, University of New Mexico, Zimmerman Library, Special Collections, Albuquerque.

18   Steinbeck's Bittersweet Thursday

1   In particular, Joseph Fontenrose attacks the conclusion of *Sweet Thursday*, which he maintains is overly sentimental and overloaded with "cheery affirmations." *John Steinbeck: An Introduction and Interpretation* (New York: Holt, Rinehart and Winston, 1962), p. 128.

2   Warren French, *John Steinbeck* (New Haven, Conn.: College and University Press, 1961), p. 157.

3   Brendan Gill, "Lean Years," *New Yorker* 30 (July 10, 1954): 71–72.

4   John Steinbeck, "Critics, Critics, Burning Bright," *Saturday Review* 33 (November 11, 1950): 20–21. Reprinted in *Steinbeck and His Critics*, ed. E. W. Tedlock, Jr., and C. V. Wicker (Albuquerque: University of New Mexico Press, 1957), p. 46.

5   Ralph Waldo Emerson, "Self-Reliance," reprinted in *The Selected Writings of Ralph Waldo Emerson*, ed. Brooks Atkinson (New York: Random House, 1950), pp. 152–53.

6   One further way in which *Sweet Thursday* differs from *Cannery Row* is that *Sweet Thursday* was deliberately written for the stage. Produced by Rodgers and Hammerstein under the title *Pipe Dream*, it created little sensation. It might be argued that the play-novelette form of *Sweet Thursday* hampered Steinbeck's ability to portray nature in the work. This argument is suspect, however, when one considers that Steinbeck does include descriptive scenes portraying nature in his other works in the same form: *Of Mice and Men*, *The Moon Is Down*, and *Burning Bright*.

7   Certain aspects of Steinbeck's Doc figure, based, of course, on Ed Ricketts, Steinbeck's personal friend, appear also in Doc Burton in *In Dubious Battle*, Dr. Winter in *The Moon Is Down*, and in the Doc of "The Snake."

8   Peter Lisca, *The Wide World of John Steinbeck* (New Brunswick, N.J.: Rutgers University Press, 1958), p. 282.

9   John Steinbeck, *Sweet Thursday*, Bantam Classics edition (New York: Bantam Books, 1961), p. 14. All further citations from *Sweet Thursday* refer to this edition and are identified by page numbers in the text.

10   John Steinbeck, *The Log from the Sea of Cortez*, Compass Books edition (New York: Viking Press, 1962), p. 29. All further citations from *The Log* refer to this edition and are identified by page number in the text.

11   Charles Metzger, "Steinbeck's Version of the Pastoral," chapter 16 in this volume.

12   John Steinbeck, *To a God Unknown*, Bantam Books edition (New York: Bantam

Books, 1960), p. 147. All further citations from *To a God Unknown* refer to this edition and are identified by page number in the text.

13 Metzger, p. 192 in this volume.

14 Lisca, p. 283.

15 F. W. Watt laments what he regards as Steinbeck taking refuge in "conventional morality." *John Steinbeck* (New York: Grove Press, 1962), p. 100. Similarly, Fontenrose attacks the novel's serious moral undertone, which, he maintains, "was deliberately written to reject the teaching of *Cannery Row* and replace it with a newer gospel." Fontenrose, pp. 128–29.

16 Lisca, p. 282.

17 Cf. Lisca, p. 281.

18 Watt, p. 101.

19 Edward Weeks, "Suzy and the Octopus," *Atlantic Monthly* 194 (August 1954): 84.

20 John Steinbeck, *Cannery Row*, Bantam Classics edition (New York: Bantam Books, 1959), p. 8. All further citations from *Cannery Row* refer to this edition and are identified by page number in the text.

21 Appropriately, Doc expresses a weak desire to join Lee in the South Sea islands; the feeble nature of his remarks indicate further his growing inertia to act on his old principles.

22 John Steinbeck, "About Ed Ricketts," in *The Log from the Sea of Cortez*, Compass Books edition (New York: Viking Press, 1962), p. xvii.

23 French suggests that Joe Elegant is really a parody of Truman Capote, for whom, French notes, Steinbeck has never had much affection. French, pp. 159–60.

24 Metzger, pp. 185–86 in this volume. For an excellent discussion of Steinbeck's use of the pastoral in *Tortilla Flat*, see Stanley Alexander, "The Conflict of Form in *Tortilla Flat*," *American Literature* 40 (March 1968): 58–66.

25 Metzger, p. 189 in this volume.

19 The Shining of Joe Saul

1 Jackson J. Benson, *The True Adventures of John Steinbeck, Writer* (New York: Viking Press, 1984), p. 664.

2 Ibid., p. 661.

3 Ibid.

4 Letter from John Steinbeck to Pascal Covici, October 28, 1948, Humanities Research Library, University of Texas, Austin.

5 Harvey Breit, "Capsule Interview," *New York Times*, October 15, 1950.

6 John Steinbeck, *In Dubious Battle* (New York: Penguin, 1966), p. 184.

7 John Steinbeck, *A Play in Story Form: Burning Bright* (New York: Penguin, 1979), p. 105. All page references to *Burning Bright* are from this edition.

8 Benson, *True Adventures*, p. 643.

9 A. C. Cawley, ed., *Everyman and Medieval Miracle Plays* (New York: E. P. Dutton, 1959), p. 217, line 358; hereinafter page number and l. for line will be cited in text.

10 "In the dark and desolate caves of the mind [is] a spawning place from which only a few forms rise to the surface. Or maybe it is a great library where is recorded everything that has happened to living matter back to the first moment where it began to live" (John Steinbeck, *Winter of Our Discontent* [New York: Bantam Books, 1962], p. 92).

11 In *The Novels of John Steinbeck: A Critical Study* (Columbia: University of Missouri Press, 1974), Howard Levant deems the language of *Burning Bright* "silly" and the play-novelette "a trivial experiment." He goes on to assert that Friend Ed is a manifestation of God, that Joe Saul is Adam, Mordeen is Eve, and Victor is the snake, playing in an "allegorical parable where life is celebrated through an awareness of death (pp. 158–63). John Ditsky muses that John Steinbeck "feels the need to make his plays dramatically effective by means of stageworthy theatrical postures, chief among them being the deaths of men both great and small," but that Friend Ed's murder of Victor is as "chilling" as Joe Saul's fathering of Victor's child is "prescriptive rationalizing." "Ritual Murder in Steinbeck's Dramas," *Steinbeck Quarterly* 11 (Summer–Fall 1978): 72–76. These comments are typical of the negative attitude toward *Burning Bright* most critics express, and with which we, for the most part, take issue.

12 *Steinbeck: A Life in Letters*, ed. Elaine Steinbeck and Robert Wallsten (New York: Viking, 1975). "I believe that everyone needs something outside himself to cling to. Actually such a thing as I have in mind is not outside yourself but rather a physical symbol that you are all right inside yourself" (pp. 363–64). Clearly, the child Mordeen gives Joe Saul is the "physical symbol" that makes Joe feel "all right inside."

13 Peter Lisca, *The Wide World of John Steinbeck* (New Brunswick, N.J.: Rutgers University Press, 1958), p. 254.

14 Warren French, *John Steinbeck* (Boston: G. K. Hall, 1975), p. 143.

15 Breit, *New York Times*, October 15, 1950.

20 Straining for Profundity

1 Joseph R. Millichap, *Steinbeck and Film* (New York: Ungar, 1983), pp. 13–26. Millichap considers *Of Mice and Men* to be the best of the Steinbeck film adaptations in terms of its fidelity to plot, character, style, and theme.

2 Brian St. Pierre, *John Steinbeck: The California Years* (San Francisco: Chronicle Books, 1983), p. 112.

3 Jackson J. Benson, *The True Adventures of John Steinbeck, Writer* (New York: Viking Press, 1984), p. 583. Although he does not make the exact connection between Steinbeck's decline as a writer and his divorce from Carol, the idea is suggested in Benson's analysis of the problems with *The Wayward Bus*. Benson comments about how rapidly Steinbeck was writing and about how poor a judge Steinbeck was of his own writing. Benson remarks, "He needed someone like Carol to tell him, 'This stuff is crap. You had better ditch it or start over.'"

4 Floyd C. Watkins, *The Flesh and the Word: Eliot, Hemingway, Faulkner* (Nashville: Vanderbilt University Press, 1971), p. 4.

5   Robert DeMott, "Steinbeck and the Creative Process: First Manifesto to End the Bringdown against *Sweet Thursday*," in *Steinbeck: The Man and His Work*, ed. Richard Astro and Tetsumaro Hayashi (Corvallis: Oregon State University Press, 1971), pp. 157–78. DeMott argues that *Sweet Thursday* is "a novel about the writing of a novel" and that though its subject may be banal, "its theme and its deep structural principle are creativity and the condition of the artist" (p. 162).

Page number quotations in the text from *Burning Bright* and *Sweet Thursday* are from the following sources, respectively: John Steinbeck, *Burning Bright* (New York: Viking Press, 1950) (referred to as *BB*, followed by page number); Steinbeck, *Sweet Thursday* (New York: Viking Press, 1954) (referred to as *ST*, followed by page number).

6   *Steinbeck: A Life in Letters*, ed. Elaine Steinbeck and Robert Wallsten (New York: Viking Press, 1975), p. 408.

7   Stefan Kanfer, "Brute Strength," *Time*, December 30, 1974, p. 53.

8   L. A. G. Strong, "Fiction," *Spectator*, August 10, 1951, p. 196.

9   Robert J. DeMott, *Steinbeck's Reading: A Catalogue of Books Owned and Borrowed* (New York: Garland, 1984), p. 39. It is not unlikely that Steinbeck knew this passage, as he owned a number of Faulkner's works and refers specifically to *As I Lay Dying* in *America and Americans*. *As I Lay Dying*, New York: Cape and Smith, 1930; *America and Americans*, New York: Viking Press, 1966.

10 Deleted pages from Jackson Benson's biography suggest that one way that Gwyn tried to hurt Steinbeck during the bitter divorce proceedings was by suggesting to him that their son John was not really his. Thus Steinbeck's personal interest in the question of parentage.

11 *Life in Letters*, p. 472.

12 Malcolm Cowley, "Steinbeck Delivers a Mixture of Farce and Freud," *PM*, January 14, 1945, p. 15.

13 Benson, *True Adventures*, p. 554.

14 The last question was the lead-in to a popular radio soap opera of the late 1940s and early 1950s, "Our Gal Sunday."

15 Ma Joad in *The Grapes of Wrath* is the singular exception in those works which are generally considered Steinbeck's best. For further discussion of the paucity of female characters in Steinbeck, see my "From Lady Brett to Ma Joad: A Singular Scarcity," in *John Steinbeck: From Salinas to the World*, ed. Shigeharu Yano et al. (Tokyo: Gaku Shobo Press), pp. 24–33.

16 The John Steinbeck Library in Salinas has a taped interview with one of the women who worked as a prostitute on Cannery Row. She married, and her children do not know of her former profession. She says that Ed Ricketts did not frequent prostitutes, although he was very friendly with them. She commented on the fact that he had many women after him. This view was also communicated in a taped interview in May 1987 in the Old Row Café with Charles Nonella, who claims to be one of the group who hung out with Mack (Gabe).

21 Steinbeck's "Deep Dissembler"

1 Joseph Fontenrose, *John Steinbeck: An Introduction and Interpretation* (New York: Holt, Rinehart and Winston, 1963), p. 130.

2 Richard Astro, *John Steinbeck and Edward F. Ricketts: The Shaping of a Novelist* (Minneapolis: University of Minnesota Press, 1973), p. 213.

3 Peter Lisca, *The Wide World of John Steinbeck* (New Brunswick, N.J.: Rutgers University Press, 1958), p. 285.

4 Fontenrose, p. 131.

5 Warren French, *John Steinbeck*, 2d ed. rev. (Boston: Twayne, 1975), p. 157.

6 Howard Levant, *The Novels of John Steinbeck: A Critical Study* (Columbia: University of Missouri Press, 1974), pp. 273, 278.

7 Ibid., p. 276.

8 Ibid., p. 276.

9 Ibid., p. 281.

10 Jackson Benson, Steinbeck's biographer, reports: "Elaine remembers that he never had more fun in his life. She could hear him while he was sitting at his table in the spare bedroom, chuckling and laughing while he wrote." See Jackson J. Benson, *The True Adventures of John Steinbeck, Writer* (New York: Viking Press, 1984), p. 785. Subsequent references to this volume are identified by *TA* and page numbers in the text.

11 *Encyclopaedia Britannica*, vol. 19 (Chicago: Encyclopaedia Britannica, 1948), pp. 836–38. For a detailed account of relations between the Hospitallers and Templars and of Enguerrand de Marigny's role in the dealings between Philip IV and the Templars and Hospitallers, see Malcolm Barber, *The Trial of the Templars* (Cambridge: Cambridge University Press, 1978).

12 Fontenrose, p. 132.

13 *The Short Reign of Pippin IV: A Fabrication* (New York: Viking Press, 1957), p. 71. Subsequent references to this novel are to this edition and identified by *Pippin* and page number in the text.

14 *America and Americans* (New York: Viking Press, 1966), p. 174.

15 French, p. 158.

16 *Steinbeck: A Life in Letters*, ed. Elaine Steinbeck and Robert Wallsten (New York: Viking Press, 1975), p. 536. Subsequent references to this volume will be identified by *Letters* and page number in the text.

17 *America and Americans*, pp. 172–73.

22 Narrative Structure

1 John Steinbeck, *The Short Reign of Pippin IV: A Fabrication* (New York: Viking Press, 1957). Hereinafter cited as *SRP*.

2 Steinbeck's political instincts were accurate and wholly appropriate. The story is possible only in a country as socially civilized and as politically anarchical as France; there was something of kingship in the government of Charles de Gaulle, which came into existence on June 1, 1958, and was formalized through a somewhat royalist constitution (for example, granting an increase in

the power of the executive branch, against the background of modern French politics) on September 28, 1958.

3   Ward Moore, "Cannery Row Revisited," *Nation* 179 (October 16, 1954): 325–27. Mr. Moore proves that Cannery Row is a real place and that many of its Steinbeckian inhabitants exist. Therefore, as in *The Short Reign of Pippin IV*, Steinbeck begins with a basis in fact that can seem an invention.

4   John Steinbeck, *The Short Reign of Pippin IV* (New York: Bantam Books, April 1958).

5   *SRP*, pp. 39, 44.

6   *SRP*, pp. 19, 21.

7   *SRP*, p. 16.

8   *SRP*, p. 16.

9   *SRP*, p. 12.

10   *SRP*, pp. 13, 12.

11   *SRP*, pp. 14–15.

12   *SRP*, p. 13.

13   Pepin the short; and possibly, too, *piper*, to catch birds with a birdcall or to cheat; or *pipi*, to urinate; or, most likely, a combination of all.

14   *SRP*, p. 14.

15   *SRP*, p. 16.

16   *SRP*, p. 17.

17   *SRP*, p. 72. The play is evidently on Adlai Stevenson's difficulty in engaging an advertising agency during the presidential campaign of 1956.

18   *SRP*, p. 74. Obviously the May Day Parade.

19   *SRP*, p. 75. The play is on the coronation of Queen Elizabeth II. Marie observes later to Pippin, who has escaped to his telescope, "*Their* queen stood and sat, stood and sat for thirteen hours without even going to the ——— Pippin, will you stop polishing that silly glass?"

20   *SRP*, pp. 92, 94.

21   *SRP*, pp. 90, 122.

22   *SRP*, p. 101. Notice the echo from *East of Eden*.

23   *SRP*, p. 111.

24   *SRP*, p. 121.

25   *SRP*, p. 129.

26   *SRP*, p. 179.

27   *SRP*, p. 179.

28   *SRP*, p. 139.

29   *SRP*, p. 175.

30   *SRP*, p. 159.

31   *SRP*, p. 160.

32   *SRP*, p. 164.

33   Lewis Gannett, "Introduction: John Steinbeck's Way of Writing," *The Portable Steinbeck* (New York: Viking Press, 1946), p. xxii.

23   Steinbeck and the Stage

1   John Steinbeck, *Burning Bright, A Play in Story Form* (New York: Bantam Books, 1951). Hereinafter referred to as *BB*.

2   *Steinbeck: A Life in Letters*, ed. Elaine Steinbeck and Robert Wallsten (New York: Viking Press, 1975), p. 132. Hereinafter referred to as *SLL*.

3   Jackson J. Benson, *The True Adventures of John Steinbeck, Writer* (New York: Viking Press, 1984), p. 358.

4   Margaret Shedd, "Of Mice and Men," *Theatre Arts Monthly* 21 (October 1937): 775.

5   Warren French, "The First Theatrical Production of Steinbeck's *Of Mice and Men*," *American Literature* 36 (January 1965): 525–27.

6   Ibid., p. 525.

7   Ibid.

8   Shedd, p. 775.

9   Ibid., p. 780.

10   Benson, p. 351.

11   John Steinbeck, *Of Mice and Men, A Play*, in *20 Best Plays of the Modern American Theatre*, ed. John Gassner (New York: Crown, 1939), p. 655.

12   Ibid., p. 656.

13   Ibid., p. 666.

14   Ibid., p. 672.

15   *New York Times*, November 24, 1937.

16   Brooks Atkinson, "Episode in the Lower Depths," *New York Times*, December 12, 1937.

17   "*Of Mice and Men* Wins Critics' Prize," *New York Times*, April 19, 1938.

18   George Jean Nathan, "Theater," *Scribner's Magazine* 103 (February 1938): 70.

19   Ibid.

20   *New York Times*, December 5, 1958.

21   Martin Bernheimer, "Opera Review," *Los Angeles Times*, March 18, 1974.

22   Benson, p. 356.

23   John Steinbeck, "Reflections on a Lunar Eclipse," *San Francisco Examiner*, October 6, 1963, p. 3. Hereinafter referred to as "Reflections."

24   Benson, pp. 489–90.

25   *Time* 41 (April 5, 1943): 54.

26   Burnes Mantle, ed., *The Best Plays of 1941–42 and the Year Book of the Drama in America* (New York: Dodd, Mead, 1942), p. 72.

27   Alfred Kazin, "The Unhappy Man from Unhappy Valley," *New York Times Book Review*, May 4, 1958, p. 1.

28   Stanley Edgar Hyman, "John Steinbeck and the Nobel Prize," *New Leader*, December 10, 1962, p. 10.

29   Benson, p. 499.

30   Mantle, *1941–42*, p. 72.

31   John Steinbeck, *The Moon Is Down* (New York: Viking Press, 1942). Hereinafter referred to as *Moon*.

32   Herman Melville, *Selected Writings of Herman Melville* (New York: Random House Modern Library, 1952), p. 880.
33   Mantle (*1941–42*) says 55 performances (p. 73) and 71 performances (p. 445).
34   Ibid., pp. 104–5.
35   *Time* 41, p. 54.
36   Benson, p. 499.
37   James W. Tuttleton, "Steinbeck in Russia: The Rhetoric of Praise and Blame," *Modern Fiction Studies* 11 (Spring 1965): 82.
38   Ibid., p. 89.
39   Benson, p. 588.
40   Ibid., p. 597.
41   John Steinbeck, *Burning Bright, Acting Edition* (New York: Dramatists' Play Service, 1951). Hereinafter referred to as *BB Acting*.
42   Thomas Fensch, *Steinbeck and Covici: The Story of a Friendship* (Middlebury, Vt.: Paul S. Ericksson, 1979), p. 130.
43   Benson, pp. 661–62.
44   Brooks Atkinson, "Burning Bright," *New York Times*, October 29, 1950.
45   L. A. G. Strong, "Fiction," *Spectator* 187 (August 10, 1951): 196.
46   John Steinbeck, "Critics, Critics Burning Bright," *Saturday Review* 33 (November 11, 1950): 20.
47   John Chapman, ed., *The Best Plays of 1950–1951 and the Year Book of the Drama in America* (New York: Dodd, Mead, 1951), p. 6.
48   Benson, pp. 655–56.
49   Ibid., p. 740.
50   Hugh Fordin, *Getting to Know Him: A Biography of Oscar Hammerstein II* (New York: Random House, 1977), p. 323. *Pipe Dream*. Music by Richard Rodgers, book and lyrics by Oscar Hammerstein II (New York: Viking Press, 1956).
51   Henry Fonda, *My Life*, as told to Howard Teichmann (New York: Signet, 1981), pp. 240, 241.
52   Fordin, p. 326.
53   Ibid., p. 327.
54   John Steinbeck, *Cannery Row* (New York: Viking Press, 1945), p. 1.
55   Fordin, p. 329.
56   Stanley Green, ed., *Rodgers and Hammerstein Fact Book* (New York: Drama Book Specialists, 1980), p. 609.
57   Richard Rodgers, *Musical Stages, An Autobiography* (New York: Random House, 1975), p. 287.

Steinbeck's Short Novels:

Comprehensive Checklist of Criticism

"Comprehensive" may more accurately describe the aim rather than the actual scope of this checklist. We have tried to include reference to every publication, in English, which deals substantially (more than just a brief reference) with one or more of Steinbeck's short novels.

We have included dissertations, but the scholar should be warned that not having access to the actual dissertations, we could rely only on the titles and published abstracts. Thus it is possible that a dissertation that should have been listed may not have been.

The list is divided into three parts: (1) books, (2) materials that refer to more than one short novel, and (3) materials that refer to one short novel. In the third section, arranged by the titles of the short novel, the parts of the books listed in the first section relevant to each short novel are given by reference to the author (and brief title if there is more than one book by the same author) and the page numbers.

Reviews of the short novels are included in both sections 2 and 3. These are, for the most part, reviews in journals or major newspapers which can be assumed to be available to the scholar. When the review was published under a byline, it will be listed by the last name of the author. Unsigned reviews are grouped together under "Rev. of," under the R's.

Credit for the extensive research required to locate the materials for this useful list and for the extensive labor needed to assemble, arrange, and edit it goes to Anne Hunsinger.

Books Books about Steinbeck's fiction and other more general books (e.g., those dealing with American fiction or modern literature) which refer to one or more of the short novels. This list includes books by a single author, books by multiple authors, published proceedings in book or monograph form, monographs (separately published shorter items in hard or soft cover), and collections of essays all about Steinbeck's work. (The parts of these works relevant to particular short novels are listed in part 3 of the checklist.)

Allen, Walter. *The Modern Novel in Britain and the United States*. New York: Dutton, 1964.

Astro, Richard. *John Steinbeck and Edward F. Ricketts: The Shaping of a Novelist*. Minneapolis: University of Minnesota Press, 1973.

Astro, Richard, and Tetsumaro Hayashi, eds. *Steinbeck: The Man and His Work.* Corvallis: Oregon State University Press, 1971.

Astro, Richard, and Joel W. Hedgpeth, eds. *Steinbeck and the Sea.* Proceedings of a conference held at Marine Science Center Auditorium, May 4, 1974. Corvallis: Oregon State University Sea Grant, 1974.

Benson, Jackson J. *The True Adventures of John Steinbeck, Writer.* New York: Viking, 1984.

Brown, Deming. *Soviet Attitudes towards American Writing.* Princeton, N.J.: Princeton University Press, 1962.

Davis, Robert Murray, ed. *Steinbeck: A Collection of Critical Essays.* Englewood Cliffs, N.J.: Prentice-Hall, 1972.

Ditsky, John. *John Steinbeck: Life, Work, and Criticism.* Fredericton, N.B., Canada: York, 1985.

Durant, Will, and Ariel Durant. *Interpretations of Life: A Survey of Contemporary Literature.* New York: Simon and Schuster, 1970.

Fensch, Thomas, ed. *Steinbeck and Covici: The Story of a Friendship.* Middlebury, Vt.: Paul S. Ericksson, 1979.

Fontenrose, Joseph. *John Steinbeck: An Introduction and Interpretation.* New York: Barnes and Noble, 1963.

French, Warren. *John Steinbeck.* 2d ed. rev. Boston: Twayne, 1975.

———. *The Social Novel at the End of an Era.* Carbondale: Southern Illinois University Press, 1966.

Fuller, Edmund. *Man in Modern Fiction.* New York: Random House, 1958.

Garcia, Reloy. *Steinbeck and D. H. Lawrence: Fictive Voices and the Ethical Imperative.* Steinbeck Monograph Series, no. 2, 1972. Muncie, Ind.: Steinbeck Society of America, Ball State University, 1972.

Gladstein, Mimi R. *The Indestructible Woman in the Works of Faulkner, Hemingway, and Steinbeck.* Ann Arbor: UMI Research Press, 1986.

Gray, James. *John Steinbeck* [pamphlet]. Minneapolis: University of Minnesota Press, 1971.

Gunn, Drewey Wayne. *American and British Writers in Mexico, 1556–1973.* Austin: University of Texas Press, 1974.

Hadley, George. *Books: Backgrounds and Foregrounds.* Mills College, Oakland, Calif.: Eucalyptus Press, 1939.

Hayashi, Tetsumaro. *John Steinbeck: A Dictionary of His Fictional Characters.* Metuchen, N.J.: Scarecrow, 1976.

———. *Steinbeck's World War II Fiction, "The Moon Is Down": Three Explications.* Steinbeck Essay Series, no. 1, 1986. Muncie, Ind.: Steinbeck Society of America, Ball State University, 1986.

———, ed. *Steinbeck and the Arthurian Theme.* Steinbeck Monograph Series, no. 5, 1975. Muncie, Ind.: Steinbeck Society of America, Ball State University, 1975.

———, ed. *Steinbeck's Literary Dimension: A Guide to Comparative Studies.* Metuchen, N.J.: Scarecrow, 1973.

————, ed. *A Study Guide to Steinbeck: A Handbook to His Major Works*. Metuchen, N.J.: Scarecrow, 1974.

————, ed. *A Study Guide to Steinbeck, Part II*. Metuchen, N.J.: Scarecrow, 1979.

————, ed. *A Study Guide to Steinbeck's "The Long Valley"*. Ann Arbor: Pierian, 1976.

Hayashi, Tetsumaro, Yasuo Hashiguchi, and Richard F. Peterson, eds. *John Steinbeck: East and West*. Proceedings of the First International Steinbeck Congress, Kyushu University, Fukuoka City, Japan, August 1974. Steinbeck Monograph Series, no. 8. Muncie, Ind.: Steinbeck Society of America, Ball State University, 1978.

Hayashi, Tetsumaro, et al., eds. *Steinbeck's Literary Dimension: A Guide to Comparative Studies*. Metuchen, N.J.: Scarecrow, 1973.

Hayashi, Tetsumaro, and Kenneth D. Swan, eds. *Steinbeck's Prophetic Vision of America*. Proceedings of the Bicentennial Steinbeck Seminar. Upland, Ind.: Taylor University Press for Steinbeck Society of America, 1976.

Hayashi, Tetsumaro, and Thomas J. Moore, eds. *Steinbeck's "The Red Pony": Essays in Criticism*. Steinbeck Monograph Series, no. 13, 1988. Muncie, Ind.: Steinbeck Society of America, Ball State University, 1988.

Hayashi, Tetsumaro, and Richard F. Peterson, eds. *Steinbeck's Women: Essays in Criticism*. Steinbeck Monograph Series, no. 9, 1979. Muncie, Ind.: Steinbeck Society of America, Ball State University, 1979.

Hoffman, Frederick J. *The Modern Novel in America, 1900–1950*. Chicago: Henry Regnery, 1951.

Hughes, R. S. *Beyond the Red Pony: A Reader's Companion to Steinbeck's Complete Short Stories*. Metuchen, N.J.: Scarecrow, 1987.

————. *John Steinbeck: A Study of the Short Fiction*. Boston: Twayne, 1988.

Jain, Sunita. *John Steinbeck's Concept of Man: A Critical Study of His Novels*. New Delhi: New Statesman, 1979.

Jones, Lawrence William. *John Steinbeck as Fabulist*. Edited by Marston LaFrance. Steinbeck Monograph Series, no. 3, 1973. Muncie, Ind.: Steinbeck Society of America, Ball State University, 1973.

Kiernan, Thomas. *The Intricate Music: A Biography of John Steinbeck*. Boston: Little, Brown, 1979.

Levant, Howard. *The Novels of John Steinbeck: A Critical Study*. Columbia: University of Missouri Press, 1974.

Lisca, Peter. *John Steinbeck: Nature and Myth*. New York: Crowell, 1978.

————. *The Wide World of John Steinbeck*. New Brunswick, N.J.: Rutgers University Press, 1958.

Lutwack, Leonard. *Heroic Fiction: The Epic Tradition and American Novels of the Twentieth Century*. Carbondale: Southern Illinois University Press, 1971.

McCarthy, Paul. *John Steinbeck*. New York: Ungar, 1980.

Marks, Lester J. *Thematic Design in the Novels of John Steinbeck*. The Hague: Mouton, 1969.

Martin, Stoddard. *California Writers: Jack London, John Steinbeck, the Tough Guys*. New York: St. Martin's Press, 1983.

Millichap, Joseph R. *Steinbeck and Film.* New York: Ungar, 1983.
Moore, Harry T. *Age of the Modern and Other Literary Essays.* Carbondale: Southern Illinois University Press, 1971.
————. *The Novels of John Steinbeck: A First Critical Study.* Chicago: Normandie House, 1939.
Owens, Louis. *John Steinbeck's Re-Vision of America.* Athens: University of Georgia Press, 1985.
Pratt, John C. *John Steinbeck.* Grand Rapids, Mich.: Eerdmans, 1970.
Rao, B. Ramachandra. *The American Fictional Hero: An Analysis of the Works of Fitzgerald, Wolfe, Farrell, Dos Passos, and Steinbeck.* Chandigarh: Bahri, 1979.
St. Pierre, Brian. *John Steinbeck: The California Years.* San Francisco: Chronicle Books, 1983.
Satyanarayana, M. R. *John Steinbeck: A Study in the Theme of Compassion.* Hyderabad: Osmania University Press, 1977.
Simmonds, Roy S. *Steinbeck's Literary Achievement.* Steinbeck Monograph Series, no. 6, 1976. Muncie, Ind.: Steinbeck Society of America, Ball State University, 1976.
Steinbeck, Elaine, and Robert Wallsten, eds. *Steinbeck: A Life in Letters.* New York: Viking Press, 1975.
Straumann, Heinrich. *American Literature in the Twentieth Century.* 3d ed. New York: Harper and Row, 1965.
Tedlock, Ernest W., Jr., and C. V. Wicker. *Steinbeck and His Critics: A Record of Twenty-five Years.* Albuquerque: University of New Mexico Press, 1957.
Thompson, Raymond H. *The Return from Avalon: A Study of the Arthurian Legend in Modern Fiction.* Westport, Conn.: Greenwood Press, 1985.
Timmerman, John H. *John Steinbeck's Fiction: The Aesthetics of the Road Taken.* Norman: University of Oklahoma Press, 1986.
Valjean, Nelson. *John Steinbeck the Errant Knight: An Intimate Biography of His California Years.* San Francisco: Chronicle Books, 1975.
Walcutt, Charles C. *Seven Novelists in the American Naturalist Tradition: An Introduction.* Minneapolis: University of Minnesota Press, 1974.
Watt, F. W. *John Steinbeck.* New York: Grove Press, 1962.
Yano, Shigeharu, et al., eds. *John Steinbeck: From Salinas to the World.* Proceedings of the Second International Steinbeck Congress, 1984. Tokyo: Gaku Shobo Press, 1986.

Items That Refer to Several Short Novels   For the most part, articles (rather than books) that discuss more than one short novel: journal articles, reviews, articles from books, articles from proceedings, articles from monographs, and dissertations.

Adams, James Donald. "Main Street and the Dust Bowl." In *Shape of Books to Come.* New York: Viking Press, 1944. Pp. 131–43.
Alexander, Stanley Gerald. "Primitivism and Pastoral Form in John Steinbeck's Early Fiction." *DAI* 26 (1965): 2201A–2A. University of Texas.

Allen, Mary. "The Cycle of Death: John Steinbeck." In *Animals in American Literature.* Carbondale: University of Southern Illinois Press, 1983. Pp. 115–34.

Anderson, Arthur Cummins. "The Journey Motif in the Fiction of John Steinbeck: The Traveler Discovers Himself." *DAI* 37 (1976): 2867A. Fordham University.

Astro, Richard. "From the Tidepool to the Stars: Steinbeck's Sense of Place." In *John Steinbeck: East and West.* Proceedings of the First International Steinbeck Congress, Kyushu University, Fukuoka City, Japan, August 1974. Steinbeck Monograph Series, no. 8. Muncie, Ind.: Steinbeck Society of America, Ball State University, 1978. Pp. 22–27. Reprinted in *Steinbeck Quarterly* 10 (1977): 5–11.

———. "Into the Cornucopia: Steinbeck's Vision of Nature and the Ideal Man." *DAI* 30 (1969): 2517A–18A. University of Washington, Seattle.

———. Introduction to *Steinbeck: The Man and His Work.* Edited by R. Astro and Tetsumaro Hayashi. Corvallis: Oregon State University Press, 1971. Pp. 1–10.

———. "Steinbeck and Ricketts: The Morphology of a Metaphysic." *University of Windsor Review* 8 (1973): 24–33.

———. "Steinbeck's Post-war Trilogy: A Return to Nature and the Natural Man." *Twentieth Century Literature* 16 (1970): 109–22.

Barreto, Pfeifer. "Similarities in Cervantes' *Don Quixote* and Steinbeck's Paisano Novels." *DAI* 42 (1981): 2657. Tulane University.

Beach, Joseph Warren. "John Steinbeck: Journeyman Artist." In *American Fiction: 1920–1940.* New York: Macmillan, 1942. Pp. 309–24. Reprinted in *Steinbeck and His Critics: A Record of Twenty-five Years.* Edited by Ernest W. Tedlock, Jr., and C. V. Wicker. Albuquerque: University of New Mexico Press, 1957. Pp. 80–91.

Beatty, Sandra. "Steinbeck's Play-Women: A Study of the Female Presence in *Of Mice and Men, Burning Bright, The Moon Is Down,* and *Viva Zapata!*" In *Steinbeck's Women: Essays in Criticism.* Edited by Tetsumaro Hayashi and Richard F. Peterson. Muncie, Ind.: Steinbeck Society of America, Ball State University, 1979. Pp. 7–16.

Bedford, R. C. "Steinbeck's Nonverbal Invention." *Steinbeck Quarterly* 18 (1985): 70–78.

Bedford, Richard C. "Steinbeck's Use of the Oriental." *Steinbeck Quarterly* 13 (1980): 5–19.

Benson, Jackson J. "John Steinbeck: Novelist as Scientist." In *Steinbeck and the Sea.* Proceedings of a conference held at Marine Science Center Auditorium, May 4, 1974. Edited by Richard Astro and Joel W. Hedgpeth. Corvallis: Oregon State University Sea Grant, 1974. Pp. 15–28. Reprinted in *Novel: A Forum of Fiction* 10 (1977): 248–64.

———. "Through a Political Glass, Darkly: The Example of John Steinbeck." *Studies in American Fiction* 12 (1984): 45–59.

Benton, Robert M. "A Scientific Point of View in Steinbeck's Fiction." *Steinbeck Quarterly* 7 (1974): 67–72.

Bleeker, Gary W. "Setting and Animal Tropes in the Fiction of John Steinbeck." *DAI* 30 (1970): 2998A. University of Nebraska, Lincoln.

Boynton, Percy Holmes. "John Steinbeck." In *America in Contemporary Fiction*. 2d ed. New York: Russell and Russell, 1943. Pp. 241–57.

Bracher, Frederick. "Steinbeck and the Biological View of Man." In *Steinbeck and His Critics: A Record of Twenty-five Years*. Edited by Ernest W. Tedlock, Jr., and C. V. Wicker. Albuquerque: University of New Mexico Press, 1957. Pp. 183–96.

Britch, Carroll, and Cliff Lewis. "Shadow of the Indian in the Fiction of John Steinbeck." *MELUS* 11 (1984): 39–58.

Brown, Daniel R. "A Monolith of Logic Against Waves of Nonsense." *Renascence* 16 (Fall 1963): 48–51.

———. "The Natural Man in John Steinbeck's Non-teleological Tales." *Ball State University Forum* 7, no. 2 (Spring 1966): 47–52.

Brown, Joyce D. C. "Animal Symbolism and Imagery in John Steinbeck's Fiction from 1929 through 1939." *DAI* 33 (1972): 1716A. Southern Mississippi University.

Burgum, Edwin Berry. "Fickle Sensibility of John Steinbeck." In *Novel and the World's Dilemma*. New York: Oxford University Press, 1947. Pp. 272–91.

———. "The Sensibility of John Steinbeck." In *Steinbeck and His Critics: A Record of Twenty-five Years*. Edited by Ernest W. Tedlock, Jr., and C. V. Wicker. Albuquerque: University of New Mexico Press, 1957. Pp. 104–18.

Carpenter, Frederic I. "John Steinbeck: American Dreamer." *Southwest Review* 26 (Summer 1940): 454–67. Reprinted in *Steinbeck and His Critics: A Record of Twenty-five Years*. Edited by Ernest W. Tedlock, Jr., and C. V. Wicker. Albuquerque: University of New Mexico Press, 1957. Pp. 68–79.

Casimir, Louis John, Jr. "Human Emotion and the Early Novels of John Steinbeck." *DAI* 27 (1966): 472A. University of Texas.

Champney, Freeman. "John Steinbeck, Californian." *Antioch Review* 7 (Fall 1947): 345–62. Reprinted in *Steinbeck and His Critics: A Record of Twenty-five Years*. Edited by Ernest W. Tedlock, Jr., and C. V. Wicker. Albuquerque: University of New Mexico Press, 1957. Pp. 135–51. Reprinted also in *Steinbeck: A Collection of Critical Essays*. Edited by Robert Murray Davis. Englewood Cliffs, N.J.: Prentice-Hall, 1972. Pp. 18–35.

Covici, Pascal, Jr. "From Commitment to Choice: Double Vision and the Problem of Vitality for John Steinbeck." *The Fifties: Fiction, Poetry, Drama*. Edited by Warren French. DeLand, Fla.: Everett/Edwards, 1970. Pp. 63–71.

———. "John Steinbeck and the Language of Awareness." *The Thirties: Fiction, Poetry, Drama*. Edited by Warren French. DeLand, Fla.: Everett/Edwards, 1967. Pp. 47–54.

Davis, Robert Murray. Introduction to *Steinbeck: A Collection of Critical Essays*. Edited by R. M. Davis. Englewood Cliffs, N.J.: Prentice-Hall, 1972. Pp. 1–17.

Ditsky, John. "Faulkner Land and Steinbeck Country." In *Steinbeck: The Man and His Work*. Edited by Richard Astro et al. Corvallis: Oregon State University Press, 1971. Pp. 11–23.

————. "Land Nostalgia in the Novels of Faulkner, Cather, and Steinbeck." *DAI* 28 (1967): 1072A. New York University.

————. "Music from a Dark Cave: Organic Form in Steinbeck's Fiction." *Journal of Narrative Technique* 1 (1971): 59–67.

————. "Ritual Murder in Steinbeck's Dramas." *Steinbeck Quarterly* 11 (1978): 72–76.

————. "Steinbeck as Dramatist: A Preliminary Account." In *John Steinbeck: From Salinas to the World*. Proceedings of the Second International Steinbeck Congress, 1984. Edited by Shigeharu Yano et al. Tokyo: Gaku Shobo Press, 1986. Pp. 13–23.

————. "Teaching the Ungreat: A Year of Steinbeck." *English Record* 22 (1972): 27–32.

Fairley, Baker. "John Steinbeck and the Coming Literature." *Sewanee Review* 50 (April 1942): 145–61.

French, Warren. Introduction to *The Novels of John Steinbeck: A Critical Study*, by Howard Levant. Columbia: University of Missouri Press, 1974. Pp. ix–xxii.

————. "John Steinbeck." In *American Winners of the Nobel Literary Prize*. Edited by W. G. French and Walter E. Kidd. Norman: University of Oklahoma Press, 1968. Pp. 193–223.

————. "John Steinbeck and Modernism." *Steinbeck's Prophetic Vision of America*. Edited by Tetsumaro Hayashi and Kenneth Swan. Proceedings of the Bicentennial Steinbeck Seminar. Upland, Ind.: Taylor University Press for Steinbeck Society of America, 1976. Pp. 35–55.

————. "John Steinbeck: From Salinas to the World." In *John Steinbeck: From Salinas to the World*. Proceedings of the Second International Steinbeck Congress, 1984. Edited by Shigeharu Yano et al. Tokyo: Gaku Shobo Press, 1986. Pp. 1–12.

————. "John Steinbeck: A Usable Concept of Naturalism." In *American Literary Naturalism: A Reassessment*. Edited by Yoshinobu Hakutani and Lewis Fried. Heidelberg: Winter, 1975. Pp. 122–35.

Frietzsche, Arthur H. "Steinbeck as a Western Author." *Proceedings of the Utah Academy of Sciences, Arts, and Literature* 42, no. 1 (1965): 11–13.

Frohock, William. "John Steinbeck's Men of Wrath." *Southwest Review* 31 (1946): 144–52.

————. "John Steinbeck: The Utility of Wrath." In *The Novel of Violence in America*. Rev. ed. Dallas: Southern Methodist University Press, 1957. Pp. 124–43.

Fukuma, Kin-ichi. "'Man' in Steinbeck's Works." *Kyushu American Literature* 7 (1964): 21–30.

Gannett, Lewis. "John Steinbeck's Way of Writing." In *Steinbeck and His Critics: A Record of Twenty-five Years*. Edited by Ernest W. Tedlock, Jr., and C. V. Wicker. Albuquerque: University of New Mexico Press, 1957. Pp. 23–37.

Geismar, Maxwell. "Further Decline of the Moderns: John Steinbeck." In *American*

Moderns: From Rebellion to Conformity. New York: Hill and Wang, 1958. Pp. 151–56.

———. "John Steinbeck: Of Wrath or Joy." In *Writers in Crisis: The American Novel Between Two Wars.* Boston: Houghton, Mifflin, 1942. Pp. 237–70.

———. "Summary." In *American Moderns: From Rebellion to Conformity.* New York: Hill and Wang, 1958. Pp. 164–67.

Gentry, Robert Wayne. "John Steinbeck's Use of Non-teleological Thinking in His Mexican American Characters." *DAI* 46, no. 10 (1986): 3033A. Baylor University.

Gibbs, Lincoln R. "John Steinbeck: Moralist." In *Steinbeck and His Critics: A Record of Twenty-five Years.* Edited by Ernest W. Tedlock, Jr., and C. V. Wicker. Albuquerque: University of New Mexico Press, 1957. Pp. 92–103.

Gladstein, Mimi Reisel. "Female Characters in Steinbeck: Minor Characters of Major Importance?" In *Steinbeck's Women: Essays in Criticism.* Edited by Tetsumaro Hayashi and Richard F. Peterson. Muncie, Ind.: Steinbeck Society of America, Ball State University, 1979. Pp. 17–25.

———. "From Lady Brett to Ma Joad: A Singular Scarcity." In *John Steinbeck: From Salinas to the World.* Proceedings of the Second International Steinbeck Congress, 1984. Edited by Shigeharu Yano et al. Tokyo: Gaku Shobo Press, 1986. Pp. 24–33.

———. "The Indestructible Woman in the Works of Faulkner, Hemingway, and Steinbeck." *DAI* 35 (1974): 1655A. New Mexico University.

Golemba, Henry L. "Steinbeck's Attempt to Escape the Literary Fallacy." *Modern Fiction Studies* 15 (1969): 231–39.

Gray, James. "A Local Habitation." In *On Second Thought.* Minneapolis: University of Minnesota Press, 1946. Pp. 133–40.

Griffith, Raymond L. "Dissonant Symphony: Multilevel Duality in the Fiction of John Steinbeck." *DAI* 33 (1972): 1723A–24A. Loyola University of Chicago.

Gurko, Leo, and Miriam Gurko. "The Steinbeck Temperament." *Rocky Mountain Review* 9 (Fall 1944): 17–22.

Hayashi, Tetsumaro. "Recent Steinbeck Studies in the United States." In *Steinbeck and the Sea.* Proceedings of a conference held at Marine Science Center Auditorium, May 4, 1974. Edited by Richard Astro and Joel W. Hedgpeth. Corvallis: Oregon State University Sea Grant, 1974. Pp. 11–13.

———. "Steinbeck's Literature Viewed From Archetypal Perspectives." *Reitaku University Journal* 39 (July 1985): 125–33.

———. "Steinbeck's Reputation: What Values Does He Communicate to Us?" In *Steinbeck's Prophetic Vision of America.* Edited by Tetsumaro Hayashi and Kenneth D. Swan. Proceedings of the Bicentennial Steinbeck Seminar. Upland, Ind.: Taylor University Press for Steinbeck Society of America, 1976. Pp. 28–34.

Holman, Hugh. "A Narrow-Gauge Dickens." *New Republic* 130 (7 June 1954): 18–20.

Hughes, Robert Saunders, Jr. "Steinbeck's Short Stories: A Critical Study." *DAI* 42, no. 7 (1982): 3157A–58A. Indiana University.

Hyman, Stanley Edgar. "Some Notes on John Steinbeck." *Antioch Review* 2 (Summer 1942): 185–200. Reprinted in *Steinbeck and His Critics: A Record of Twenty-five Years.* Edited by Ernest W. Tedlock, Jr., and C. V. Wicker. Albuquerque: University of New Mexico Press, 1957. Pp. 152–66.

Jackson, Joseph Henry. Introduction to *The Short Novels of John Steinbeck,* by John Steinbeck. New York: Viking Press, 1953. Pp. vii–xv.

Jain, Sunita G. "John Steinbeck's Concept of Man." *DAI* 33 (1972): 2937A–38A. University of Nebraska, Lincoln.

Jones, Claude E. "Proletarian Writing and John Steinbeck." *Sewanee Review* 48 (October 1940): 445–56.

Jones, Lawrence W. "'A Little Play in Your Head': Parable Form in John Steinbeck's Post-war Fiction." *Genre* 3 (1970): 55–63.

———. "Steinbeck and Emile Zola." In *Steinbeck's Literary Dimension: A Guide to Comparative Studies.* Edited by Tetsumaro Hayashi. Metuchen, N.J.: Scarecrow, 1973. Pp. 138–46.

Kennedy, John S. "John Steinbeck: Life Affirmed and Dissolved." In *Steinbeck and His Critics: A Record of Twenty-five Years.* Edited by Ernest W. Tedlock, Jr., and C. V. Wicker. Albuquerque: University of New Mexico Press, 1957. Pp. 119–34.

Krause, Sydney J. "Steinbeck and Mark Twain." *Steinbeck Quarterly* 6 (1973): 104–11.

Levant, Howard. Preface to *The Novels of John Steinbeck: A Critical Study.* Columbia: University of Missouri Press, 1974. Pp. 1–9.

———. "Three Play-Novelettes." In *The Novels of John Steinbeck.* Pp. 130–63.

Levidora, I. "The Post-war Books of John Steinbeck." *Soviet Review* 4, no. 2 (Summer 1963): 3–13.

Lewis, Clifford L. "John Steinbeck: Architect of the Unconscious." *DAI* 34 (1973): 781A. University of Texas, Austin.

Lewis, R. W. B. "John Steinbeck: The Fitful Daemon." In *Steinbeck: A Collection of Critical Essays.* Edited by Robert Murray Davis. Englewood Cliffs, N.J.: Prentice-Hall, 1972. Pp. 163–75.

Lieber, Todd M. "Talismanic Patterns in the Novels of John Steinbeck. *American Literature* 44 (1972): 265–75.

Lisca, Peter. "The Art of John Steinbeck: An Analysis and Interpretation of Its Development." *DAI* 16, no. 5 (1956): 965. University of Wisconsin.

———. "Escape and Commitment: Two Poles of the Steinbeck Hero." In *Steinbeck: The Man and His Work.* Edited by Richard Astro and Tetsumaro Hayashi. Corvallis: Oregon State University Press, 1971. Pp. 75–88.

———. "John Steinbeck: A Literary Biography." In *Steinbeck and His Critics: A Record of Twenty-five Years.* Edited by Ernest W. Tedlock, Jr., and C. V. Wicker. Albuquerque: University of New Mexico Press, 1957. Pp. 3–22.

———. "Keynote Address: New Perspectives in Steinbeck Studies." *University of Windsor Review* 8 (1973): 6–10.

———. "Steinbeck and Ernest Hemingway." In *Steinbeck's Literary Dimension: A*

Guide to Comparative Studies. Edited by Tetsumaro Hayashi. Metuchen, N.J.: Scarecrow, 1973. Pp. 46–54.

———. "Steinbeck and Hemingway: Suggestions for a Comparative Study." *Steinbeck Newsletter* 2, no. 1 (1969): 3–9.

———. "Steinbeck's Image of Man and His Decline as a Writer." *Modern Fiction Studies* 11 (1965): 3–10.

———. "A Survey of Steinbeck Criticism, to 1971." In *Steinbeck's Literary Dimension: A Guide to Comparative Studies.* Edited by Tetsumaro Hayashi. Metuchen, N.J.: Scarecrow, 1973. Pp. 148–67.

———. "Teaching Steinbeck." *A Study Guide to Steinbeck: A Handbook to His Major Works.* Edited by Tetsumaro Hayashi. Metuchen, N.J.: Scarecrow, 1974. Pp. 1–4.

McCarthy, Kevin M. "The Name Is the Game." In *The Linguistic Connection.* Edited by Jean Casagrande. Lanham, Md.: University Press of America, 1983. Pp. 161–70.

McTee, James David. "Underhill's Mystic Way and the Initiation Theme in the Major Fiction of John Steinbeck." *DAI* 36 (1976): 6102A. East Texas State University.

Magny, Claude-Edmonde. "Steinbeck, Or the Limits of the Impersonal Novel." In *Steinbeck and His Critics: A Record of Twenty-five Years.* Edited by Ernest W. Tedlock, Jr., and C. V. Wicker. Albuquerque: University of New Mexico Press, 1957. Pp. 216–27.

Marks, Lester Jay. "A Study of Thematic Continuity in the Novels of John Steinbeck." *DAI* 22 (1961): 4351. Syracuse University.

Marshall, Margaret. "Writers in the Wilderness." *Nation* 149 (25 November 1939): 576–79.

Metzger, Charles R. "Steinbeck's Mexican Americans." In *Steinbeck: The Man and His Work.* Edited by Richard Astro and Tetsumaro Hayashi. Corvallis: Oregon State University Press, 1971. Pp. 141–55.

Moore, Ward. "*Cannery Row* Revisited: Steinbeck and the Sardine." *Nation* 179 (16 October 1954): 325–27.

Morsberger, Robert E. "In Defense of 'Westering.'" *Western American Literature* 5 (1970): 143–46.

———. "Steinbeck on Screen." In *A Study Guide to Steinbeck: A Handbook to His Major Works.* Edited by Tetsumaro Hayashi. Metuchen, N.J.: Scarecrow, 1974. Pp. 258–98.

———. "Steinbeck's Films." In *John Steinbeck: From Salinas to the World.* Proceedings of the Second International Steinbeck Congress, 1984. Edited by Shigeharu Yano et al. Tokyo: Gaku Shobo Press, 1986. Pp. 45–67.

———. "Steinbeck's Happy Hookers." *Steinbeck Quarterly* 9 (1976): 101–15. Reprinted in *Steinbeck's Women: Essays in Criticism.* Edited by Tetsumaro Hayashi and Richard F. Peterson. Muncie, Ind.: Steinbeck Society of America, Ball State University, 1979. Pp. 36–48.

Murray, Edward. "John Steinbeck: Point of View and Film." In *The Cinematic*

Imagination: Writers and the Motion Picture. New York: Ungar, 1972. Pp. 261–77.

Nakayama, Kiyoshi. "John Steinbeck and Yasunari Kawabata." In *John Steinbeck: From Salinas to the World.* Proceedings of the Second International Steinbeck Congress, 1984. Edited by Shigeharu Yano et al. Tokyo: Gaku Shobo Press, 1986. Pp. 68–82.

———. "An Oriental Interpretation of Steinbeck's Literature and Thought." In *John Steinbeck: East and West.* Proceedings of the First International Steinbeck Congress, Kyushu University, Fukuoka City, Japan, August 1974. Steinbeck Monograph Series, no. 8. Edited by Tetsumaro Hayashi, Yasuo Hashiguchi, and Richard F. Peterson. Muncie, Ind.: Steinbeck Society of America, 1978. Pp. 71–82.

Nevius, Blake. "Steinbeck: One Aspect." *Pacific Spectator* (Summer 1949): 302–10. Reprinted in *Steinbeck and His Critics: A Record of Twenty-five Years.* Edited by Ernest W. Tedlock, Jr., and C. V. Wicker. Albuquerque: University of New Mexico Press, 1957. Pp. 197–205.

Nossen, Evon. "The Beast-Man Theme in the Work of John Steinbeck." *Ball State University Forum* 7, no. 2 (Spring 1966): 52–64.

Oliver, H. J. "John Steinbeck." *Australian Quarterly* 23 (June 1951): 79–83.

Owens, Louis Dean. "A New Eye in the West: Steinbeck's California Fiction." *DAI* 42 (1982): 4002A. University of California, Davis.

Oxley, William. "The Sick Novel." In *A Salzburg Miscellany: English and American Studies 1964–1984.* Edited by Woldried Haslauer. Salzburg: Institut fur Anglistik und Amerikanistik, University of Salzburg, 1984. 2:117–29.

Prescott, Orville. "Squandered Talents: Lewis, Steinbeck, Hemingway, O'Hara." In *In My Opinion: An Inquiry into the Contemporary Novel.* Indianapolis: Bobbs-Merrill, 1952. Pp. 50–74.

Rascoe, Burton. "John Steinbeck." *English Journal* 27 (1938): 205–16. Reprinted in *Steinbeck and His Critics: A Record of Twenty-five Years.* Edited by Ernest W. Tedlock, Jr., and C. V. Wicker. Albuquerque: University of New Mexico Press, 1957. Pp. 57–67.

Raymund, Bernard. "John Steinbeck." In *Writers of Today.* Edited by Denys Val Baker. London: Sidgwick, 1946. Pp. 122–38.

Redman, Ben Ray. "The Case of John Steinbeck." *American Mercury* 64 (May 1947): 624–30.

Richards, Edmund C. "The Challenge of John Steinbeck." *North American Review* 243 (Summer 1957): 405–13.

Roane, Margaret C. "John Steinbeck as a Spokesman for the Mentally Retarded." *Wisconsin Studies in Contemporary Literature* 5 (Summer 1964): 127–32.

Rosenstone, Robert A. "Steinbeck's America: Myth and Reality." *Kyushu American Literature* 17 (September 1976): 85–86.

Ross, Woodburn O. "John Steinbeck: Earth and Stars." In *Steinbeck and His Critics: A Record of Twenty-five Years.* Edited by Ernest W. Tedlock, Jr., and C. V. Wicker. Albuquerque: University of New Mexico Press, 1957. Pp. 167–82.

———. "John Steinbeck: Naturalism's Priest." In *Steinbeck and His Critics: A Record of Twenty-five Years.* Edited by Ernest W. Tedlock, Jr., and C. V. Wicker. Albuquerque: University of New Mexico Press, 1957. Pp. 206–15.

Rundell, Walter, Jr. "Steinbeck's Image of the West." *American West* 1 (Spring 1964): 4–17, 79.

Sargent, Raymond Matthews. "Social Criticism in the Fiction of John Steinbeck." *DAI* 42 (1981): 706A. Arizona State University.

Seixas, Antonia. "John Steinbeck and the Non-teleological Bus." In *Steinbeck and His Critics: A Record of Twenty-five Years.* Edited by Ernest W. Tedlock, Jr., and C. V. Wicker. Albuquerque: University of New Mexico Press, 1957. Pp. 275–80.

Shimomura, Noboru. "Steinbeck and Monterey: Theme and Humor in the 'Monterey Trilogy.'" In *John Steinbeck: From Salinas to the World.* Proceedings of the Second International Steinbeck Congress, 1984. Edited by Shigeharu Yano et al. Tokyo: Gaku Shobo Press, 1986. Pp. 103–12.

Simmonds, Roy S. "Steinbeck and World War II: The Moon Goes Down." *Steinbeck Quarterly* 17 (1984): 14–34.

Slochower, Harry. "Promise of America." In *No Voice is Wholly Lost . . . Writers and Thinkers in War and Peace.* Edited by Harold Slochower. New York: Creative Age, 1945. Pp. 299–308. Reprinted in *Literature and Philosophy between Two World Wars: The Problem in a War Culture.* Edited by Harold Slochower. New York: Citadel Press, 1964. Pp. 299–308.

Smith, Donald B. "The Decline in John Steinbeck's Critical Reputation Since WW II: An Analysis and Evaluation of Recent Critical Practices with a Suggested Revision." *DAI* 28 (1967): 1449A. University of New Mexico.

Smith, Thelma May, and Ward L. Miner. "Steinbeck." In *Transatlantic Migration: The Contemporary American Novel in France.* Durham, N.C.: Duke University Press, 1955. Pp. 161–78.

Spies, George H. III. "Steinbeck and the Automobile." *Steinbeck Quarterly* 7 (1974): 18–24.

Spilka, Mark. "Of George and Lennie and Curly's Wife: Sweet Violence in Steinbeck's Eden." *Modern Fiction Studies* 20 (1974): 169–79.

Sreenivasan, K. "The Novels of Steinbeck: A Study of His Image of Man." Ph.D. diss. University of Kerala, India, 1977.

Steinbeck, John. "My Short Novels." *English Journal* 43 (1954): 147.

Stovall, Floyd. "Contemporary Fiction." In *American Idealism.* Port Washington, N.Y.: Kennikat Press, 1943. Pp. 137–66.

Swan, Kenneth D. "John Steinbeck: In Search of America." *Steinbeck's Prophetic Vision of America.* Edited by Tetsumaro Hayashi and Kenneth D. Swan. Proceedings of the Bicentennial Steinbeck Seminar. Upland, Ind.: Taylor University Press for Steinbeck Society of America, 1976. Pp. 12–27.

———. "The Merit of John Steinbeck: A Wide-Ranging Debate." In *Steinbeck's Prophetic Vision of America.* Edited by Tetsumaro Hayashi and Kenneth D. Swan. Proceedings of the Bicentennial Steinbeck Seminar. Upland, Ind.: Taylor University Press for Steinbeck Society of America, 1976. Pp. 56–84.

———. "Perspectives on the Fiction of John Steinbeck: A Critical Review of Two

Prominent Critics—Peter Lisca and Warren French." *DAI* 35 (1974): 1673A–74A. Ball State University.

Taylor, Horace P., Jr. "The Biological Naturalism of John Steinbeck." *DAI* 22 (1961): 3674. Louisiana State University.

———. "The Biological Naturalism of John Steinbeck." *McNeese Review* 12 (Winter 1960–61): 81–97.

———. "John Steinbeck—The Quest." *McNeese Review* 16 (1965): 33–45.

Tedlock, Ernest W., Jr., and C. V. Wicker. Introduction to *Steinbeck and His Critics: A Record of Twenty-five Years.* Edited by Tedlock and Wicker. Albuquerque: University of New Mexico Press, 1957. Pp. xi–xii.

TeMaat, Agatha. "John Steinbeck: On the Nature of the Creative Process in the Early Years." *DAI* 36 (1976): 5306A. University of Nebraska, Lincoln.

Tokunaga, Masanori. "A Return to Nature: Steinbeck's Search for American Civilization." *Kyushu American Literature* 17 (1976): 20–24.

Tuttleton, James W. "Steinbeck in Russia: The Rhetoric of Praise and Blame." *Modern Fiction Studies* 11 (Spring 1965): 79–89.

Wagenknecht, Edward Charles. "Two Kinds of Novelists: Steinbeck and Marquand." In *Cavalcade of the American Novel: From the Birth of the Nation to the Middle of the Twentieth Century.* New York: Holt, 1952. Pp. 438–48.

Walcutt, Charles Child. "Later Trends in Form: Steinbeck, Hemingway, Dos Passos." In *American Literary Naturalism: A Divided Stream.* Minneapolis: University of Minnesota Press, 1956. Pp. 258–89.

Waldmeir, Joseph J. "John Steinbeck: No Grapes of Wrath." In *A Question of Quality: Popularity and Value in Modern Creative Writing.* Edited by Louis Fuller. Bowling Green: University Popular Press, 1976. Pp. 219–28.

Wallis, Prentiss B., Jr. "John Steinbeck: The Symbolic Family." *DAI* 27 (1966): 1842A–43A. University of Kansas.

Weeks, Donald. "Steinbeck against Steinbeck." *Pacific Spectator* 1 (Autumn 1947): 447–57.

Whicher, G. E. "Proletarian Leanings." In *Literature of the American People: An Historical and Critical Survey.* Edited by Arthur Hobson Quinn. New York: Appleton, 1951. Pp. 954–62.

Whipple, Thomas King. "Steinbeck: Through a Glass, though Brightly." In *Study out the Land: Essays.* Berkeley: University of California Press, 1943. Pp. 105–11.

Woodress, James. "John Steinbeck: Hostage to Fortune." *South Atlantic Quarterly* 63 (Summer 1964): 385–97.

Yarmus, Marcia D. "The Hispanic World of John Steinbeck." *DAI* 46, no. 1 (1985): 146A. New York University.

———. "John Steinbeck's Hispanic Character Names." *Literary Onomastics Studies* 13 (1986): 193–204.

———. "John Steinbeck's Toponymic Preferences." In *From Oz to the Onion Patch.* Edited by Edward Callary. Dekalb, Ill.: North Central Name Society, 1986. 1: 147–60.

Zane, Nancy Elizabeth. "Steinbeck's Heroes: 'The Individual Mind and Spirit of Man.'" *DAI* 43 (1982): 1549A. Ohio University.

Materials That Refer to One Short Novel Journal articles, reviews, articles from books, articles from proceedings, articles from monographs, dissertations, and parts of books (indicated by page numbers) that refer to one short novel, arranged by novel.

Tortilla Flat

Alexander, Stanley. "The Conflict of Form in *Tortilla Flat*." *American Literature* 40 (1968): 58–66.
Allen, Walter. *Modern Novel*, p. 163.
Astro, Richard. *Steinbeck and Ricketts . . . Shaping*, pp. 3, 97, 109–12, 117.
Benet, William Rose. Rev. of *TF*. *Saturday Review of Literature* 12 (1 June 1935): 12.
Benson, Jackson J. *True Adventures*, pp. 41–42, 52, 61, 92, 120, 174, 224, 270, 274–80, 288, 309–10, 317, 318, 323–25, 364–66.
Bhargava, Rajul. "*Tortilla Flat*: A Revaluation." In *John Steinbeck: From Salinas to the World*, ed. Shigeharu Yano et al., pp. 123–29.
Chamberlain, John. Rev. of *TF*. *Current History* 42 (July 1935): 7.
Colby, Harriet. Rev. of *TF*. *New York Herald Tribune Books*, 2 June 1935, p. 4.
Ditsky, John. "From Oxford to Salinas: Comparing Faulkner and Steinbeck." *Steinbeck Newsletter* 2, no. 3 (1969): 51–55.
———. *John Steinbeck: Life, Work, and Criticism*, pp. 7, 18, 20, 27, 28.
———. "Steinbeck and William Faulkner." In *Steinbeck's Literary Dimension: A Guide to Comparative Studies*, ed. Tetsumaro Hayashi, pp. 28–45.
Durant, Will, and Ariel Durant. *Interpretations*, pp. 43–44, 46.
Ewen, A. J. Rev. of *TF*. *Books and Bookman*, November 1962, p. 75.
Fensch, Thomas. *Steinbeck and Covici*, pp. 9, 11–12, 15, 49–50, 52–54, 88, 198, 223.
Fontenrose, John. *Introduction and Interpretation*, pp. 30–41, 50, 107.
French, Warren. *John Steinbeck*, 2d ed., pp. 23–24, 62–63, 68, 70–75, 76, 77, 82, 106, 117, 126, 129, 170, 173.
———. *Social Novel*, pp. 46, 168.
———. "Steinbeck and J. D. Salinger." In *Steinbeck's Literary Dimension*, ed. Tetsumaro Hayashi, pp. 105–15.
Fuller, Edmund. *Man in Modern Fiction*, p. 33.
Garcia, Reloy. *Steinbeck and D. H. Lawrence*, p. 14.
Gibbs, Lincoln R. "John Steinbeck, Moralist." *Antioch Review* 2 (1942): 172–84.
Gray, James. *John Steinbeck*, pp. 27–28.
Hadley, George. *Books*, pp. 9, 11.
Hayashi, Tetsumaro. *Dictionary*, pp. 28, 31, 40, 42–43, 51–52, 53–54, 55, 57–60, 62, 74, 75, 80, 81, 99, 102, 112, 113, 114, 120, 124, 125, 128, 131–32, 133, 134, 138–39, 146, 147, 148–54, 158–60, 161–62, 166, 167–68, 169–70, 173, 175–76, 183, 184–86, 194, 202, 205.
Hoffman, Frederick J. *Modern Novel*, p. 151.

Jackson, Joseph Henry. "John Steinbeck: A Portrait." *Saturday Review of Literature* 16 (25 September 1937): 11–12, 18.

Jain, Sunita. *Concept of Man*, pp. 2, 3, 24–29, 89, 90, 91, 93.

Jones, Lawrence William. *JS as Fabulist*, p. 16.

Justus, James H. "The Transient World of *Tortilla Flat*." *Western Review: A Journal of the Humanities* 7 (1970): 55–60.

Kiernan, Thomas. *Intricate Music*, pp. 178, 189–91, 196–202, 217–18, 226–27.

Kinney, Arthur F. "The Arthurian Cycle in *Tortilla Flat*." *Modern Fiction Studies* 11 (1965): 11–20. Reprinted in *Steinbeck: A Collection of Critical Essays*, ed. Robert Murray Davis, pp. 36–46.

———. "*Tortilla Flat* Revisited." In *Steinbeck and the Arthurian Theme*, ed. Tetsumaro Hayashi, pp. 12–24.

Levant, Howard. "The First Public Success." In *The Novels of John Steinbeck: A Critical Study*, pp. 52–73.

———. "*Tortilla Flat*: The Shape of John Steinbeck's Career." *PMLA: Publications of the Modern Language Association of America* 85 (1970): 1087–95.

Lisca, Peter. *Nature and Myth*, pp. 2, 4, 54–62, 112, 220.

———. *Wide World*, pp. 7, 8, 72–91, 199, 202, 204, 206, 224.

Lutwack, Leonard. *Heroic Fiction*, pp. 62, 65.

McCarthy, Paul. *JS*, pp. 14, 38–45, 48, 49, 97, 98, 140, 149.

Mangione, Jerre. Rev. of *TF*. *New Republic* 83 (1935): 285.

"Manuscripts III: *Tortilla Flat*, by John Steinbeck." *Library Chronicle of the University of Texas* 3 (1971): 80–81.

Marks, Lester J. *Thematic Design*, pp. 42, 47, 89–91, 93.

Marsh, Fred T. Rev. of *TF*. *New York Times*, 2 June 1935, p. 6.

Martin, Stoddard. *California Writers*, pp. 88–91, 94, 102, 107, 143.

Millichap, Joseph R. *Film*, pp. 5, 11, 61–69, 87, 94, 177.

Miyagawa, Hiroyuki. "On Steinbeck's *Tortilla Flat*." *Chu-Shikoku Studies in American Literature* 20 (1984): 88–100.

Moore, Harry T. *Novels of JS*, pp. 36–39.

Neville, Helen. Rev. of *TF*. *Nation* 140 (19 June 1935): 720.

Owens, Louis. "Camelot East of Eden: John Steinbeck's *Tortilla Flat*." *Arizona Quarterly* 38 (1982): 203–16.

———. *Re-Vision*, pp. 160, 161, 164–77, 180, 209.

Plomer, William. Rev. of *TF*. *Spectator* 155 (1935): 960.

Pratt, John C. *JS*, pp. 17, 32–33, 35.

Rao, B. Ramachandra. *American Fictional Hero*, pp. 62–63.

Rev. of *TF*. *Chicago Daily Tribune*, 1 June 1935, p. 14.

Rev. of *TF*. *Saturday Review* (London) 160 (23 November 1935): 501.

Rev. of *TF*. *Time* 39 (18 May 1942): 84.

Rev. of *TF*. "On Monkey Hill." *Times* (London) *Literary Supplement*, 21 December 1935, p. 877.

St. Pierre, Brian. *California Years*, pp. 63–65.

Satyanarayana, M. R. *Compassion*, pp. 8, 9, 23, 104.

Simmonds, Roy S. *Steinbeck's Literary Achievement*, pp. 7, 10, 12, 16–19, 20, 21, 32.

Simpson, Arthur L., Jr. "Steinbeck's *Tortilla Flat* (1935)." In *Study Guide to Steinbeck*, ed. Tetsumaro Hayashi, pp. 214–43.
Steinbeck, Elaine, and Robert Wallsten. *Letters*, pp. 88, 96–97, 98, 102, 105, 116, 462.
Straumann, Heinrich. *American Literature*, p. 114.
Street, Webster. "John Steinbeck: A Reminiscence." In *Steinbeck: The Man and His Work*, ed. Richard Astro and Tetsumaro Hayashi, pp. 35–41.
Thompson, Raymond H. *Avalon*, pp. 20–21.
Timmerman, John H. *Aesthetics*, pp. 72, 110, 134–41, 145–57, 166, 167, 168, 172, 176, 194, 229, 231.
Uchida, Shigeharu. "Sentimental Steinbeck and His *Tortilla Flat*." *Kyushu American Literature* 7 (1964): 8–12.
Valjean, Nelson. *Errant Knight*, pp. 22, 147–48.
Walcutt, Charles C. *Seven Novelists*, pp. 206, 226, 227–28, 233.
Watt, F. W. *Steinbeck*, pp. 7, 23, 38–42, 79.

Of Mice and Men

Allen, Walter. *Modern Novel*, pp. 163–64.
Astro, Richard. *Steinbeck and Ricketts . . . Shaping*, pp. 104–7, 108, 173, 181.
Atkinson, Brooks. Rev. of *Of M & M*. New York Times, 24 November 1937, p. 20.
———. Rev. of *Of M & M*. New York Times Book Review, 12 December 1937, p. 11.
Bellman, Samuel I. "Control and Freedom in Steinbeck's *Of Mice and Men*." *CEA Critic: An Official Journal of the College English Association* 38 (1975): 25–27.
Benson, Jackson J. *True Adventures*, pp. 39, 325–32, 349, 350–52, 357–59, 363–65, 372, 376, 383, 393, 394–95, 407–8.
Brighouse, Harold. Rev. of *Of M & M*. Manchester Guardian, 14 September 1937, p. 5.
Brown, Deming. *Soviet*, p. 79.
Brown, John Mason. "Mr. Steinbeck's *Of Mice and Men*." In *Two on the Aisle: Ten Years of the American Theatre in Performance*. 2d ed. Port Washington, N.Y.: Kennikat Press, 1966. Pp. 183–87.
Calverton, V. F. "Steinbeck, Hemingway, and Faulkner." *Modern Quarterly* 11, no. 4 (Fall 1939): 36–44.
Canby, Henry S. Rev. of *Of M & M*. Saturday Review of Literature 15 (27 February 1937): 7.
Cardullo, Robert. "The Function of Candy in *Of Mice and Men*." *Notes on Contemporary Literature* 12 (1982): 10.
———. "On the Road to Tragedy: The Function of Candy in *Of Mice and Men*." University of Florida, Department of Classics/Comparative Drama, Conference Papers. *All the World: Drama Past and Present*. 2 vols. Edited by Karelisa V. Hartigan. Washington, D.C.: University Press of America, 1982. 2:1–8.
Court, Franklin E. "*Of Mice and Men* (Play) (1937)." In *Study Guide to Steinbeck*, ed. Tetsumaro Hayashi, pp. 155–67.
Dacus, Lee. "Lennie as Christian in *Of Mice and Men*." *Southwestern American Literature* 4 (1974): 87–91.

Davidson, Richard A. "An Overlooked Musical Version of *Of Mice and Men*."
    Steinbeck Quarterly 16 (1983): 9–16.
Ditsky, John. *John Steinbeck: Life, Work, and Criticism*, pp. 18, 30.
Durant, Will, and Ariel Durant. *Interpretations*, pp. 44–45.
Dusenbury, Winifred Loesch. "Homelessness." *The Theme of Loneliness in Modern
    American Drama*. Gainesville: University of Florida Press, 1960. Pp. 44–51.
Everson, William K. "Thoughts on a Great Adaptation." *The Modern American Novel
    and the Movies*. Edited by Gerald Peary and Roger Shatzkin. New York: Ungar,
    1978. Pp. 63–69.
Feied, Frederick V. "Steinbeck's Depression Novels: The Ecological Basis." *DAI* 32
    (1971): 427A–28A. Columbia University.
Fensch, Thomas. *Steinbeck and Covici*, pp. 13–15, 114, 136, 139, 223.
Fontenrose, Joseph. *Introduction and Interpretation*, pp. 53–59, 140.
French, Warren. "End of a Dream." In *Steinbeck: A Collection of Critical Essays*, ed.
    Robert Murray Davis. Pp. 63–69.
———. "The First Theatrical Production of Steinbeck's *Of Mice and Men*." *Ameri-
    can Literature* 36 (1965): 525–27.
———. *John Steinbeck*, 2d ed., pp. 24, 60, 76, 86, 87–91, 116, 126, 129, 134–35,
    145, 170, 173.
Ganapathy, R. "Steinbeck's *Of Mice and Men*: A Study of Lyricism Through
    Primitivism." *Literary Criterion* 5 (1962): 101–4.
Garcia, Reloy. *Steinbeck and D. H. Lawrence*, pp. 15–16.
Goldhurst, William. "*Of Mice and Men*: John Steinbeck's Parable of the Curse of
    Cain." *Western American Literature* 6 (1971): 123–35.
Goodrich, Norma L. "Bachelors in Fiction, through John Steinbeck and Jean
    Giono." *Kentucky Romance Quarterly* 14 (1967): 367–78.
Gray, James. *John Steinbeck*, pp. 21–22.
Gurko, Leo. "*Of Mice and Men*: Steinbeck as Manichean." *University of Windsor
    Review* 8 (1973): 11–23.
Gwen, A. J. Rev. of *Of M & M*. *Books and Bookman*, December 1962, p. 41.
Hadley, George. *Books*, pp. 9, 11.
Hayashi, Tetsumaro. *Dictionary*, pp. 39, 42, 44, 56, 128–29, 173, 202.
Hirose, Hidekazu. "From Doc Burton to Jim Casy: Steinbeck in the Latter Half of
    the 1930's." In *John Steinbeck: East and West*, ed. Tetsumaro Hayashi, Yasuo
    Hashiguchi, and Richard F. Peterson, pp. 6–11.
Hughes, R. S. *Beyond the Red Pony*, pp. 5–6, 33.
———. *Study of the Short Fiction*, p. 91.
Hwang, Mei-shu. "*Of Mice and Men*: An Experimental Study of the Novel and the
    Play." *Tamkung Journal/Tan-Chaing Hueh Pao: Language, Literature, and History*
    11 (1973): 225–40.
Hyman, Stanley Edgar. "John Steinbeck: Of Invertebrates and Men." In *The
    Promised End: Essays and Reviews*. Cleveland: World Press, 1963. Pp. 17–22.
Isaacs, E. J. R. "*Of Mice and Men*." In *Theatre Arts Anthology: A Record and a Prophecy*.
    Edited by Rosamond Gilder et al. New York: Theatre Arts Books, 1950. Pp.
    644–46.

Jain, Sunita. *Concept of Man*, pp. 2, 3, 36, 37–42, 44, 45, 91, 93, 94.

Jones, Lawrence William. *JS as Fabulist*, pp. 5, 7, 17.

Kauffmann, Stanley. "Mice and Men." In *Persons of the Drama: Theatre Criticism and Comment*. New York: Harper and Row, 1976. Pp. 156–59.

Kiernan, Thomas. *Intricate Music*, pp. 207–11, 220–23, 226–28.

Levenson, Samuel. "The Compassion of John Steinbeck." *Canadian Forum* 20 (1940): 185–86.

Lisca, Peter. "Motif and Pattern in *Of Mice and Men*." *Modern Fiction Studies* 2 (1956–57): 228–34.

———. *Nature and Myth*, pp. 2, 76–86, 124, 155.

———. *Wide World*, pp. 7, 12, 110, 117, 130–43, 159, 191, 193, 206, 255, 279.

Lutwack, Leonard. *Heroic Fiction*, pp. 62, 63, 65.

McCarthy, Paul. *JS*, pp. 10, 15, 41, 57–64, 139, 140, 142.

Magny, Claude-Edmonde. "Steinbeck, or the Limits of the Impersonal Novel." In *The Age of the American Novel*. New York: Ungar, 1972. Pp. 161–77.

Marks, Lester J. *Thematic Design*, pp. 42, 58–65, 68.

Martin, Stoddard. *Tough Guys*, pp. 8, 14–15, 107, 210.

Millichap, Joseph R. *Film*, pp. 2–3, 5, 13–26, 170–72, 176–77.

Moore, Harry T. *Novels of JS*, pp. 48–52.

Morsberger, Robert E. "Play It Again, Lennie and George." *Steinbeck Quarterly* 15 (1982): 123–26.

O'Hara, Frank Hurburt. "Melodrama with a Meaning." In *Today in American Drama*. Chicago: University of Chicago Press, 1939. Pp. 142–89.

Ohnishi, Katsue. "Why Must Lennie Be Killed?" *Kyushu American Literature* 22 (1981): 85–87.

Owens, Louis. *Re-Vision*, pp. 99, 100–106, 177, 209.

Paul, Louis. Rev. of *Of M & M*. *New York Herald Tribune Books*, 28 February 1937, p. 160.

Pizer, Donald. "John Steinbeck and American Naturalism." *Steinbeck Quarterly* 9 (1976): 12–15.

Pratt, John C. *JS*, pp. 23, 36, 40.

Rao, B. Ramachandra. *American Fictional Hero*, pp. 54–55, 57, 66–68.

Rev. of *Of M & M*. *Commonweal* 27 (10 December 1937): 191.

Rev. of *Of M & M*. *Literary Digest* 124 (18 December 1937): 34.

Rev. of *Of M & M*. *London Mercury* 36 (October 1937): 595.

Rev. of *Of M & M*. *Newsweek* 9 (27 February 1937): 39.

Rev. of *Of M & M*. *Theatre Arts* 21 (October 1937): 774–81.

Rev. of *Of M & M*. *Theatre Arts* 22 (January 1938): 13–16.

Rev. of *Of M & M*. *Time* 29 (1 March 1937): 69.

Rev. of *Of M & M*. *Time* 30 (6 December 1937): 41.

Rev. of *Of M & M*. *Times* (London) *Literary Supplement*, 2 October 1937, p. 714.

St. Pierre, Brian. *California Years*, pp. 75, 83–85.

Satyanarayana, M. R. *Compassion*, pp. 49, 55, 69, 71, 72, 135.

Shurgot, Michael W. "A Game of Cards in Steinbeck's *Of Mice and Men*." *Steinbeck Quarterly* 15 (1982): 38–43.

Simmonds, Roy S. *Steinbeck's Literary Achievement,* pp. 2, 6, 24.
Slater, John F. "Steinbeck's *Of Mice and Men* (Novel) (1937)." In *Study Guide to Steinbeck,* ed. Tetsumaro Hayashi, pp. 129–54.
Steele, Joan. "A Century of Idiots: *Barnaby Rudge* and *Of Mice and Men.*" *Steinbeck Quarterly* 5 (Winter 1972): 8–17.
―――. "Steinbeck and Charles Dickens." In *Steinbeck's Literary Dimension,* ed. Tetsumaro Hayashi, pp. 16–27.
Steinbeck, Elaine, and Robert Wallsten. *Letters,* pp. 5, 114, 120, 123–24, 129, 132, 134, 135, 179, 562.
Straumann, Heinrich. *American Literature,* pp. 114–15.
Thompson, Ralph. Rev. of *Of M & M. New York Times,* 27 February 1937, p. 15.
Thompson, Ralph. Rev. of *Of M & M. New York Times,* 2 March 1937, p. 19.
Timmerman, John H. *Aesthetics,* pp. 37, 56, 72, 94–101, 111, 144, 145, 166, 187.
Valjean, Nelson. *Errant Knight,* pp. 60, 158–59.
Van Doren, Mark. Rev. of *Of M & M. Nation* 144 (6 March 1937): 275.
―――. "Wrong Number." In *Private Reader: Selected Articles and Reviews.* New York: Holt, Kraus Reprint Collection, 1968. Pp. 255–57.
Walcutt, Charles C. *Seven Novelists,* pp. 221–22.
Walter, Eda Lou. Rev. of *Of M & M. New York Times Book Review* 7 (28 February 1937): 7, 20.
Watt, F. W. *Steinbeck,* pp. 8, 58–62.
Weeks, Donald. Rev. of *Of M & M. Atlantic Monthly* 159 (April 1937): n.p., between 384–85.
Worsley, T. C. Rev. of *Of M & M. New Statesman* 20 (19 October 1940): 396.
Wyatt, Bryant N. "Experimentation as Technique: The Protest Novels of John Steinbeck." *Discourse* 12 (1969): 143–53.
Wyatt, Euphemia. Rev. of *Of M & M. Catholic World* 146 (January 1938): 468–69.
Young, Stark. Rev. of *Of M & M. New Republic* 93 (15 December 1937): 170–71.

The Red Pony

Astro, Richard. "Something that Happened: A Non-teleological Approach to 'The Leader of the People.' " *Steinbeck Quarterly* 6 (1973): 19–23. Reprinted in *Study Guide to Steinbeck's "The Long Valley,"* ed. Tetsumaro Hayashi, pp. 105–11.
―――. *Steinbeck and Ricketts . . . Shaping,* pp. 68–69, 106, 108, 114, 146.
Autrey, Max L. "Men, Mice, and Moths: Gradation in Steinbeck's 'The Leader of the People.' " *Western American Literature* 10 (1975): 195–204.
Benson, Jackson J. *True Adventures,* pp. 9, 255, 262, 281–82, 284–85, 330, 360, 382, 483, 489, 629.
Benton, Robert M. "Realism, Growth, and Contrast in 'The Gift.' " *Steinbeck Quarterly* 6 (1973): 3–9. Reprinted in *Study Guide to Steinbeck's "The Long Valley,"* ed. Tetsumaro Hayashi, pp. 81–88.
―――. "Steinbeck's *The Long Valley.*" In *Study Guide to Steinbeck,* ed. Tetsumaro Hayashi, pp. 69–86.

Ditsky, John. *John Steinbeck: Life, Work, and Criticism*, pp. 18, 25.

Fensch, Thomas. *Steinbeck and Covici*, pp. 9, 15, 48–50, 99, 223.

Fontenrose, John. *Introduction and Interpretation*, pp. 63–66.

French, Warren. *John Steinbeck*, 2d ed., pp. 17, 62–68, 75, 76, 91, 125, 134, 135, 167, 168, 170, 171, 173.

———. *Social Novel*, p. 141.

Garcia, Reloy. *Steinbeck and D. H. Lawrence*, p. 14.

Gierasch, Walter. "Steinbeck's *The Red Pony* II: The Great Mountains." *Explicator* 4 (March 1946): 39.

Gladstein, Mimi. "'The Leader of the People': A Boy Becomes a 'Mensch.'" In *Steinbeck's "The Red Pony": Essays in Criticism*, ed. Tetsumaro Hayashi and Thomas J. Moore, pp. 27–37.

Goldsmith, Arnold L. "Thematic Rhythm in *The Red Pony*." *College English* 26, no. 5 (February 1965): 391–94. Reprinted in *Steinbeck: A Collection of Critical Essays*, ed. Robert Murray Davis, pp. 70–74; and in *John Steinbeck: A Study of the Short Fiction*, ed. R. S. Hughes, pp. 166–71.

Gray, James. *John Steinbeck*, pp. 7, 22, 43.

Grommon, Alfred H. "Who Is 'The Leader of the People'?: Helping Students Examine Fiction." *English Journal* 48 (1959): 449–61, 476.

Hayashi, Tetsumaro. *Dictionary*, pp. 40, 62, 67, 75, 78, 163, 180, 181–82.

Houghton, Donald E. "'Westering' in 'Leader of the People.'" *Western American Literature* 4 (1969): 117–24.

Hughes, R. S. *Beyond the Red Pony*, pp. 1, 3, 90–103, 123.

———. "The Black Cypress and the Green Tub: Death and Procreation in Steinbeck's 'The Promise.'" In *Steinbeck's "The Red Pony": Essays in Criticism*, ed. Tetsumaro Hayashi and Thomas J. Moore, pp. 9–16.

———. *Study of the Short Fiction*, pp. 15, 53–62, 80.

Jain, Sunita. *Concept of Man*, pp. 3, 48, 53–58, 94.

Jones, Lawrence William. *JS as Fabulist*, p. 17.

Kiernan, Thomas. *Intricate Music*, pp. 20–21, 184–86, 219.

Levant, Howard. "John Steinbeck's *The Red Pony*: A Study in Narrative Technique." *Journal of Narrative Technique* 1 (1971): 77–85.

Lisca, Peter. *Nature and Myth*, pp. 1, 5, 191, 195–200.

———. *Wide World*, pp. 22, 23, 63, 97, 100, 101, 102, 103, 104, 105–7, 118, 170, 182, 190, 222.

McCarthy, Paul. *JS*, pp. 2, 30–32, 84, 111, 140.

Marks, Lester J. *Thematic Design*, pp. 16–18.

Martin, Bruce K. "'The Leader of the People' Reexamined." *Studies in Short Fiction* 8 (1971): 423–32.

Millichap, Joseph R. *Film*, pp. 11, 94, 107–21, 167–68, 177.

———. "Realistic Style in Steinbeck's and Milestone's *Of Mice and Men*." *Literature/Film Quarterly* 6 (1978): 241–52.

Moore, Harry T. *Novels of JS*, pp. 34–35.

Owens, Louis. *Re-Vision*, pp. 7, 32, 34, 46–58, 77, 86, 105, 107, 196, 209.

Pearce, Howard D. "Steinbeck's 'The Leader of the People': Dialectic and Symbol." *Papers on Language and Literature: A Journal for Scholars and Critics of Language and Literature* 8 (1972): 425–26.

Peterson, Richard F. "The Grail Legend and Steinbeck's 'The Great Mountains.'" *Steinbeck Quarterly* 6 (1973): 9–15. Reprinted in *Study Guide to Steinbeck's "The Long Valley*," ed. Tetsumaro Hayashi, pp. 89–96.

Rao, B. Ramachandra. *American Fictional Hero*, pp. 64–65, 68.

Rev. of *Red Pony. Chicago Sun Book Week*, 16 September 1945, p. 2.

Rev. of *Red Pony. New York Herald Tribune Books*, 4 November 1945, p. 6.

Rev. of *Red Pony. Time* 30 (11 October 1937): 79.

Satyanarayana, M. R. "'And then the Child Becomes a Man': Three Initiation Stories of John Steinbeck." *Indian Journal of American Studies* 1 (1971): 87–93.

———. *Compassion*, pp. 19, 25–30, 134.

Shuman, R. Baird. "Initiation Rites in Steinbeck's *The Red Pony*." *English Journal* 59 (1970): 1252–55.

Simmonds, Roy S. "The First Publication of Steinbeck's 'The Leader of the People.'" *Steinbeck Quarterly* 8 (1975): 13–18.

———. "The Place and Importance of 'The Great Mountains' in *The Red Pony*." In *Steinbeck's "The Red Pony": Essays in Criticism*, ed. Tetsumaro Hayashi and Thomas J. Moore, pp. 17–26.

———. *Steinbeck's Literary Achievement*, pp. 11, 26–27.

———. "Steinbeck's *The Pearl*: A Preliminary Textual Study." *Steinbeck Quarterly* 22, nos. 1 and 2 (Winter/Spring 1989): 16–34.

Steinbeck, Elaine, and Robert Wallsten. *Letters*, pp. 58, 71, 73, 78, 82, 83, 85, 139, 225.

Tammaro, Thomas M. "Erik Erikson Meets John Steinbeck: Psychosocial Development in 'The Gift.'" In *Steinbeck's "The Red Pony": Essays in Criticism*, ed. Tetsumaro Hayashi and Thomas J. Moore, pp. 1–9.

Thompson, Ralph. Rev. of *Red Pony. New York Times*, 29 September 1937, p. 21.

Timmerman, John H. *Aesthetics*, pp. 35, 73–75, 97, 159.

Tsuboi, Kiyohiko. "Two Jodys: Steinbeck and Rawlings." In *John Steinbeck: From Salinas to the World*, pp. 83–96.

Valjean, Nelson. *Errant Knight*, p. 35.

Walcutt, Charles C. *Seven Novelists*, pp. 207, 222, 242.

Walter, Edith H. Rev. of *Red Pony. New York Times Book Review* 6 (10 October 1937): 7.

Watt, F. W. *Steinbeck*, pp. 3–4, 18–19, 21, 46–49.

West, Philip J. "Steinbeck's 'The Leader of the People': A Crisis in Style." *Western American Literature* 5 (1970): 137–41.

Woodward, Robert H. "The Promise of Steinbeck's 'The Promise.'" In *Study Guide to Steinbeck's "The Long Valley*," ed. Tetsumaro Hayashi, pp. 97–103.

———. "Steinbeck's 'The Promise.'" *Steinbeck Quarterly* 6 (1973): 15–19.

Work, James G. "Coordinate Forces in 'The Leader of the People.'" *Western American Literature* 16 (1982): 279–89.

Yano, Shigeharu. "Psychological Interpretation of Steinbeck's Women in *The Long*

Valley." In *John Steinbeck: East and West,* ed. Tetsumaro Hayashi, Yasuo Hashiguchi, and Richard Peterson, pp. 54–60.

The Moon Is Down

Adey, Alvin. Rev. of *Moon. Current History* 2 (April 1942): 143–44.
Astro, Richard. *Steinbeck and Ricketts . . . Shaping,* pp. 4, 149–57, 158, 159, 176, 181, 192, 195, 229, 245.
Benson, Jackson J. *True Adventures,* pp. 487–88, 497–500, 503, 507, 646.
Brighouse, Harold. Rev. of *Moon. Manchester Guardian,* 26 June 1942, p. 3.
Brown, Deming. *Soviet,* pp. 139–40.
Burnham, David. Rev. of *Moon. Commonweal* 36 (24 April 1942): 14.
Butler, E. M. Rev. of *Moon. Catholic World* 155 (May 1942): 254–55.
Chamberlain, John. Rev. of *Moon. New York Times,* 6 March 1942, p. 19.
Clancy, Charles J. "Steinbeck's *The Moon Is Down.*" In *A Study Guide to Steinbeck, Part II,* ed. Tetsumaro Hayashi, pp. 100–121.
Cousins, Norman. Rev. of *Moon. Saturday Review of Literature* 25 (14 March 1942): 6.
Ditsky, John. *John Steinbeck: Life, Work, and Criticism,* pp. 8, 20, 26.
———. "Steinbeck's 'European' Play-Novella: *The Moon Is Down.*" *Steinbeck Quarterly* 20 (1987): 9–18.
Duffus, R. C. Rev. of *Moon. New York Times Book Review* 6 (8 March 1942): 1, 27.
Duffy, Charles. Rev. of *Moon. Commonweal* 35 (1942): 569–70.
Fadiman, Clifton. Rev. of *Moon. New Yorker* 18 (7 March 1942): 52.
Fensch, Thomas. *Steinbeck and Covici,* pp. 32, 36, 41.
Fontenrose, Joseph. *Introduction and Interpretation,* pp. 98–101.
French, Warren. "After the *Grapes of Wrath.*" *Steinbeck Quarterly* 8 (1975): 73–78.
French, Warren. *John Steinbeck,* 2d ed., pp. 27–28, 104, 106–8, 109–10, 125, 126, 127, 171.
Garrison, W. W. Rev. of *Moon. Christian Century* 59 (29 April 1942): 561–62.
Gassner, John. Rev. of *Moon. Current History* 2 (May 1942): 228.
Gunther, John. Rev. of *Moon. New York Herald Tribune Books,* 8 March 1942, p. 1.
Hayashi, Tetsumaro. *Dictionary,* pp. 27, 30, 32, 36, 51, 54, 65, 96, 101, 109, 114, 115, 117, 134, 145, 154, 176, 183–84, 207.
———. "Steinbeck's Political Vision in *The Moon Is Down:* A Shakespearean Interpretation." *Kyushu American Literature* 24 (1983): 1–10.
———. "Steinbeck's *The Moon Is Down:* A Shakespearean Explication." *Reitaku University Journal* 36 (December 1983): 1–14.
John, S. B., and C. A. Burns. "The Mirror of the Stage: Vichy France and Foreign Drama." In *Literature and Society: Studies in Nineteenth and Twentieth Century French Literature Presented to R. J. North.* Edited by C. A. Burns. Birmingham: Goodman for University of Birmingham, 1980. Pp. 200–213.
Jones, Lawrence William. *JS as Fabulist,* p. 18.
Kiernan, Thomas. *Intricate Music,* pp. 258–59.
Krutch, Joseph Wood. Rev. of *Moon. Nation* 145 (11 December 1937): 663.
Lisca, Peter. *Nature and Myth,* pp. 21, 200–203, 208.

———. *Wide World*, pp. 8, 119, 186–96.
Marks, Lester J. *Thematic Design*, pp. 29, 98–105, 113.
Marshall, Margaret. Rev. of *Moon. Nation* 154 (7 March 1942): 286.
Millichap, Joseph R. *Film*, pp. 5, 60, 69–76, 177.
Moore, Harry T. *Age of the Modern*, pp. 86–87.
Morsberger, Robert E. "Steinbeck's Zapata: Rebel versus Revolutionary." In *Steinbeck: The Man and His Work*, ed. Richard Astro and Tetsumaro Hayashi, pp. 43–63.
O'Brien, Kate. Rev. of *Moon. Spectator* 169 (10 July 1942): 44.
Pratt, John C. *JS*, pp. 15–16.
Rev. of *Moon. Booklist* 38 (15 March 1942): 252.
Rev. of *Moon. Bookmark* 3 (May 1942): 17.
Rev. of *Moon. Catholic World* 155 (May 1942): 253.
Rev. of *Moon. Christian Science Monitor*, 6 March 1942, p. 18.
Rev. of *Moon. Library Journal* 67 (15 February 1942): 182.
Rev. of *Moon. Library Journal* 67 (1 September 1942): 739.
Rev. of *Moon. Life* 12 (6 April 1942): 32–34.
Rev. of *Moon.* "Moon Is Halfway Down." *New Republic* 106 (18 May 1942): 657.
Rev. of *Moon. Newsweek* 19 (20 April 1942): 72.
Rev. of *Moon. New York Herald Tribune Books*, 8 March 1942, p. 1.
Rev. of *Moon. New Yorker* 18 (7 March 1942): 59; 18 (4 April 1942): 63.
Rev. of *Moon. Time* 34 (9 March 1942): 84.
Rev. of *Moon. Times* (London) *Literary Supplement*, 20 June 1942, p. 305.
Rev. of *Moon. Yale Review* 31 (Spring 1942): 8.
Satyanarayana, M. R. *Compassion*, pp. 99–104.
Simmonds, Roy S. *Steinbeck's Literary Achievement*, pp. 9–10, 24–25.
Stegner, Wallace. Rev. of *Moon. Boston Globe*, 11 March 1942, p. 19.
Steinbeck, Elaine, and Robert Wallsten. *Letters*, pp. 233, 235, 236, 237, 238, 239, 590, 767–68.
Straumann, Heinrich. *American Literature*, pp. 115–16.
Thurber, James. Rev. of *Moon. New Republic* 106 (16 March 1942): 370.
Timmerman, John H. *Aesthetics*, pp. 183–87, 267.
Toynbee, Philip. Rev. of *Moon. New Statesman and Nation* 23 (20 June 1942): 408–9.
Van Doren, Mark. Rev. of *Moon. Nation* 154 (18 April 1942): 468.
Watt, F. W. *Steinbeck*, pp. 77–79.
Weeks, Donald. Rev. of *Moon. Atlantic Monthly* 169 (April 1942): n.p., between 398–99.
Young, Stark. Rev. of *Moon. New Republic* 106 (11 May 1942): 638.

Cannery Row

Adams, J. Donald. Rev. of *CR. New York Times Book Review* 9 (14 January 1945): 1, 2.
Alexander, Stanley. "*Cannery Row:* Steinbeck's Pastoral Poem." In *Steinbeck: A Collection of Critical Essays*, ed. Robert Murray Davis, pp. 135–48.
Allen, Walter. *Modern Novel*, pp. 163.

Astro, Richard. *Steinbeck and Ricketts . . . Shaping*, pp. 3, 4, 20, 108, 159–60, 169, 173, 177, 186, 190, 194–205, 213, 214, 246.

Benson, Jackson J. "John Steinbeck's *Cannery Row:* A Reconsideration." *Western American Literature* 12 (1977): 11–40.

———. *True Adventures*, pp. 39, 153, 193–95, 224, 245–46, 429, 432, 553–56, 560–63, 564, 926.

Benton, Robert M. "The Ecological Nature of Cannery Row." In *Steinbeck: The Man and His Work*, ed. Richard Astro and Tetsumaro Hayashi, pp. 131–39.

Brown, Deming. *Soviet*, pp. 162, 178.

Cousins, Norman. Rev. of *CR. Saturday Review of Literature* 28 (17 March 1945): 14.

Ditsky, John. *John Steinbeck: Life, Work, and Criticism*, p. 20.

Fausset, Hugh. Rev. of *CR. Manchester Guardian*, 9 November 1945, p. 3.

Fensch, Thomas. *Steinbeck and Covici*, pp. 10, 35–38, 40, 41, 42–44, 74, 133–34, 137, 194, 197, 223.

Fontenrose, Joseph. *Introduction and Interpretation*, pp. 95, 101–8, 127, 128, 130.

French, Warren. *John Steinbeck*, 2d ed., pp. 18, 20, 28–29, 32, 41, 111, 112–24, 125, 127, 130, 148–49, 154–55, 156, 164, 167, 168, 171, 172, 173.

———. *Social Novel*, pp. 46, 168.

Fuller, Edmund. *Man in Modern Fiction*, pp. 28, 105.

Garcia, Reloy. *Steinbeck and D. H. Lawrence*, pp. 12, 31.

Gladstein, Mimi R. *Indestructible Woman*, pp. 90–92.

Gray, James. *John Steinbeck*, pp. 34–36.

Hampson, John. Rev. of *CR. Spectator* 175 (2 November 1945): 418–19.

Hayashi, Tetsumaro. *Dictionary*, pp. 26, 27, 31, 37–38, 43, 44, 50, 63–65, 66, 67, 72, 74, 75, 76–77, 95, 96–97, 107, 109, 118, 120, 121, 122, 179, 203, 205.

Hedgpeth, Joel W. "Philosophy on Cannery Row." In *Steinbeck: The Man and His Work*, ed. Richard Astro and Tetsumaro Hayashi, pp. 89–129.

Hoffman, Frederick J. *Modern Novel*, p. 151.

Hughes, R. S. *Beyond the Red Pony*, pp. 15, 112–14, 123.

———. *Study of the Short Fiction*, pp. 70–72, 80.

Jain, Sunita. *Concept of Man*, pp. 3, 68–72.

Jones, Lawrence William. *JS as Fabulist*, pp. 4, 18–20, 21, 31–32.

———. "Poison in the Cream Puff: The Human Condition in *Cannery Row*." Edited by Marston LaFrance. *Steinbeck Quarterly* 7 (1974): 35–40.

Kiernan, Thomas. *Intricate Music*, pp. 267–70, 273–76.

Krutch, Joseph Wood. Rev. of *CR. New York Herald Tribune Weekly Book Review*, 31 December 1955, p. 1.

Levant, Howard. " 'Is' Thinking." In *The Novels of John Steinbeck: A Critical Study*, pp. 164–84.

Lisca, Peter. "*Cannery Row* and the Tao Teh Ching." *San Jose Studies* 1 (1975): 21–27.

———. *Nature and Myth*, pp. 2, 111–23, 125, 126, 152, 205, 206–8.

———. *Wild World*, pp. 104, 197–217, 224, 228, 277, 279, 280, 283.

Longaker, Mark. Rev. of *CR. Catholic World* 160 (March 1945): 570–71.

McCarthy, Paul. *JS*, pp. 97–105, 140.

Marks, Lester J. *Thematic Design*, pp. 89, 90, 92–99.

Marshall, Margaret. Rev. of *CR*. *Nation* 160 (20 January 1945): 75–76.
Martin, Stoddard. *California Writers*, pp. 93–98, 100–103.
Matthiessen, F. O. Rev. of *CR*. *New York Times Book Review* 7 (31 December 1944): 1.
Mayberry, George. Rev. of *CR*. *New Republic* 112 (15 January 1945): 89–90.
Metzger, Charles R. "Steinbeck's *Cannery Row*." In *Study Guide to Steinbeck*, ed. Tetsumaro Hayashi, pp. 19–28.
Millichap, Joseph R. *Film*, pp. 5, 90–92, 153, 172–75, 177.
Owens, Louis. *Re-Vision*, pp. 31, 36, 160, 161, 163, 164, 177, 178–90, 191, 192, 193, 194, 209.
Pratt, John G. *JS*, pp. 40–41.
Prescott, Orville. Rev. of *CR*. *New York Times*, 2 January 1945, p. 17.
Rao, B. Ramachandra. *American Fictional Hero*, pp. 63, 64.
Rev. of *CR*. *Booklist* 41 (1 January 1945): 140.
Rev. of *CR*. *Chicago Sun Book Week*, 7 January 1945, p. 6.
Rev. of *CR*. *Commonweal* 41 (26 January 1945): 378.
Rev. of *CR*. *New Yorker* 20 (6 January 1945): 62.
Rev. of *CR*. *Time* 45 (1 January 1945): 62.
Rev. of *CR*. *Times* (London) *Literary Supplement*, 3 November 1945, p. 521.
Rothman, Nathan L. "A Small Miracle." *Saturday Review of Literature* 27 (30 December 1944): 5.
Satyanarayana, M. R. *Compassion*, pp. 52–53, 104, 105.
———. "Indian Thought in Steinbeck's Works." In *John Steinbeck: From Salinas to the World*, pp. 113–22.
Simmonds, Roy S. *Steinbeck's Literary Achievement*, pp. 2, 7, 10, 11, 12, 19–21, 29–30, 32.
Steinbeck, Elaine, and Robert Wallsten. *Letters*, pp. 265, 270, 273, 276, 467, 474, 588.
Straumann, Heinrich. *American Literature*, p. 116.
Tarp, Fred. "John Steinbeck: Some Reflections." In *Steinbeck and the Sea*, ed. Richard Astro and Joel W. Hedgpeth, pp. 29–33.
Timmerman, John H. *Aesthetics*, pp. 13–14, 156–68, 169, 172, 177, 187.
Toynbee, Philip. Rev. of *CR*. *New Statesman and Nation* 30 (24 November 1945): 356–57.
Valjean, Nelson. *Errant Knight*, p. 99.
Walcutt, Charles G. *Seven Novelists*, pp. 206, 233, 234, 235.
Watt, F. W. *Steinbeck*, pp. 15, 79–84.
Wilson, Edmund. Rev. of *CR*. *The New Yorker* 20 (6 January 1945): 62.
Wooster, Harold A. Rev. of *CR*. *Library Journal* 70 (1 January 1945): 32.

The Pearl

Astro, Richard. *Steinbeck and Ricketts . . . Shaping*, pp. 169–72, 177, 182, 189.
Baker, Carlos. Rev. of *Pearl*. *New York Times Book Review* 7 (30 November 1947): 4.
Bartel, Roland. "Proportioning in Fiction: *The Pearl* and *Silas Marner*." *English Journal* 56 (1967): 542–46, 560.

Beatty, Sandra. "A Study of Female Characterization in Steinbeck's Fiction." *Steinbeck's Women: Essays in Criticism*, ed. Tetsumaro Hayashi and Richard F. Peterson, pp. 1–6.

Benson, Jackson J. *True Adventures*, pp. 543, 560–61, 564–65, 568–69.

Brown, Deming. *Soviet*, pp. 177–78.

Corin, Fernand. "Steinbeck and Hemingway: A Study in Literary Economy." *Revue des Langues Vivantes* 24 (January–April, 1958): 60–75, 153–60.

Cox, Martha H. "Steinbeck's *The Pearl*." In *Study Guide to Steinbeck*, ed. Tetsumaro Hayashi, pp. 107–28.

Ditsky, John. *John Steinbeck: Life, Work, and Criticism*, pp. 21, 30.

Falkenberg, Sandra. "A Study of Female Characterization in Steinbeck's Fiction." *Steinbeck Quarterly* 8 (1975): 50–56.

Farrelly, John. Rev. of *Pearl*. *New Republic* 117 (23 December 1947): 28.

Fensch, Thomas. *Steinbeck and Covici*, pp. 10, 35–37, 39, 42, 46–49, 70.

Fontenrose, John. *Introduction and Interpretation*, pp. 88, 140.

French, Warren. *John Steinbeck*, 2d ed., pp. 29, 126–30, 153, 171.

Garcia, Reloy. *Steinbeck and D. H. Lawrence*, pp. 12, 14, 15.

Geismar, Maxwell. Rev. of *Pearl*. *Saturday Review of Literature* 30 (22 November 1947): 14.

Gladstein, Mimi R. *Indestructible Woman*, pp. 86–89.

———. "Steinbeck's Juana: A Woman of Worth." In *Steinbeck's Women: Essays in Criticism*, ed. Tetsumaro Hayashi and Richard F. Peterson, pp. 49–52.

Gray, James. *John Steinbeck*, pp. 29–30.

Gunn, Drewey Wayne. *American and British Writers*, pp. 200–202.

Hamby, James A. "Steinbeck's *The Pearl*: Tradition and Innovation." *Western Review* 7 (1970): 65–66.

Harcourt-Smith, Simon. Rev. of *Pearl*. *New Statesman* 36 (6 November 1948): 400–402.

Hayashi, Tetsumaro. *Dictionary*, pp. 55–56, 65, 110, 113, 154, 177, 183.

———. "*The Pearl* as the Novel of Disengagement." *Steinbeck Quarterly* 7 (1974): 84–88.

Hunter, Anne. Rev. of *Pearl*. *Commonweal* 47 (23 January 1948): 377.

Jain, Sunita. *Concept of Man*, pp. 3, 73–81, 94.

———. "Steinbeck's *The Pearl*: An Interpretation." *Journal of the School of Languages* 6 (1978–79): 138–43.

Jones, Lawrence William. *JS as Fabulist*, pp. 21–22.

Karsten, Ernest E., Jr. "Thematic Structure in *The Pearl*." *English Journal* 54 (1965): 1–7.

Kiernan, Thomas. *Intricate Music*, p. 269.

Kingery, Robert E. Rev. of *Pearl*. *Library Journal*, 1 November 1947, p. 1540.

Krause, Sydney J. "*The Pearl* and Hadleyburg: From Desire to Renunciation." *Steinbeck Quarterly* 7 (1974): 3–17.

Levant, Howard. "The Natural Parable." In *The Novels of John Steinbeck: A Critical Study*, pp. 185–206.

Lisca, Peter. *Nature and Myth*, pp. 123–41.

————. "Steinbeck's Fable of the Pearl." In *Steinbeck and His Critics: A Record of Twenty-five Years*, ed. Ernest W. Tedlock, Jr., and C. V. Wicker, pp. 291–301.
————. *Wide World*, pp. 8, 104, 135, 218–30, 279.
McCarthy, Paul. *JS*, pp. 108–9, 140.
Marks, Lester J. *Thematic Design*, pp. 105–7.
Martin, Stoddard. *California Writers*, p. 143.
Metzger, Charles R. "The Film Version of Steinbeck's *The Pearl*." *Steinbeck Quarterly* 4 (1971): 88–92.
————. "Steinbeck's *The Pearl* as a Nonteleological Parable of Hope." *Research Studies* 46 (1978): 98–105.
Meyer, Michael John. "Darkness Visible: The Moral Dilemma of Americans as Portrayed in the Early Short Fiction and Later Novels of John Steinbeck." *DAI* 47 (1986): 179A. Loyola University of Chicago.
Millichap, Joseph R. *Film*, pp. 93, 95, 96–107, 122, 177.
Morris, Harry. "*The Pearl*: Realism and Allegory." *English Journal* 52 (1963): 487–95, 505. Reprinted in *Steinbeck: A Collection of Critical Essays*, ed. Robert Murray Davis, pp. 149–62.
Nagle, J. M. "View of Literature Too Often Neglected: *The Pearl*." *English Journal* 58 (1969): 399–407.
Owens, Louis. *Re-Vision*, pp. 35–46, 86, 196.
Pratt, John C. *JS*, pp. 14, 15.
Prescott, Orville. Rev. of *Pearl*. *New York Times*, 24 November 1947, p. 21.
Rao, B. Ramachandra. *American Fictional Hero*, pp. 73–75.
Rev. of *Pearl*. "At Home and Abroad." *Times* (London) *Literary Supplement*, 6 November 1948, p. 621.
Rev. of *Pearl*. *Booklist* 44 (15 December 1947): 152.
Rev. of *Pearl*. *Chicago Sun Book Week*, 23 November 1947, p. 7.
Rev. of *Pearl*. *Newsweek* 31 (8 March 1948): 83–84.
Rev. of *Pearl*. *New Yorker* 23 (27 December 1947): 59.
Rev. of *Pearl*. *San Francisco Chronicle*, 14 December 1947, p. 16.
Rev. of *Pearl*. *Time* 50 (22 December 1947): 90.
Rev. of *Pearl*. *Time* 51 (1 March 1948): 84.
Satyanarayana, M. R. *Compassion*, pp. 88–90, 92, 106, 107.
Scoville, Samuel. "The Weltanschauung of Steinbeck and Hemingway: An Analysis of Themes." *English Journal* 56 (1967): 60–63, 66.
Shimomura, Noboru. "Guilt and Christianity in *The Pearl*." *Chu-Shikoku Studies in American Literature* 16 (1980): 19–31.
Simmonds, Roy S. *Steinbeck's Literary Achievement*, pp. 7, 10.
Smith, Stevie. Rev. of *Pearl*. *Spectator* 181 (29 October 1948): 570.
Steinbeck, Elaine, and Robert Wallsten. *Letters*, pp. 269, 273, 274, 279, 281, 283.
Straumann, Heinrich. *American Literature*, pp. 116–17.
Surgue, Thomas. Rev. of *Pearl*. *New York Herald Tribune*, 7 December 1947, p. 4.
Tarr, E. Whitney. "Steinbeck on One Plane." *Saturday Review of Literature* 30, no. 2 (20 December 1947): 20.
Timmerman, John H. *Aesthetics*, pp. 10–11, 56, 194–209.

Tokunaga, Masanori. "The Biological Descriptions in *The Pearl* and Their Mean-
ings." *Kyushu American Literature* 16 (1975): 13–16.
VanDerBeets, Richard. "A Pearl Is a Pearl Is a Pearl." *CEA Critic* 32 (April 1970): 9.
Walcutt, Charles C. *Seven Novelists*, pp. 229–30.
Waldron, Edward E. *"The Pearl* and the *Old Man and the Sea:* A Comparative
Analysis." *Steinbeck Quarterly* 13 (1980): 98–106.
Watt, F. W. *Steinbeck*, pp. 23, 84–89.
Weeks, Edward. Rev. of *Pearl. Atlantic* 180 (December 1947): 138–39.

Sweet Thursday

Astro, Richard. *Steinbeck and Ricketts . . . Shaping*, pp. 4, 180, 181, 193–206, 213–
15, 222, 223.
——. "Steinbeck's Bittersweet Thursday." *Steinbeck Quarterly* 4 (1971): 36–48.
Baker, Carlos. Rev. of *ST. New York Times Book Review* 7 (13 June 1954): 4.
Barron, Louis. Rev. of *ST. Library Journal* 79 (1 June 1954): 1052.
Benson, Jackson J. *True Adventures*, 193–94, 745, 767, 779–82, 908–9.
Boyle, Robert H. Rev. of *ST. Commonweal* 60 (9 July 1954): 351.
Brown, Deming. *Soviet*, p. 178.
DeMott, Robert. "Steinbeck and the Creative Process: First Manifesto to End the
Bringdown against *Sweet Thursday*." In *Steinbeck: The Man and His Work*, ed.
Richard Astro and Tetsumaro Hayashi, pp. 157–78.
Ditsky, John. *John Steinbeck: Life, Work, and Criticism*, pp. 22, 25, 28, 29.
Fensch, Thomas. *Steinbeck and Covici*, pp. 10, 74, 133, 194.
Fontenrose, Joseph. *Introduction and Interpretation*, pp. 127–30.
French, Warren. *John Steinbeck*, 2d ed., pp. 20, 32, 154–57, 172.
Fuller, Edmund, *Man in Modern Fiction*, pp. 28, 33.
Garcia, Reloy. *Steinbeck and D. H. Lawrence*, p. 5.
Gill, Brendan. Rev. of *ST. New Yorker* 30 (July 1954): 63–64.
Gladstein, Mimi R. *Indestructible Woman*, pp. 91–92.
Gray, James. *John Steinbeck*, pp. 6–7.
Hayashi, Tetsumaro. *Dictionary*, pp. 26, 27, 30–31, 32, 35–36, 38, 40, 41, 44, 50,
56, 62, 66, 68–69, 71, 72–73, 76, 77, 78, 79, 80–81, 95–96, 97, 99, 101, 103–4,
113, 118–19, 120–21, 122, 123, 127, 139, 161, 163–64, 165, 168, 171–72, 176,
178, 180, 184, 196, 203–4, 206, 207.
Holman, Hugh. Rev. of *ST. New Republic* 130 (7 June 1954): 18–20.
Hughes, Riley. *Rev. of ST. Catholic World* 179 (April 1954): 393–94.
Hughes, R. S. *Beyond the Red Pony*, pp. 69–70, 117–18.
——. *Study of the Short Fiction*, p. 75.
Jones, Lawrence William. *JS as Fabulist*, pp. 20–21, 31–32.
Kiernan, Thomas. *Intricate Music*, p. 302.
Levant, Howard. "Hooptedoodle." In *The Novels of John Steinbeck: A Critical Study*,
pp. 259–72.
Lisca, Peter. *Nature and Myth*, pp. 178, 204–8, 210, 211.

————. *Wide World*, pp. 205, 206, 276–84, 290.

Lutwack, Leonard. *Heroic Fiction*, p. 65.

McCarthy, Paul. *JS*, p. 125.

Marks, Lester J. *Thematic Design*, pp. 132–34.

Martin, Stoddard. *California Writers*, pp. 13, 100–103, 143.

Metzger, Charles R. "Steinbeck's Version of the Pastoral." *Modern Fiction Studies* 6 (1960): 115–24.

Millichap, Joseph R. *Film*, pp. 153–54, 173.

Owens, Louis. *Re-Vision*, pp. 160, 161, 164, 185, 190–96.

Poore, Charles. Rev. of *ST*. *New York Times*, 10 June 1954, p. 29.

Pratt, John C. *JS*, p. 18.

Rev. of *ST*, *Booklist* 50 (15 April 1954): 309; 50 (15 June 1954): 401.

Rev. of *ST*. *Manchester Guardian*, 26 October 1954, p. 4.

Rev. of *ST*. *Nation* 179 (10 July 1954): 37.

Rev. of *ST*. *New Yorker* 30 (10 July 1954): 63.

Rev. of *ST*. *Times* 63 (14 June 1954): 120–21.

Rev. of *ST*. *Times* (London) *Literary Supplement*, 26 November 1954, p. 753.

Richardson, Maurice. Rev. of *ST*. *New Statesman and Nation* 48 (6 November 1954): 589–90.

Rugoff, Milton. Rev. of *ST*. *New York Herald Tribune Books*, 13 June 1954, p. 1.

Simmonds, Roy S. *Steinbeck's Literary Achievement*, pp. 2, 7, 10, 11, 12.

————. "Steinbeck's *Sweet Thursday*." In *Study Guide to Steinbeck, Part II*, ed. Tetsumaro Hayashi, pp. 139–64.

Steinbeck, Elaine, and Robert Wallsten. *Letters*, pp. 472–73, 603.

Timmerman, John H. *Aesthetics*, pp. 12–13, 21, 110, 144, 168–82, 185, 187, 229.

Walcutt, Charles G. *Seven Novelists*, pp. 206, 207, 233, 234.

Watt, F. W. *Steinbeck*, pp. 13–14, 15, 99–101.

Webster, Harvey Curtis. Rev. of *ST*. *Saturday Review* 37 (12 June 1954): 11.

Weeks, Edward. Rev. of *ST*. *Atlantic* 194 (August 1954): 82.

Burning Bright

Astro, Richard. *Steinbeck and Ricketts . . . Shaping*, pp. 4, 180, 181–87, 189, 192, 193, 195, 205, 229.

Atkinson, Brooks. Rev. of *BB*. *New York Times Book Review*, 29 October 1950, p. 2.

Benson, Jackson J. *True Adventures*, pp. 643–45, 655–56, 660, 661–66, 669.

Brooke, Jocelyn. Rev. of *BB*. *New Statesman* 42 (18 August 1951): 184–85.

Cousins, Norman. Rev. of *BB*. *Saturday Review* 33 (28 October 1950): 26–27.

Cox, Martha Heasley. "Steinbeck's *Burning Bright*." In *Study Guide to Steinbeck, Part II*, ed. Tetsumaro Hayashi, pp. 46–62.

Ditsky, John. *John Steinbeck: Life, Work, and Criticism*, pp. 10, 11, 21, 29.

————. "Steinbeck's *Burning Bright*: Homage to Astarte." *Steinbeck Quarterly* 7 (1974): 79–84.

Fensch, Thomas. *Steinbeck and Covici*, pp. 48, 127–30, 136–38, 139–40, 146, 147, 187, 190.

Fontenrose, John. *Introduction and Interpretation*, pp. 115–17.

French, Warren. *John Steinbeck*, 2d ed., pp. 20, 59, 137, 138–40, 143, 151, 153–54, 156, 157, 168, 169, 171, 173.

Gladstein, Mimi R. *Indestructible Woman*, pp. 92, 98.

Gray, James. *John Steinbeck*, pp. 28–29.

Hayashi, Tetsumaro. *Dictionary*, pp. 74–75, 134, 171, 194.

Jackson, Joseph Henry. Rev. of *BB*. *This World, San Francisco Chronicle*, 27 October 1950, p. 16.

Jones, Lawrence William. *JS as Fabulist*, pp. 6, 12.

Kerr, Walter. Rev. of *BB*. *Commonweal* 53 (10 November 1950): 120.

Kiernan, Thomas. *Intricate Music*, pp. 292–94, 302.

Larder, John. Rev. of *BB*. *New Yorker* 26 (28 October 1950): 52–53.

Lisca, Peter. *Nature and Myth*, pp. 154–60, 170, 179.

———. *Wide World*, pp. 205, 207, 248–60, 269. 270, 272.

Lockridge, Richard. Rev. of *BB*. *New York Herald Tribune Books*, 22 October 1950, p. 4.

McCarthy, Paul. *JS*, pp. 107, 109.

Marshall, Margaret. Rev. of *BB*. *Nation* 171 (28 October 1950): 396.

Millichap, Joseph R. *Film*, p. 121.

Morris, Alice S. Rev. of *BB*. *New York Times Book Review* 7 (22 October 1950): 4.

Nathan, George Jean. "*Burning Bright.*" In *Theatre Book of the Year, 1950–51: A Record and an Interpretation*. New York: Knopf, 1951. Pp. 67–70.

Pratt, John G. *JS*, pp. 7, 15–16, 36–37.

Prescott, Orville. Rev. of *BB*. *New York Times*, 20 October 1950, p. 25.

Rev. of *BB*. *Booklist* 47 (1 September 1950): 3.

Rev. of *BB*. *Booklist* 47 (1 November 1950): 98.

Rev. of *BB*. *Newsweek* 36 (30 October 1950): 78.

Rev. of *BB*. *New York Times Book Review* 6 (1950): 7, 26.

Rev. of *BB*. *Theatre Arts* 34 (December 1950): 16.

Rev. of *BB*. *Time* 56 (30 October 1950): 58.

Satyanarayana, M. R. *Compassion*, pp. 67, 68, 110, 111.

Simmonds, Roy S. *Steinbeck's Literary Achievement*, p. 24.

"Staging a Story." Rev. of *BB*. *Times Literary Supplement*, 18 August 1951, p. 513.

Steinbeck, Elaine, and Robert Wallsten. *Letters*, pp. 380–81, 402, 405, 408, 411, 412–13, 414, 516.

Strong, L. A. G. Rev. of *BB*. *Spectator* 187 (10 August 1951): 196.

Timmerman, John H. *Aesthetics*, p. 187–88, 252–53, 258.

Walcutt, Charles C. *Seven Novelists*, p. 228.

Watt, F. W. *Steinbeck*, pp. 23, 91–93.

Wyatt, Euphemia Van Rensselaer. Rev. of *BB*. *Catholic World* 172 (December 1950): 228.

Yarmus, Marcia D. "Federico Garcia Lorca's *Yerma* and John Steinbeck's *Burning Bright*: A Comparative Study." *Garcia Lorca Review* 11 (1983): 75–86.

The Short Reign of Pippin IV

Astro, Richard. *Steinbeck and Ricketts . . . Shaping*, pp. 54, 213–14, 215–16, 224, 229.
Benson, Jackson J. *True Adventures*, pp. 767, 785–86, 794, 803, 807, 815.
Bois, William. Rev. of *Pippin*. *New York Times*, 15 April 1957, p. 27.
Ditsky, John. *John Steinbeck: Life, Work, and Criticism*, pp. 10, 22, 30.
———. "Some Sense of Mission: Steinbeck's *The Short Reign of Pippin IV* Reconsidered." *Steinbeck Quarterly* 16 (1983): 79–89.
Fensch, Thomas. *Steinbeck and Covici*, pp. 10, 195–98.
Fontenrose, Joseph. *Introduction and Interpretation*, pp. 130–32.
French, Warren. *John Steinbeck*, 2d ed., pp. 33, 154, 157–58, 166, 172.
———. *Social Novel*, pp. 46, 168.
George, Daniel. Rev. of *Pippin*. *Spectator* 198 (31 May 1957): 726–27.
Hayashi, Tetsumaro. *Dictionary*, pp. 26, 50, 63, 66, 73, 76, 77, 78, 79, 86, 97–99, 108, 109, 110, 113, 115–16, 121, 124–25, 127–28, 129, 131, 144, 146–47, 152, 154, 166, 168, 169, 171, 176, 181, 191, 194.
Hughes, Riley. Rev. of *Pippin*. *Catholic World* 185 (July 1957): 312.
Hughes, R. S. *Study of the Short Fiction*, p. 76.
Janeway, Elizabeth. Rev. of *Pippin*. *New York Times Book Review* 7 (14 April 1957): 6.
Johnson, Pamela Hansford. Rev. of *Pippin*. *New Statesman* 54 (13 July 1957): 61–62.
Jones, Lawrence William. *JS as Fabulist*, p. 28.
Kiernan, Thomas. *Intricate Music*, pp. 306–8.
Levant, Howard. "Jeu d'esprit." In *The Novels of John Steinbeck: A Critical Study*, pp. 273–87.
Lisca, Peter. *Nature and Myth*, pp. 208–12.
———. *Wide World*, pp. 206, 285–88.
McCarthy, Paul. *JS*, p. 125.
Marks, Lester J. *Thematic Design*, pp. 132–34.
Millichap, Joseph R. *Film*, pp. 160–61, 177.
Moore, Harry T. *Age of the Modern*, pp. 82, 84–85.
———. *Novels of JS*, pp. 100–101.
———. Rev. of *Pippin*. *New Republic* 136 (27 May 1975): 23–24.
Owens, Louis D. "Winter in Paris: John Steinbeck's *Pippin IV*." *Steinbeck Quarterly* 20 (1987): 18–25.
Pratt, John C. *JS*, p. 17.
Ray, David. Rev. of *Pippin*. *Nation* 184 (20 April 1957): 346–47.
Redman, Ben Ray. Rev. of *Pippin*. *Saturday Review* 40 (13 April 1957): 14.
Rev. of *Pippin*. *Booklist* 53 (1 March 1957): 345.
Rev. of *Pippin*. *Booklist* 53 (15 April 1957): 428.
Rev. of *Pippin*. *Bookmark* 16 (May 1957): 191.
Rev. of *Pippin*. *Canadian Forum* 37 (July 1957): 89.
Rev. of *Pippin*. "King for a Day." *Times* (London) *Literary Supplement*, 7 June 1957, p. 345.
Rev. of *Pippin*. *Manchester Guardian*, 4 June 1957, p. 4.

Rev. of *Pippin*. *New Yorker* 33 (13 April 1957): 164.
Rev. of *Pippin*. *Time* 69 (15 April 1957): 15.
Smith, Eleanor T. Rev. of *Pippin*. *Library Journal* 82 (15 March 1957): 753.
Steinbeck, Elaine, and Robert Wallsten. *Letters*, pp. 524, 537–38, 541.
Timmerman, John H. *Aesthetics*, pp. 211, 258.
Watson, Phil. "Steinbeck's Whimsy." Rev. of *Pippin*. *San Jose Mercury-News Maga-zine*, 21 April 1957, p. 8.
Watt, F. W. *Steinbeck*, pp. 101–2.
Weeks, Edward. Rev. of *Pippin*. *Atlantic* 200 (July 1957): 83–84.

Contributors

RICHARD ASTRO is Provost and Academic Vice President at the University of Central Florida. He is the coeditor of *Steinbeck: The Man and His Work* (with Tetsumaro Hayashi), coeditor (with Joel Hedgpeth) of the proceedings of a Sea Grant College Conference, *Steinbeck and the Sea,* and author of the influential *John Steinbeck and Edward F. Ricketts: The Shaping of a Novelist.* Among his many articles on Steinbeck's work are "Steinbeck's Post-war Trilogy: A Return to Nature and the Natural Man," published in *Twentieth Century Literature* (April 1970), and "Steinbeck and Ricketts: Escape or Commitment in the Sea of Cortez," in *Western American Literature* (Summer 1971).

CARROLL BRITCH is Professor of Drama and English and Director of Theatre at Springfield College in Massachusetts. He is coauthor of *Speech Acts: Hints and Samples;* coauthor (with Cliff Lewis) of "Shadow of the Indian in the Fiction of John Steinbeck," published in *Melus* (Winter 1984); and coeditor (also with Lewis) of the forthcoming *Rediscovering Steinbeck.*

JOHN DITSKY is Professor of English at the University of Windsor, Ontario, Canada. He is a poet and the author of *John Steinbeck: Life, Work, and Criticism,* and the editor of *Critical Essays on Steinbeck's "The Grapes of Wrath."* He has also published more than a dozen essays on Steinbeck, including "Music from a Dark Cave: Organic Form in Steinbeck's Fiction," in the *Journal of Narrative Technique,* and "Words and Deeds in *Viva Zapata!*" in *Dalhousie Review.*

JOSEPH FONTENROSE at the time of his death was Emeritus Professor of Classics at the University of California, Berkeley. He is best known to Steinbeck scholars for his *John Steinbeck: An Introduction and Interpretation.* A leading authority on the subject of oracles, his other books include *Python: A Study of Delphic Myth and Its Origins, The Cult and Myth of Pyrros at Delphi, The Ritual Theory of Myth,* and *Didyma: Apollo's Oracle, Cult, and Companions.*

WARREN FRENCH is Emeritus Professor of English, Indiana University, and Honorary Professor of American Studies, University of Wales, Swansea. He has had an enormously productive career as scholar, critic, and editor. Among his books are two editions (1961 and 1975) of *John Steinbeck, Frank Norris, A Companion to "The Grapes of Wrath," The South in Film, Jack Kerouac,* and *J. D. Salinger Revisited.*

ROBERT GENTRY is Instructor of English at Texas State Technical Institute at Waco. His dissertation, written for Baylor University in 1986, was "John Steinbeck's Use of Non-teleological Thinking in His Mexican American Characters."

MIMI REISEL GLADSTEIN is Professor of English at the University of Texas, El Paso, and author of *The Indestructible Woman in Faulkner, Hemingway, and Steinbeck* and *The Ayn Rand Companion*. Among her articles are "Ayn Rand and Feminism: An Unlikely Alliance" in *College English*, and "Mothers and Daughters in Endless Procession: Faulkner's Use of the Demeter/Persephone Myth" in *Faulkner and Women*.

WILLIAM GOLDHURST is Professor of Humanities at the University of Florida. He is the author of *F. Scott Fitzgerald and His Contemporaries* and the editor of *Contours of Experience*. He is the author of many articles, including "The Hyphenated Ham Sandwich of Ernest Hemingway and J. D. Salinger: A Study in Literary Continuity" in the *Fitzgerald/Hemingway Annual*.

TETSUMARO HAYASHI, as founder of the International John Steinbeck Society and editor of *Steinbeck Quarterly*, has been the guiding light of Steinbeck studies for more than two decades. Among his many publications are *A Study Guide to Steinbeck: A Handbook to His Major Works, Herman Melville: Research Opportunities and Dissertation Abstracts*, and *John Steinbeck on Writing*. He is also Steinbeck's primary bibliographer. His most recent volume in that series is *A New Steinbeck Bibliography: 1971–1981*.

ROBERT S. HUGHES, JR., is Assistant Professor of English at the University of Hawaii and author of *Beyond the Red Pony: A Reader's Companion to Steinbeck's Complete Short Stories* and *John Steinbeck: A Study of the Short Fiction*. Among his articles are "Steinbeck's Stories at the Houghton Library" in *Harvard Library Bulletin*, and "Steinbeck's *Travels with Charley* and *America and Americans:* 'We have never slipped back—never'" in *Steinbeck Quarterly*.

HOWARD LEVANT is a full-time poet who earlier, as critic and professor, published *The Novels of John Steinbeck: A Critical Study* and several articles on Steinbeck, including "*Tortilla Flat:* The Shape of John Steinbeck's Career" in *PMLA*.

CLIFF LEWIS is Professor of English and American Studies at the University of Lowell, Massachusetts. He is the coeditor (with Carroll Britch) of the forthcoming *Rediscovering Steinbeck*, and author of "The Short Happy Life of Francis Macomber" in *Études Anglaisez*.

PETER LISCA, who lives in Florida, has been a pioneer in Steinbeck studies. He is the author of two highly respected books: *The Wide World of John Steinbeck* and *John Steinbeck: Nature and Myth*. He is the editor of *"The Grapes of Wrath": Text and Criticism* and *From Irving to Steinbeck: Studies in American Literature*. Among his many articles on modern fiction is his *"The Grapes of Wrath* as Fiction" published in *PMLA*.

ANNE LOFTIS is a historian and free-lance writer based in Menlo Park, California. She is the author of *California, Where the Twain DID Meet*, and coauthor of *The Great Betrayal: The Evacuation of the Japanese-Americans During World War II* (with Audrie

Girdner) and of *A Long Time Coming: The Struggle to Unionize America's Farm Workers* (with Dick Meister).

CHARLES R. METZGER is Emeritus Professor of English, University of Southern California. He is the author of *Emerson and Greenough, Thoreau and Whitman, F. Scott Fitzgerald's Psychiatric Novel: Nicole's Case, Dick's Case*, and *The Silent River*, a memoir of an Artic adventure.

MICHAEL J. MEYER is Assistant Professor of English at Concordia College, Wisconsin. His dissertation, "Darkness Visible: The Moral Dilemma of Americans as Portrayed in the Early Short Fiction and Later Novels of John Steinbeck," was written at Loyola University of Chicago. He is currently working on a book about Steinbeck's career after *East of Eden*.

ROBERT E. MORSBERGER is Professor of English at California State Polytechnic University, Pomona. He is the coauthor (with Katherine M. Morsberger) of *James Thurber, Lew Wallace: Militant Romantic*, and editor of John Steinbeck's *Viva Zapata!* (publication of the screenplay). He has written well over a hundred articles on literature and on film, including " 'The Minister's Black Veil': 'Shrouded in a Blackness Ten Times Black,' " in the *New England Quarterly*, and "Melville's 'The Bell-Tower' and Benvenuto Cellini," published in *American Literature*.

LOUIS OWENS is Associate Professor of English at the University of New Mexico. He has written *John Steinbeck's Re-Vision of America* and (with Tom Colonnese) *American Indian Novelists: An Annotated Critical Bibliography*. He has also edited the forthcoming *The Grapes of Wrath: Trouble in the Promised Land*, and is the new coeditor of *American Literary Scholarship*.

ROY S. SIMMONDS is a literary scholar and biographer living in Essex, England. He is the author of *The Two Worlds of William March* and compiler of *William March: An Annotated Checklist*. He has published a monograph, *Steinbeck's Literary Achievement*, and is the author of a number of articles on Steinbeck, including "The Original Manuscripts of Steinbeck's 'The Chrysanthemums,' " which appeared in the *Steinbeck Quarterly*.

MARK SPILKA is Professor of English and Comparative Literature at Brown University and editor of *Novel: A Forum on Fiction*. He is the author of several books, including *The Love Ethic of D. H. Lawrence, Dickens and Kafka: A Mutual Interpretation*, and *Hemingway's Quarrel with Androgyny*. Among his many articles are "The Necessary Stylist: A New Critical Revision" in *Modern Fictions Studies*, and "Quentin Compson's Universal Grief" in *Contemporary Literature*.

JOHN H. TIMMERMAN is Professor of English at Calvin College in Michigan. Among his many books are *John Steinbeck's Fiction: The Aesthetics of the Road Taken* and *Other Worlds: The Fantasy Genre*. He is the author of "John Steinbeck's Use of the Bible: A Descriptive Bibliography of the Critical Tradition" in *Steinbeck Quarterly*, and of "Steinbeck's Place in the Modern Epistolary Tradition" in the forthcoming *Essays in Criticism: Steinbeck's Posthumous Works*, plus more than fifty other articles on various literary subjects.

ACC-3629
6/22/94

15.7

'Γ

Library of Congress Cataloging-in-Publication Data
The Short novels of John Steinbeck : critical essays /
edited by Jackson J. Benson.
Includes bibliographical references.
ISBN 0-8223-0988-2. — ISBN 0-8223-0994-7 (pbk.)
1. Steinbeck, John, 1902–1968—Criticism and interpretation.
I. Benson, Jackson J.
PS3537.T3234Z8666 1990
813'.52—dc20   89-27255 CIP